From Byzantine to Norman Italy

From Byzantine to Norman Italy

*Mediterranean Art and Architecture
in Medieval Bari*

Clare Vernon

I.B. TAURIS
LONDON • NEW YORK • OXFORD • NEW DELHI • SYDNEY

I.B. TAURIS
Bloomsbury Publishing Plc
50 Bedford Square, London, WC1B 3DP, UK
1385 Broadway, New York, NY 10018, USA
29 Earlsfort Terrace, Dublin 2, Ireland

BLOOMSBURY, I.B. TAURIS and the I.B. Tauris logo are trademarks of
Bloomsbury Publishing Plc

First published in Great Britain 2023
This paperback edition published 2024

Copyright © Clare Vernon, 2023

Clare Vernon has asserted her right under the Copyright, Designs and Patents Act, 1988, to be identified as Author of this work.

For legal purposes the Acknowledgements on p. viii constitute an extension of this copyright page.

Series design by Rebecca Heselton
Cover image: Decorations of west portal of pontifical Basilica di San Nicola in Bari, Puglia, Italy. (© dimamoroz/Adobe Stock)

All rights reserved. No part of this publication may be reproduced or transmitted in any form or by any means, electronic or mechanical, including photocopying, recording, or any information storage or retrieval system, without prior permission in writing from the publishers.

Bloomsbury Publishing Plc does not have any control over, or responsibility for, any third-party websites referred to or in this book. All internet addresses given in this book were correct at the time of going to press. The author and publisher regret any inconvenience caused if addresses have changed or sites have ceased to exist, but can accept no responsibility for any such changes.

A catalogue record for this book is available from the British Library.

A catalog record for this book is available from the Library of Congress.

ISBN: HB: 978-1-7883-1506-7
PB: 978-0-7556-3577-1
ePDF: 978-0-7556-3574-0
eBook: 978-0-7556-3575-7

Series: New Directions in Byzantine Studies

Typeset by Deanta Global Publishing Services, Chennai, India

To find out more about our authors and books visit www.bloomsbury.com and sign up for our newsletters.

For Aly, just in case.

Contents

List of illustrations	viii
Acknowledgements	xii
Introduction: A Mediterranean city, c. 1000–1130	1

Part 1 Byzantine Bari and Canosa

1 Life in Byzantine Bari	9
2 The Byzantine palace: Building Constantinople on the frontier	14
3 Bari cathedral and 'Lombard' patronage under Byzantine rule	21
4 Canosa cathedral: 'Minister with light', how to be an archbishop	42

Part 2 The Church of San Nicola, Bari

5 The crypt: Enter St Nicholas and the Normans	55
6 A throne of Solomon: Classicism, crusade, slavery	81
7 Architecture: A temple of Solomon	102
8 Portal sculpture: The secular, the sacred and the sacramental	111
9 Elias of Bari: Benedictine, bishop, builder	129
10 Pavements: Adriatic connections underfoot?	137

Part 3 The Tomb of Bohemond I, Prince of Antioch

11 Crusader architecture: Constance of France and her Holy Sepulchre	157
12 Made in Italy: Innovations in bronze	179
13 Inscribing a crusader legacy	194
Conclusion: Connections and retrospection	199
Notes	203
Bibliography	232
Index	263

Illustrations

Map

1	Map of Southern Italy showing key places mentioned in the text	2
2	Map of Mediterranean showing key places mentioned in the text	3
3	Map of Bari in the Byzantine and Norman periods	11
4	Map of Canosa in the Byzantine and Norman periods	43

Figure

1	Crypt of San Nicola, Bari, plan	17
2	Capital 26 with cornucopia, crypt of San Nicola, Bari	17
3	Capital 6 with basket weave, crypt of San Nicola, Bari	18
4	Capital 27 with inverted palmette, crypt of San Nicola, Bari	18
5	Figure of Holy Wisdom from the Byzantine palace, probably early eleventh century. Museo Nicolaiano, Bari	19
6	'Star Mantle' given by Melus of Bari to Emperor Henry II	22
7	Late antique mosaic pavement, Bari cathedral	25
8	Burial crypt, Bari cathedral	26
9	Hall crypt, Bari cathedral	27
10	Current baptistery, Bari cathedral	27
11	Ambo, Bari cathedral	28
12	South portal, Bari cathedral	29
13	Byzantine tombstone with pseudo-Arabic ornament. Discovered in Bari cathedral, now in the castle	30
14	Trapezoid capital, Pinacoteca Provincial, Bari	31
15	Trapezoid capital, Pinacoteca Provincial, Bari	32
16	Rylands Exultet, Anastasis detail 1	34
17	Rylands Exultet, Anastasis detail 2	35
18	Chorus of the Winds, Bari Exultet 1	37
19	Emperors from Bari Exultet 1, Museo Diocesano, Bari	39
20	Frates Karissimi prayers from Exultet 1, Bari	40
21	Plan of Canosa cathedral as it was c. 1100	44
22	Canosa cathedral, nave	44
23	Exposed pendentive dome in the south transept, Canosa cathedral	45
24	Reconstruction of the plan of Justinian's Holy Apostles in Constantinople by Nikolaos Karydis	46
25	Ambo by Acceptus, Canosa cathedral	47

26	Episcopal throne, Canosa cathedral	48
27	Episcopal throne, Monte Sant'Angelo	50
28	Crypt, San Nicola	64
29	Shrine of St Nicholas	64
30	Medallion that sealed the relic chamber, shrine of St Nicholas, Bari	65
31	Reverse, medallion that sealed the relic chamber, shrine of St Nicholas, Bari	65
32	Salerno crypt	66
33	Salerno cathedral, crypt, plan	66
34	Canosa throne, detail of elephant	68
35	Canosa throne, detail	68
36	Elephant from the Charlemagne chess set	69
37	Capital 13, crypt, San Nicola, Bari	70
38	Lion doorknocker, the David Collection, Copenhagen, inventory number 50/2000	70
39	Borradaile Oliphant	71
40	Copy of the Borradaile Oliphant in the Pinacoteca Provinciale, Bari. Detail of dragon eating his tail	72
41	Copy of the Borradaile Oliphant in the Pinacoteca Provinciale, Bari. Detail of peacocks drinking	73
42	Peacocks and pinecone fountain, capital 14, San Nicola	73
43	Clephane Horn	74
44	Capital 18, crypt, San Nicola, Bari	76
45	Preening peacocks, capital 14, crypt, San Nicola	76
46	Bronze pine cone, in the Vatican Museums	77
47	The fountain at the centre of the atrium of Old St Peter's	77
48	Capital 9, crypt, San Nicola, Bari	78
49	San Clemente, apse mosaic, Rome	79
50	Drawing of the Bari throne, side view. Heinrich Wilhelm Schulz, *Denkmäler der Kunst des Mittelalters in Unteritalien* (Dresden, 1860) Atlas, plate 6	82
51	Bari throne and sanctuary pavement	83
52	Bari throne	83
53	Bari throne, detail of the back	84
54	Goslar throne, Kaiserpfalz, Stiftskirche St. Simon und Judas, Goslar, bronze	85
55	Krodo altar, Stadtmuseum, Goslar, bronze and brass	86
56	The Cramond Lioness	89
57	*Front of a Sarcophagus with Female Portrait in a Medallion above Two Theatrical Masks, and Lion Devouring a Boar at Each Extremity*, CE 250–275	89
58	Salerno cathedral, entrance to atrium	90
59	Bari throne, detail of the front	92
60	Capital with figures of different ethnicities, originally from Troia, *c.* 1225 to 1250, Metropolitan Museum of Art, New York, limestone	92
61	Sarcophagus depicting the labours of Hercules with kneeling telamons in the bottom corners, Galleria Borghese, Rome	93

62	Orestes sarcophagus with telamon supports, Roman, Musei Vaticani, Rome	93
63	Fragment of the Arcus Novus, showing a Barbarian prisoner, third century, Boboli Gardens, Florence	94
64	Portrait Vessel, imperial Roman, Asia Minor? ceramic with lead glaze, Menil Collection, Houston Texas	95
65	Theatrical mask depicting an African slave, made in Sicily, c. 350 BCE, British Museum, 1926,0324.96, 22 x 20cm, terracotta	96
66	Muse sarcophagus with theatrical masks, Nelson-Atkins Museum of Art, object number 87-21, marble, third century. Excavated at Vigna Casali, Rome	96
67	Fatimid textile with lattice pattern from Fayoum, silk and linen, 12 x 18cm, Musée du Louvre, museum number E 9963	97
68	Fatimid textile, with lattice pattern and inscription dating it to the caliphate of al-Mustansir, 1081–94, linen and silk, Cleveland Museum of Art, John L. Severance Fund 1950.536	97
69	Fatimid wood carving, 68 x 18 x 5cm, Musée du Louvre, museum number OA 4062	98
70	Telamons on the trumeau at Sainte Marie d'Oloron in the Pyrenees	101
71	Plan, San Nicola, Bari	103
72	Nave, San Nicola, Bari	103
73	Plan of Salerno cathedral	104
74	North façade, San Nicola, Bari	105
75	East façade, San Nicola, Bari	105
76	Plan of Sana Maria delle Grazie, Grado	106
77	Speyer cathedral, south elevation	107
78	West façade, San Nicola, Bari	108
79	West portal, San Nicola, Bari	112
80	South portal, San Nicola, Bari	113
81	North portal, San Nicola, Bari	114
82	Piacenza cathedral, west façade	114
83	Arthurian archivolt, north portal, San Nicola, Bari	115
84	Arthurian archivolt, Modena cathedral, porta della pescheria	115
85	Capital, south portal, San Nicola, Bari	118
86	Oxen, west portal, San Nicola, Bari	120
87	Classical cornice reused in the west portal of San Nicola	120
88	Coffer motif on west portal, San Nicola, Bari	121
89	Telamons at the base of the west portal, San Nicola, Bari	121
90	Elephant at the base of the west portal, San Nicola, Bari	122
91	Grape harvest, west portal, San Nicola, Bari	123
92	Grape harvest, Santa Costanza, Rome	123
93	Angels on the west portal of San Nicola, Bari	124
94	*Sol invictus*(?), west portal, San Nicola, Bari	127
95	Detail from the Girona Tapestry	127
96	Liturgical gloves, Museo dei Vescovi, Canosa	131
97	Elias's tomb, San Nicola	132

98	Sanctuary steps, San Nicola, Bari	139
99	Drawing of the sanctuary in 1647	140
100	*Opus sectile* around the shrine of St Nicholas, crypt, San Nicola, Bari	142
101	Quincunx, *opus sectile*, south apse of the crypt, San Nicola, Bari	142
102	*Opus sectile* panel by the altar at Hosios Loukas, Boethia	143
103	Pavement of the south church of the Pantocrator monastery, Constantinople	144
104	Pavement, St John of Studion, Constantinople	144
105	San Vitale, Ravenna, mosaic pavement	145
106	Gattola's drawing of the Montecassino pavement	146
107	Sanctuary pavement, upper basilica, San Nicola, Bari	147
108	Griffin, sanctuary pavement, San Nicola, Bari	148
109	Roundel, sanctuary pavement, San Nicola, Bari	149
110	Roundel, St Nicholas, Myra	150
111	*Opus sectile* panel, St Nicholas, Myra	151
112	Sanctuary, St Nicholas, Myra	152
113	Templon, San Nicola, Bari	152
114	Bohemond's burial chapel	160
115	Semi-capital on Bohemond's burial chapel	161
116	Early photograph of Bohemond's burial chapel. Late nineteenth century?	162
117	Engraving of Bohemond's burial chapel	162
118	Interior, Bohemond's burial chapel	163
119	Interior of the dome, Bohemond's burial chapel	163
120	Interior of the apse, Bohemond's burial chapel	164
121	Tomb of Alberada of Buonalbergo, SS Trinità di Venosa	169
122	Hypothetical reconstruction of the aedicule as it may have been in *c.* 1100, Holy Sepulchre, Jerusalem	172
123	The Antioch artophorion, Aachen cathedral	173
124	Dome of the Rock, Jerusalem	174
125	Wall painting of the crucifixion in the south transept, Canosa cathedral	177
126	Wall painting of the crucifixion, detail, south transept, Canosa cathedral	177
127	Doors to Bohemond's burial chapel	180
128	Doors to Bohemond's burial chapel	181
129	Back of the doors to Bohemond's burial chapel	182
130	Detail of doors to Bohemond's burial chapel, showing the missing Marian relief	186
131	Detail of the doors to Bohemond's burial chapel, showing one of the Arabic medallions	187
132	Star interlace medallion from the doors to Bohemond's burial chapel	188
133	Kneeling figures, doors to Bohemond's burial chapel	189
134	Trio of figures, doors to Bohemond's burial chapel	189
135	Original design of the Canosa doors, hypothetical reconstruction by the author	190
136	God introduces Eve to Adam, Monreale	192
137	Angel with Adam and Eve, Porte Miègeville, St Sernin, Toulouse	192

Acknowledgements

One night in 2007, I slept on the deck of the ferry from Patras to Bari. Later that day, still cold and windswept, I walked into Trani cathedral and was captivated. I had written my undergraduate dissertation on the Cappella Palatina and was on my way to Sicily, when I was waylaid by the churches of Puglia, which were a complete surprise to me. Fifteen years later, still captivated, I have a lot of people to thank for helping me to understand them better. This book is very loosely based on my doctoral research, which was funded by the AHRC. I would never have finished the thesis, let alone the book, without Paul Binksi's gentle and wise guidance and Lucy Donkin and Claudia Bolgia's insightful critiques in the viva.

Early drafts of parts of the book were presented at the International Medieval Congress, the Cambridge Medieval Art Seminar, British Archaeological Association, the Northern Network for the Study of the Crusades and Birkbeck's Murray Seminar, and I thank the audiences for their very helpful feedback. My students at Birkbeck on the module 'Artistic Encounters in the Medieval Mediterranean' have been the very best teachers. Their questions, ideas and enthusiasm improved this book no end. John McNeill, Eric Fernie, Nikolaos Karydis, Will Wooton, Jelena Bogdanovic and Bissera Pentcheva generously allowed their images to be published. Kate Cook and Andy Fox helped me translate some of the inscriptions. All the errors remain mine, of course. Rachel Winchcombe, Francesca Young Kaufman, John McNeill, Rosa Bacile and Laura Varnam read sections of the manuscript.

Above all, I need to thank many people for their moral support and scholarly community: Emma Edwards, Rosa Bacile and Francesca Young Kaufman for talking things through and cheering me on; Liz Gloyn, Amelia Dowler, Tony Keen and Ellie Mackin Roberts for days and long lunches in the British Library; Sophie Jones, Imogen Woodberry and Laura Cushing-Harries for Shut Up and Write at Birkbeck; Kate Cook, Josh Nudell, Andy Fox, Christine Plastow and Ellie Mackin Roberts on Slack during the coronavirus lockdowns; Lisa Morriss and Lily Green for Monday mornings on Zoom (an hour a week made all the difference!).

When women succeed in writing books, it's often because other women take on extra domestic work. I could not have written this book if it weren't for the women who have helped me take care of my mother: Lindsay Saint-Alme, Catherine Le Fur, Jemma Carnell, Sanda, Yinka, Ying Suen and Isobel Taylor. Aly, Nick and Syd have been endlessly patient in the face of my obsession with medieval churches and have given me much-needed breaks so I could write or rest. Bohemond the cat mainly just walked on the keyboard.

Introduction

A Mediterranean city, c. 1000–1130

In May of 1087, a group of sixty-two sailors from Bari arrived home with cargo they had stolen from the city of Myra: the relics of St Nicholas. The arrival of the ship caused chaos and violence, as different factions fought for control of the relics. Ultimately, it led to the construction of a new church and to international prestige for Bari that would last for centuries. The arrival of the ship is re-enacted every year, when a statue of St Nicholas is borne on the shoulders of local sailors and dances joyfully through the streets of the city, to the port. It is then taken out to sea, where it stays all day, returning in the evening accompanied by dozens of fishing boats for a ceremonial entrance into Bari, a re-enactment of the arrival in 1087. Three days of feasting and celebration conclude when the relics of St Nicholas emit a miraculous, healing manna that is collected and venerated by the faithful and, traditionally at least, distributed to pilgrims. Since St Nicholas is also the patron saint of Russia and one of the most popular saints among Orthodox Christians, his shrine in Bari is an important centre of ecumenical dialogue between the Catholic and Orthodox churches. In the era of post-Soviet ecumenism, St Nicholas has become a bridge between eastern and western Christianities. This is apt because the church has always been a meeting point for different cultures. Even while the site was still a building site, eastern and western clergy gathered in it to try to resolve the differences that had caused the schism between them.

It is fitting that Bari's biggest religious festival connects the church to the sea because connections to the Adriatic and the wider Mediterranean have shaped Bari's history. Bari has always been defined by its port, even more so before the advent of air travel, the formation of the state of Italy and its twentieth-century orientation towards the European Union. It has always been a city that looked out to sea and beyond the sea to other lands. It has been a pit stop for travellers, a destination for merchants and a prize for conquerors and pirates. This book explores how that mentality of looking out to sea shaped its art and architecture in the medieval period. The following chapters place Bari in a Mediterranean context for the first time, arguing that patrons and artists were constantly responding to and seeking out Mediterranean connections through visual culture.

This book explores the art and architecture in the neighbouring cities of Bari and Canosa in the period c. 1000–1130 (Map 1). Although the title of the book refers only to Bari, the two cities cannot be studied separately. The two cathedrals were co-cathedrals in a joint archdiocese and were interdependent in terms of ecclesiastical structures, culture and artistic production. At the turn of the millennium, both cities were part of the Byzantine Empire and Bari was the capital of the Italian imperial

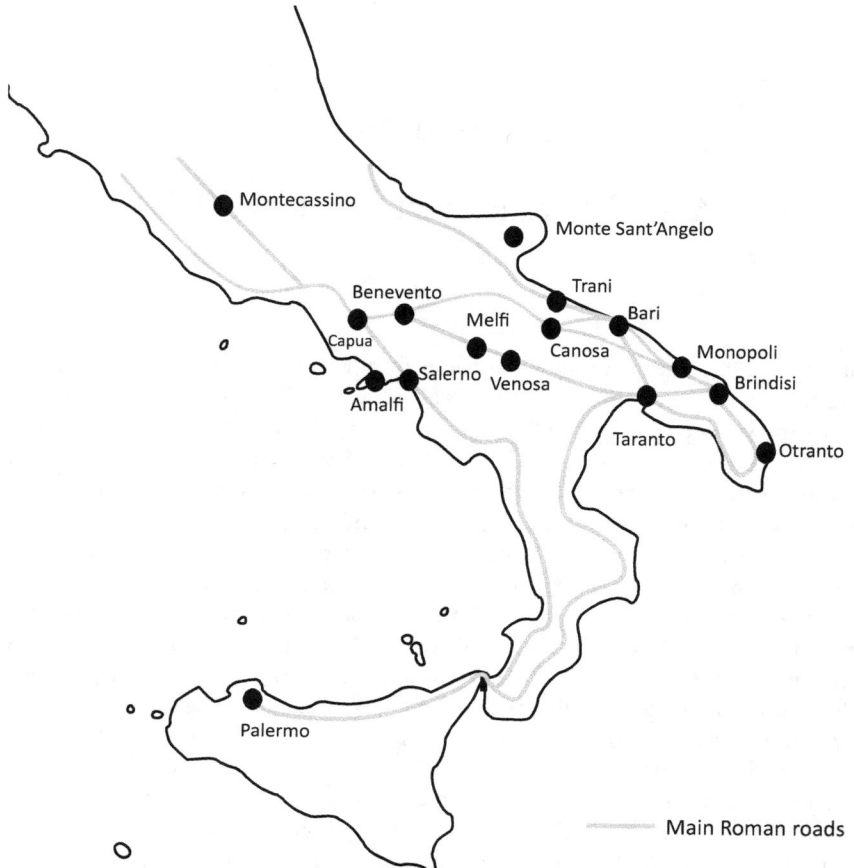

Map 1 Map of Southern Italy showing key places mentioned in the text. Drawn by the author.

provinces. Over the course of the eleventh century, the whole of southern Italy was conquered by the Normans. The Normans (and other northern French immigrants), under the leadership of the Hauteville dynasty, established first the Duchy of Apulia and then, from 1130, the Kingdom of Sicily. This book deals with the period of the conquest and consolidation of Norman rule, stopping before the establishment of the kingdom in 1130, when Norman authority in southern Italy entered a new phase.

Although the Norman conquest was a dramatic political shift in many ways, for Bari and Canosa it meant swapping one foreign ruler for another. Both the Normans and the Byzantines took a 'hands-off' approach to ruling the archdiocese, allowing a strong sense of independent civic identity to flourish in both eras. The Norman conquest was disruptive, politically and economically; it caused anxiety and threatened Bari's commercial success. But the people of Bari used the disruption as an opportunity to assert their autonomy and to form new social, religious and commercial relationships,

Introduction

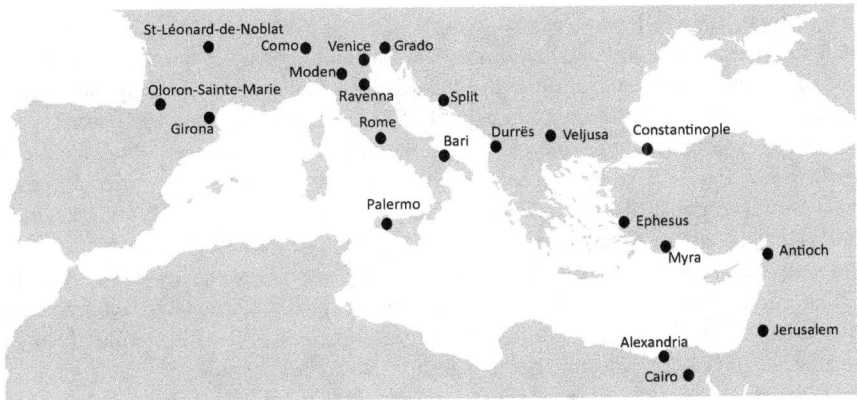

Map 2 Map of Mediterranean showing key places mentioned in the text. Drawn by the author.

largely through the construction of a major new church for St Nicholas. The conquest was not the only dramatic change that took place in this period. The interrelated events of the first crusade and the ecclesiastical Gregorian Reform movement also had a big impact on the archdiocese and its visual culture.

The aim of this book is to explore Mediterranean connections in the art and architecture of these two cities (Map 2). In doing so, it makes a contribution to five overlapping scholarly fields: Byzantine art, Norman Italy, the crusades, the international Romanesque and medieval Mediterranean studies. Art historical studies of Norman Italy have so far been dominated by the court of Roger II in Palermo, partly for good reason because Palermo offers a rich array of well-preserved and enticing evidence.[1] To a lesser extent Campania has also been a focus, particularly the abbey of Montecassino and ivory carving in Amalfi and Salerno, but the mainland remains under-researched in comparison to Palermo.[2] The period before Roger II has been neglected across Sicily and the mainland. Mainland artistic centres – such as Mileto, Venosa, Otranto, Monte Sant'Angelo, Trani and Bari – have received some attention, particularly from local scholars, but not as much as they deserve.[3] It is important to elucidate the period before 1130 not only to contextualize, and therefore better understand, the court in Palermo, but also in its own right because it offers a different picture of Mediterranean art in this period. While studies of Palermo are limited to courtly art, the mainland gives us more scope to explore different kinds of communities, patrons and artists (cathedral, monasteries, merchants, laity and non-royal Normans). This book and other mainland studies add diversity to our understanding of Norman Italy, which is currently narrowly dominated by the royal court.

Bari is geographically and intellectually peripheral in scholarship on Norman Italy, and it occupies a similarly peripheral position in Byzantine studies (geographically, it is caught between the two and on the periphery of both). In recent decades Byzantine art historians have moved away from the traditional focus on Constantinople, to think more broadly about what constitutes Byzantine art and how the provinces and frontiers related to, or were independent of, the capital.⁴ For the western fringes of the empire, Sicily has tended to dominate that discussion, particularly studies of mosaics.⁵ Apulia, in some ways more of a 'frontier zone' than Sicily because it was actually part of the empire, has received little attention as part of Byzantine art history. The few scholars who have explored the question of how Apulia fits into Byzantine art – mostly in the 1970s and 1980s – have largely concluded that it was not very Byzantine, although more recent work has discussed the blurry line between 'Byzantine and 'not Byzantine'.⁶ This study of Bari and Canosa takes a broad approach to Byzantine art, incorporating not only the narrowest definition (through the Byzantine governor's palace in Bari, which might be considered 'pure' Byzantine art) but also the broadest, encompassing Byzantium's continued cultural influence long after the end of Byzantine rule (through *opus sectile* pavements, mosaics and Byzantium's allure for crusaders).

When seen through a Western lens, the material covered in this book has been considered as Romanesque. In the 1920s, Arthur Kingsley Porter used San Nicola in Bari as one of his examples in *Romanesque Sculpture of the Pilgrimage Roads*, in support of his theories about artists and iconographies travelling from shrine to shrine across Western Europe.⁷ Since then the architecture and architectural sculpture of Bari and Canosa have been included in broad international studies of Romanesque architecture.⁸

The Italian scholarship tends to refer to *il Romanico Pugliese*, the 'Apulian Romanesque', and is dominated by the idea of regional Romanesque styles, often categorized according to the boundaries of the regions in the modern Italian nation state, rather than according to medieval boundaries (this approach is encapsulated by Jaca's rigorous series, *Italia Romanica*).⁹ The question of whether the art of Bari and Canosa is Romanesque is as fraught as the question of whether it is Byzantine and is entirely dependent on how the terms are defined.¹⁰ If Romanesque is the art of the Latin church in the central Middle Ages then the material in this book is certainly Romanesque. But the term Romanesque, with its focus on the Latin church, can obscure the diverse influences on Apulia, including from Byzantium and the Fatimid Empire, and I have therefore avoided using it here.

Although Romanesque can be too narrow a term to describe Apulian visual culture, this book does illuminate the intersections between art and the issues facing the Latin church. One of the major themes of this book is the ways in which Benedictine networks facilitated artistic production, enabled innovation and produced erudite inscriptions that merged visual and literary culture. Another theme pertinent to the Latin church is the intersection of art and the Gregorian Reform movement. In art history, there is some debate about whether or not Gregorian Reform had an impact on art and architecture.¹¹ But there is no doubt that the reform movement coincided with a renewed interest in early Christian art and some have seen art as a key tool of the reformers.¹² This book makes a contribution to that debate, arguing that San Nicola should be included in what we might call 'reforming art'. Recent research on the movement has stressed local variations, and Bari is emblematic of that. San Nicola is not typical of reforming art because of the particular local circumstances, but it is nonetheless participating in the retrospective gaze back to early Christianity and other reform issues.

Gregorian Reform is closely related to the schism between the eastern and western churches, the Latinization of southern Italy after the Norman conquest and the expansion of the Latin church through the first crusade. One of the conclusions of this book is that the first crusade had a significant impact on the art and architecture of San Nicola and Bohemond's burial chapel in Canosa. Although some art historians have touched on the subject, nobody has written the art history of the first crusade. The term 'crusader art' usually refers to the art produced in the crusader states, mostly from the middle of the twelfth century onwards.[13] Broadly speaking the first crusade is the dominion of military, social and literary historians. As this book will show, art history should be part of that conversation as well.

In the last twenty years, the new field of 'medieval Mediterranean studies' has emerged out of Peregrine Horden and Nicholas Purcell's influential book, *The Corrupting Sea: A Study of Mediterranean History*, and focusing on the interconnectedness of the Mediterranean region, across political and religious boundaries.[14] In some ways the focus on connectivity solves some of the problems discussed earlier in parcelling art into categories like Romanesque or Byzantine. But, as Horden and Purcell themselves note, in other ways it creates as many problems than it solves. There were as many connections in and out of the Mediterranean as there were within it, and a Mediterranean focus can be as limiting as a Byzantine, Latin or Islamic focus. But, since southern Italy is at the centre of the Mediterranean Sea, the Mediterranean focus works in its favour. Seen through a Mediterranean lens Apulia, which is on the periphery of so many other fields, is suddenly at the centre of a network of connections. Yet, with very few exceptions, Apulia's place in the wider Mediterranean has not been investigated.[15] This book will incorporate Bari into medieval Mediterranean studies.

The book is divided into three parts. Part one examines Bari and Canosa during the period of Byzantine rule, from c. 1000 until the Norman conquest of Bari in 1071. It explores the visual culture surrounding the Byzantine governor's palace; the reconstruction of Bari cathedral; Latin manuscript production; the use of textiles as diplomatic gifts and the commissioning of new liturgical furniture for Canosa cathedral. Byzantine Bari was a place where Greek and Latin cultures came into contact with one another and where the distinction between the two could be blurred. These chapters evaluate how the majority-Lombard population and the Byzantine officials chose to engage with each other culturally and how the Lombard population retained their distinctive Latin identity while also appropriating elements of Byzantine culture. Unfortunately, artistic and contextual evidence from the Byzantine period is far from plentiful. The Byzantine palace and the eleventh-century cathedral are no longer standing, and Canosa cathedral was altered quite significantly in the post-medieval period. This means that Part 1 is necessarily short and the conclusions are partial and sometimes tentative. Nonetheless, surviving sculptural fragments, manuscripts, archaeology and documents do allow us to piece together a picture of artistic production during the Byzantine period, which significantly enhanced our understanding of the culture on the western frontier of the Byzantine Empire.

Evidence for the Norman period is much more ample, with two major monuments still standing: the church of San Nicola and the burial chapel of Bohemond I of Antioch. Part 2 focuses on the most ambitious and well-known building project in

Bari's history: the basilica of San Nicola. When the citizens of Bari stole the relics of St Nicholas and brought them back to Bari, they demolished the Byzantine governor's palace and built a church to house the relics in its place. The chapters in Part 2 chart how the construction project changed as it progressed. It began as a civic enterprise, a symbolic appropriation of the site of Byzantine authority but, as time went on, it incorporated the ideas of the first crusade, the Gregorian Reform movement and new influences introduced by crusaders, pilgrims and merchants.

Part 3 focuses on Canosa and the burial chapel of Bohemond I, Prince of Antioch. Bohemond was the lord of Bari and Canosa and the son of the Norman ruler Robert Guiscard. He was also the leader of the southern Italian contingent of the first crusade. During the crusade he became the ruler of Antioch in the Levant. When he died in Italy, he was buried in a small chapel in Canosa cathedral. In Part 3 I will argue that the chapel was commissioned by his widow, Constance of France, and that it is an imitation of the aedicule, Christ's empty tomb, in the Holy Sepulchre in Jerusalem. The chapel has a pair of bronze doors which are notable as the first cast in southern Italy in the Middle Ages.

This book reminds us that Mediterranean history has always been a story of connections across the sea, but the course of those connections did not always run smoothly. Mediterranean connectivity looks different from an Apulian perspective than it does from Sicily. The plentiful studies of Norman Palermo emphasize the relationship between art and monarchy, in the context of a court that is often portrayed as successful and stable. Bari and Canosa may not be among the great metropolises of the Mediterranean; they cannot compete with Constantinople, Cairo, Cordoba or Palermo, but therein lies the value of this book. Studying smaller, less influential cities demonstrates how more 'ordinary' urban communities negotiated the transformations and continuities of the era. Looking at a single archdiocese through Byzantine rule, the Norman conquest and the first crusade enables us to understand change over time, through several eras. The history of Bari and Canosa is one in which art was often used to manage and mitigate conflicts, disruptions and anxieties. In all three parts of this book, we see the construction of new buildings instigated by a threat (a threat to the Byzantine frontier, a threat to Bari's economy, a threat to Constance of France's authority). This book sets out to amplify our understanding of southern Italian art by redirecting some scholarly focus away from the royal Palermo and towards the mainland and the period of the conquest. In doing so, the picture becomes messier and less glamorous and evidence is more fragmented and challenging to interpret, but the buildings are no less interesting. They help us to understand what it is like to live on the periphery of an empire, through a time of tumultuous change.

Part 1

Byzantine Bari and Canosa

1
Life in Byzantine Bari

The first part of this book explores the archdiocese of Bari and Canosa during the Byzantine period (up to the Norman conquest in 1071). This first chapter provides some brief political, social and cultural context by painting a picture of life in Bari under Byzantine rule. Chapter 2 discusses the Byzantine palace complex, built by Byzantine officials as an administrative and military citadel. The palace was an enclave of Greek culture and was conceived as a miniature version of the Great Palace in Constantinople. Chapter 3 looks at the wider community in Bari, addressing Lombard culture and Lombard reactions to Byzantine rule, looking in particular at the patronage of the Lombard rebels Melus and Argyros and the construction of the new cathedral from 1025 onwards. Chapter 4 moves to Canosa, examining the liturgical furniture commissioned for the cathedral, which helps us to understand the role of Lombard bishops under Byzantine rule.

Since antiquity Bari has been a commercial port, a city bustling with travellers and merchants, where products from all over the Mediterranean were bought and sold. In Roman times it was much smaller and less influential than Brindisi to the south, which was the main port for shipping to the east. Ancient Bari was also eclipsed by its inland neighbour, the city of Canosa, the provincial capital, which prospered as a centre of wool production.[1] In the early Middle Ages, Bari and Canosa, like the rest of Italy, were caught in the tug of war between the Byzantine Empire and the Germanic Lombards. The Lombards established the Duchy of Benevento in the sixth century, only for the Byzantines to reconquer Apulia in the ninth century. Our story begins at the turn of the second millennium, with Bari under Byzantine rule.

Government and population

The east coast of Italy was strategically important for the Byzantine Empire because whoever controlled the entrance to the Adriatic controlled the *via Egnazia*, the road that ran through the Balkans to Constantinople. The Byzantine priority was to maintain military control of the region. They established the administrative province of *Lombardia*, led by a military governor and a small number of officials who were sent from Constantinople for short periods, on average for four years.[2] The capital was initially Benevento but was transferred to Bari in 985.[3] The population of Bari remained mostly Lombard, Latin rite Christians who used Latin as their liturgical and administrative language and were able to maintain their own legal system even under Byzantine rule.[4] The Lombard aristocracy retained much of their power and adopted elements of Byzantine culture for prestige.[5]

There were, however, tensions between the Byzantines and the local population, which erupted periodically into revolts. Two major revolts in 1009 and 1017 were led by a nobleman called Melus, who was Lombard but may have had some Armenian heritage.[6] When the revolts failed, Melus went into exile at the court of the Holy Roman Emperor, while his son Argyros was taken hostage by the Byzantines and sent to be educated in Constantinople. Argyros encapsulates the complex relationship between Lombards and Byzantines. Despite having been educated in Greek in the imperial capital, as an adult he was initially as anti-Byzantine as his father, returning to Italy to proclaim himself a duke and leader of the Lombard population, but later he switched sides and became an imperial official.[7] His pragmatism is probably fairly typical of the Lombard attitude to the Byzantine government.

Although it was mostly Lombard, Bari, like most port cities, had a diverse population. Southern Italians were mobile, and documentary sources are full references to people living away from where they were born and families scattered across the region.[8] In addition to the transient Byzantine officials and soldiers who came from all over the empire, there were other minorities, including sizeable Armenian and Jewish communities.[9] Jews were mostly artisans, many of whom worked in the textile trade, particularly in dyeing.[10] Conversion between faiths sometimes happened, including Archbishop Andrew, who converted to Judaism while on a trip to Constantinople and went to live in a Jewish community in Egypt.[11] There may have been small communities of foreign merchants with accommodation and warehouses in Bari. The eleventh-century St Mark's church is known as 'of the Venetians' and may indicate that Venetian merchants lived or stayed in that area of the city. Similarly, the church of San Pietro (now called 'La Vallisa') was known colloquially as 'Raveddise' in reference to the city of Ravello in Campania, whose merchants may have had a colony in Bari.[12] Cypriots were associated with the church of Santa Pelagia, and there may also have been a community from Dalmatia.[13]

In the ninth century Bari had briefly been an Arab emirate and, like other southern Italian cities, spent the central Middle Ages in constant contact with its Muslim neighbours, both through trade and through the threat of piracy. Raids and pillaging by Arab pirates caused a great deal of fear, destruction, enslavement of southern Italians and depopulation of some rural areas.[14] Although the city had been re-Christianized after the fall of the emirate and it was rare for Arab merchants to travel to Europe, it is likely that small numbers of Muslim traders and travellers from Sicily, North Africa and further afield would have been a common sight on the streets of Byzantine and Norman Bari.[15]

Topography

The medieval city (Map 3) occupies a small peninsula jutting out into the Adriatic. The most prominent landmarks in Byzantine Bari were the cathedral and governor's palace, which will be the subjects of the next chapters. Other churches included those now known

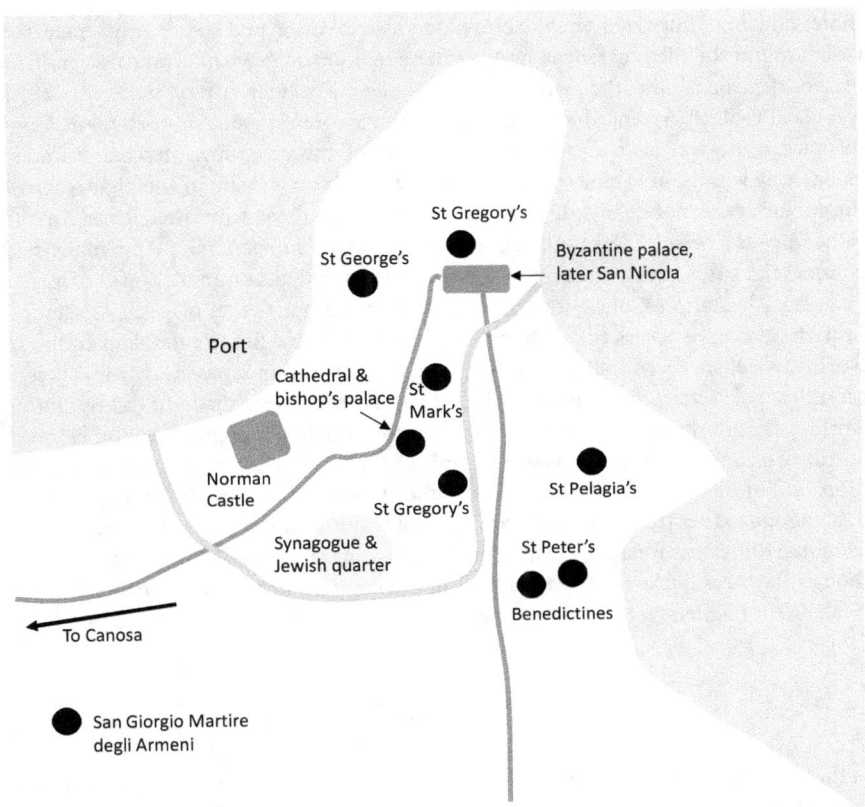

Map 3 Map of Bari in the Byzantine and Norman periods. Drawn by the author.

as Santa Teresa dei Maschi, San Martino, Santa Pelagia, Santa Maria del Buonconsiglio, Santa Maria del Carmine, San Pietro and San Giorgio.[16] Outside the walls was a Benedictine monastery with a fortified tower, which was a dependency of the powerful abbey of Montecassino.[17] The city was crowded; medieval authors noted how narrow the streets and alleys were and how the urban landscape was dotted with small gardens.[18] Disputes between neighbours were often about water, particularly the disposal of waste water into communal alleys and courtyards.[19] Interestingly, most houses were still single storey so, unlike other cities, Byzantine Bari does not seem to have had the population density or the civic competitiveness to building upwards in a display of *campanilismo*.[20]

Commerce

Maritime commerce drove the economy. The ports of the southern Adriatic exported agricultural staples and raw materials (such as wheat, oil and timber) from the fertile hinterland and imported manufactured goods, luxuries and exotic raw materials from around the Mediterranean and further afield, through Mediterranean terminals of the 'silk roads' and the African trade routes.[21] The majority of trade in staples was local (within Apulia, the Adriatic or to other southern Italian ports), but long-distance trade was also a very significant part of the economy. Merchants traded extensively with Islamic cities. Many documents mention 'Amalfitan' merchants across the Mediterranean, but this did not refer narrowly to those from the city of Amalfi; rather, it was a broader term indicating southern Italians in general.[22] 'Amalfitans' had commercial bases (*fonduqs*, community warehouses with accommodation) in Durrës, Palermo, Alexandria, Constantinople and Jerusalem, among other places.[23] Alexandria in particular gave access to products from Cairo, the Red Sea, Yemen and India. In North Africa, southern Italians sold staples like grain and purchased luxuries such as ceramics, gold, clothing, rugs and spices.[24] Similar sales were made in the Byzantine world, particularly Constantinople, where southern Italian merchants sold their wine and olive oil and purchased glass and ceramics.[25] But trade with Constantinople became more and more complex. The Byzantine authorities saw southern Italian merchants as a threat due to the strength of their commercial relationships with Islamic cities and so sought to limit their wealth by restricting their trading rights in Constantinople.[26] Even though Bari was a provincial capital within the empire, merchants from Apulia were treated as foreigners in terms of paying import and export taxes.[27]

The church

In the early eleventh century, the eastern and western churches were still in communion with each other, although the differences between them were becoming more and more pronounced and diplomatic relations between the pope and the eastern patriarch were becoming more and more strained and they would officially split in 1054. Within Byzantine Italy there was already an ecclesiastical split: dioceses in Calabria and Salento – which were more culturally and linguistically Greek – saw the patriarch of Constantinople as their spiritual leader to whom they owed obedience, whereas the dioceses in northern Apulia, including Bari, were loyal to the pope.[28] Thus, in Bari and Canosa, despite political governance from Constantinople, religious governance came from Rome. This division sometimes caused confusion and tension. Liturgical practices, however, were very mixed, and there was nothing like the strict divide between Greek and Latin practice that we see today.[29]

Bishops and archbishops were chosen by the local population; then the Byzantine authorities vetoed unsuitable anti-Byzantine candidates and sent them into exile, whereupon the local population proposed another candidate and the process continued until they found a mutually agreeable person. If no bishop could be found then the diocese was joined together with a neighbouring one, which happened reasonably frequently. The Byzantine state accepted Latin Bishops but limited their secular powers, so that Italian Bishops had a different, theoretically more purely spiritual, role in the community than their counterparts in other parts of the empire.[30] In practice, however, as we shall see, bishops often took on a more political role in their communities. They could be a subversive presence, sometimes antagonizing the Byzantines, but more often they supported the Byzantine authorities.

A vignette

A document from 1028 records the marriage of a woman called Alferada, who was, as far as we can tell, a fairly typical bourgeois citizen of Bari in the early eleventh century.[31] She was a Lombard by heritage; her very distant ancestors had migrated from northern Europe many centuries earlier. Her community was governed by Byzantine officials who came from Constantinople for a few years then left again. They brought with them battalions of soldiers from all over the empire. There were tensions between the officials and the Lombard community, and the Byzantines were able to retreat to their fortified citadel when rebellions erupted. Alferada worshipped God in Latin, in a church draped in eastern textiles. When her neighbour emptied his chamber pot onto her vegetable patch, the dispute was settled according to Lombard law. Her family's livelihood depended, directly or indirectly, on trade and shipping. In the marketplace she brought plentiful supplies of olive oil and wheat from the local countryside, artisanal products made in Bari and a few luxuries from around the Mediterranean. While shopping she heard dialects from elsewhere in Italy, Greek, Arabic, Hebrew, Armenian, Slavic and other languages of the pilgrims waiting to embark for the Holy Land. In her kitchen she flavoured her food with eastern spices, and on her wedding day she wore a dress made of eastern silk.

2

The Byzantine palace

Building Constantinople on the frontier

In Bari today, the most significant medieval landmark is the church dedicated to St Nicholas that was built in the Norman period. Under Byzantine rule, the site was occupied by the governor's palace, the citadel known in some sources as the 'Court of the Catepan' (from *Katepano*, governor), demolished to make way for the church. Although evidence is very limited, from texts, archaeological investigations, salvaged sculptural fragments and careful contextualization we can draw some conclusions about the palace and its place in Italo-Byzantine culture.

The earliest piece of evidence for the palace's existence comes from the Venetian chronicler John the Deacon, who mentions it in passing when describing how Venice sent ships to help the Byzantine navy repel an attempted Arab invasion in 1003.[1] During the twentieth-century restorations of the church of San Nicola, another piece of evidence came to light: a Greek inscription which had been set into the wall of the church.[2]

> With great effort and wisdom, the most powerful [governor] Basil Mesardonites, best of the nobles, who belongs to the imperial family, has used great technical skill to raise this building, to restore it as if it were new, with brick and stone. Having also built fortifications, he has built a vestibule to keep the soldiers free of fear [of attack] and a palace for glory and pride. Motivated by sincere devotion he has erected the church of St Demetrios, built in stone, so that, like a lighthouse, it shines clearly in its powerful glory for all those who live here and those who shall live here.[3]

The inscription refers to Basil Mesardonites, governor of Byzantine Italy from 1010 to 1017.[4] At that time, the Byzantines were facing significant rebellions from the Lombard population and incursions from the Lombard principality of Benevento along the northern border. The local Lombard population had always been sporadically hostile to Byzantine rule, but minor rebellions had been put down. More serious problems came with Melus's first revolt in 1009, which began in Bari and spread to neighbouring cities. It took several years and an influx of imperial troops for Mesardonites to quell the rebellion and force Melus into exile (although he would later return in 1017).[5] This context explains the alterations described in the inscription: the palace was damaged in a revolt and needed to be restored and fortified in durable materials.

Some of Mesardonites's fortifications survive. The base of the north tower of San Nicola is constructed with a different, rougher masonry than the rest of the tower. The type of blocks used is datable to much earlier than the construction of the church.[6] Excavations beneath the San Nicola Museum have revealed a section of the perimeter wall of the citadel, part of Mesardonites's fortifications.[7] Excavations around the periphery of San Nicola have revealed tantalizing fragments of the former palace, showing that it was a citadel with public, domestic, religious and industrial buildings constructed from the late ninth century to the early eleventh century.[8] It had its own cemeteries and workshops for metalworking and other trades. The date of the earliest structures means that there was probably some kind of Byzantine administrative building in Bari even before the capital was transferred from Benevento in 985. Geophysical surveys have found structures beneath the crypt of San Nicola, but it is impossible to discern their function or any architectural features. They are approximately 1 metre below the floor level of the crypt, so they could be underground storerooms for the Byzantine palace or even earlier structures, possibly Roman.[9]

The citadel contained five churches, dedicated to the Holy Wisdom, St Basil, St Gregory, St Eustratios and St Demetrios.[10] The dedications are revealing and very imperial in character. The Holy Wisdom is an obvious allusion to the cathedral in Constantinople and was probably the governors' main chapel. The dedication to St Basil of Cappadocia can be seen as an homage to the emperor, Basil II (958–1025), during whose long rule most of the palace complex was probably built. There are a few possible candidates for St Eustratios, but the most likely is the Armenian, Eustratios of Sebasteia, the leader of the so-called 'Holy Five', martyrs. Basil II had a particular devotion to St Eustratios of Sebasteia, who was depicted in Basil's *menologium* manuscript and whose head relic Basil donated to the Lavra monastery on Mount Athos.[11] St Eustratios was an appropriate patron, not only because of the emperor's devotion to him, but also because of his hagiography. He was an Armenian who served the Byzantines as a civil servant and possibly a soldier. He may have had particular meaning to the units of Armenian soldiers who were sent to Bari to quash the Lombard rebellions.[12]

The dedication to St Gregory is more complex. It is first attested in a document from 1015, when the priest, Melus, donated to the church some money he had inherited.[13] Later, in the post-Byzantine period, it was a private chapel belonging to the Adralistos family.[14] Some scholars have assumed that the dedication is for St Gregory the Illuminator, evangelist to the Armenians (because Melus is an Armenian name?), but it seems to me equally likely that the dedication was for St Gregory of Nyssa, brother of St Basil.[15] There is still a church of St Gregory adjacent to San Nicola. Presumably it is on the site of the original Byzantine chapel, but it was rebuilt in the late twelfth century.[16]

Saint Demetrios is a military saint and was a protector of the Byzantine army, an apt dedication in a citadel that also functioned as an army barracks.[17] Likewise, Eustratios of Sebasteia and his four companions are usually depicted in icons and manuscripts as protectors of churches, so they were good patrons for a fortified citadel, at a time when the Byzantine authorities felt threatened by the local population.[18] The inscription commemorating Mesardonites's fortifications and renovations mentions, poetically, that the church of St Demetrios shone like a lighthouse. This could be a subtle allusion to the Pharos, the 'lighthouse' church within the Great Palace in Constantinople. Mesardonites wanted his citadel to echo the palace in the imperial capital.

Mesardonites's inscription also tells us that he built a vestibule to keep his soldiers safe, which is another allusion to Constantinople. The main entrance to the Great Palace was the Chalke Gate and behind it was a vestibule with barracks to the side.[19] Nino Lavermicocca has argued that some of the enigmatic structures at the east end of San Nicola are the remnants of Mesardonites's vestibule.[20] This theory is no more than a hypothesis, but it would mean that the main entrance was on the east side, a sea gate rather than a monumental entrance facing into the city.[21] If this were indeed the case, it would mirror the governor's palace at Apollonia in Libya, where the principal façade and monumental entrance were oriented towards the sea, so that the most impressive view of the palace was reserved for approaching ships.[22] Another example is the much earlier palace of Diocletian across the Adriatic at Split, where the land walls were fortified and imposing but the sea façade was unfortified with an open arcade on the upper storey.

In general, we know little about middle Byzantine governors' palaces. Very few were built in this period because, in most provinces, the late antique buildings were still in use, for example in Caesarea, where the governor continued to use the Roman praetorium as his residence. It contained a basilical audience hall that also served as a law court; a private residence for the governor; gardens and courtyards; a bath house and administrative buildings.[23] Where new governor's palaces were built, most continued to be modelled on late antique prototypes.[24] Where late antique buildings remained in use they were altered very little during the middle Byzantine period. A good example, already mentioned earlier, is in Apollonia in Libya, where the late antique palace has been excavated. The palace revolved around a central atrium, surrounded by a chapel, a hall for secular ceremonies and an entrance vestibule, with access to a public audience hall. The chapel was essential for governing the province: relics (presumably of a local saint), had been moved from the nearby cathedral at Cyrene and would have been used for swearing oaths, as part of governing the local population.[25] It is not known whether any of the five chapels in Bari contained relics, but it is reasonable to suppose they did. The link between St Demetrios and the Pharos insinuated in Mesardonites's inscription might indicate that relics had been brought from Constantinople to be housed in St Demetrios, the Pharos being the great imperial repository of relics, particularly the Passion relics.[26]

In the church of San Nicola and the attached museum, we can see some of the sculpture that once adorned the Byzantine palace. Much of the salvaged sculpture is in the crypt of San Nicola. Thanks to Gioia Bertelli's meticulous analysis of the crypt capitals and their models, they can be divided into four groups. Figure 1 shows a plan of the crypt, which was built in the 1080s. The two groups of capitals pertinent in this chapter are those in blue and yellow. The yellow group were carved in the sixth century, mostly in the eastern Mediterranean.[27] For example, capitals 26 (Figure 2) and 28, which are decorated with pairs of cornucopia, goat's horns overflowing with flowers and fruit as a symbol of abundance and fertility, and are similar in style to the sculpture recovered from the sixth-century church of St Polyeuktos in Constantinople.[28] One of them is supported by a spiral column, of the type often used in late antique ciboria.[29] Another example is capital 6, featuring typical Byzantine basket weave (Figure 3). Basket weave is found on Byzantine capitals from the fourth to the tenth centuries but was particularly common in late antiquity, for example in Hagia Sophia and

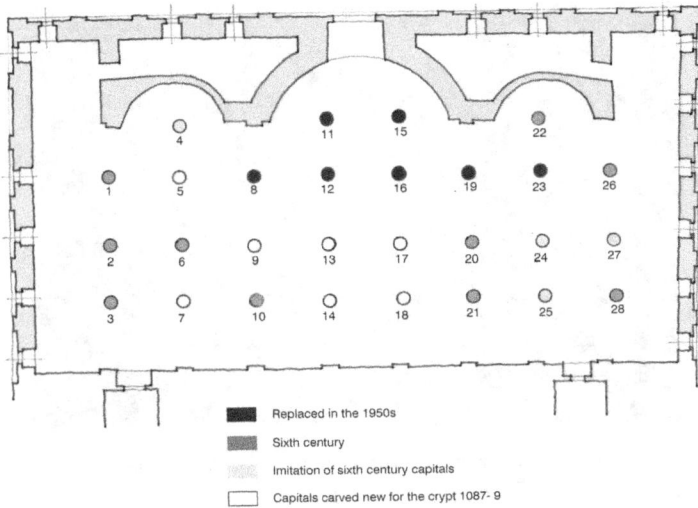

Figure 1 Crypt of San Nicola, Bari, plan. Drawn by Elisabeth Kendall.

Figure 2 Capital 26 with cornucopia, crypt of San Nicola, Bari. Photo: John McNeill.

Ravenna. This group of capitals are not uniform, they have not been collected from a single source, but rather they display influences from various parts of the eastern Mediterranean. This implies that they have been collected through trade by a patron who collaborated with merchants to piece together a collection of capitals selected specifically for their sixth-century date and eastern Mediterranean origin. Transporting stone and stone sculpture around the Mediterranean was practical and fairly common. Stone is excellent ballast to make ships more sturdy and was therefore a desirable cargo.[30] My hypothesis is that these spoliate capitals were collected by Mesardonites or

Figure 3 Capital 6 with basket weave, crypt of San Nicola, Bari. Photo: author.

Figure 4 Capital 27 with inverted palmette, crypt of San Nicola, Bari. Photo: author.

one of the other governors, through collaboration with Baresi merchants and used in the construction of the chapels in the palace, in order to create buildings that reflected the contemporary interest in Constantinople in late antique art and culture.

The group of spoliate capitals was amplified by copies of sixth-century capitals, marked on the plan in blue. They are very similar to the sixth-century group, but they were carved in the tenth or eleventh century.[31] Capitals 24 and 27 (Figure 4) conform

Figure 5 Figure of Holy Wisdom from the Byzantine palace, probably early eleventh century. Museo Nicolaiano, Bari. Photo: Sailko via Wikimedia.

to a sixth-century Byzantine design, known as the inverted palmette type, which is also found at St Menas in Egypt. They were carved as a pair, but they are of different heights, to accommodate spoliate columns of different heights. I find it likely that these imitations were commissioned by Mesardonites or one of his colleagues to blend in with the spoliate group described earlier. They were probably carved in Bari for the Byzantine palace as a way of expanding the collection of sixth-century material.

A more few pieces of sculpture came to light during the restoration of San Nicola and are now in the museum. There are some fragments of epistyles and a small capital featuring a Greek cross and the monogram of the patron, the *patrikios* Leo, a high-ranking official.[32] Most were reliefs which had been flipped over and re-used as paving stones in the new church. The most interesting depicts a winged figure with a book on her lap, sitting on a faldstool (a classical *sella curulis*) with clawed feet (Figure 5), probably a depiction of the Holy Wisdom.[33] Depictions of Holy Wisdom are not always easy to identify since there was no established iconography for the Holy Wisdom in Byzantine art in this period; the standardization of the iconography developed later in early modern icons. A mosaic in the narthex of Hagia Sophia depicts Christ as Holy Wisdom, in line with early Byzantine theology.[34] But other personifications of Wisdom are comparable to the Bari panel.[35] In the tenth-century Paris psalter, commissioned by Constantine VII Porphyrygenitos (913–959), Wisdom is a female figure in classicizing dress, standing with a book tucked under her arm.[36] In the Arsenal Bible, made in

Acre in the 1250s but based on earlier Byzantine and French models, Wisdom is a winged woman in classicized dress, seated next to Solomon, who is reading an open book.[37] Presumably, the relief in Bari once adorned the eponymous chapel, where it not only reminded the governors and other civil servants of the great cathedral at the heart of the empire but also evoked something of the culture of the capital. Wisdom's classicizing seat and dress, evocative of imperial commissions like the Paris psalter, reflect the revival of late antiquity in contemporary Constantinople.[38]

Putting together these disparate pieces of evidence, we can see that the Byzantine officials who built and lived in the palace complex saw it as a little piece of Constantinople, even a miniature version of the Great Palace. This was manifested even in its orientation towards the east, looking back to Constantinople rather than towards the city of Bari. Although it was a newly built citadel, it was probably modelled on late antique palaces that were standard elsewhere in the empire. The dedications of the churches evoke an imperial identity and the commemorative inscription makes implicit comparisons with the Great Palace in the capital. Those churches were decorated with sculpture that echoed the artistic trends in the Byzantine capital.

For the small number of Greek officials, the palace was an enclave during their short posting to the frontier, and they did little to engage culturally with the population beyond its fortified walls. Beyond the palace in Bari, Byzantine officials rarely acted as patrons of the visual arts. There is only one example from Bari itself: a Byzantine official called Pothos Argyros built a Greek monastery on the periphery of Bari in 1032.[39] Emperor Constantine Monomachos instructed a Greek monk to found a monastery dedicated to St Nicholas, to whom the emperor had a particular devotion, in the 1040s or 1050s.[40] Outside Bari, one of the governors commissioned some paintings for a cave church built by a local called Vitalis.[41] At Otranto, where the majority of the population were Greek-rite Christians, there was more patronage from Byzantine officials, most notably at San Pietro.[42]

It is notable that the most significant act of patronage by a Byzantine governor of Bari took place in Greece. The church of Panagia Chalkeon in Thessaloniki was built in 1028 by Christopher, governor of Bari and the Italian province. The church is typical of eleventh-century architecture in the Balkans, displaying no links to Bari. The patronage was a family affair, Christopher and his wife Maria were buried there, and Maria and their three children are mentioned in the dedicatory inscription over the door.[43] Christopher probably built the church in his home province during his retirement. Like other Byzantine officials, he probably saw little reason to engage with art or build a legacy in Italy. Byzantine officials were sent to Bari only for short periods, and it was seen primarily as a military outpost. The governor's palace is therefore exceptional, the only building in Byzantine Bari to be 'purely' Byzantine.

3

Bari cathedral and 'Lombard' patronage under Byzantine rule

In an article in 1974, Hans Belting asked the question, was there any Byzantine art in Byzantine Italy? His conclusion was that, under Byzantine rule, southern Italian art was decidedly not Byzantine in style (although he did conclude that manuscripts in Bari began to show Byzantine influence from c. 1000).[1] In 1988 Anabel Wharton compared the architecture and painting in four Byzantine provinces, including Apulia, concluding that southern Italy was distinctive because of its lack of artistic engagement with Constantinople. The distance from the capital, proximity to Rome and the popularity of Latin Christianity made southern Italy artistically different from other provinces, which were highly dependent on Constantinople.[2] Belting and Wharton were typical of art historians of the mid- to late-twentieth century in defining 'Byzantine art' as the art of Constantinople. Their interest in the provinces was in how art from Constantinople was received and imitated, mirroring the way that historians thought about the political relationship between centre and peripheries in the empire.[3] In this framework, Constantinople was the centre of innovation which 'fed' the provinces, an idea which is now considered problematic.[4] Art historians now tend to argue for a more expansive definition of Byzantine art, in which the provinces were artistic centres in their own right and each developed their own way of engaging or not engaging with Constantinople, according to their own needs.[5]

In 2012, Linda Safran described art in Apulia as being in the 'fuzzy space' between Byzantine and not Byzantine, arguing for 'Byzantineness' to be seen as spectrum. Safran and others are in favour of the term 'Byzantinizing' as a way of acknowledging the vagueness and messiness of categorizing art on the periphery of the empire.[6] This chapter will explore the messiness of that fuzzy space by delving into the artistic agency of the Lombard community during the period of Byzantine rule. We will look at the patronage of the rebel leader Melus and his son Argyros, before turning our attention to the cathedral of Bari, the spiritual and civic hub of the city for the Lombard population.

Melus and Argyros as patrons

Melus was a Lombard nobleman, an influential figure in Bari, who led a series of rebellions against the Byzantines in 1009 and 1017, along with his brother-in-law

Dattus. The Norman writer William of Apulia claimed that Melus recruited a group of Norman pilgrims to help his cause, thus instigating Norman migration to southern Italy, but the story is probably a literary device to boost the impression of Norman legitimacy. At a local level the rebellions began with the resentment of the Lombard population but on a bigger scale, they were part of the tug of war between the Byzantine Empire and the Holy Roman Empire over territory in southern Italy. Melus ended up in exile and fled to the court of Holy Roman Emperor in Bamberg to form an anti-Byzantine alliance with Henry II. He took part in a meeting between the pope and the emperor to plan an attack on Byzantine territories.[7] Melus commissioned a garment known as the 'star mantle' (Figure 6), which he gave to Henry in an act of what Anna Muthesius calls 'silken diplomacy', the use of textiles as gifts to build political networks and achieve political goals.[8]

The mantle was a semicircle of purple twill silk, decorated with gold thread embroidery. The purple ground was replaced in the sixteenth century when the embroidery was cut out and remounted as appliqué on the current electric blue damask.

During the alteration, the arrangement of the embroidery was changed a little, particularly the inscription along the hem, which reads, 'Ornament of Europe, Emperor Henry, you are blessed. May the king who rules forever increase your realm'. Above that is a smaller inscription reading 'Description of the whole world. May Ishmael who commissioned it rest in peace', implying that Melus died before the mantle was completed (he also went by the name Ishmael).[9] The imagery includes saints, evangelists, astrological constellations, personifications of the sun and the moon and Christ in Majesty at the centre.

Figure 6 'Star Mantle' given by Melus of Bari to Emperor Henry II. Photo: Allie Caulfield via Wikimedia.

The mantle is generally included in books on Ottonian art and is more rarely connected to southern Italy.[10] There has been some debate about whether it was made in Germany or Italy but the current consensus is that it was probably made in Regensberg, Bavaria.[11] In favour of the Regensberg provenance are the similarities to other embroideries made in the same workshop and to Ottonian manuscripts.[12] Added to this is the fact that Melus left his home in Bari, fleeing from the Byzantines (who had his fellow rebel Dattus drowned in the port of Bari), and would not have been able to stop to commission a mantle in Apulia. Nonetheless, the act of patronage should be considered in relation to the art history of Bari. In consultation with the embroiderers and perhaps with Henry's courtiers, Melus must have chosen the imagery and the inscription.[13] Melus probably purchased the purple silk and gold thread in Apulia and took it with him to Regensberg, but both were likely to have been manufactured in Constantinople, where they were purchased by merchants from the Apulian port cities. The gold thread on the roughly contemporary Hungarian coronation mantle was manufactured in Constantinople, as was the thread on the twelfth-century mantle of Roger II.[14] Since Melus decided to use imperial purple silk, he probably also chose gold thread from Constantinople too (probably purchased from the same merchant). In this period, gold thread embroidery was a way that Europeans would emulate Byzantine woven textiles, despite not having the expertise or machinery to reproduce them in woven form.[15]

The idea for an imperial mantle depicting the cosmos was originally Roman but would have been perceived as Byzantine by Melus. The Capitoline Temple of Jupiter contained star mantles presented to the emperors to commemorate military victories They signified the emperor's dominion over the whole world, and that idea was continued in Byzantine culture.[16] However, the nuance of star mantles was slightly different in northern Europe and Henry II may have interpreted the gift in a different way than its giver intended. Both Charles the Bald and Henry II's predecessor, Otto III, donated star mantles to St Denis and St Alessio in Rome respectively.[17] Henry II did not keep the mantle that Melus gave him but instead donated it to the cathedral of Bamberg to be used as a vestment. Benjamin Anderson argued that in German culture the apotheosis of the emperor implied in the imagery was considered inappropriate for secular regalia. The idea of the ruler as having dominion over the whole cosmos was considered an example of Byzantine arrogance and the astrological imagery more fitting for the ecclesiastical sphere.[18] If this theory is correct, then we see a cultural misunderstanding played out in the gift. Melus, steeped in Mediterranean culture, gave the mantle with a Byzantine mentality, misunderstanding Western ideas about the power of the emperor.

Whether or not the iconography was considered inappropriate by the recipient, the giving of the mantle had a clear political significance for both parties. The gift sealed a contract between Melus and the emperor. In return for Melus proclaiming allegiance to the Holy Roman Empire, Henry made him Duke of Apulia.[19] If Melus had lived, he would have joined Henry's military campaigns in Italy in the hope of conquering Bari for the Holy Roman Empire and ruling the city himself in place of the Byzantine governor. The mantle therefore signifies the intended transfer of Bari from one empire to another. Melus's gift, made with Byzantine imperial silk and Byzantine gold thread, imitating a Byzantine woven textile, symbolized Melus offering the emperor a piece of the Byzantine Empire.

Melus's son Argyros was also a shrewd diplomat. Argyros, held hostage by the Byzantines in Constantinople after his father's rebellions, returned to Bari in *c.* 1040 full of his father's anti-Byzantine politics. During further upheaval in the 1040s, Argyros persuaded the Normans, who were by now gaining territory in southern Italy, to appoint him duke of Apulia, just as his father had persuaded Henry II to do the same. Presumably Argyros offered to help secure Bari for the Normans in return for the title. Mysteriously, Argyros then switched sides and offered his loyalties to the Byzantines, who eventually made him governor of the Italian province. As governor, he continued to use the title Duke, rather than the Byzantine Katepan, because it was a rank recognized by both the Lombards and the Byzantines.[20] In 1054 Argyros travelled to Constantinople to take part in negotiations between the Byzantines and representatives of the Holy Roman Emperor, regarding an anti-Norman alliance.[21]

Argyros was concerned with maintaining and building upon his father's legacy. He was concerned about the tomb of his father, who had died in Bamberg, and he wrote to Henry III asking him to make sure it was well maintained.[22] He also participated in silken diplomacy, just like his father, by donating money and silk to the abbey of Farfa near Rome. The donation document, written in both Latin and Greek, tells us that the silk was a mantle embroidered with gold (made in Bari, presumably?) – similar therefore to the one commissioned by his father – and was probably re-purposed by the monastery as an ecclesiastical vestment, which may have been Argyros's intention, in reference to Henry II's donation of the star mantle to Bamberg cathedral.[23] Argyros's donation should be seen as part of a desire to build an alliance with Holy Roman Emperor Henry III, who was a patron of both Farfa and Santa Maria di Tremiti (on an island off the coast of northern Apulia), where Argyros also made donations.[24] Argyros was, therefore, hedging his bets by building alliances with both the Byzantine and Holy Roman emperors.

In their dealings with both empires, Melus and Argyros were always pragmatic. Their aim seems to have been to secure as much independence and 'self-determination', to borrow a modern term, for the Lombard population of Bari as possible, allying themselves with whichever empire seemed to be providing the best terms at the time. The fine silks they commissioned were intended to imitate prestigious Byzantine woven silks. Silk was a tool they used to build alliances with the Holy Roman Empire, perhaps leveraging Bari's connections with the Byzantine Empire. Although neither the star mantle nor the Farfa mantle is in Bari today, they are nonetheless part of the way that Bari projected its identity into the wider world, and that identity was one that leveraged Byzantine culture.

Bari cathedral

We now turn our attention to Bari cathedral, which must have been the focal point of the Lombard community under Byzantine rule. There have been three cathedrals in Bari, all on the same site, built in the sixth, eleventh and twelfth centuries. It is the eleventh-century building that concerns us here, although there is very little evidence for what it looked like. The early Christian cathedral had a basilical plan with a single apse and an impressive mosaic floor (Figure 7).[25] In 1034, Archbishop Bisantius decided to replace it, but rather than demolish the existing church, he preserved it as a burial crypt and built the new cathedral on top of it (Figure 8).[26] The burial crypt was in use throughout the Middle Ages and has now been opened up again.

Archbishop Bisantius was an important civic leader. In the *Annales of Bari*, he is described as 'a most pious father to the fatherless, founder of the holy church of Bari, guardian of the city, a defender who was fearless and frightful against all the Greeks'.[27] This refers to tensions between the Byzantine authorities and the Lombard population and to Bisantius's civic and pastoral leadership of the Lombard population. Bisantius may have been involved in Melus's revolts and in a continuing anti-Byzantine movement in the 1020s. But he also collaborated with the governor Pothos Argyros in the foundation of the Greek monastery dedicated to the Theotokos, St John the Evangelist and St John the Baptist in 1032, and he must have been on cordial terms with the Byzantines for them to approve his appointment as archbishop.[28] Somehow he managed to walk the delicate line between resisting Byzantine rule and not antagonizing the Byzantine authorities.

Unfortunately, Bisantius could not make much progress with his cathedral because he died a year after it was begun. The tension between Greeks and Lombards continued with his successor, Romuald, who was said to have been 'elected by all the people'.[29] He must have been anti-Byzantine, more so than his predecessor and less diplomatic, because the Byzantine authorities disapproved of his appointment and exiled him to

Figure 7 Late antique mosaic pavement, Bari cathedral. Photo: Author.

Figure 8 Burial crypt, Bari cathedral. Photo: John McNeill.

Constantinople. This was a common strategy for the Byzantine officials, who often vetoed episcopal candidates if they were likely to be hostile (one wonders how Bisantius managed to hold onto his mitre).[30] Next in line was Nicholas, who was approved by the Byzantine authorities. The majority of the work on the new cathedral must have been completed during Nicholas's episcopacy (1035–62), although the original vision was Bisantius's. Archbishop Nicholas was given the title *protosynkellus*, a Byzantine title probably given in recognition of his loyalty to the empire.[31]

The new cathedral was built about twenty years after the fortification of the governor's palace. The construction project may have been a response to the fortifications and the failure of Melus's rebellions. It could have been a way for the Lombards to assert themselves and strengthen their community without antagonizing the governor. But we should be cautious about assuming that the Lombard community felt straightforward animosity towards the Byzantine authorities and towards the governor's palace complex. In reality the Lombards' attitude towards the Byzantines was more nuanced. Not only did Bisantius collaborate with Pothos Argyros in the foundation of the Greek monastery but a Latin priest called Peter left all of his property to the church of St Eustratios in the Byzantine palace. Peter obviously felt an affinity with the eastern saint and with the church building and did not view that as antithetical to his Lombard identity.[32] These two examples of cross-cultural patronage show that there was nothing like an ecclesiastical schism in Bari, and the Byzantine authorities may well have approved or even supported the reconstruction of the cathedral.

The cathedral built by Bisantius and Nicholas lasted less than a century before King William I ordered its destruction along with most of the city (except San Nicola), as punishment for Bari's rebelliousness in 1156. The current cathedral is a late-twelfth-

Figure 9 Hall crypt, Bari cathedral. Photo: John McNeill.

Figure 10 Current baptistery, Bari cathedral. Photo: Author.

century building, which defiantly rose from the ashes of the king's destruction and was modelled on the basilica of San Nicola. Today, the cathedral has four parts: there are two subterranean spaces (the late antique church–turned–burial crypt and a late-twelfth-century hall crypt, Figure 9) and the main church, which is modelled on the architecture of San Nicola (1087–c. 1106; see Part 2).[33] There is also a room to the southwest that was possibly part of the Byzantine-era cathedral (Figure 10). Today it is used as a baptistery but was possibly part of a tower or treasury built by Bisantius and Nicholas.

The destruction in 1156 seems to have been extensive. The chronicler Hugo Falcandus tells us that even the city walls were 'brought down to ground level . . . the most powerful city of Apulia, celebrated by fame and immensely rich, proud in its noble citizens and remarkable in the architecture of its buildings now lies transformed into piles of rubble'.[34] Falcandus's description implies total demolition, but his aim was to portray William I as a barbaric despot, and it was in his interests to exaggerate. The architecture may have been completely destroyed, but a careful look at the sculpture in the current cathedral tells us that some of it was salvaged from the rubble. Some was re-employed by the twelfth-century builders, and some came to light in a fragmentary state during twentieth-century restorations. Various fragments have been reused in the current ambo (Figure 11) and other liturgical furnishings.

Figure 11 Ambo, Bari cathedral. Photo: Author.

Some of the material that has come to light is late antique spolia that Bisantius and Nicholas used in their cathedral. That spolia was imported from the eastern Mediterranean, just like in the Byzantine palace. The twelfth-century crypt is mostly covered in Baroque cladding, but one column has been exposed and it is topped with a capital from the fifth or sixth century, of a type found on the Adriatic, Greece and Sicily.[35] The column bases on the south portal are also sixth-century spolia, similar to sculpture from Constantinople in the era of Justinian (Figure 12).[36] A sixth-century tombstone with a Greek inscription had been used as part of the sacristy pavement in the post-medieval period (Figure 13). A pseudo-Arabic border had been added to it, probably in the eleventh century.[37] The presence of this tombstone in the cathedral is interesting. One would expect to find a Greek tombstone in the Byzantine palace complex, but it is more surprising in the context of the Latin rite cathedral and it demonstrates that the Lombard population engaged with Greek culture. The similar artistic vocabulary across both sites indicates more harmony than discord, at least in terms of visual and religious culture.

Figure 12 South portal, Bari cathedral. Photo: Author.

Figure 13 Byzantine tombstone with pseudo-Arabic ornament. Discovered in Bari cathedral, now in the castle. Photo: Author.

John of Trani

It is a shame we do not have more evidence for how the Lombard communities in Bari and Canosa related to the Byzantine authorities. To flesh out our understanding of Archbishops Bisantius and Nicholas and their artistic patronage, we can look at the life and patronage of Archbishop John of Trani, about whom we have more information. Being part of the Byzantine Empire was generally economically and politically advantageous. The majority of Apulian bishops had good relationships with the Byzantine authorities and supported the empire against the Normans.[38] The bishops of Troia and Acerenza were killed fighting against the Normans in 1041.[39] Trani was a particularly pro-Byzantine city, but it nonetheless switched sides and supported Melus in the revolt of 1017, along with many other cities.[40] John became archbishop around 1053, and he is known for two things: for promoting a local cult and for his loyalty to the empire.

John was rewarded for his loyalty to Byzantium with the title *Synkellus*, which is recorded in his epitaph. The title was a great honour, usually bestowed only on high-ranking priests who served under the Patriarch of Constantinople, but was sometimes given by the emperor to bishops and occasionally to laymen.[41] However, his loyalty to the empire at a time of schism and the encroaching Norman conquest was his downfall. In 1063 he was deposed by Pope Alexander II for simony and 'ostentation', which was probably a euphemism for being too close to the Byzantines.[42] He found himself on the fault line between east and west on another occasion when Archbishop Leo of Ohrid sent him a letter attacking Latin practices such as the use of unleavened bread for the Eucharist and fasting on Saturdays in Lent. The letter, which is a key document in history of the rapid decline in the relationship between the eastern and western churches, was then translated into Latin by Cardinal Humbert de Silva Candida and disseminated in Latin clerical circles.[43] On this occasion, John of Trani was the conduit for communication between eastern and western clerics, showing Apulia's important role on the frontier between the two.

John wrote an account of the *translatio*, move, of the relics of St Leucius, the first bishop of Brindisi, whose relics were shared between Trani and Brindisi.[44] In doing so he revitalized Leucius's cult and promoted his own cathedral in Trani as an important site in the sacred topography of Apulia. Like Bisantius and Nicholas of Bari, he was a patron who commissioned new liturgical furnishings for his cathedral: an ambo, inscribed 'let the priest John possess paradise', a templon screen and an episcopal throne, all now in fragments in the diocesan museum.[45] There are also a few fragments of an architrave by Acceptus, with the same vegetal scroll as the door jambs at Bari cathedral.[46]

John and his contemporaries in Bari were bishops on a frontier. The fact that the pope saw John as a threat to papal primacy indicates that the Latin church viewed them as having split loyalties. Their episcopal colleagues in the east saw them as advocates for Latin practices but also as 'go-betweens', people with a foot in both camps who could facilitate dialogue with the Latins. They walked a precarious line between two major powers in the Mediterranean, while also strengthening and promoting their own local communities.

Trapezoid capitals and silk

There is a group of finely carved capitals in and around Bari with links to portable objects. These capitals are trapezoid (known in Italian as *a stampella*, crutch capitals), of the type designed for templons, galleries and cloisters (Figures 14 and 15). In Bari

Figure 14 Trapezoid capital, Pinacoteca Provincial, Bari. Photo: Author.

Figure 15 Trapezoid capital, Pinacoteca Provincial, Bari. Photo: Author.

they were present in the eleventh-century cathedral and the roughly contemporary cloister of San Benedetto.[47] The examples from the cathedral are now distributed between the Pinacoteca Provinciale, the castle and reused in the galleries of the present cathedral. Similar capitals have also come to light at Canosa cathedral, the cloister of Santa Maria di Colonna in Trani and the lost cloister of San Benedetto in Polignano.[48] The capitals feature pairs of addorsed animals with bands of beads on their wings and tails looped around their hind legs. Fritz Volbach asserted confidently but vaguely that the sculptors drew inspiration from ivories, but I cannot find any examples of ivories with the same features.[49] The looped tail is characteristic of middle Byzantine stone sculpture, while the beading on the winged creatures derives from Byzantine and Islamic woven silks, for example, the shroud of St Germanus and the shroud of St Siviard.[50] Transposing textile motifs into stone happened in other southern Italian port cities at this time, for example on the parapet screens from Sant'Aspreno al Porto in Naples and the relief panels from Sorrento cathedral.[51] Textiles were among the most lucrative commercial goods handled by Italian merchants, and the transposition of textiles designs into cathedrals and monasteries highlights international trade as the bedrock of the city's economy. Many foreign silks were used in ecclesiastical settings, as vestments; curtains to veil the sanctuary; wall hangings; shrouds; and to wrap relics. When sculptors used the same motifs in stone, it created a unified aesthetic in the church, amplifying the impact of the luxurious textiles, as if the whole church were wrapped in silk.[52] The homogeneity of this group of capitals indicates that they were carved by a single workshop, based in Bari, in the c. 1040s. The prevalence of these capitals in Benedictine cloisters points to a workshop of Latin monastic sculptors. It is likely that this workshop was based in San Benedetto in Bari.

Manuscripts

San Benedetto in Bari is more artistically significant than it is usually given credit for. Not only did it produce an important workshop of sculptors, it also had a thriving scriptorium. Although illuminated manuscripts from Bari are not plentiful, there are enough of them to indicate that there was an active Latin scriptorium, staffed by skilled illuminators. Manuscripts from the Benedictine scriptorium Bari and the surrounding area are easy to identify because the scribes developed their own version of the Beneventan script, known as the 'Bari type' (which later spread across the Adriatic to Dalmatia).[53] Here I will limit myself to discussing a few examples produced during Byzantine rule. Unsurprisingly, the illuminators of Bari were predominantly influenced by their Benedictine brothers in the influential scriptoria at Benevento, San Vincenzo al Volturno, Salerno and Montecassino. One of the best known manuscripts from Byzantine era Bari is a Morgancap document, dated 1028, in which Melus gives his wife Alferada (whom we met in Chapter 1) a quarter of his wealth, as was the Lombard custom. The document is illustrated with a depiction of the couple standing under an arch with birds perched on it. The illumination is very much in keeping with manuscripts from the Lombard principalities and shows no Byzantine influence.[54] Likewise, the copy of Ovid's *Metamorphoses* (*c*. 1050) is very Lombard in character.[55]

On the other hand, the liturgical scrolls produced in Bari (two Exultets and a Benedictional) do show some Byzantine influence. Scrolls had long since been replaced by the codex as the standard form of manuscript, so their reintroduction in Southern Italy in the late tenth century was an anomaly, probably part of the revival of interest in the antique.[56] The first liturgical scrolls (an Exultet and a Pontifical) were commissioned by Landulf of Benevento to commemorate his promotion to archbishop in 969.[57] The scrolls were used at a moment of high emotion and drama during the Easter vigil. The vigil took place at dusk, as the light was fading. The Easter fire was lit outside the church, from which the bishop lit a candle, which he carried into the nave. The deacon processed to the altar to collect the Exultet scroll then ascended the ambo, where he sang the *lumen Christi* (light of Christ), with the people responding *deo gratias* (thanks be to God). The deacon sang the opening line of the Exultet hymn 'rejoice now angelic choirs of the heavens' as the bishop lit the paschal candle and then the flame was passed through the congregation as they lit their candles, gradually illuminating the church.[58] As Landulf's new Exultet scroll was unfurled for the first time to its full length of 7 metres, it must have made a big impression on the community. Although the images are small, the object as a whole is almost monumental, rivalling the size of the massive spoliate columns in Benevento cathedral.

The Bari scrolls seem to have been inspired by Landulf's, but they are not derivative of it; the Bari illuminators sought out their own iconographic models and added and subtracted certain scenes.[59] For example, the chanting of the exultet hymn and lighting of the paschal candle, a pivotal scene in the Beneventan scroll and in the liturgy, are absent from the Bari manuscript. The first scroll made in Bari is now in the John Rylands Library in Manchester, dated to *c*. 1000.[60] Thomas Kelly categorized it as unknown provenance, but the script is Bari type and the Rylands library catalogue now attributes it to Bari or the Terra di Bari.[61] Since it is only partially preserved, the liturgical scenes

Figure 16 Rylands Exultet, Anastasis detail 1. Photo: John Rylands Library, University of Manchester.

have been lost, leaving us with only the illuminated 'E' at the beginning of *exultet*, the 'V' at the beginning of *vere dignum* ('it is truly fitting'), the Crucifixion, Anastasis, Nativity and praise of the bees (bees are lauded in the text for making the wax for the paschal candle). The Anastasis is particularly elaborate and interesting, unusually explored over two images. In the first (Figure 16), Christ, holding a scroll, stands on top of a chained, naked figure (presumably the devil), driving a spear through his skull. The background is a cityscape, a crenelated arch flanked by towers and other buildings, populated by a crowd watching Christ's triumph. In the second scene (Figure 17), Christ pulls the souls out of Limbo, again observed by a crowd. In this second scene the cityscape has become part of the underworld, with flaming naked bodies impaled on the city walls.

The images on the scroll are highly self-referential. The crowd are mostly laymen in short tunics, with a few monks in darker brown tunics. Thomas Kelly imagined that many of the monks who worked on the Exultet scrolls were also deacons, so the scrolls may have been written and illuminated by the very men who sang from them.[62] The depictions of the monks in the crowd watching the Anastasis may even be 'portraits' of the illuminators-deacons who made and used the scroll. Christ carries a scroll, not only indicating that he is *logos*, but also alluding to the scroll upon which he is depicted and the moment of the proclamation of his resurrection on Holy Saturday. In the image on the scroll, he is watched by a congregation of contemporary Baresi, the same people who would watch the unfurling of the scroll and hear the Exultet hymn at the Easter vigil liturgy. In the

Figure 17 Rylands Exultet, Anastasis detail 2. Photo: John Rylands Library, University of Manchester.

image, Christ's triumph and resurrection are depicted as taking place in Bari, signifying that the resurrection of Christ that takes place during the liturgy of the Easter vigil in the urban cathedral *is* the resurrection (rather than merely symbolic of it). The image makes Christ's resurrection in Bari visible to the faithful of Bari. Like most of the great feasts of the church, the Exultet hymn disrupts the linearity of time, transporting the congregation to the moment of the resurrection.[63] At the vigil liturgy, the people of Bari would have seen themselves, as a community, reflected in the images on the scroll. That gave the scroll, not just a religious significance, but also a community and civic significance.

The remaining two scrolls were produced as a pair: an Exultet (known as Bari Exultet 1 because a second was produced during the Norman period) and a Benedictional. For much of their history they were sewn together into a continuous manuscript, although they were made as separate scrolls.[64] The Benedictional contains the parts of the vigil liturgy led by the bishop, prayers before the Exultet hymn and for baptism after it.[65] The Exultet can be fairly securely dated to *c*. 1025 and the episcopate of Archbishop Bisantius. The date of the Benedictional is more uncertain, with Thomas Kelly dating it to *c*. 1024, just before the Exultet, whereas Penelope Mayo and Nino Zchomeldise date it to the era of Archbishop Nicholas in the middle of the century.[66] I am inclined to follow Kelly in viewing the scrolls as part of the same commission by Archbishop Bisantius because of their stylistic similarities and the precedent, set by Landulf, of an archbishop commissioning a pair of scrolls.

In Landulf's scrolls and the Rylands scroll, the text and images are intended to be viewed together. The images are placed just above the relevant piece of text, so that the text functions a bit like a caption. The deacon would be able to see each image just before he sang the related text and perhaps the images functioned as a memory prompt or a way of infusing the singing with more devotion and emotion. As the deacon unravelled the scroll, the parts he had already sung would hang over the edge of the ambo, eventually trailing on the floor (unless an assistant was standing by to re-roll it). The Bari Exultet 1 and the Benedictional represent a second phase in the development of the Exultet scroll, in which the illustrations have been inverted, so that they are upside down to anyone reading the text. Consequently, as the scroll hung from the ambo, the images could be seen by the congregation the right way up.

As Thomas Kelly has emphasized, although the images were the right way round for congregational viewing, they would not have been particularly visible to the congregation. Kelly argued that in the dim church, just after dusk, lit only by the paschal candle and the candles of the congregation, the images would have been difficult to make out. Furthermore, the images remain in the same position in the manuscript, just above the relevant text, meaning that the congregation would see each image only once the deacon had moved on to a new verse, so the images were always well 'behind' the chant. For Kelly this means that the scroll was not intended to be viewed by the congregation during the liturgy. The inversion of the images was a good idea that slightly increased the lay engagement with the hymn but not significantly.[67] However, Bissera Pentcheva has stressed that medieval art embraces partial visibility and many, if not most, liturgical art was designed to be viewed in low light and by candlelight.[68] In the Exultet scrolls, the gold highlights, the shadows, the gradual movement of the scroll, the disconnect between the visible images and the verse being sung, the separation between the lay and clerical spaces are all part of the mystery and emotion of the ritual.

There may have been other, extra-liturgical, opportunities for viewing the scrolls. The Deesis image on the Benedictional is significantly more worn than the others. This may be because it is at the end of the scroll, and so was subject to more wear and tear, but it could also be because it was frequently touched and kissed. Kelly emphasized that these scrolls were the property of the bishop and he may have used them for private prayer throughout the year, particularly the Deesis, which was accessible by unrolling the scroll only a little.[69] The Deesis signifies the moment during the three hours on the cross when Christ entrusted John and Mary to each other as a Christian family and is therefore an image that could be particularly associated with Good Friday. Perhaps the scroll was displayed or partially displayed on Good Friday, for veneration by the faithful. It could have been hung or placed on a long table. This would give another opportunity for the community to view the images, this time up close, in better lighting conditions, and would mean that when they saw them in flickering candlelight during the Vigil, they could conjure up the details in their minds, as well as marvel at the evocative gold highlights.

One of the exciting aspects of the Exultet scrolls is that, since they are unique to southern Italy at a particular moment in time, many of the images do not have prototypes and the illuminators had to be inventive in their depictions of the texts. In the Bari Exultet 1, two such images are the depictions of Earth and the Chorus of the

Winds. The depiction of Earth illustrates the passage 'may the earth rejoice illuminated by such splendours', depicted as a woman in an ornate silk tunic standing in a meadow between two trees with animals at her feet.[70] The Chorus of the Winds is a circular image with Christ at the centre, surrounded by personifications of the twelve winds who blow towards Christ through musical horns (Figure 18). The image signifies the wind as the breath of God the creator. Sophia Germanidou sees this image as inspired by Neoplatonic ideas, but most scholars have associated it with Christ Pantocrator in church domes.[71] The Chorus of the Winds image was made *c*. 1025 when the sixth-century cathedral was still standing and that cathedral was almost certainly a standard early Christian basilica, without a dome. It is possible that the Chorus of the Winds image was inspired by a Pantocrator image in one of the churches in the Byzantine palace. Some of those churches were probably very small, simple chapels, but the Holy Wisdom was probably a cross-in-square church with a dome. The Chorus of the Winds could be another example of the complex and nuanced relationship between Greeks and Lombards in Bari, in which the Lombards were sometimes resistant to Byzantine rule but also willing to appropriate elements of Byzantine culture to create a hybrid and distinctive identity for themselves.

Bissera Pentcheva, on the other hand, has emphasized different aspects of the Chorus of the Winds image, noting its strangeness and the emphasis on breath in a manuscript so focused on the act of chanting.[72] For Pentcheva, the enactment of the Exultet is a 'performative icon' and an 'icon of sound', in which the deacon temporarily becomes *imago dei* (in the image of God), his song literally breathing life and the Holy Spirit into the space through his chant and ritual action. The Chorus of the Winds image is a manifestation of this idea. While the deacon breathes life into Christ through

Figure 18 Chorus of the Winds, Bari Exultet 1. Photo: Bissera Pentcheva.

his song marking the resurrection, the winds breathe life into the image of Christ on the scroll.[73] This is another example of self-referentiality in the Bari scrolls, further evidence that the Rylands scroll was produced in the same scriptorium as the Exultet 1.

Alongside a possible connection between the Chorus of the Winds image and the Byzantine churches of Bari, there is further evidence of Greek influence on the scroll. Although Bisantius was inspired by the Benevento scrolls, his illuminators have made the Bari Exultet their own, partly by drawing on models in Byzantine art.[74] Unlike the other Latin manuscripts produced in Byzantine Bari, the Exultet shows extensive Greek influence. While the Anastasis scene in the Beneventan scroll is modelled on prototypes from early medieval Rome, the one on the Bari scroll is related to the Anastasis at Hosios Loukas.[75] The Benevento scrolls have a geometric border, but the Bari scrolls have busts of saints in the borders (Figure 18). The saints, who are identified by Greek inscriptions, are very Byzantine in character, including St John Chrysostom, St Basil, St Gregory of Nazianzus, St Procopius and Holy Wisdom.[76]

Further Byzantine influence comes in the depiction of Byzantine emperors. The text of the Exultet includes prayers for the pope and bishop and for the emperor. In the Benevento scroll, the authorities are represented by the Holy Roman Emperor Otto II, crowned by angels, with his army below him and Archbishop Landulf surrounded by his clergy and laity. In the Bari scroll, the Holy Roman Emperor has been replaced with the contemporary Byzantine co-emperors who ruled Bari, Basil II (976–1025) and Constantine VIII (976–1028) (Figure 19). The illuminators must have had access to other images of Basil II and Constantine VIII because their facial features have been rendered faithfully, in line with other contemporary depictions.[77] They wear their *loros* costume, which was worn by emperors in Hagia Sophia for major religious festivals, including Easter. The emperors are therefore appropriately dressed for their appearance during the Easter vigil, even though the Greek rite has no equivalent of the Exultet. The fact they are wearing the *loros* may be a coincidence, since it was widely depicted in imperial portraits, despite being seldom worn.[78] Although the imperial portraits are, in many ways, faithful to Byzantine conventions, they contain Western misunderstandings of imperial iconography. They hold their insignia in their left hand, rather than the correct right hand. In their right hands they hold small crosses, something reserved only for saints in Byzantine iconography.

Another oddity is that the bishop is wearing Greek vestments, an *omophorion* and an *epimanikion* and a man with a child, assumed to be a layman, is also wearing an *omophorion*. Belting interpreted this as the illuminator drawing on a Greek model without adapting it to Latin customs.[79] This is curious because, while the subtleties of imperial portraiture may plausibly have been lost on a Latin monk on the edge of the empire, monks in Bari would certainly have met Greek clergy and been aware of the differences in vesting. It is difficult to believe that a Benedictine monk in cosmopolitan Bari would have dressed a layman in an *omophorion*. It is a curious detail and one that is difficult to explain. The Latin bishop wearing Greek vestments is also interesting and points to Bari as a 'fuzzy' space, in which Greek and Latin practices were not strictly delineated.

Nino Zchomeldise has noted that a curiosity of the Bari Exultet 1 is the diminished role of the bishop in the illuminations. Other scrolls put the bishop centre stage, but here

Figure 19 Emperors from Bari Exultet 1, Museo Diocesano, Bari. Photo: Age of Stock.

he is limited to two images: the prayers for the pope and bishop and the prayers known as *fratres karisimmi*, in which the deacon asks those present, the 'dear brothers', to pray with him.[80] Landulf of Benevento was depicted surrounded by a crowd of clergy and laity, whereas Bisantius of Bari is accompanied only by a pair of deacons in the prayers for bishop and clergy (the four laymen are a later addition to the manuscript, making this originally a very clerical scene). Bisantius is seated on an ornate throne, wearing the conical episcopal hat, in the orans posture. His throne is decorated with a plump striped (silk?) cushion and the legs are carved with an inverted palmette motif. Both the bishop, seated on his throne, and the deacon, chanting on the ambo, are pushed to the sides of the image (Figure 20). At the centre is another cleric holding the paschal candle standing under a canopy which presumably represents the cathedral. A third cleric swings his censer, evoking the multisensory experience of the liturgy. The bishop is seated behind the others; he seems to be hovering in mid-air, presumably to show that his throne was raised up in the sanctuary behind the altar. I agree with Zchomelidse that the Bari Exultet 1 does downplay the role of the bishop in comparison to the Beneventan manuscript, but the Benedictional puts him centre stage. This probably reflects the use of the scrolls: the Exultet was used by the deacon, but the Benedictional was used by the bishop.

The bishop is also depicted twice in the Benedictional: in the procession and in the blessing of the font. Here he is much more prominent, particularly in the procession,

Figure 20 Frates Karissimi prayers from Exultet 1, Bari. Photo: Sailko via Wikimedia.

where he leads the way, followed by his clergy and flock. Both are heart-warming, very human scenes that convey the joy and excitement of Easter, with children riding on their parents' shoulders and a baby tenderly handed over for baptism, cradled in the arms of a priest. Penelope Mayo has pointed out that the jugs of water to fill the font are marked with the keys of St Peter, the sword of St Paul, the ox of St Luke and the lion of St Mark. Mark and Luke were followers of Peter and Paul respectively, so the symbols draw attention to the gospels, to the transmission of Christian knowledge and authority and particularly to apostolic succession, an unbroken thread which led to Archbishop Bisantius. This link is stressed again in the *vere dignum* initial where Christ is flanked by the busts of Peter and Paul in the borders.[81] The subtle emphasis on apostolic succession underscores Archbishop Bisantius's role as being *in persona Christi* during the liturgy.

Penelope Mayo interpreted the commissioning of both scrolls as part of the tense relationship between Byzantines and Lombards in Bari.[82] Bisantius's re-construction of the cathedral and the commissioning of the scrolls can both be seen as an assertion of Lombard identity in the Byzantine city, in the wake of the rebellions, the Byzantine campaign against them and the fortification of the Byzantine palace. But the scrolls, like other aspects of the Byzantine-Lombard relationship, are complex. The Exultet is specific to the Latin rite and the idea of an Exultet scroll was invented in the Lombard royal city of Benevento by a Lombard archbishop, so the Bari scrolls are a declaration of affiliation with that culture. They also manifest the liturgical differences between eastern and western Christianity, emphasizing that the Lombards celebrated Easter differently from their Greek neighbours. Yet, the scrolls are not 'purely' Lombard; the artists have used of Byzantine artistic models, Byzantine saints, Greek text and included Byzantine emperors. While in some sense setting his community apart from the Byzantine authorities, Archbishop Bisantius was also acknowledging – even celebrating? – the fact that Byzantine culture was part of Barese identity.

At San Benedetto, the sculpture in the cloister roughly coincided with the illumination of Bari Exultet 1 and the Benedictional (or possibly with the Rylands Exultet, if the cloister were built earlier). San Benedetto in Bari is not usually thought of as one of the great Benedictine cultural powerhouses, but perhaps it should be. Out of it came a new form of script, some extraordinary manuscripts, possibly a workshop of sculptors and the influential figure Abbot Elias, later Archbishop of Bari, whom we shall meet in Chapter 5.

Partial integration with Byzantine culture was what made Bari distinctive among the Lombard cities of central and northern Apulia. The Baresi may have seen themselves as superior to the princely court in Benevento because of their easier access to eastern culture. Byzantine art was a beautiful and prestigious tool that they could make use of. In Melus and Argyros's silken diplomacy, in the trapezoid capitals and in Bisantius's cathedral and scrolls, we see the Baresi using Byzantine visual culture for their own ends. In this sense, Bari can be compared to the court of Roger II in Palermo and to other provinces that appropriated Byzantine culture to suit their own purposes. 'Byzantinizing' is indeed a useful term to describe the art of the Lombard community in Bari. Their art could be described as Lombard with Byzantinizing elements. But regardless of how we categorize it, there was a nuanced engagement with Greek culture. It is not, as Hans Belting might have portrayed it in the 1970s, straightforward emulation and admiration of trends from Constantinople. There is a tension and even an animosity in Lombard engagement with Greek culture, which is as much a part of the history of the Byzantine Empire as the Byzantine palace.

4

Canosa cathedral

'Minister with light', how to be an archbishop

Archbishops Bisantius and Nicholas could not give all their attention to Bari cathedral because theirs was a joint archdiocese in which the co-cathedrals of Bari and Canosa had equal status. Let us now trace their footsteps on the journey they must have made often, along the via Traiana to Canosa (Map 4), to see what was happening in a different kind of city. Just like in Bari, very little remains extant from the Byzantine period and the works of art that do remain are plagued with complex issues of dating and scant contextual evidence. Any discussion will necessarily be incomplete and fragmented. Nonetheless, it is worth piecing together the evidence we have because it reveals that Canosa cathedral was an important monument, modelled on the Holy Apostles in Constantinople and that the cathedral clergy commissioned a new set of liturgical furniture in the Byzantine period that may hint at tensions between the cathedral clergy and the episcopate. This chapter is dominated by two bishops: the sixth-century Sabinus, a saintly bishop and ideal patron of churches, and Nicholas, the contemporary archbishop who may have been struggling to manage his two communities.

Canosa had been a large and prosperous city in antiquity. The city was located on the via Traiana and on the Ofanto river, where there was an emporium, which effectively made Canosa a small port city, even though it is 20km inland.[1] The city's patron saint is the sixth-century bishop Sabinus, who will be significant in Part 2 of this book because he was also the patron saint of Bari and his relics played a role in the competition between the two cities. Sabinus is significant in this chapter because he was a prolific patron and builder of churches. His church-building projects were partly inspired by two trips he made to Constantinople, one with Pope John I in 525 and another when he led the delegation of Italian bishops to the Council of 536.[2] In Canosa, Sabinus built San Pietro, SS. Cosma e Damiano and baptistery of San Giovanni, and he may have embellished the fourth-century cathedral of Santa Maria, adjacent to his new baptistery.[3] Most significantly, it has recently come to light that Sabinus also built a new cathedral for Canosa (still in use as the cathedral today, although much amplified). The building was long thought to have been built in the Byzantine or Norman periods, but recently discovered evidence dates it to the sixth century.

It is worth laying out the reasons for the re-dating of the cathedral. The idea that Canosa cathedral dates to the eleventh century began with Ferdinando Ughelli, who

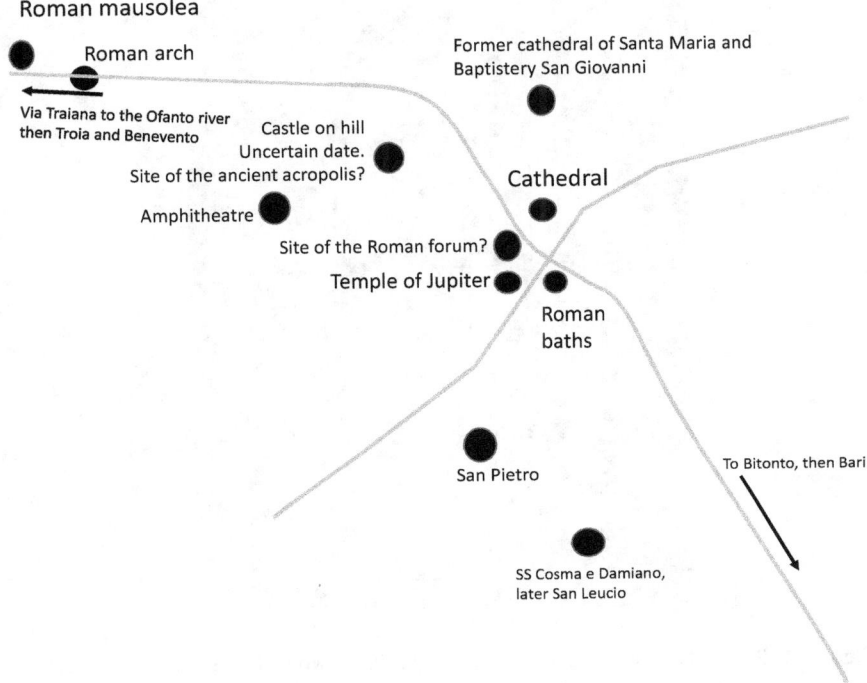

Map 4 Map of Canosa in the Byzantine and Norman periods. Drawn by the author.

claimed that the cathedral of Canosa was re-built by Archbishop Nicholas in the 1030s or 1040s.[4] Although there was no documentary evidence to support this, it was considered a plausible idea that the cathedral would have been re-built after the partial destruction of the city in an Arab raid in the tenth century and the stylistic ambiguity of the architecture meant that the cathedral was, for a long time, considered contemporary to Bisantius and Nicholas's cathedral in Bari.[5] In reality, Ughelli probably transposed Nicholas's re-building of Bari cathedral onto Canosa.

Until recently, scholars interpreted the architectural evidence in agreement with Unghelli's assertion that the cathedral was built by Archbishop Nicholas.[6] But during recent restorations, tiles were found on the roof of the cathedral bearing the monogram of St Sabinus, identical to the tiles used in the Sabinus's other churches.[7] In light of the new evidence, it is easy to see that the architecture is very much in keeping with its sixth-century date. It is composed of five bays, arranged in the T shape typical of late antique churches (Figures 21 and 22). The cathedral is often described as having five domes, although they are not really domes at all, but pendentive domes (sometimes called sail vaults) (Figure 23).[8] Pendentive domes such as this were a particular feature of early Byzantine architecture, St John at Ephesus and Hagia Eirene being the most notable examples.[9] When Constantine's Holy Apostles was rebuilt by Empress Theodora, the central space was covered by a proper dome on a drum but the other bays were covered by shallow pendentive domes.[10]

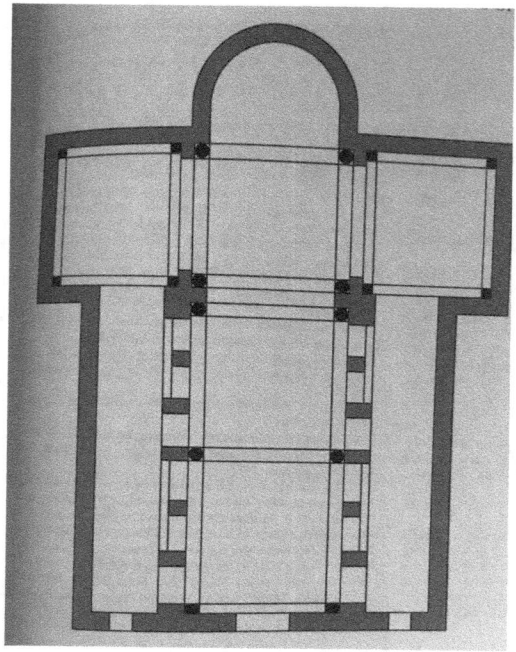

Figure 21 Plan of Canosa cathedral as it was *c.* 1100. Drawn by Eric Fernie.

Figure 22 Canosa cathedral, nave. Photo: John McNeill.

Figure 23 Exposed pendentive dome in the south transept, Canosa cathedral. Photo: John McNeill.

The similarities to contemporary architecture in Constantinople indicate that Sabinus modelled his new cathedral on the magnificent churches he had seen on his journeys to Constantinople in 525 and 536. His second visit coincided with the extensive re-building projects that took place following the fire of 532. He would have seen Emperor Justinian's Hagia Sophia as it was nearing completion (it was consecrated in 537). The council he attended was held in the Chalkoprateia church, just a hundred metres from the cathedral, so Sabinus would have been able to observe the construction on a daily basis.[11] The building that Sabinus saw had an experimental and innovative shallow dome with windows. It was almost a pendentive dome but the pendentives were separated from the dome by a cornice and windows.[12]

Even before the discovery of St Sabinus's tiles, Anne Wharton Epstein argued that Canosa cathedral was modelled on the Holy Apostles in Constantinople (Figure 24) and her argument is strengthened by the new dating.[13] The five domes of the Holy Apostles were arranged in a Greek cross formation, while Canosa cathedral has a T-shaped plan, to accommodate a Latin liturgy. Wharton argued that the T-shaped plan would not have sullied Canosa's status as a copy.[14] Drawing on Krautheimer's idea that medieval copies reproduce only key features of their prototype, Wharton argued that the presence of five domes would have been enough to constitute a copy.[15] The foundation stone for Justinian's Holy Apostles was laid in by Empress Theodora in 536, and the church was finished in 550. Although Sabinus could not possibly have seen the finished church, he may have been present for the laying of the foundation stone, an event that would surely have made a lasting impression.

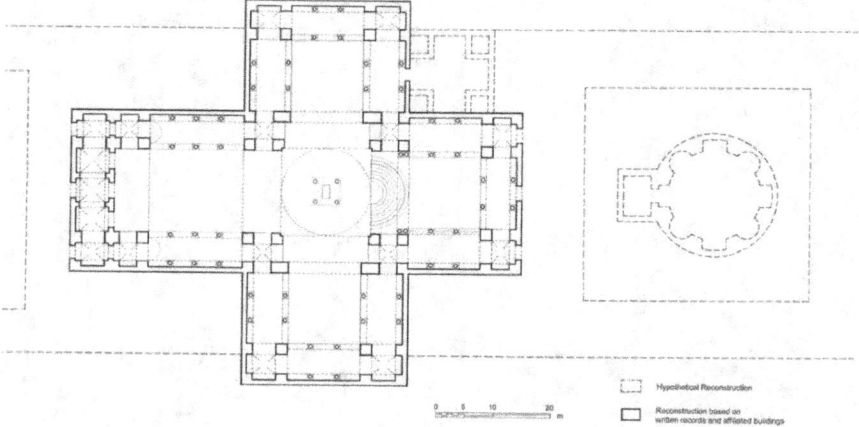

Figure 24 Reconstruction of the plan of Justinian's Holy Apostles in Constantinople by Nikolaos Karydis.

Sabinus may also have had the opportunity to discuss the plans for the new church with the architect Anthemius of Tralles, who had also worked on Hagia Sophia and he may have kept himself informed of the construction progress once he returned home to Italy.

Just as Bari had a monument that emulated Constantinople, in the form of the Byzantine palace, Canosa too had its own piece of Constantinople, its own Holy Apostles, built in Canosa's heyday. The recent re-dating means we can no longer include it in the corpus of Byzantine and Norman cathedrals. But we can consider the significance it would have had in the Byzantine period. The association with the Holy Apostles seems to have been part of the collective memory in Canosa, preserved partly in the cathedral's dedication, to St John the Evangelist and St Paul.[16] In 1101, it was re-dedicated to St Sabinus which, I shall argue in Chapter 9, was a response to rivalry with Bari and an assertion that Canosa had a closer connection to St Sabinus than Bari did. In Part 3 of this book, we will return to Canosa cathedral, to explore the tomb of the crusader, Bohemond I, in a chapel attached to the south transept. The location of Bohemond's burial was purposefully chosen because of the link to Constantinople and the Holy Apostles as the burial church of the Byzantine Empire.

Raffaella Cassano has raised the possibility that Canosa cathedral had a sixth-century nucleus that was enlarged in the eleventh century by Archbishop Nicholas.[17] Although this is possible, and would neatly solve some of the complex dating issues, the eighteenth-century additions make it very difficult even to guess what kind of architectural changes Nicholas might have made. There are two capitals in the south transept that were certainly carved in the eleventh century and may have been part of a refurbishment.[18] Although any architectural interventions in the eleventh century remain a mystery, we do have good evidence for sculptural additions to the church during the era of Archbishop Nicholas: an ambo and an episcopal throne.

Acceptus's ambo and throne

The Canosa ambo takes the form of a box, raised up on columns, with a lectern from which the scriptures were read (Figure 25).[19] Presumably, it was originally accessed by a wooden staircase. It is inscribed on the west side, 'by the command of my lord Guitbert, the venerable priest, I Acceptus, sinner and archdeacon, made this work'.[20] Acceptus and his workshop are well-known sculptors who worked across northern Apulia in the 1030s and 1040s.[21] His earliest securely dated work is a now-fragmentary ambo from Siponto inscribed with the date 1039.[22] He made a second ambo for the shrine at Monte Sant'Angelo in 1041 (also fragmentary), and he also carved the door jambs for the cathedral of Bari, which he decorated with the same vegetal scroll as the ambos. A further piece of sculpture (architrave or jamb) of unknown provenance is now in the Bode Museum in Berlin.[23]

The Canosa ambo must have been made towards the end of Acceptus's career, since he was an archdeacon. Archdeacons in this period were highly educated, senior clerics who were attached to a cathedral; the role was often a stepping stone to the episcopate.[24] Indeed, Jean-Louis-Alphonse Huillard-Bréholles argued that Acceptus was the same man who later became bishop of Ruvo and was present at the inauguration of Montecassino in 1071, which is entirely possible.[25] Leslie Cavell has suggested that archdeacons in Burgundy in this period were responsible for the cathedral building,

Figure 25 Ambo by Acceptus, Canosa cathedral. Photo: John McNeill.

its maintenance and decoration.[26] This is interesting in light of Acceptus's role as both archdeacon and sculptor. Pina Belli D'Elia has suggested that he did not carve the Canosa ambo himself but, as the archdeacon of Canosa, he financed it.[27] However, the ambo is stylistically in keeping with Acceptus's other work and must have been made by his workshop. Moreover, the inscription seems to attribute a financing role to Guitbert, who was presumably a fellow member of the cathedral clergy.

The other major artistic acquisition made by Canosa cathedral in the eleventh century is the episcopal throne, distinctive because it rests on the backs of elephants (Figure 26). Episcopal thrones, like ambos, were a key part of the choreography of the liturgy, when the bishop was present. The bishop would stand in front of his throne facing east during the *kyries*, turn back to the people to for the start of the *Gloria*, then east again while the *Gloria* was sung. He would move forward to receive the offertory before going to the altar and return to his throne after the Eucharist. Popes administered the Eucharistic bread to the clergy from their throne, and it is possible that bishops did the same.[28] Episcopal thrones were, therefore, visual and topographical symbols for episcopal authority.

The upper part of the Canosa throne, composed of the seat, back and the armrests, is made of the same marble as the ambo and features the same diamond decoration. On the front of the seat are two eagles, extremely similar to the eagle on the ambo,

Figure 26 Episcopal throne, Canosa cathedral. Photo: John McNeill.

allowing us to be fairly confident that they were sculpted by the same person. Along the top is an inscription, which must have been carved before the separate pieces were assembled, because some of the letters extend into the joints.[29] The inscription takes the form of a reminder or supplication to the archbishop to govern his flock in an enlightened manner.

> O bishop, after you obtain this eternal seat, through which the outward voice speaks things to the interior, through which you should minister in the form of light, prevail with light, do not lack light.[30]

The lower part of the throne, including the elephants which support the seat, is made of a different marble, and the sculptural style is different. On the outside of the right-hand armrest is a second inscription, 'Ursus [was the] instructor, Romuald was the maker of this.'[31] Pina Belli D'Elia has proposed the highly plausible theory that Acceptus made the throne in the 1040s and then archbishop Ursus (1080–1089) commissioned Romuald to replace Acceptus's base with the elephant base.[32] Thrones carried by majestic animals were standard in antiquity and ultimately came from the Sassanian Empire via imperial Rome. They were easily adapted to Christianity since Solomon's throne had also rested on lions.[33] Acceptus's gabled seat is very similar to the Monte Sant'Angelo throne, which has been dated to *c.* 1020–1050 and could well have been made by Acceptus, although he has not 'signed' it in the inscription (Figure 27).[34] The Monte Sant'Angelo throne rests on a pair of lions, so perhaps the Canosa throne originally did too. Since the elephant base seems to belong to the 1080s, I will discuss it in Chapter 5, in the context of the sculpture made during the episcopate of Ursus, and limit myself here to a discussion of Acceptus's sculpture and inscription.

The lettering of the inscription seems identical to that on the ambo so we can conclude that both inscriptions were composed by Acceptus. The inscription is striking and scholarly, in keeping with Acceptus's erudite bilingual (Greek and Latin) inscription on the ambo of Siponto.[35] The corpus of Acceptus's inscriptions presents him as highly educated, humble and pious, deeply concerned for the theological orthodoxy of the churches he worked in. Other Apulian thrones have much more perfunctory inscriptions. The Bari throne, which we will look at in Chapter 6, has a more pragmatic inscription, bluntly informing the viewer that the 'bishop of Bari and Canosa sits in this seat' and similarly, the later Monte Sant'Angelo inscription makes a straightforward statement about the throne being the seat of the archdiocese.[36] The Canosa inscription is much more complex and theologically rich. It is addressed to the bishop, instructing him on how to carry out the duties of his office, the 'eternal seat' stressing that he is a temporary occupant, part of a lineage that stretches back to the apostles and forwards into eternity. It is written on the inside of the armrests and gable, meaning that it wraps itself around the body of the seated bishop, impossible for him to ignore the message admonishing him to govern well.[37] The content touches upon two theological ideas. The first, relatively straightforward, is the idea of a spiritual tension between light and dark, that would have been familiar to all medieval Christians. God created light and separated it from darkness in Genesis, Christ is light in the

Figure 27 Episcopal throne, Monte Sant'Angelo. Photo: Paolo Monti via Wikimedia.

New Testament and Christians are the 'children of the light'.[38] The inscription, with a repetition of 'light' three times, perhaps subtly echoes John 12:36, 'while you have the light, believe in the light, that you may be children of the light.'[39]

The second idea is that of the external voice and the contrast with 'the interior'. In medieval theology, the 'external voice' or similar phrases were used to describe the prophets, saints, angels and writers of scripture, whose voices were used by God to speak through. This is sometimes contrasted with an interior voice or inner understanding. St Augustine wrote of the inner word or 'word of the heart', which is always truth and the incarnate Christ as the external manifestation of the divine.[40] Similar ideas were explored by Peter Abelard, who preached about the external human voice that spreads the work of God and connected it to the inner truth of the Holy Spirit.[41] Probably most influential of all was Gregory the Great's commentary on the *Book of Job*, in which he explains how God speaks through the voices of the prophets. He gives the example of the angel who appeared to Moses, who served as an 'external voice' of God, but is also described *as* God because 'acting from within, he made the speaking effective. Therefore the angel is guided from within'.[42] Gregory the Great's commentary was read extremely widely; Montecassino had at least two copies, including one illuminated copy commissioned by Abbot Theobald (1022–35), probably a decade or so before the throne was made.[43]

What the inscription seems to be conveying is that the bishop's (external) voice is the vehicle God uses to enhance the inner understanding of the bishop's flock and the bishop is to embody the light of Christ through his episcopate in general, and more specifically, through his preaching. The allusion to preaching is there, not only with the 'external voice', but also in the throne itself because early Christian bishops (and presumably also those in the eleventh century) preached from their thrones, which were understood as 'teaching chairs'.[44] The inscription is concerned with the orthodoxy or perhaps the pastoral nature of the bishop's preaching. It is significant that the new liturgical furniture made by Acceptus was commissioned by the priest Guitbert, not by the archbishop, and that Archbishop Nicholas is not mentioned by name in the inscriptions. The new liturgical furniture seems to have been a project of the cathedral clergy, without the bishop's involvement. The passive-aggressive undertones in the inscription perhaps hint at tensions between the cathedral clergy and Archbishop Nicholas. We can only speculate about the reasons – perhaps Nicholas was too focused on Bari and was considered absent and neglectful by the community in Canosa, perhaps he was considered too close to the Byzantine authorities or perhaps he was accused of some lack of orthodoxy, as the inscription seems to insinuate.

Archbishop Nicholas was, at the time, busy re-building Bari cathedral, and the new sculpture at Canosa could be not only an expression of displeasure with the archbishop himself, but also a response to Bari's new cathedral. Commissioning new liturgical furniture could be a way of 'keeping up' with rival Bari, and also with other Lombard cathedrals – Trani, Siponto and Monte Sant'Angelo – that were also being decorated with new sculpture around the time. Some of the trapezoid capitals made by the Benedictine workshop in Bari have also been found in Canosa, indicating that Canosa was indeed making an effort to join in with artistic trends in Bari. Bari was the only city to completely re-build its cathedral in this period, but all these cathedrals acquired new liturgical furniture in the first half of the eleventh century. Together with the new invention of the Exultet scroll in Bari, these new works of art must have significantly enhanced and enlivened the liturgical life of Lombard communities, perhaps pointing to a renewal of liturgy and preaching as part of the nascent Gregorian Reform movement.

Conclusion to Part 1

The limited evidence makes it difficult to accurately assess the art and architecture of the archdiocese of Bari and Canosa under Byzantine rule. The two large new buildings constructed in this period, the governor's palace and Bari cathedral, are no longer standing. Canosa cathedral turns out to have been built several centuries earlier. There are therefore no major buildings still extant. What we have instead are tantalizing snippets of surviving evidence: fragments of sculpture, inscriptions, liturgical furniture and, best-preserved, the liturgical scrolls. To this material evidence, we can add some texts which enable some limited contextualization. The patchy nature of the evidence is one of the reasons that previous scholarship has been brief and has tended towards the descriptive rather than attempting to draw overarching conclusions. I have attempted to tease out some meaningful conclusions, but they are necessarily tentative. The Byzantine officials probably had little connection to Apulia and mostly limited their patronage to the governor's palace and a few Greek monasteries. The palace was a bastion of Byzantine culture, an island in a largely non-Greek city. The Lombard communities in both Bari and Canosa created art that was broadly Lombard, drawing inspiration from the Lombard heartlands of Benevento and Monte Sant'Angelo, but they also made use of their access to Byzantine culture and appropriated aspects of it as their own. Canosa was much more Lombard in Character, but in Bari we find the Lombard community creating a hybrid culture and creating a distinctive identity as a port city on the edge of the empire, neither fully Byzantine nor fully Lombard.

Part 2

The Church of San Nicola, Bari

5

The crypt

Enter St Nicholas and the Normans

Over the course of the eleventh century a dramatic change took place in the south of the Italian peninsula. At the beginning of the century, the region was split between the Byzantines, Lombards and Arabs. By the time it ended, the Norman Hauteville family, led by Robert Guiscard, had conquered and, to some extent unified, southern Italy. Part 2 of this book deals with Bari in the Norman period, looking specifically at the construction of the basilica of San Nicola. This chapter explores the Norman conquest, the theft of the relics of St Nicholas and the foundation of the new church. The next chapter examines the episcopal throne, arguing that it is a throne of Solomon that commemorates the victories of the first crusade. The Solomonic theme continues in Chapter 7, which argues that the architecture was conceived as a temple of Solomon. Chapter 8 argues that the portals were inspired by northern Italian sculpture and reflect lay responses to the Gregorian Reform movement. Chapter 9 looks at Archbishop Elias as a civic leader and his tomb in the crypt of San Nicola. After Elias's death, Bari entered a new era with the appointment of Abbot Eustasius as rector of San Nicola and Riso as archbishop. Chapter 10 explores the pavements of San Nicola commissioned by Elias and Eustasius and analyses Bari's artistic relationships with Greece and other areas of the Adriatic.

When the Normans conquered Bari, the monument to imperial power, the governor's palace, was demolished and replaced with a church dedicated to St Nicholas. This was a dramatic change in the urbanism of the city that bolstered the existing civic identity of the local community that we have already seen in Part 1 of this book. In this chapter, I will examine the transition from Byzantine to Norman rule, the foundation of the new church and the construction and consecration of the crypt. We will see how the foundation of the church was fraught with conflict as different factions in the city tussled for power in the new political era. Ultimately, the Lombard community asserted their autonomy and commercial prowess through the construction of the new church.

The Norman conquest and its impact on Bari

Spurred by social and political upheaval in Northern France, young Normans migrated to southern Italy in the early eleventh century to fight as mercenaries in the ongoing conflicts between Lombards, Byzantines and Arabs. Gradually they began to transition from mercenaries to conquerors, marrying into the Lombard nobility and taking land for themselves. The Hauteville brothers emerged as leaders: Drogo, William Ironarm, Roger and, the youngest, Robert 'Guiscard', 'the cunning', who became the outright leader around the middle of the century. They began to be acknowledged as rulers from the 1050s and Robert Guiscard was invested as Duke of Apulia and Calabria by Pope Nicholas II in 1059 in the city of Melfi, which had effectively become the Normans' first capital city.[1] Bari was one of the last mainland cities to fall to the Normans in 1071, after a three-year siege.[2] When they finally took control of the city, the Normans allowed the Byzantine governor and his entourage to return peacefully to Constantinople and adopted a 'hands-off' approach to ruling Bari, choosing not to make it their capital.[3]

Guiscard delegated the daily governing to Lizius, probably a Norman, and Maurelianus, probably a local Lombard from Bari, who was given the Byzantine imperial title *katepan*. Other administrative officials were elected by the Baresi and their appointments ratified by the Normans; some were given Byzantine titles.[4] This delegated and collaborative approach to governing may have been because Guiscard had no interest in Bari, but it may also have been due to the distinctive character of the city. As we saw in the early chapters of this book, the Baresi were accustomed to a high degree of independence during Byzantine rule through their own ecclesiastical and legal systems. Guiscard may have brought them to their knees with a three-year siege, but he needed their cooperation in order to govern. The use of Byzantine titles not only provided continuity but also perhaps gave the impression of increased autonomy for the local community. For the local leader Maurelianus to be a *katepan* meant that he had symbolically replaced the imperial governor, even if the Normans now had ultimate control of the city.

Under Byzantine rule, Bari had been a provincial capital, arguably the most important city in southern Italy, which brought prestige and prosperity. After the conquest, Bari's status changed. Guiscard initially exempted the citizens from paying tribute (they must have had nothing to give anyway after the siege) but later extracted high taxes, which caused anxiety.[5] Although it is difficult to quantify, it is important to consider the economic impact of the Norman conquest. The long siege and change of government caused economic instability because it disrupted both local and long-distance trade.[6] Just as the merchants had got back on their feet in the 1080s, Guiscard imposed high taxes and conscripted the Baresi to serve in his military campaigns in the Balkans and Sicily.[7]

At the same time, Bari was increasingly overshadowed commercially by the ascendency of Venice. The Venetians gained further commercial advantages from Byzantium by providing military help to expel the Normans from the Balkans. In recognition of Venetian help, Alexios I granted them extensive privileges: imperial titles and stipends for the Doge and Patriarch of Grado; funding for Venetian churches; land in Constantinople and tax exemptions within the empire. These privileges are documented in a chrysobull issued sometime before 1092, but they had been granted and put into practice from 1082. The chrysobull specifically forbids the Venetians from carrying goods for Amalfitans, Jews and the Lombards of Bari.[8] This shows that no longer being part of the empire put Bari at an economic disadvantage and contributed to Venice's growing dominance in the Adriatic.

When Guiscard died in 1085, there was further political upheaval. When he repudiated his Norman first wife Alberada, he disinherited her son, Bohemond, in favour of his second, half-Lombard son, Roger Borsa. After their father's death, Bohemond challenged his half-brother's succession and a civil war broke out. Roger Borsa remained in control of Bari until September of 1089, when he ceded it to Bohemond.[9] Bohemond continued his father and brother's light-touch government of the city. Like them he appointed *katepan*, a representative to handle his affairs. The *katepan* had no power in the general running of the city; his role was simply to protect Bohemond's property and interests. Before issuing documents or making decisions he had to show his seal to many of the prominent citizens.[10] None of the *katepans* were from Bari.[11] Bohemond's *katepans* often gave gifts to prominent citizens in recognition of their continued loyalty; in other words Bohemond needed the cooperation of the very independent-minded local elite in order to hold onto the city.[12]

During Byzantine rule, there may have been tension between Greeks and Lombards, but it had been a period of stability and prosperity. The Norman conquest was a seismic change which threatened the city's economy and disrupted power structures and social networks. Despite the decline and instability, the conquest provided an opportunity for the Lombard community to assert more autonomy. In order to recover and thrive in the new Norman duchy, the Baresi needed to forge new relationships with the Normans and their proxies, but the upheaval and economic uncertainty may also have prompted them to create new trade networks, social relationships and religious structures.

Saints, relics and pilgrims in and around Bari before 1087

In southern Italy in the later eleventh century there was a renewed emphasis on relics and shrines. The threat of first Arab and then Norman raids, particularly in coastal cities, had meant that relics were frequently hidden to keep them safe. Once the conquest was complete, relics could be re-instated and shrines could be restored. There were a series of 'rediscoveries' of lost relics; often bishops unearthed the relics of their predecessors during the construction of a new cathedral. To cite just three examples: St Cataldus of Taranto, St Matthew in Salerno and St Secundinus of Troia. Desiderius unveiled his new shrine to St Benedict in 1071, and his friend Alfanus, archbishop of Salerno, followed suit, collaborating with Guiscard in the re-construction of the shrine of St Matthew, which was consecrated by Gregory VII in 1085. The Venetians, Bari's great commercial rivals, were building themselves an ambitious new cathedral to house the relics of St Mark, which had also been lost and were found during construction. More and more of Bari's rival neighbours could boast accessible relics and newly built shrines.

One potential way to mitigate the decline in prestige and wealth, which came with no longer being a provincial capital in the Byzantine Empire, was for Bari to re-brand itself as a pilgrimage destination. The Adriatic coast of Apulia already attracted significant numbers of local and long-distance pilgrims. A hundred kilometres north of Bari is Monte Sant'Angelo, the most important shrine to St Michael the Archangel in Latin Europe. Pilgrims came from as far afield as Germany, France, England and Greece and included Holy Roman Emperors Otto III and Henry II and Pope Leo IX.[13] Many visited Monte Sant'Angelo as part of a longer pilgrimage, en route from Rome to the Holy Land, embarking from ports such as Bari, Trani or Otranto.[14] Attracting more of those pilgrims to Bari, and away from the other ports, would be advantageous.

It was unfortunate that Bari did not possess an alluring shrine. Bari's patron saint had long been St Sabinus, who they shared with rival Canosa. Bari claimed to possess his relics, but they had been lost (they would later be rediscovered in the cathedral in 1091). Sabinus had been bishop of Canosa not of Bari which weakened their link to him. Furthermore, Sabinus was a local bishop saint, unknown outside Apulia. During the Byzantine period devotion to the Latin bishop St Sabinus probably fostered a distinctive Lombard identity which was much needed. But after the Norman conquest the local cult was less useful. They needed a new patron, and at some unknown point, they decided to adopt St Nicholas.

St Nicholas, the early Christian bishop of Myra in Asia Minor, whose cult had spread quickly throughout the Byzantine Empire and then to Russia and Western Europe, was one of the most widely venerated saints in the Middle Ages. By the eleventh century his cult was established in southern Italy, and he was widely venerated in Bari by both Lombards and Greeks.[15] In Byzantine Bari there were already five churches and a monastery dedicated to him.[16] The monastery was founded by a Basilian monk called John, on the instructions of Emperor Constantine IX Monomachos (1042–55), who also responsible for the restorations to St Nicholas's shrine in Myra.[17] There are also a number of wall paintings of the saint in the region surrounding Bari, all painted in the eleventh century, demonstrating his widespread veneration: at Santa Marina in Muro Leccese; in the Rock church of San Nicola near Mottola; and in the rock church of SS Maria & Cristina in Carpignano Salentino.[18] By 1080s, St Nicholas had become more than just a saint among many. He was depicted on Robert Guiscard's seal, where he was explicitly identified as the patron saint of Bari.[19] His presence on Guiscard's seal could mean that adopting Nicholas as patron was encouraged, fostered or even initiated by Guiscard. In Salerno, Guiscard had promoted the cult of St Matthew as part of his strategy to consolidate Norman power, and he may have adopted a similar policy in Bari with St Nicholas.[20]

Theft of the relics and foundation of the new church

In 1087, merchants from Bari stole the relics of St Nicholas from Myra and brought them back to Bari. His long-standing veneration and his earlier adoption as patron saint raise the question of how long the Baresi had been planning the theft. Although the sources paint a picture of a spontaneous event, it is likely that it was premeditated and desired years in advance. The same year that the Byzantines lost Bari, they suffered a far greater defeat at the battle of Manzikert, which allowed the Seljuks to conquer most of Anatolia in the 1070s, including Myra.[21] Muslim control of Myra left the shrine of St Nicholas vulnerable, giving Christians from elsewhere an excuse to steal the relics and claim that St Nicholas was better off in a Christian city. There is plausible evidence that Bari was in competition with Venice and Genoa to acquire the relics.[22] Re-homing St Nicholas from Muslim territory could be interpreted as an act of proto-crusading, but it can also be seen as declaration of commercial superiority. Whichever city succeeded in taking the relics would be lauded for their international connections, skilled sailors and shrewd merchants.

The story of the arrival of the relics in Bari is narrated in two contemporary local texts. When analysed in tandem, they reveal a power struggle for control of the relics between Archbishop Ursus (who we have already met as the second patron of the throne at Canosa) and Elias, abbot of the monastery of San Benedetto. The earlier account, written in support of Elias, was composed soon after the arrival of the relics, in either 1087 or 1088, by a cleric named Nicephorus, at the request of a group of prominent citizens of Bari. Nicephorus narrates that, while in Antioch selling wheat, a group of merchants from Bari heard rumours that the Venetians were planning to steal the relics of St Nicholas from Myra and made the impromptu decision to take them for themselves when they sailed past Myra on their way home.[23]

When they got home to Bari, the arrival of the ship carrying the relics sparked a debate about how and where they should be housed. The merchants informed the citizens that they had made a pledge to erect a church for the saint on the site of the Byzantine palace. Elias supported the merchants, but others disagreed, arguing that they should be housed in the cathedral, under the jurisdiction of the Archbishop.[24] The debate was temporarily resolved when Elias offered to take care of the relics at San Benedetto until the citizens reach a decision. Nicephorus writes that Ursus, who had been away at Canosa, returned to Bari and insisted that they be moved immediately to the episcopal palace, provoking a violent conflict, during which two men were killed. In the end, Elias moved the saint to the church of St Eustratios, in the former Byzantine palace complex, where they began to work miracles. Nicephorus's account characterizes Ursus as an absent archbishop who provoked violent protest when he tried to appropriate the relics for himself. This characterization is supported by other sources. Ursus was indeed an outsider in Bari, possibly even a Norman puppet; he had been the bishop of Rapolla before being promoted by Robert Guiscard to archbishop of Bari and Canosa, with the approval of Gregory VII.[25] He preferred Canosa (where he commissioned the base of the episcopal throne) and was rarely in Bari.[26] He worked so hard for the Norman cause that he was often exhausted.[27] Ultimately, in this version of events, the pro-Norman outsider Ursus is unsuccessful and Elias, the 'people's choice', takes control of the precious relics.

The relics were stolen by a group of sixty-two merchants, who formed a society and were granted privileges, including allocated seating and burial plots in the new church. Some of those privileges were passed on to their descendants.[28] The names of those in the society reveal that the theft was an enterprise that crossed social boundaries, from simple sailors to merchants and Lombard noblemen (the latter probably the financiers rather than active participants).[29] One of the members was a Slav, called Stefanus, whose right to a burial plot was confirmed by Elias in 1095. His funerary inscription is still visible on the south side of the west façade. Stefanus, like many Slavs in Bari, may have been enslaved (we will return to slavery in Chapter 6). On the East façade is the grave of Stefanus of Taranto.[30] The inclusion of both of these men shows co-operation not just across social classes, encompassing the cosmopolitan diversity of the city but also from beyond Bari. The theft was an economic and civic enterprise that involved the whole city and social networks across Apulia.

The second text was commissioned by Ursus himself, to defend himself against Nicephorus's negative portrayal, and was written by the Archdeacon John, probably a year or so later.[31] According to John, Ursus was not in Canosa but in Trani, waiting to embark upon a pilgrimage to the Holy Land. This paints him in a different light, making him look pious rather than partisan. When he heard about the arrival of the saint, he returned to Bari and found the relics already housed in St Eustratios, and the citizens squabbling over them. John claims that Ursus agreed immediately that a new church should be built on the site of the Byzantine palace and that it was Ursus who entrusted the relics to Elias and ordered him to oversee the construction of the basilica. Thus, according to John, Ursus acted as the ultimate patron of the new basilica and guardian of the relics while Elias is cast in the role of deputy, to whom the project management was delegated.

Together these two texts paint a picture of conflict between rival factions vying for ownership of the relics. Louis Hamilton has argued that the arrival of the relics *caused* the conflict between different factions, but my reading of the texts is that the tug of war over the relics stirred up existing tensions.[32] A sense of civic independence, rebelliousness and tension between Bari and Canosa were issues already simmering during the Byzantine era. Francesco Nitti di Vito, who was archdeacon of the Basilica in the 1930s, was convinced that the endings of both Nicephorus and John's accounts had been altered in the twelfth century to reflect a later conflict between the monastery and the cathedral, so we should not rely too heavily on their depiction of the conflict.[33] However, the picture of a strong local community in tension with a pro-Norman outsider archbishop tallies very well with everything else we know about Bari in this period and the subsequent ascent of Elias as a civic leader (which will be discussed later). It also seems to confirm Nicephorus and John's basic narrative about the conflict. Nitti di Vito also believed that a fourteenth-century Russian manuscript contained the original and accurate account of the events, written within a decade or so of the events. The Russian account begins with a description of the poor state of the tomb in Myra and of the Turkish invasions. Nicholas appeared to a priest in Bari, asking to be moved. The grain-selling expedition to Antioch was a ruse to acquire the relics. In Antioch, the expedition became more urgent when they learned of the competition from Venice. The relics were placed in the church of St John the Baptist at the Sea while the new church was built.[34] Patrick Geary agreed that Nicephorus and John's accounts are told through a later lens, but was equally wary of the Russian account which only exists in the much later manuscript.[35] There are, however, aspects of the Russian manuscript that are very plausible, such as the premeditation and the Muslim control of Myra as a motivating factor.

The relics arrived on the ninth of May. The texts of Nicephorus and John the Deacon tell us that pilgrimage began immediately. The relics arrived on Saturday and by Wednesday local pilgrims began to arrive and healing miracles began soon after.[36] The flow of pilgrims has been constant since that Wednesday. Local pilgrims were soon joined by long-distance travellers but Bari probably never became a destination in its own right. A stop in Bari was usually part of a longer journey to the Holy Land, unless the pilgrim was local.[37] In June, the new duke, Roger Borsa, and his half-brother Bohemond, who had recently reached a tentative and temporary ceasefire, co-signed a document donating the Byzantine palace to Ursus and granting him permission to build the new church on the site. Duke Roger also granted Ursus significant land in and around Bari and rights over the Jews of the city.[38] Duchess Sichelgaita, Guiscard's widow, had already given the archbishop rights over the Jews a year earlier, so perhaps the confirmation by Roger Borsa and Bohemond indicates that Jewish taxes were intended to help finance the building.[39] Bohemond and Roger Borsa's document either gives credence to Archdeacon John's claim that Ursus was the patron of the new church or shows that the Normans supported their ally Ursus in his attempt to take control of the building project after Elias and the citizens had begun it. Either way, although the theft may have been a mercantile enterprise, the construction of the church required collaboration between Lombards and Normans.

Elias began work immediately, no doubt aided by the gifts that were offered to St Nicholas by the many local pilgrims who began to visit.[40] Nicephorus tells us that

> That church [of St Eustratios] together with churches of other saints, was razed to the ground some days later. On their sites and on some other space from the same court, the people of Bari erected the most glorious and magnificent church in honour of the most blessed Nicholas and of those saints. This project was managed, from the beginning, by Abbot Elia together with some of the nobles of Bari. It was at the request of the archbishop himself and of all the citizens that he had charge of the holy body.[41]

The churches of the Byzantine palace complex had survived and were used until 1087, but the rest had already been demolished and left as open space, wasteland waiting to be filled. This indicates that, at some point between 1071 and 1087, the Baresi, either with or without Norman support, had demolished the secular parts of the palace, perhaps as an act of symbolically obliterating the traces of Byzantine rule and re-appropriating the site. When, eventually, the churches needed to be demolished, they transferred the dedications en masse to the new church. The continuity of dedications mitigated the upheaval of regime change: although the Baresi wanted to remove the symbols of Byzantine authority, they did not want to lose the saints they had come to rely on (remember the Latin priest Peter who made donations to St Eustratios in Chapter 3). Perhaps there was also an element of harnessing the might of imperial power. The very imperial saints were powerful protectors, advocates and intercessors worth keeping. Nicholas himself was also a Byzantine saint, so the new church created an agglomeration, a 'pantheon' of Byzantine saints, adopted by a small city facing a brave new world. In the midst of Nicephorus's account, the various factions within the city are at odds – he tells a story of an evil archbishop trying to take control of relics that belong to the people – but by the end he paints a picture of unity: the construction of the church is a civic enterprise and all involved are united by Elias's leadership of the project, with the blessing of Archbishop Ursus and the Norman rulers. The site of Byzantine imperial power has been appropriated by the Lombard population.

Consecration

A mere seventeen months later, in October 1089, the crypt of the new church was consecrated. Ursus had died in Canosa in the spring of 1089, leaving Elias as the most prominent clergyman.[42] In September, Pope Urban II held a council in Melfi. Bohemond and Roger Borsa, acting together once again, sent a delegation that included Elias, to invite the Pope to Bari, to consecrate the church and invest Elias as the new archbishop.[43] Urban accepted, partly he said, because he had a particular devotion to St Nicholas, who was a favourite of all the reforming popes, as an example of a model bishop.[44] Urban would go on to play a continuing role in the life of the church and San Nicola was a nexus where his dual projects of reform and crusade would meet. Urban's approval of St Nicholas as a patron demonstrates the shrewd decision made by the Baresi who stole the relics. Nicholas was a proto-ecumenical saint from the start, equally beloved of Byzantine emperors and popes. Urban invested Elias as archbishop in the cathedral and, the following day, he went to the new basilica, where he interred the relics of St Nicholas beneath the altar in the crypt, which had been built in a mere seventeen months. Although the documentary evidence claims that the invitation was initiated by Bohemond and Roger Borsa, it is much more likely to have been Elias's idea. Consecrations were important events that created communal memories, especially for Benedictines like Elias and Urban II. In Benedictine houses consecration anniversaries were celebrated and special sermons were sometimes composed to mark them.[45] The Benedictine connection between Elias and Urban is significant and will be explored in subsequent chapters, especially in relation to Gregorian Reform.

The papal consecration of San Nicola echoed the consecration in 1085 of Salerno cathedral by Gregory VII, at the request of Robert Guiscard, an event that augmented Guiscard's legitimacy and status.[46] While Melfi had been the first Norman stronghold, Guiscard later married into the Lombard royal family and moved his court to Salerno, where he could boost his legitimacy by portraying himself as the successor to the Lombard Dukes.[47] In the early years of his rule in Salerno, Guiscard developed a collaborative relationship with Archbishop Alfanus (not coincidentally, another Benedictine), with whom he promoted the cult of St Matthew and re-built the cathedral.[48] A similar pattern has emerged in Bari. The Norman rulers were instrumental in promoting both cults and in the foundation and construction of both churches, but in collaboration with local leaders. A key difference, however, is that the Norman involvement at Salerno cathedral was much more explicit – Guiscard is mentioned no fewer than three times in the inscriptions on the entrances at Salerno – whereas at Bari there is no reference to the Normans on the building itself, their involvement must be pieced together from texts and context.[49] Norman involvement in

Bari is implicit, the new cult and church are constructed with the Normans permission and sometimes with their collaboration, but their involvement is never overtly manifested in the building itself.

The crypt and shrine

The relics emit a miraculous, sweet-smelling and healing manna, which is removed annually on the 9th of May and distributed to pilgrims. Archaeologists working on the original church of St Nicholas at Myra have discovered a system of pipes and troughs for liquid. It is thought that, in Myra, the relics may have been immersed in water that was then distributed as a contact relic.[50] When the relics reached Bari they began to produce the miraculous liquid, thus enabling the cult to function in Bari in a similar way to how it had functioned in Myra. We shall see in Chapter 10 that some of the designs for the pavements may also have been inspired by the church in Myra. The intimate knowledge of the shrine in Myra and the way the cult had functioned may be additional evidence that the relics' theft was premeditated for several years. It may also support the Russian *translatio* text's claim that the relics arrived in Bari accompanied by some of the monks who had been the custodians in Myra. It may also indicate that a sense of continuity in cultic practice and aesthetic was a factor in attracting pilgrims to the new shrine. It was very common in the Middle Ages for relics to be naturally perfumed, and indeed the relics of St Sabinus also emitted a sweetly scented manna, along with an intense light (providing another sense of continuity for the faithful of Bari).[51] Pleasant scent was considered indicative of authenticity.[52] So, the scent of the manna was part of the proof that the bones acquired by the Baresi were genuine, which was crucial to the success of the shrine because the Venetians had also managed to steal some of the bones and had set up a rival shrine at San Niccolò al Lido.

The crypt today, like the whole church, is a product of extensive restorations in the twentieth century (Figures 1 and 28). From the eighteenth century until the 1950s, the crypt was encased in stucco decoration and the side apses were walled up. Changes in sea levels meant that it was frequently flooded and inaccessible. Franco Schettini's restorations in the middle of the twentieth century made it water-tight and stripped away the post-medieval decoration.[53] The area around the altar had suffered the most damage, and some of the capitals had to be replaced. The altar has a semi-circular opening in the west side, which allows pilgrims to kiss or touch the tomb slab beneath it (Figure 29). The slab has a hole at the centre, which penetrates down to the relic casket below. The hole in the closure slab was sealed by a metal disc on hinges so that it could be lifted.[54] It is decorated on both sides with a bust of St Nicholas and an inscription, 'pray for us, O, Saint Nicholas, so that we are worthy of the promise of Christ' (Figures 30 and 31).[55] The relic casket was opened in the 1950s and the relics examined and authenticated by representatives from the Vatican.

The crypt is a hall crypt that seems to have been modelled on the crypt at Salerno cathedral and needs to be analysed in conjunction with Salerno (Figures 32 and 33).[56] The two crypts have similar proportions and are accessed by lateral staircases from the north and south aisles of the nave, with one functioning as an entrance and the other

Figure 28 Crypt, San Nicola. Photo: author.

Figure 29 Shrine of St Nicholas. Photo: Palickap via Wikimedia.

Figure 30 Medallion that sealed the relic chamber, shrine of St Nicholas, Bari. Photo: Author.

Figure 31 Reverse, medallion that sealed the relic chamber, shrine of St Nicholas, Bari. Photo: Author.

an exit, facilitating the orderly flow of pilgrims around the building without disturbing liturgies (whether or not the pilgrims followed the prescribed route is another matter. Medieval writers usually describe shrines as being more chaotic than their designers intended). Bari has much shallower apses, behind which are two small, windowed rooms – presumably for vesting and storage – accessed via recessed bays to the north and south. The major difference between the two crypts is the placement of the shrine. At Salerno, the shrine is located in the centre of the space allowing it to be entirely surrounded, and circumnavigated, by the faithful, whereas at Bari, it is in the apse,

Figure 32 Salerno crypt. Photo: Mentnafunnagan via Wikimedia.

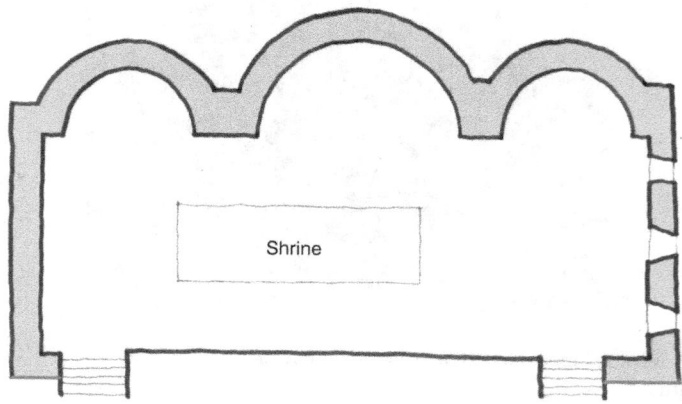

Figure 33 Salerno cathedral, crypt, plan. Drawn by Elisabeth Kendall.

mirroring more closely the liturgical arrangement in the church above. At Salerno the designers have prioritized access to the shrine and the easy circulation of crowds of pilgrims. A procession to the shrine was a key part of the Easter vigil liturgy in Salerno, and the crypt overall seems to have been designed to accommodate processions, rather than the mass.[57] The arrangement at Bari places more emphasis on creating a vertical axis between the altar-shrine in the crypt and the main altar above.

A hall crypt is a more or less rectangular subterranean space, supported by columns with an apse or apses in the east. Unlike the annular crypts and small *confessios*, in which shrines were usually housed in late antiquity and the early Middle Ages, a hall crypt is suitable for full liturgies and larger crowds and can function as a church within a church. Possibly the earliest hall crypt is Santa Maria in Cosmedin in Rome, built by Hadrian I as part of the eighth-century project to bring relics from the catacombs into the city churches.[58] But this kind of crypt would not become standard until the eleventh century. The introduction of this kind of crypt in Salerno and Bari is innovative and probably came from northern Europe, rather than from Santa Maria in Cosmedin: plausible comparisons can be made with the crypts at Speyer cathedral, St Cyriakus at Gernrode and examples in Normandy.[59] There are further links between Speyer cathedral and the architecture of the rest of San Nicola, and this northern European influence will be discussed further in Chapter 7. There are two plausible and interconnected theories about what drove the introduction of hall crypts into southern Italy: a desire for additional liturgical spaces or a desire to create spaces that emulate the tombs of the martyrs.[60] San Nicola seems to have been designed with both of these in mind. The placement of the shrine in the main apse, mirroring the design of the sanctuary in the church above, makes the space ideal for celebrating mass, giving the church a second, fairly large space for daily and festal liturgies. We have already seen that certain aspects of the church emulated the saint's original tomb in Myra and contributed to proving the authenticity of the relics. The subterranean shrine would have added another layer of authenticity, especially for pilgrims who had visited the early Christian sites in Rome on their way to the Adriatic.

Romuald the sculptor

In Chapter 4 we encountered the episcopal throne in Canosa, to which we will now briefly return (Figure 26). The seat of the throne was made by Acceptus during the episcopacy of Archbishop Nicholas. The elephant base, however, was commissioned by Archbishop Ursus and sculpted by Romuald, both Lombards judging by their names (Figures 34 and 35). Underneath the inscription are a pair of griffins drinking from a fountain, flanked by anthropomorphic feline masks. Both the iconography and style are very similar to some of the crypt capitals at San Nicola in Bari. Ursus became archbishop in 1078 and died in 1089, the year the crypt was consecrated. It is therefore a very reasonable supposition that Romuald sculpted both the Canosa elephants and the crypt capitals and then went on to work elsewhere at San Nicola (particularly on the east window, which is supported by elephants similar to the Canosa throne). Stylistically Romuald's work bears similarities to the trapezoid capitals in San Benedetto and Bari and Canosa cathedrals. Tentatively, I would suggest that Romuald was trained in the workshop that carved the trapezoid capitals and that he may also have carved the capitals at Santa Maria di Colonna.

The elephant can be seen as a Christological symbol and there are several examples of them supporting episcopal thrones.[61] But Romuald's stylistic influences were decidedly Islamic. Romuald's elephants are domestic, rather than wild, animals. They are wearing beaded ornamental saddlecloths and harnesses around their necks

Figure 34 Canosa throne, detail of elephant. Photo: Author.

Figure 35 Canosa throne, detail.

decorated with a vegetal design. The ridges on their head and trunk may represent ceremonial headdresses. This way of decorating elephants' bodies comes from the court ceremonial of Fatimid Cairo, where the caliphs processed through the streets of Cairo, accompanied by elephants, giraffes and soldiers, all of whom were clothed in opulent silks.[62] Elephant figurines were made and displayed at the court in Cairo, made of materials like amber, silver and gold.[63] Adorned elephants were depicted on ceramics and textiles.[64] The beading on the Canosa elephants' saddles is similar to the beading on the wings on the trapezoid capitals, themselves inspired by eastern Mediterranean silks. The Charlemagne chess set, made in Amalfi or Salerno in the 1080s, include elephants with saddlecloths and body ornament very similar to the Canosa throne (Figure 36). The Charlemagne chess set as a whole is considered to be closely related to Fatimid ivories and was probably modelled on a Fatimid chess set imported to Italy after the sack of the Fatimid treasuries.[65] The chess elephants have very flat trunks and compact heads because the sculptor was limited by the width of the ivory tusk. The Canosa elephants are more elongated but have the same flat, very straight trunks, perhaps indicating that Romuald was copying directly from a chess piece or another ivory figurine.

As well as textiles and ceramics, Romuald drew from metalwork. Capital 13 in the crypt of San Nicola is similar to a door knocker in the David Collection in Copenhagen (Figures 37 and 38). The capital features a lion mask, of a kind found on many medieval door knockers, but particularly similar to the example in Copenhagen. The David Collection knocker was made in the eleventh century, probably in Sicily, where it was probably attached to the door of a mosque. The lion head is surrounded by an Arabic inscription of the *basmala* and the *shahada*, written in the first person,

Figure 36 Elephant from the Charlemagne chess set. Photo: Poulpy via Wikimedia.

Figure 37 Capital 13, crypt, San Nicola, Bari. Photo: Author.

Figure 38 Lion doorknocker, the David Collection, Copenhagen, inventory number 50/2000. Photographer: Pernille Klemp.

so that when the knocker knocks, the lion roars out the Islamic invocation of God and the profession of faith.[66] The Copenhagen lion and capital 13 are also similar to the lions on the episcopal throne at San Nicola (see Chapter 6). A capital in the roughly contemporary crypt at Otranto has a similar lion mask, more obviously copied from a door knocker because it has the ring in its mouth. Richard Camber has suggested that medieval sculptors in southern Italy may have worked across both stone and bronze, which raises the possibility that Romuald also made small bronze objects like door knockers that were probably attached to wooden doors.⁶⁷ One such door knocker is in the museum of San Nicola, although it is very different stylistically to the lions in the crypt and in Copenhagen.

Oliphants

We can also add ivories to the list of objects from which Romuald drew inspiration. In the Pinacoteca Provinciale in Bari is a resin copy of the Borradaile Oliphant, displayed with the hypothesis that the original was made in Bari (Figure 39).⁶⁸ The provenance of oliphants is uncertain; some scholars attribute them to Fatimid Egypt, others to southern Italy, most commonly to Salerno or Amalfi.⁶⁹ Others have urged art historians to move away from provenance, towards a focus on reception and shared Mediterranean culture.⁷⁰ The move away from the traditional art historical focus on provenance is a sensible and fruitful one, especially for secular objects that belong to the 'shared culture of objects' of Mediterranean courts, as Oleg Grabar put it.⁷¹ However, site-specific studies like this one benefit from being able to anchor objects in a particular place, even speculatively. There is a tendency to link all southern Italian ivories to Salerno-Amalfi because of the group in Salerno cathedral and Maurus de Comite Maurone's commissioning of the Farfa Casket, but in reality ivory must have been carved in other cities as well.⁷² Although oliphants are most commonly associated with Salerno-Amalfi, a few scholars have connected oliphants to the coastal cities of Apulia.⁷³ Although there is stronger evidence for Amalfitan merchants' access to the trans-Saharan ivory trade, merchants from Bari would have been able to procure ivory (at the very least they could have purchased it from Amalfitan traders, who were certainly present in Bari).⁷⁴

The Borradaile Oliphant is one of a group decorated with animals in interlaced circles, a pattern that comes from textiles, as if the horns were shrouded in silk: one

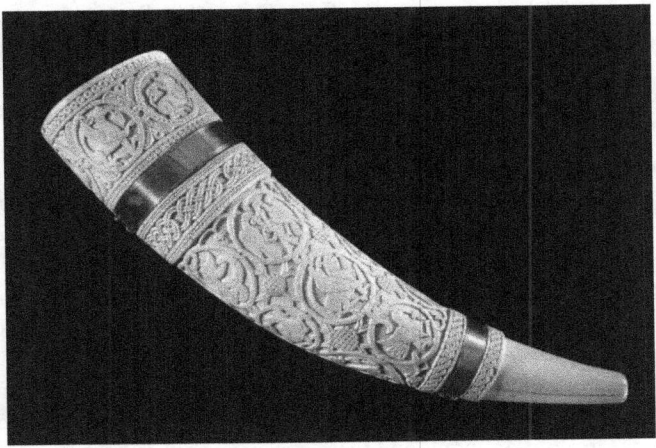

Figure 39 Borradaile Oliphant. Photo: British Museum.

Figure 40 Copy of the Borradaile Oliphant in the Pinacoteca Provinciale, Bari. Detail of dragon eating his tail. Photo: Author.

precious material wrapped in another. The group includes the examples in the Victoria and Albert Museum, the National Museum of Scotland and the Metropolitan Museum of Art.[75] The Borradaile Oliphant has bands of beading at the top, another nod to textiles. The other decorative bands are interlace, similar to the illuminated initials on Lombard manuscripts. A good example is the dragon eating his own tail (Figure 40). Another good comparison is the illuminated T from a fragment of a homily written in Bari type script, recently sold at Sotheby's, in which a dragon with a bird head holds its body in its beak. The peacocks drinking from a fountain (Figure 41) are comparable to crypt capital 14 (Figure 42) and the overall imagery of birds and animals is similar to the crypt capitals more generally. The idea that the Borradaille Oliphant may have been carved in Bari, or in the same cultural milieu, is plausible. Romuald certainly seems to have been familiar with contemporary ivory carving and may even have worked in both stone and ivory.

Another oliphant that has been linked to San Nicola is the Clephane Horn (Figure 43).[76] It was included in the catalogue of eleventh-century sculpture in Apulia, *Puglia XI Secolo: Alle Sorgenti del Romanico* and Herman Fillitz and Anthony Eastmond have suggested that the clothing worn by the figures on the Clephane Horn is similar to the episcopal throne in San Nicola (see Chapter 6 for the throne).[77] The vegetal bands are similar to Acceptus's vegetal scrolls on the door jambs of Bari cathedral. The horn is decorated with scenes from the hippodrome in Constantinople, similar to the images at the base of the fourth-century obelisk of Theodosius in the Hippodrome itself, with chariot races, animal fights, wrestling and the obelisks on the central spina. Although the depiction of the hippodrome would seem to tie the Clephane Horn to Constantinople, it is a red herring. Stylistically it does not fit, there is no evidence for other oliphants in Constantinople and there may have been a shortage of ivory in the capital, making it unlikely that large ivory objects like oliphants were made there.[78]

Figure 41 Copy of the Borradaile Oliphant in the Pinacoteca Provinciale, Bari. Detail of peacocks drinking. Photo: Author.

Figure 42 Peacocks and pinecone fountain, capital 14, San Nicola. Photo: John McNeill.

The Clephane Horn is considered to be part of the 'Byzantine group' of four oliphants. They have similar imagery, of chariots or hunting, but are stylistically not at all Byzantine and are very diverse.[79] The closest relation to the Clephane Horn is the oliphant in St Vitus' Cathedral in Prague; the imagery is similar but the style is completely different. The Prague horn includes animal roundels, linking it to that group. The other two oliphants loosely associated with the Prague and Clephane

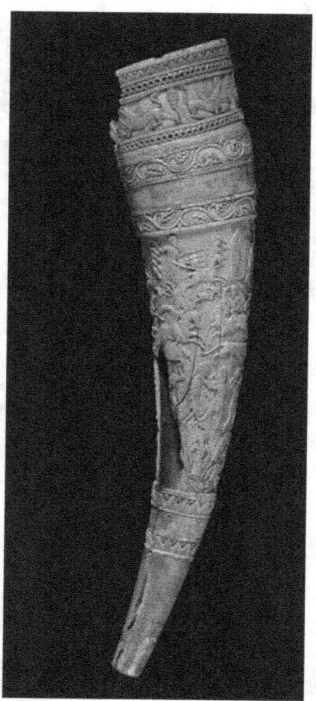

Figure 43 Clephane Horn. Photo: British Museum.

horns are in the Jászberény Museum and the National Museum of Copenhagen, but they are quite different with generalized hunting scenes.[80] The imagery on the Clephane Horn is archaicizing, not a depiction of contemporary reality.[81] By the eleventh century, the Hippodrome had become a primarily ceremonial imperial space, with chariot races, by then an archaic sport almost more of a ceremony than a race, taking place only on special occasions. One of its functions was hosting receptions of foreign diplomats, so it had perhaps more of a reputation abroad than it did in Constantinople by this time.[82] Anthony Eastmond has described the 'Byzantine' oliphants as 'Byzantium at second hand'.[83] Bari is a much more likely place of production than Constantinople, given that there is so much more evidence for oliphants being made in southern Italy.

In the middle Byzantine period, the idea of the Hippodrome and its late antique glamour seems to have been more attractive to foreigners than to the people of Constantinople. Charioteers are depicted on the shroud of Charlemagne.[84] The Hippodrome was depicted in the eleventh-century wall paintings in Kyiv cathedral. The images in Kyiv were part of a strategy to elevate the status of Kyiv and its ruler, from provincial backwater on the periphery of the empire to internationally recognized city.[85] In Kyiv the foreign concept of chariot racing had to be explained to the local community, but for people who saw the Clephane Horn in Italy, chariot racing signified ancient Rome and the Hippodrome's prototype, the Circus Maximus.[86] The Clephane

Horn evokes Constantinople but, like much Byzantinizing art in southern Italy, it may be using Constantinople to evoke Rome.

Eastmond has pointed out that oliphants seem to have been valued above all in northern Europe and certainly did not stay in their place of production (there are no Mediterranean clusters of oliphants, although nineteenth-century collecting could have broken them up, if they existed). Eastmond speculates that perhaps oliphants were made in southern Italy to be 'marketed' to northern Europeans as souvenirs of their visit to the Mediterranean.[87] Indeed their production seems to have coincided with increased pilgrimage and the crusades. Bari, as a Byzantine capital, would be a good place to market objects like the Clephane and Prague horns that evoke a nostalgia for the glamour of Constantinople in its heyday. There is good reason to believe that many oliphants – including the three discussed here – were made in Bari and had connections to the stone-carving workshops at San Nicola and the cathedral.

The crypt as paradise

We saw in Chapter 2 how spolia from the Byzantine palace was reused in the crypt. Broadly speaking the spoliate capitals have been placed on the peripheries of the crypt, with capitals carved in the 1080s at the centre. Similarly, the most colourful columns have also been placed at the centre. Also in Chapter 2, we saw that other pieces of Byzantine sculpture were used as paving in the upper church. Pushing Byzantine material to the peripheries of the space was perhaps a conscious decision to visually manifest the demise of Byzantine power, part of the Lombard community's appropriation of the site and a declaration of autonomy. The capitals newly carved for the crypt between 1087 and 1089 can be dated by their stylistic homogeneity and similarity to contemporary sculpture elsewhere in Apulia, such as the triangular frames for the pine cones on capitals 5 and 18 (Figure 44), which can also be found at Sant'Andrea dell'Isola in Brindisi, built from 1060 onwards and the bi-corporate lions on capital 17 which echo their counterparts on capitals at nearby Bitetto and in a micro-mosaic from the Benedictine convent at Conversano.[88]

The iconography of the capitals in the Bari crypt – a variety of foliage, cornucopia, diverse and sometimes fantastical animals – together symbolizes the safety, fertility and abundance of a garden, evoking the imagery of paradise. Romuald and Elias were drawing on early Christian art, which often evoked paradise through an abundance of natural imagery. This links Bari to the contemporary Gregorian Reform movement, which sought to return the Latin church to its early Christian state. Two capitals in particular have been modelled on images commissioned by reformers, ultimately derived from early Christian models. The peacocks on the east face of capital 14 sit on a branch, one preening the other (Figure 45). On the north face is a griffin and on the south face, a pair of peacocks 'kiss' above a vase with a pine cone inside it and below an anthropomorphic lion spurts water (Figure 42). The iconography recalls the fountain that stood in the atrium of Old St Peter's, at the centre of which was an antique bronze pine cone, 4 metres tall (now relocated to inside the Vatican, Figure 46). A sixteenth-century drawing shows the pine cone surrounded by eight porphyry columns,

Figure 44 Capital 18, crypt, San Nicola, Bari. Photo: Author.

Figure 45 Preening peacocks, capital 14, crypt, San Nicola. Photo: Author.

surmounted by lunettes decorated with a pair of gilded peacocks (Figure 47).[89] The pine cone was a symbol of new life, while the supposedly incorruptible flesh of peacocks associated them with immortality and mythical griffins with the wonders of paradise.[90] These symbols were placed at the centre of the atrium at Old St Peter's, known as the *paradisus*, conjuring up the garden of paradise. Old St Peter's was a particular source of inspiration for artists and patrons who participated in Gregorian Reform.

Figure 46 Bronze pine cone, in the Vatican Museums. Photo: Dcastor via Wikimedia.

Figure 47 The fountain at the centre of the atrium of Old St Peter's. Drawing: Cronaca, now in the Ufizzi.

On the vegetal capitals, pine cones are a popular motif. The most interesting is capital 9 (Figure 48), with a vine divided into four spirals, a design remarkably similar to the apse mosaic at San Clemente in Rome (*c*. 1100) (Figure 49). The apse mosaic at San Clemente is thought to have drawn inspiration from the apse mosaic at Salerno cathedral, which now only survives in fragments.[91] The ultimate model for both is the early Christian mosaic in the Lateran baptistery.[92] The crypt capitals as a whole seem to chime with the spirit of the apse inscription at San Clemente, 'we shall symbolise the church of Christ by that vine, which the law makes to be arid, but the cross makes to be flourishing'.[93] Given the other links between San Nicola and Salerno, it is very plausible that Romuald copied part of the Salerno apse mosaic on capital 9.

The general evocation of early Christian art and the specific links to Rome and Salerno are the first indication of one of the major arguments of this book: that Elias of Bari was an adherent of the Gregorian Reform movement and that San Nicola reflects his reforming ideology. 'Gregorian Reform' is a term coined in the nineteenth century to describe a movement within the Latin church in the eleventh and twelfth centuries named after Pope Gregory VII, one of many reforming popes of the era.[94] The aim of the movement, like so many church reforms, was to return the church to the state of perceived 'purity' of the first few centuries of Christianity, a process they called *renovatio*, renewal. The reformers sought to undo the 'corruptions' of the early Middle Ages principally though changes in canon law and ecclesiastical structures.[95] The first crusade can be seen as a product of Gregorian Reform, and we shall see connections between the two in subsequent chapters.[96]

In southern Italy, the movement is generally associated with Montecassino and Salerno.[97] Bari is rarely connected with the reformers, despite the involvement of Urban II. Most histories of medieval Bari understandably focus on its distinctive sense of civic independence and its relationships with the Byzantines and the Normans. As far as we can tell from the documentary evidence, Bari was not a hub of administrative or legislative reform. But, as we shall see in the following chapters, ideas of *renovatio* are present in San Nicola, beginning with the crypt capitals, links to Salerno and the

Figure 48 Capital 9, crypt, San Nicola, Bari. Photo: Author.

Figure 49 San Clemente, apse mosaic, Rome. Photo: Dnalor 01 via Wikimedia

papal consecration. The fact that St Nicholas was an early Christian saint and the desire to imitate the fourth-century church in Myra also tallied with a reform agenda.

Conclusion

The Norman conquest was a big change for the city of Bari, and San Nicola is a physical manifestation of that change. The demolition of the Byzantine palace and the erection of a Latin church on its site made a momentous statement about the transfer of power. But it was not the straightforward transfer from Byzantine to Norman authority that we might expect. Instead it was a more complex change in which the local community asserted their independent civic identity, partially through the project of stealing the relics of St Nicholas and building him a church. The foundation of the church and the construction of the crypt were characterized by a complex, and often fraught, web of relationships. The project was initiated by the merchants of Bari, supported by the whole local community. The Norman rulers gave their consent and participated in oblique ways but were not active patrons. Archbishop Ursus seems to have been the representative of Norman interests, who was in conflict with the local Lombard, mercantile community. Romuald, the mason who probably sculpted the crypt capitals, was a local Lombard who drew inspiration from the recently completed Salerno cathedral and from the luxury portable objects that circulated in the Mediterranean and were a crucial part of Bari's economy. Elias began his involvement as the merchants' representative and project manager of the building site but became the archbishop and overall patron when Ursus died. It was Elias, in collaboration with the Normans, who invited Urban II to consecrate the church, thus bringing the new church further into the orbit of the Gregorian Reform movement. What we can see very clearly in the foundation of San Nicola are the twin concerns of the renewal of the Latin church and the preservation of international commercial networks across the Mediterranean.

6

A throne of Solomon

Classicism, crusade, slavery

From the crypt, we now move up into the main basilica to look at the throne that stands in the apse. After the consecration of the crypt and the internment of the relics, work began in earnest on the upper church. Elias was now archbishop, and the throne was made *c.* 1100 as his episcopal throne. It bears some similarities to the Canosa throne, made in two stages for Archbishops Nicholas and Ursus, particularly in drawing on luxury portable objects from the eastern Mediterranean. While the Canosa throne was concerned with the preaching and pastoral ministry of the archbishop, the Bari throne evokes King Solomon and Archbishop Elias's role as an ecclesiastical judge. The throne combines the authority of classical spolia and the Solomonic tradition with ideas about the contemporary world at the dawn of the twelfth century, particularly the first crusade and slavery.

As we saw in the previous chapter, in 1089 Pope Urban II had travelled to Bari to consecrate the crypt of the basilica and to ordain Abbot Elias as archbishop of the joint archdiocese of Bari and Canosa. Nearly a decade later, Urban returned to convene a church council. The council of 1098 was primarily to discuss the issues that separated the eastern and western churches, and it took place during the first flush of Latin crusader victories in the eastern Mediterranean. The location of the council was no coincidence. St Nicholas, an eastern saint migrated west, had become for the papacy an instrument through which they hoped to heal the rift with the eastern churches (the Great Schism had taken place in 1054). In 1091, just two years after the relics arrived in Bari, Urban II had sent one of his small bones to the rulers of Kyiv as an offering of reconciliation.[1] Nicholas was an ideal saint to heal ecumenical rifts (a role he continues to play today). At the Council of Nicaea in 325, in the debate about the nature of the Trinity, St Nicholas was a vehement defender of orthodox ideas about the nature of Christ and his relationship to the Trinity and opponent of the Arian heresy. In the eleventh century, one of the points of divergence between eastern and western Christianity was the question of the *filioque*, another debate about the nature of the Trinity. Urban II chose the shrine of St Nicholas to discuss this and other issues, perhaps in an attempt to hark back to the ecumenical councils of the early church.[2]

As well as the *filioque* and other esoteric issues, the Council of Bari had a more practical purpose. Urban II was very concerned with papal primacy, the supremacy of the Bishop of Rome over the eastern Mediterranean patriarchs. One of his priorities was to persuade the Greek-rite clerics in southern Italy to recognize papal primacy. He had minimal interest in imposing the Latin rite on the south; liturgical divergence was not important to him. Authority was what concerned Urban and he wanted his own authority to be universally recognized in the Italian peninsula (and indeed some Greek clergy had submitted to papal authority at the Council of Melfi, although others resisted).[3]

On arrival in Bari, Urban commissioned an episcopal throne for Elias, as the *Anonymous Chronicle of Bari* narrates.[4]

> On the 3rd October 1098, Pope Urban arrived, bringing with him numerous Archbishops and Bishops, Abbots and Counts; they entered Bari and were greeted with great reverence and he [Urban] prepared a marvellous throne in the church of St Nicholas for our Archbishop Elias.[5]

This throne now stands in the main apse, inscribed as belonging to Elias, 'The illustrious and good patron, Elias, Bishop of Bari and Canosa, sits in this seat' (Figures 50–53).[6]

As we saw in Chapter 4, the earlier Apulian episcopal thrones at Canosa and Monte Sant'Angelo were made of marble panels, assembled after carving, like today's flat-pack furniture. The panel construction, practical and economical, meant that a sizeable throne could be made from smaller pieces of marble. The Bari throne is a

Figure 50 Drawing of the Bari throne, side view. Heinrich Wilhelm Schulz, *Denkmäler der Kunst des Mittelalters in Unteritalien* (Dresden, 1860) Atlas, plate 6.

Figure 51 Bari throne and sanctuary pavement. Photo: Author.

Figure 52 Bari throne. Photo: Author.

much more decadent object since it is carved from a single block of marble. The large size and roughly square proportions indicate that it was carved from a section of a Roman column shaft from a prestigious public building, most likely from Rome.[7] A 'marvellous' throne such as this would take time to carve and the chronicle implies that

Figure 53 Bari throne, detail of the back. Photo: Paolo Monti via Wikimedia.

it was made in Bari. The most likely scenario is Urban brought the marble with him to Bari, where he presented it as a gift to Elias and commissioned a local sculptor to make a throne from it. Possibly Urban instructed the sculptor in conjunction with Elias.

This was a time when Roman law was being revived and the popes began to assert that they were the legal owners of antiquities in Rome. By the 1140s, popes were claiming that the use and transportation of ancient spolia was their particular prerogative as the rightful successors of Roman emperors and similar ideas maybe have been circulating fifty years earlier during the pontificate of Urban II.[8] When Urban made a gift of a prestigious piece of Roman spolia, it sent the message about the power and supremacy of the papacy over the physical remains and land of the Roman Empire. Possibly, the gift also carried undertones of papal primacy. Using spolia to assert that he was the successor to Constantine, as well as successor to St Peter, may have been part of Urban's strategy to persuade the recalcitrant Greek clerics at the Council of Bari to recognize his authority over them.

Dating the throne

Together, the inscription on the throne and the passage in the chronicle seem to me to be sufficient evidence that the throne in the apse is the same one commissioned by Urban II at the Council of Bari in 1098. However, much of the scholarship on the throne has focused on questioning that date, so before we look at the throne in more detail, it is necessary to first set out the various theories about its date. The first scholars to write about the throne – André Grabar, Géza de Francovich and Arthur Kingsley Porter – believed it to date to *c.* 1100, immediately after the Council of Bari.[9] But the date was contested later in the twentieth century for two reasons: First, the majority of eleventh-century sculpture in Apulia is aniconic and it is rare (but not unknown) to find representations of human figures. Second, the figures on the throne display extraordinary naturalism, which was too precocious for *c.* 1100. On the basis of style alone Pina Belli D'Elia dated the throne to the 1160s, claiming that the reference to Elias in the inscription was intended to preserve his memory long after his death (despite the fact that the inscription refers to Elias in the present tense).[10] This theory was accepted and replicated by some, but rejected and critiqued by others, on the grounds that stylistic parallels do exist *c.* 1100 and that the later memorialization of Elias is far-fetched.[11] The earlier dating is further supported by the influence of the throne on sculpture at Bury St Edmunds in England in the 1130s.[12] Partly in light of these critiques, Belli D'Elia came to favour of a date in the 1120s, on the basis of comparisons with sculpture in Modena, Monopoli and a capital in the Pinacoteca Provinciale in Bari.[13] My own view is that the throne was commissioned by Urban II and was begun at the Council of Bari in 1098. In fact, the comparable sculpture at Monopoli can be securely dated, by an inscription, to *c.* 1107, making it more and more likely that the throne was carved before Elias's death in 1105.[14] The most convincing comparisons, local and international, date it firmly to the period just after the Council of Bari.

Another comparison that helps us to date the throne is the bronze imperial throne of Goslar, which rested on four kneeling telamons.[15] It was made sometime around 1100 and later dissembled. The open latticework back and armrests, which bear some similarity to the Bari throne, were mounted on a marble base *c.* 1200 (Figure 54). The telamons

Figure 54 Goslar throne, Kaiserpfalz, Stiftskirche St. Simon und Judas, Goslar, bronze. Rabanus Flavus via Wikimedia Commons.

Figure 55 Krodo altar, Stadtmuseum, Goslar, bronze and brass, Rabanus Flavus via Wikimedia Commons.

were re-purposed to support an altar, known as the Krodo altar (Figure 55). They are strikingly similar to the Bari throne, resting on one knee while supporting their burden on their shoulders. Like their counterparts in Bari, the Krodo telamons are figures of different ethnicities (two have tightly coiled hair, as medieval European artists depicted Africans). In light of the similarity between the two thrones, Millard Hern hypothesized that the Goslar throne is earlier and that the Bari throne was made by a German working in Rome for Urban II.[16] Although Hern's comparison with the Goslar throne is certainly striking, her theory seems unlikely. The Bari throne does not resemble any contemporary sculpture in Rome. As we have seen, Elias's throne was probably commissioned in Bari and belongs to the culture of southern, rather than central, Italy. If there is a link between the two objects, the influence is more likely to have gone the other way, from Bari to Goslar. Bari had many international visitors – pilgrims, crusaders, merchants, diplomats and other travellers all passed through the port. The throne exerted an iconographical and stylistic influence from Sicily to Bury St Edmunds and Goslar.

Solomonic allusions

Elias's throne was intended to echo the throne of Solomon. The biblical passages on Solomon's throne describe it as made of gilded ivory, raised up on six steps, a pair of lions on each step and another pair of lions stood on either side of the armrests. It had a gold footstool and a rounded back.[17] There were many Solomonic thrones in the medieval Mediterranean, not exact copies of the biblical prototype, but they reflected some of its key features.[18] The Bari throne follows the prototype more closely than others. It is made of a bright white marble, a material that gives the same visual effect as ivory, without the fragility of ivory. Marble allowed the sculptors to create a piece of liturgical furniture which was larger, more durable and more monumental.[19] I have not noticed traces of gilding, but parts of the throne may originally have been gilded. It is raised up on the sanctuary platform by three steps, rather than twelve, and while the steps do not have lions on them, the footstool does. The polygonal, gabled backrest of the throne is an approximation of Solomon's rounded backrest. Modern translations of the bible describe a pair of lions on either side of Solomon's 'armrests', but the vulgate uses the Latin word *manus*, hands. The sculptor of the Bari throne has taken the 'hands' literally and sculpted a pair of telamons supporting the seat with their hands and, just behind them, a pair of lionesses. There are enough similarities here to say that the Bari throne was intended to be Solomonic, especially when seen together with the Solomonic references on the west façade of the basilica and on Elias's tomb, which will be discussed in subsequent chapters.

The most impressive of all medieval 'thrones of Solomon' was famous automaton throne in the Great Palace in Constantinople where, for centuries, it impressed and intimidated Byzantine courtiers and foreign dignitaries alike. Made in the ninth century, it stood in the Magnaura Hall and was described as a *thronos Solōmonteios*.[20] The Byzantine emperors, particularly the Macedonian dynasty, were seen as chosen rulers of a chosen people and therefore belonging to the tradition of Old Testament Kings, including Solomon.[21] Another Solomonic throne was made in Constantinople in the sixth century, for Maximium, the archbishop of Ravenna, this time in ivory.[22] There may also have been Solomonic associations with some of the other southern Italian thrones. The earlier eleventh-century thrones at Monte Sant'Angelo, Canosa, Siponto and Trani all rested on majestic beasts, a possible allusion to Solomon's throne.[23] The same is true of Gregory VII's papal throne at Salerno, which rested on spoliate lions.

Allegra Iafrate's work has shown that descriptors like *thronos Solōmonteios*, corresponding Latin terms like *opus salomonis* and similar ideas in Islamic art, should be translated as 'with Solomonic qualities', rather than 'of Solomon'. She argues that medieval patrons, artists and audiences understood these objects sometimes as direct references to Solomon himself but also more broadly as exemplifying the extremely high quality of Solomon's patronage. For an object to be 'Solomonic', it needed to be beautiful and demonstrate the impeccable technical skill of the artist who made it.[24] The Byzantine throne not only linked the emperors to the Old Testament kings, it also demonstrated that artistic excellence was common to both. Beauty, technical skill and provoking a reaction of awe and wonder were part of what made the Byzantine throne Solomonic. The same is surely true of the Bari throne, which may not be as impressive as the imperial throne but is one of the most beautiful and technically impressive works of art from the period. The sculptor was undoubtedly one of the most talented artists of his generation.

Urban II's gift to Elias is therefore imbued with two overarching meanings about heritage and authority. The spoliate marble signifies a connection between ancient Rome and the continuing authority of the papacy, not an explicit statement about papal primacy but an implicit reminder about the foundations and scope of papal authority. The allusion to King Solomon evokes the still more ancient heritage of the

Old Testament, a heritage that would have been very pertinent at the moment when the crusader armies were conquering the site of Solomon's temple in Jerusalem. It is significant that Elias's new throne was made not for the cathedral but for San Nicola. The Byzantine palace, on the site, would have had an audience hall, probably with some kind of simple 'throne', possibly placed in an apse, from which the governor governed and administered justice. With the construction of San Nicola meant that the authority of the Byzantine Empire had been symbolically replaced by St Nicholas, the Latin Church and Archbishop Elias in his throne.

Fed to the lions: Protection, justice and judgement

The current position of the throne, in the centre of the main apse, must surely be its original location. The throne is carved in the round, with an inscription that wraps around it, obviously intended to be viewed from all angles, with an *opus sectile* pavement that fans out around it. The apse itself is now obscured by the sixteenth-century tomb of Bona Sforza but originally, it would have had a synthronon (a bench for the clergy in the apse), like the one in the crypt below. The usual early Christian arrangement was to incorporate the episcopal throne into the synthronon, as seen in the late antique examples further up the Adriatic, at Aquiliea and Torcello, where the clerical bench was up against the wall of the apse and the throne was built into the bench. In this arrangement, the bishop was flanked by his clergy, mirroring images of Christ flanked by his apostles. This arrangement is also found in Bari cathedral, where the late-twelfth-century throne is built up against the apse wall. The different arrangement at San Nicola, with the freestanding throne sitting in front of the synthronon, is an innovation. Instead of the clergy fanning out on either side of their archbishop, Elias chose to sit in front of them, where they could see him and the back of his throne.

On the back of the throne, in an emotive scene, two terrified men are attacked by lionesses. The lions grip their heads with outstretched claws and sink their teeth into the skulls of their prey. Both the naturalism and the iconography come from classical sculpture. The most direct parallel comes from the northern fringe of the Roman Empire. The Cramond lioness (Figure 56) is a sandstone sculpture which was once part of the tomb of an elite Roman soldier on the Scottish border. A lioness sinks her teeth into the skull of a naked captive who has his hands tied behind his back. Despite its location on the northernmost border of the Roman Empire, the Cramond lioness is skilfully carved and would have been based on a prototype from the heart of the empire, quite possibly Rome itself.[25] Pairs of hunting lions are common on tomb sculpture from the first and second centuries, where their strength and agility may symbolize victory over death (Figure 57).[26]

In medieval sculpture, rather than symbolizing victory over death, hunting lions seem most often to serve an apotropaic function. The Byzantine automaton throne was described by Luitprand of Cremona as 'guarded by lions', who not only protected the emperor but also ensured that only worthy successors of Solomon were able to sit in it.[27] In other words, the lions were like body guards, protecting the office that

Figure 56 The Cramond Lioness. Photo by Kim Traynor via Wikimedia Commons.

Figure 57 *Front of a Sarcophagus with Female Portrait in a Medallion above Two Theatrical Masks, and Lion Devouring a Boar at Each Extremity*, A.D. 250–275, Marble, J. Paul Getty Museum, Villa Collection, Malibu, California, Gift of Gordon McLendon, 77.AA.65.

the occupant held, as much as they protected a particular emperor.[28] Hunting lions flanking doorways – including the side doors at San Nicola – play a similar role of guarding the vulnerable liminal area of the church. The lions on the back of the Bari throne certainly seem to be apotropaic. They face the apse, directly behind which were the protective city wall and beyond it, mere metres from the throne, the dangers of the sea and the wider world. The apse pavement is framed along the curve by a pseudo-Arabic mosaic which, I have argued elsewhere, was also apotropaic, an additional protective barrier in a place where the sacred space of the church came so close to the unprotected world beyond the city.[29] The capitals on the templon screen, populated with similar, equally ferocious, lions were carved by the sculptor of the throne, so that these apotropaic symbols wrap around both sides of the high altar.[30]

On the other hand, the lionesses on the Bari throne seem to be more than just protective. It is unusual to find lions with human, rather than animal prey and the particularly violent, emotive nature of the imagery seems to emphasize the plight of the men, rather than the strength of the lions. This is made clear if we compare the Bari lions to others, for example the lions flanking the door to the atrium of Salerno cathedral, where the lions stand tall and strong with small, lifeless prey between their paws (Figure 58) – at Salerno the prey is incidental and symbolic, whereas at Bari the viewer empathizes with the plight of the people being eaten. Although the throne is close to a liminal zone of the church – the usual position for apotropaic imagery – it has been placed so that it can be seen by the clergy during the liturgy. As the clergy sat behind their archbishop during a long liturgy, how did they feel when their gaze inevitably fell on the back of the throne? A natural response would be trepidation. From their position in the synthronon, the clergy could see not only the attacking lions but also the central part of the inscription, '[in this] seat the patron, the bishop of Bari'.[31] Part of the role of an archbishop was to act as a judge in the ecclesiastical court, policing the conduct of the clergy. King Solomon was renowned for his wisdom in judgement, and the medieval idea of the throne of Solomon evoked ideas of justice and judgement. In Constantinople, the automaton throne stood in the Magnaura Hall, which functioned partly as a law court, where the emperor sat in judgement, embodying Solomon in his role as perfect judge.[32] The lions on the throne could be a depiction of the Roman practice of sentencing convicts to death by wild animals, *damnatio ad bestias*; big cats in particular were used for this method of execution, as seen in the mosaics at El Djem in Tunisia. Giovanna de Appolonia has argued that lions flanking church portals also have associations with both civic and ecclesiastical justice in northern Italy, where law courts were often convened in front of churches, with the judge sitting in the doorway, flanked by lions.[33] In Bari, there is a specific and

Figure 58 Salerno cathedral, entrance to atrium. Photo: Author.

concrete link between lions and justice: in Piazza Mercantile, the site of the medieval marketplace and probably an open air law court, is a spoliate Roman lion with some medieval re-carving, including a collar inscribed 'guardian of justice'.

Both Urban II and Archbishop Elias were responsible for justice when they acted as ecclesiastical judges. Elias probably had no official role in the civic administration of the city, but he was a powerful figurehead and he did act as the judge in the ecclesiastical court.[34] The pope was the supreme judge of the church, and this was emphasized in canon law manuals from the late eleventh century, especially in Gregory VII's *Dictatus Pape*.[35] Urban II emphasized his role as supreme judge in the 'Gregorian' reforms, predominantly through canon law.[36] Urban held eleven councils in his eleven years as pope; at each he promulgated new canons and repeated the canons promulgated at previous councils. He also asserted his place at the top of the ecclesiastical hierarchy by dominating the councils, unlike his predecessors who fostered debate and usually approved the outcome of the synod's discussions.[37] The reform movement, which sought *renovatio* largely through legal reform and implementation, was partly concerned with regulating clerical behaviour. Issues such as implementing clerical celibacy and preventing clerical violence were legislated and policed by the reformers.[38] The lions on the back of the Bari throne need to be viewed through this lens. The unfortunate souls being devoured by lions could represent those who transgress canon law. The throne, commissioned by the pope as supreme judge, given to Archbishop Elias, the local judge, sends a message to the clergy sitting behind it to behave themselves.

Classicism and slavery

The front of the throne was less visible than the back. It would have been visible to the clergy as they processed in and out of the sanctuary and during the liturgy. It is not visible from the nave so the laity could only glimpse it from afar, by standing in the aisles and craning their necks. On the front of the throne are three figures: two telamons supporting the seat and one figure in the centre (Figure 59). The telamons wear loin cloths, and they are kneeling on one knee, struggling beneath the weight of the stone seat, which rests on their hunched shoulders. Their faces are extraordinarily expressive, contorted in grimaces, mouths open and brows furled. The viewer becomes caught up in the emotional drama of the scene, in a way that is unusual for sculpture of this date in Apulia. The telamons are very similar to the hapless men on the back of the throne. Their ethnicity is significant as at least three of the five figures are African. The telamon on the south side of the throne has tightly coiled hair, as do the two figures at the back. The hair is very similar to depictions of Africans from the early thirteenth century, for example the four-headed capital from Troia cathedral (Figure 60) and the bust of Johannes Maurus in Lucera.[39] The thirteenth-century sculptures have large lips and wide noses in comparison to depictions of Europeans. The curly haired telamon on the Bari throne has less pronounced facial features, but nonetheless his ethnicity is clear. The ethnicity of the telamon on the north side of the throne is more difficult to discern. His hair is wavy, rather than coiled, but his facial features are very similar

Figure 59 Bari throne, detail of the front. Photo: Author.

Figure 60 Capital with figures of different ethnicities, originally from Troia, c. 1225–50, Metropolitan Museum of Art, New York, limestone. Image in the public domain.

to the other telamon. He could be an African or perhaps a depiction of a different ethnicity. The angels on the Monopoli archivolt, carved by the same artist, also have deep, pronounced grooves for their hair, and the same centre parting as the wavy-haired telamon, but their hair is less wavy.

Like the imagery on the back of the throne, the telamons are inspired by classical sculpture. In ancient southern and central Italy, kneeling telamons seem to have been particularly associated with theatrical seating, for example at the Odeon at Pompeii and the theatre at Pietrabbondante. Medieval builders certainly had access to Roman theatres, for example at Venosa, where the Roman amphitheatre was spoliated to build the nearby abbey church of the SS. Trinità, so the Bari sculptor could have been influenced by theatrical seating.[40] However, some of the closest parallels to the Bari telamons are found on tomb sculpture and sarcophagi (figures 61 and 62). It is possible that the Bari telamons were modelled on a classical throne, as André Grabar hypothesized, but no classical thrones have survived and there is no evidence that any survived into the Middle Ages. A sarcophagus seems like a more likely model.

The idea of one or more sarcophagi as sources is further supported by sculptural parallels from the later Middle Ages. Two of the royal sarcophagi in Palermo bear resemblances to the Bari throne: the so-called sarcophagus of Frederick II (carved in the mid-twelfth century, long before Frederick's birth, more likely the original tomb of Roger II) is supported by pairs of lions, two of which hold human prey between their paws. As we have seen, lions with human prey are much more rare than animal prey, so this example is significant. The so-called sarcophagus of Roger II (which again was

Figure 61 Sarcophagus depicting the labours of Hercules with kneeling telamons in the bottom corners, Galleria Borghese, Rome. Burkhard Mücke via Wikimedia commons.

Figure 62 Orestes sarcophagus with telamon supports, Roman, Musei Vaticani, Rome.

almost certainly not made for Roger) is supported by kneeling telamons, so similar to the throne that the sculptor must have had a connection to Bari.[41] Another example is the Pugliese sculptor Nicola Pisano's *Arca di San Domenico*, the shrine of St Domenic, which was originally supported by trios of classicizing telamons.[42] These examples show that medieval sculptors seem to have associated telamons most often with tombs, probably because they copied them from Roman sarcophagi.

In both classical and medieval depictions, kneeling telamons represent captive or enslaved people.[43] In Roman sculpture, the captives were often 'Barbarians' or other vanquished populations from the fringes of the Roman Empire. Their subjugated strength, harnessed to support imperial monuments, was a visual manifestation of the vastness and invincibility of the empire.[44] Captives were often displayed in victory processions in Rome, so their depiction on monuments either depicted or recalled such processions.[45] An example is the victory monument that commemorated Augustus's victories in the East, which rested on a tripod carried by three kneeling Persians.[46] Other examples are the kneeling prisoner on the Arcus Novus in Rome (figure 63) and the 'captives' façade' in Corinth.[47]

The features of the Bari telamons have been carefully copied from classical depictions of African slaves, from both ancient Greece and Rome. Similarities can be seen in the treatment of the tightly coiled hair on a ceramic jug in the Menil Collection (Figure 64).[48] The jug is from Asia Minor, but a very similar object was found in Apulia.[49] The open-mouthed grimaces on the faces of both telamons can be compared

Figure 63 Fragment of the Arcus Novus, showing a Barbarian prisoner, third century, Boboli Gardens, Florence. Photo by Sailko, via Wikimedia Commons.

Figure 64 Portrait Vessel, imperial Roman, Asia Minor? ceramic with lead glaze, Menil Collection, Houston Texas. Photographer: Paul Hester.

to ancient theatrical masks, some of which represent African slaves (Figure 65 is an example from Sicily).[50] Theatrical masks would not have been available to medieval sculptors to copy (the vast majority of extant masks have been found in situ in ancient sites), but masks found their way into more monumental Roman sculpture, including sarcophagi (Figure 66).

Connections to Fatimid art

If some elements of the throne are rooted in the medieval appreciation of classical sculpture, others are the fruit of Bari's relationships with Islamic culture. The armrests have been cut in a radiating lattice, reminiscent of Islamic window grills (e.g. at San Cataldo in Palermo and in the Great Mosque of Damascus).[51] The front of the seat, just above the telamons heads, is decorated with a lattice pattern inhabited by animals and birds. It would originally have been inlaid with coloured mastic to make the design stand out. This is a skeumorph, a design which imitates another material; here the stone carving is imitating a cushion, the lattice pattern being very common in contemporary Fatimid textiles (Figures 67 and 68). Merchants from Bari and other Adriatic ports traded in such textiles, which were both highly portable and highly profitable.

The elephants in the 'Charlemagne' chessmen are adorned with similar lattice textiles (Figure 36). The 'Charlemagne' chessmen were modelled on a chess set imported from Fatimid Cairo, quite possibly some of the many luxury objects which flooded the

Figure 65 Theatrical mask depicting an African slave, made in Sicily, *c.* 350 BCE, British Museum, 1926,0324.96, 22 x 20cm, terracotta. Jastrow via Wikimedia Commons.

Figure 66 Muse sarcophagus with theatrical masks, Nelson-Atkins Museum of Art, object number 87-21, marble, third century. Excavated at Vigna Casali, Rome. Daderot via Wikimedia Commons.

Italian market in the wake of the sack of the Fatimid treasuries in the 1060s.[52] The men riding the elephant have tightly coiled hair, indicating that they, like the figures on the throne, are African. An important part of the ceremonial life in the Fatimid court were processions through Cairo in which courtiers, soldiers and animals – including

Figure 67 Fatimid textile with lattice pattern from Fayoum, silk and linen, 12 x 18cm, Musée du Louvre, museum number E 9963.

Figure 68 Fatimid textile, with lattice pattern and inscription dating it to the caliphate of al-Mustansir, 1081–94, linen and silk, Cleveland Museum of Art, John L. Severance Fund 1950.536.

elephants – were dressed in opulent silks. The Fatimid army included regiments of enslaved black soldiers, as depicted in the chess pieces.[53]

The link to Fatimid ivories brings us to the final figure at the base of the throne. Between the telamons is a man half-heartedly helping to support the seat. In stark contrast to his enslaved neighbours, he is finely dressed in a tunic with intricate beading at the cuffs and neckline, pointy shoes and a ridged conical hat. He carries a stick and is looking upwards. He is part of the world of the telamons but set apart from them by his clothing, his stance and his facial expression, which is one of serene curiosity, in contrast to the telamons' exertion. Rowan Dorin has convincingly argued that this man's clothing identifies him as a Muslim.[54] His little stick, pointy shoes, pointy ridged hat and tunic with a billowing triangular fold in the skirt are identical to figures seen in Fatimid wood carvings (e.g. Figure 69).[55] Who is this enigmatic figure and why is he depicted between the telamons? Pina Belli D'Elia saw him as a Christian pilgrim to the shrine of St Nicholas, but his Muslim identity precludes that.[56] André Grabar suggested

Figure 69 Fatimid wood carving, 68 x 18 x 5cm, Musée du Louvre, museum number OA 4062.

he might be the slave supervisor for the telamons, which fits with his position between them and his half-hearted attempt to help support the seat.[57] Both Grabar and Dorin have written about the triumphal nature of the iconography at the base of the throne. Grabar argued that they serve to indicate the power of the occupant.[58] Dorin has linked this discourse of power to the Muslim figure and to the first crusade. He writes that the 'subjugated Muslim' and enslaved telamons at Elias's feet can be seen as part of the 'fervent triumphalism' that characterized the crusading fervour of the 1090s.[59] However, this interpretation is not borne out visually in the sculpture. The telamons are indeed vanquished, but the Muslim does not look completely subjugated.

Reading the throne in the context of contemporary slavery

The throne contains several layers of meaning. The enslaved telamons on the throne are iconographically and stylistically inspired by classical sculpture, so on one level, this is a retrospective monument that harnesses the authority of antiquity through spolia and classical models. But Grabar's intriguing ideas that the central, Fatimid figure might be their supervisor adds an extra contemporary dimension to the throne. Can we read the throne in relation to medieval, as well as classical, slavery? Although the telamones are not depictions of contemporary figures, the original audience may have projected contemporary understandings of slavery onto them. In order to explore this further, it is worth setting out how slavery worked in the Mediterranean *c.* 1100. In the central Middle Ages, the Islamic caliphates, with their robust economies, were the biggest market for slave trading, closely followed by the Byzantine Empire.[60] Both retained some of the conventions of ancient Roman slavery, with a legal distinction between a free and an unfree person, but in practice there were many ambiguities and different ways of being 'unfree'.[61] In Latin Europe, 'freedom' could be even more ambiguous.[62] The slave trade operated in three main ways: commerce, piracy and war. The people enslaved through piracy were mainly Black Africans and Slavs from eastern Europe and Rus, who were kidnapped by organized groups of pirates. For example, in the tenth century, the Venetians kidnapped people in Dalmatia and sold them to the Fatimids.[63] Muslims and Christians were theoretically not allowed to enslave their co-religionists but in practice that 'rule' was often not adhered to, especially with captives taken in war.[64]

As Romney David Smith and Sarah Guérin have shown, one of the ways that the Italian port cities were able to participate in long-distance Mediterranean trade networks was through slave trading. Prices were much higher in the eastern Mediterranean, so an Italian merchant could buy a person in Italy and sell them in Egypt for three times the price.[65] Italian merchants loaded their ships with agricultural staples, such as oil and grain, timber and humans then sold those 'commodities' in the eastern Mediterranean – in places like Cairo, Alexandria and Constantinople. With the profits, they could buy valuable luxury items, like silk, spices, gold, pearls, precious stones, ivory, rock crystal and perfume, all in high demand in Italy. There was a little profit in bulk agricultural products (you could trade a whole ship full of grain for roughly two silk robes); considerably more profit in timber; and a lot of profit in humans. Italian merchants mainly acquired enslaved Slavs from the Balkans. Sometimes they enslaved Arabs through war (e.g. during the conquest of Sicily), and sometimes they traded other Italians who were captured in war. An Italian merchant bringing enslaved people into the caliphate needed a middle man or broker in order to sell them.[66] Because of the high prices, selling just a few people could give a merchant the contacts, knowledge and enough capital to set himself up as a specialist trader in luxury goods, like Fatimid and Byzantine silks or ivory and gold from sub-Saharan Africa.[67] Thus the art market in Italy was dependent on the slave trade. The slave trade was a gateway to luxury goods and materials.

Everything I have said about Italian merchants in general applies to Bari specifically. In fact we have more documentary evidence of slavery in Bari than in most Italian cities, which might indicate a particularly strong involvement in the trade. Bari has notoriously few documentary sources in general so to find such a high concentration of references to slavery is surprising. References to human trafficking begin in the ninth century, when Bernard the monk saw ships from Bari, loaded with slaves, in the port of Taranto and an anonymous rabbi from Bari wrote a Hebrew poem about young men who were sold for more than gold. In 925 Arab pirates raided Otranto and enslaved some of the inhabitants, who they then sold in the market in Bari.[68]

Around the time the throne was made we have a flurry of legal documents about domestic slaves in Bari, owned by the local elite and merchant classes. Where the enslaved person's nationality is recorded, it is always Slavic. The Latin word for slave, inherited from the Romans, is *servus*. It was gradually replaced by the word *sclavo* (for Slav, because the Slavic people were the most commonly enslaved people in Italy), the root of the modern English and Italian. One of the very earliest uses of the word is from Bari in a sale contract from 1088.[69] Another example from Bari is a Slavic woman and her daughter who were sold in 1121 and the dispute over Maria, Bulgarian woman, and her son Lupo, who were freed by a judge.[70] Interestingly, the usual ritual for manumission involved the slave processing around an altar, attested in a document from Bari written in 1103.[71] This adds an extra poignancy to the slaves on the throne, so close to the high altar in San Nicola.

I began this chapter with Urban II and the council he convened in the midst of the first crusade. I'd like to return to Urban now, considering the iconography of the throne within a crusading context. If the throne was made following the council of 1098, it was probably in the process of being carved when the crusaders conquered Jerusalem in 1099. A large contingent of the first crusade came from southern Italy, led by Bohemond, who prayed at San Nicola before he set sail. When Bohemond captured the tent of Kerbogha of Mosul in the battle of Antioch, he sent the tent back to Bari as a donation to this church. I have argued elsewhere that the pseudo-Arabic border on the sanctuary pavement may be a design taken from Kerbogha's tent.[72] San Nicola was, therefore, steeped in crusading ideas, as a site closely associated with Urban II, Bohemond and crusaders from Bari and elsewhere who embarked for the Holy Land from the Adriatic ports.

Slavery was part of the rhetoric that surrounded the first crusade. Urban II's speech at Clermont, which inaugurated the crusade, probably included references to it. The account of Balderic, archbishop of Dol, tells us that Urban described the Christians of the Holy Land as subjugated: 'they are flogged and exiled as slaves for sale in their own land. Christian blood, redeemed by the blood of Christ, has been shed, and Christian flesh, akin to the flesh of Christ, has been subjected to unspeakable degradation and *servitude*.'[73] This imagery is repeated in Urban's letter to the crusaders in Flanders in 1095 where he writes that Eastern Christians were 'grasped in intolerable servitude'.[74] The crusaders saw themselves as the liberators of the eastern Christians (even if eastern Christians did not agree), but during the crusade, they also became enslavers of Muslims. At the siege of Ma'arra in 1098, Bohemond took many captives. Some were sold in the market at Antioch, while others were forced to fight for the crusaders.[75] Some of them probably ended up in Italy eventually – to speculate a little, Bohemond sent Kerbogha's tent to San Nicola, and it is not too much of a stretch to imagine that it was accompanied by captives. Are those captives alluded to or even explicitly depicted on the throne?

The *Gesta Francorum*, the earliest and therefore most authoritative account of the crusade, written by a southern Italian follower of Bohemond, recounts that during the battle over Jerusalem, Muslims and Jews were herded onto the Temple Mount and some were slaughtered, but many of the younger people were enslaved. The *Gesta* notes that they were divided between Gaston of Beert and Bohemond's nephew, Tancred.[76] The episode on the Temple Mount is particularly significant for the iconography of the throne. When news of the conquest of Jerusalem arrived in Bari, perhaps that news arrived on ships carrying captive Muslims and Jews. In the new, unfinished, basilica – already adorned with the tent of a vanquished enemy – a throne was being carved from marble donated by the pope who had initiated the crusade.

Figure 70 Telamons on the trumeau at Sainte Marie d'Oloron in the Pyrenees. Myrabella via Wikimedia Commons.

Archbishop Elias, in the midst of his ambitious building project, adopted Solomon, the great temple builder, as a role model. The slaves on his throne perhaps evoked the slaves captured on the Temple Mount, possibly also drawing on contemporary society in Bari, where slavery was part of the city's social and economic identity. But the classicizing African slaves on the throne are not depictions of contemporary Arabs or Jews captured in Jerusalem or Slavs captured in Dalmatia or Bulgaria. The telamons are a rhetorical trope rather than portraits or depictions of the crusade. Telamons in Romanesque sculpture are often 'Other' in a generalized, ambiguous way. They could be Muslims, Jews or mythologized versions of slaves, like the telamons on the portal of Sainte Marie d'Oloron in the Pyrenees, who are dressed as Muslims, like their counterparts in Bari, with the addition of chains around their waist (figure 70). In Bari, the careful copying of classical models adds another layer of meaning, the evocation of the ancient figures opens up the possibility of a link with the Old Testament, with the Jews who helped Solomon to build his temple, another way that the throne might focus the viewer's attention on the recent crusading victories.[77] Seen through this lens, the sanctuary of San Nicola, with the throne and the pseudo-Arabic mosaic, becomes a victory monument to the first crusade that references Roman victory monuments.

7

Architecture

A temple of Solomon

The Solomonic theme is a thread that runs through San Nicola. Not only is the throne a Solomonic throne, Elias was explicitly compared to Solomon in his epitaph (as we shall see in Chapter 9). In this chapter, I will argue that the basilica as a whole was conceived as an evocation of the Temple of Solomon in ancient Jerusalem.

Although the upper church of the basilica was not consecrated until 1197, it must have been finished by 1106 when Paschal II declared 'the building is now perfect'.[1] It began to influence the design of other cathedrals before it was even finished, for example at Bitonto from the 1090s.[2] In the twelfth century, the design spread across central Apulia and into Dalmatia.[3] Elias oversaw the construction in conjunction with the master masons, some of whose names are recorded on the façades of the building. Chief among them seems to have been *Magister An[...] de Fumarello*, whose partially legible name is inscribed on the north jamb of the west portal (his name is assumed to be Angelus but could have been Andreas).[4] Angelus's workshop included Ansaldus, Taddeo and Basil, sculptors who worked on the portals, as well as the Magistri Blasii (brothers? Or father and son?) and Magister Madus, who made one of the lancet windows 'at his own cost' as a votive offering.[5] The names do not reveal much about the identity or training of the masons. *De Fumarello* may be toponymic in a generic way, probably somewhere between the Latin *flumen* and the modern Italian *fiumarella*, meaning river or stream. Today, it is particularly associated with a river near Cantanzaro in Calabria, but Angelus's name could have been derived from any river. The inclusion of Basil, essentially a Greek name, is interesting and may point to a Byzantine background, but one would assume that Greek names were fairly popular among the Lombards in Apulia (even the arch anti-Byzantine Melus gave his son a Greek name).

Angelus's building has survived relatively intact with a few additions: following an earthquake in the fifteenth century, an arcade was built across the nave to strengthen the structure; in the sixteenth century, the tomb of Bona Sforza, duchess of Bari, was erected in the main apse; and later the nave was given a baroque ceiling.[6] In its essence, the church broadly follows the design of a late antique basilica.[7] It is, for example, similar to Old St Peter's, on a much more modest scale. It has a subtly T-shaped plan, with very shallow transepts and a long nave, supported by spoliate columns, most of which are made of dark granite and probably came from the Byzantine palace (Figures 71 and 72).[8]

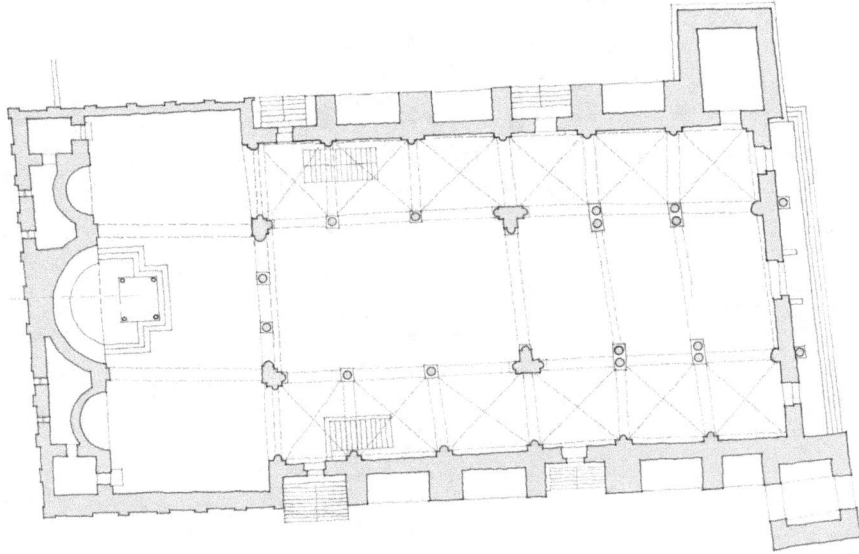

Figure 71 Plan, San Nicola, Bari. Drawn by Elisabeth Kendall.

Figure 72 Nave, San Nicola, Bari. Photo: Saiko via Wikimedia.

In their emulation of Constantinian basilicas, Elias and Angelus were following the example of Desiderius at Montecassino and Sant'Angelo in Formis and Alfanus at Salerno.⁹ However, the end result at San Nicola is quite different to the extant Salerno and Sant'Angelo in Formis (Figure 73). Part of the difference comes from San Nicola's deep arcades to the north and south that act as buttresses to strengthen the structure

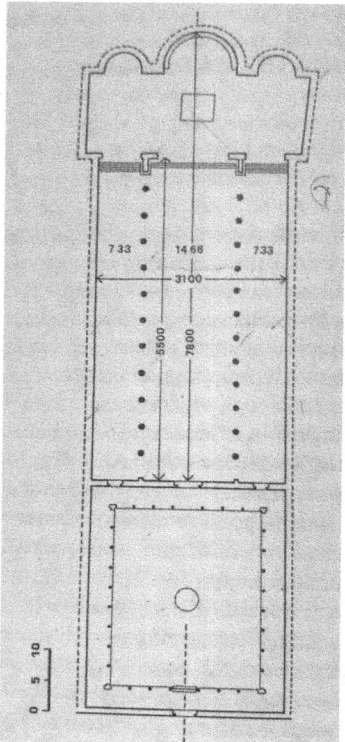

Figure 73 Plan of Salerno cathedral. Drawn by Armando Schiavo.

(Figure 74). The spaces between the buttresses were originally intended for tombs for the members of the Society of St Nicholas, those who had been involved in the *translatio* of the relics in 1087. In the post-medieval period they were walled off and turned into chapels, accessible from inside the church, but this was reversed during the renovations in the 1950s.[10] But the biggest differences between San Nicola and Montecassino and Salerno are the innovative and unusual features in at the east and west ends.

Mystery of the flat east end

At the east end of San Nicola, the apses are encased within a flat wall, hiding them on the exterior and making it difficult to identify the building as a church (Figure 75). The apses are continuous from the crypt below, so the flat wall encasing them must have been planned from the inception of the design.[11] This is a highly unusual and puzzling feature, Romanesque and Byzantine churches of this period tend to have apses that are boldly articulated on the exterior of the building. The closest parallels geographically

Figure 74 North façade, San Nicola, Bari. Photo: Author.

Figure 75 East façade, San Nicola, Bari. Photo: Sailko via Wikimedia.

are Santa Maria delle Grazie in Grado (sixth century) (Figure 76) and the early Christian 'Basilica E' at Concordia Sagittaria, both at the top of the Adriatic.[12] Bearing in mind the constant traffic between Adriatic ports and the many early Christian influences at San Nicola, a late antique model from the northern Adriatic is plausible, even though it seems somewhat random. The flat east end also appears at San Benedetto in Brindisi and at the cathedral of Bitonto which are both slightly later and must both be modelled on San Nicola. San Nicola evokes late antiquity in many ways, and the east end seems to be another example of that.

The original design for the east end of the church included a pair of slender transept towers. The towers are part of the internal plan but were never built beyond the height of the transepts. As Pina Belli D'Elia has noted, the design of the towers is similar to northern European architecture.[13] The best example is Speyer cathedral (1040s) (Figure 77).[14] We have already seen in Chapter 5 that Speyer could have been the model for the crypts at Salerno and Bari. Together, the flat east wall and towers would have given the church an imposing, fortress-like appearance. Even without the towers, the building looks sturdy, impenetrable and is difficult to identify as a church from the sea. Perhaps this was part of the aim. In demolishing the Byzantine palace, the citizens of Bari had lost a fortified structure, part of their defences against attack. They had also secured a promise from the Normans not to build a new castle, which was broken by Bohemond in the 1090s. The new church, built virtually against the seawall, would have been highly visible from out at sea, perhaps giving the deliberate impression that the city was more fortified and less vulnerable than it was.

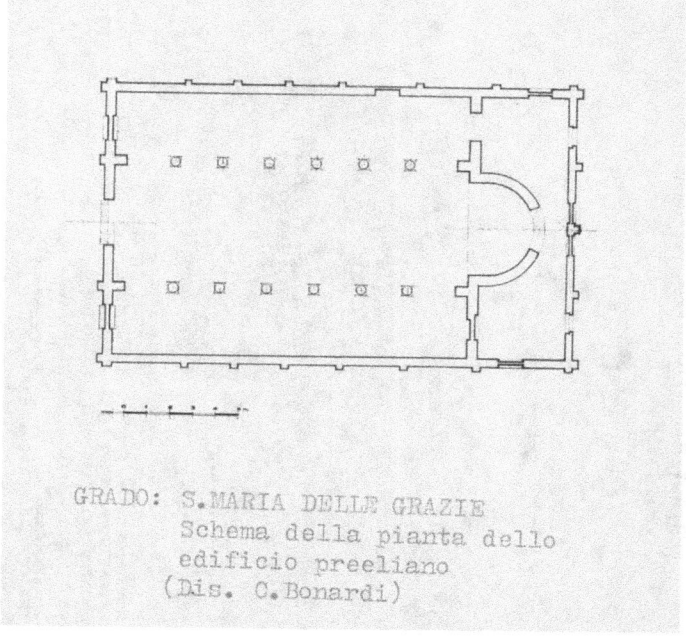

Figure 76 Plan of Sana Maria delle Grazie, Grado. Photo: C. Bonardi, University of Bologna.

Figure 77 Speyer cathedral, south elevation. Photo: Sail Over via Wikimedia.

The west end

The west end also has towers, which are asymmetrical. The north tower is almost an independent structure, with delicate blind arcading in keeping with the rest of the building and a pair of windows that mirror the windows on the façade. Although Pina Belli D'Elia thinks this is a pre-existing tower belonging to the Byzantine palace, it seems to me to have been designed in unison with the church.[15] The tower housed the chapel of SS Peter and Paul, which served as a burial chapel for the clergy until the seventeenth century.[16] The south tower is quite different (see Chapter 1). It has been attached, much less elegantly to the church, cutting into the southwest corner. The base of the south tower is made of large, roughly cut blocks, in contrast to the smooth fine ashlars of the rest of the building. The rougher, more utilitarian stonework makes the tower look like a military building rather than a church. This tower, it seems to me, is a better candidate for being retained from the Byzantine palace complex.

Solomonic meaning

The basilicas at Montecassino and Salerno were preceded by atria, as was the custom in early Christian Rome. San Nicola does not have a formally constructed atrium, although the piazza in front of the church is semi-enclosed and has always functioned as a space for pilgrims to congregate. Opposite the west façade is the so-called portico of the pilgrims, which was built later than the church, possibly in the late twelfth or thirteenth

Figure 78 West façade, San Nicola, Bari. Photo: Elio Pallard via Wikimedia.

century. Pina Belli D'Elia hypothesized that Elias had originally intended to build a portico on the west façade. As evidence for this she cited the two columns attached to the façade which do not support anything (Figure 78).[17] I do not think that the design of the façade and portals would have accommodated such a portico. The contemporary buildings with porticoes or atria, such as Salerno cathedral and Sant'Angelo in Formis, and their late antique models, such as San Lorenzo fuori le Mura, have simple façades with a row of three windows above the portico. The façade of San Nicola is much more elaborate; there is not space for a portico to be attached to the façade. As we shall see in the following chapter the portal design comes from the churches of northern Italy, particularly Emilia Romagna, none of which have atria or porticoes.

The purpose of the non-supporting columns is therefore a mystery. The columns are dark granite, with spoliate capitals from the fourth or fifth century, probably carved in Constantinople and therefore quite possibly salvaged from the Byzantine palace.[18] It is a feature that was not incorporated into the other Apulian cathedrals that followed Bari, with the exception of Ruvo di Puglia, where four columns have been incorporated into the façade and Sant'Agostino in Andria, where a pair of columns stand about a metre in front of the façade.

At Bari, the columns may be explained as a reference to Solomon's temple. King Solomon commissioned two bronze pillars with capitals that were placed in the porch of his temple; one was named Joachim, the other Boaz.[19] Next to the temple was a fountain called the Molten Sea which was supported by twelve oxen, and the bases of the fountain were decorated with lions, oxen and cherubim.[20] The tradition of placing a pair of columns on or near the main façade of a church in reference to Solomon's temple was begun by Justinian at the Nea Ekklesia in Jerusalem and appears throughout the Middle

Ages in certain places.²¹ As late as *c.* 1230 two columns inscribed *Iachim* and *Boaz* were placed outside Wurtzburg cathedral (the columns at Wurtzburg were dismantled in 1644 and are now inside the cathedral).²² Pairs of non-structural columns on the exterior of the main façade can also be found at the cathedrals of Siena, Piacenza, San Marco in Venice.²³ The columns outside San Marco are known as the *pilastri acritani*; they were taken from the church of St Polyeuktos in Constantinople by the Venetians in or after 1204 and set up in the Piazzetta next to San Marco. St Polyeuktos also contained Solomonic overtones.²⁴ Furthermore, at the abbey of Notre-Dame des Moreaux near Poitiers, the portal (*c.* 1142) was flanked by two bishops: one standing on an ox, the other on a lion.²⁵ The archivolt was inscribed 'as was the entrance to the temple of the holy Solomon, so the entrance of this is placed between an ox and a lion'.²⁶ The Lateran in Rome has a strong association with Solomon; in the Middle Ages it was the supposed home of the temple treasures that were brought to Rome by Emperor Titus after he destroyed the temple. Benjamin of Tudela, in the 1160s, described seeing two bronze columns there, inscribed 'Solomon the son of David', which exuded moisture annually.²⁷

In Bari the main portal canopy is supported by oxen, while the other portals are supported by lions and in the sunshine the dark granite has a dull shine–like bronze. As we saw in the previous chapter, Elias's throne emulated Solomon's and in Chapter 9 we shall see that Elias's epitaph explicitly compared him to Solomon. The Temple had proportions of 1:3. This corresponds to San Nicola, where the width of the church is roughly a third of its length. However these proportions were so widely employed in church-building, and it is impossible to know when they were intended symbolically or not.²⁸

The idea of comparing a patron as Solomon and a church to the temple of Jerusalem is an extremely common one in the Middle Ages, so much so that it may not have any particular significance for the individual site. However, given San Nicola's construction in the context of the first crusade, it is worth exploring how this aspect of the church might have been understood in *c.* 1100. From the crusader conquest of Jerusalem, the Temple Mount took on a new significance. In the Byzantine period, it had not been a focal point of Christian piety and almost disappeared from the sacred topography of the city. Its ruined state symbolized the victory of the New Covenant over the old, and thus the Holy Sepulchre became the sole focus of Christian devotion.²⁹ Eusebius began the trope of comparing patrons to Solomon when he conflated the Constantinian church-building programme with Solomon's temple-building in his panegyric speech at the dedication of the church of Tyre, stressing that the church had superseded the temple.³⁰

After the crusaders conquered Jerusalem, the Temple Mount was integrated into the sacred and administrative topography of the city and took on a significant role in Christian devotion. The shift may have begun as early as Urban II's instigation of the crusade. Balderic of Dol (writing *c.* 1108), in his account of Urban's speech at Clermont, claims that Urban mentioned the liberation of the temple along with the Holy Sepulchre, as the goal of the crusade and Ekkehard of Aura claimed the same thing, writing in 1115.³¹ Godfrey of Bouillon, who led the conquest and became the first king of Jerusalem, established his court on the Temple Mount. Godfrey used the al-Aqsa mosque as his palace, and the Dome of the Rock was turned into a church which served as the seat of the new Latin patriarch, Daimbert of Pisa.[32] The crusaders called the al-Aqsa mosque the temple or palace of Solomon, *templum salomonis* or *palatium salamonis*, and they called the Dome of the Rock the temple of the lord, *templum domini*. Most crusaders were aware that the Dome of the Rock was not actually the temple built by Solomon, but they did believe that it occupied the same site and replicated its basic form.[33] The crusader kings were crowned in the Holy Sepulchre, then processed to the *templum domini*, to place the crown upon the altar (commemorating the presentation of the Christ at the temple), then held a feast in the *templum Salomonis*.[34] This topography, in which the Holy Sepulchre and the Temple Mount became, together, the most sacred sites in the city, was also reflected in pilgrim itineraries and other events. Pilgrims began to visit the Temple Mount immediately after the Holy Sepulchre.[35] In 1101 (according to a text written before 1109), the Holy Fire failed to appear in the Holy Sepulchre at Easter, so the Patriarch ordered everyone to process barefoot to the *templum domini*, where they prayed for the Holy Fire, which duly appeared in the Holy Sepulchre.[36] The feast of the conquest of Jerusalem, on the 15th of July, was also marked by a procession from the Holy Sepulchre to the *templum domini*.[37]

Churches can never be recreations of the Temple of Solomon because, in medieval theology, it was important that the Old Testament temple had been superseded by the New Testament and the Church. The ruins of Old Testament sites were proof of the existence of the New Covenant. But the references to the temple in medieval churches helped to emphasize the victory of the New Covenant.[38] If the episcopal throne is, in some ways, a victory monument for the first crusade, so too is the church itself. But the construction of San Nicola was underway from 1087, long before the proclamation of the crusade in 1095. While it is possible that the church was conceived as a Temple of Solomon from 1087, all of the Solomonic aspects – the throne, the columns on the façade, Elias's epitaph – date to much later in the building project, all probably around the time of the Council of Bari in 1098 and the conquest of Jerusalem in 1099. It seems likely therefore that the conceptualization of the building changed over the course of construction. The church began with a focus on re-appropriating the site of Byzantine government and the shrine of St Nicholas as a manifestation of Bari's civic identity. But from 1095, and even more so from the first crusader victories in 1098, it began to reflect crusader ideology, under the influence of Pope Urban II, Bohemond, who was lord of Bari, and the pilgrims and crusaders who embarked from the Adriatic ports. In responding to the crusade, Bari was also moving away from the early use of Salerno cathedral as a model.

8

Portal sculpture

The secular, the sacred and the sacramental

San Nicola has seven entrances: three portals in the main façade and four lateral doors. The main portal in the west façade is the liturgical, ceremonial entrance (Figure 79), while the lateral doors were designed for everyday use. Probably, the smaller, undecorated doors at the east end were for clerical use, giving Elias and his brothers direct access to the sanctuary for mass and the liturgy of the hours, without being disturbed by the throng of pilgrims. The larger doors at the west end of the north and south facades were for lay use (Figures 80 and 81). To avoid congestion, it is likely that there was a 'one-way system' in place, whereby pilgrims would enter via the north door, walk along the north aisle then descend into the crypt, exiting to the south. The sculpted portals reflect the different functions of each door.

The portals are porch-portals, an innovative architectural feature in which the sculpted doorframe was covered by a single- or double-storey canopy supported by column-bearing animals (or atlas figures). The design was probably inspired by early Christian porches in Rome. Its invention is usually attributed to the sculptor Wiligelmus at Modena cathedral (before *c.* 1106) and replicated soon afterwards at Cremona (before *c.* 1117) and Piacenza (before *c.* 1120) (Figure 82).[1] The portals at San Nicola were almost certainly finished before 1106, meaning that this new form of portal appeared at Bari and Modena more or less contemporaneously and indeed could have been invented in Bari rather than Modena.

Portals for the laity: From King Arthur to the New Jerusalem

On the north portal of San Nicola (Figure 81), there seems to be a mingling of early Christian paradisal imagery with symbols of temptation and potential evil and secular imagery, all aimed at the laity. There are inhabited vine scrolls, fantastical creatures, palmettes and peacocks drinking from fountains topped with pine cones, which echo the paradisal imagery of the crypt, discussed in Chapter 5. But here it is mixed with images of secular life. On either side of the lintel are figures engaged in agricultural work: on the left, a man is harvesting wheat; and on the right, another is picking something from a tree. Pina Belli D'Elia saw this as harvesting grapes from a vine,

Figure 79 West portal, San Nicola, Bari. Photo: Palickap via Wikimedia.

but the solid trunk of the tree makes it more likely to be olives. Belli D'Elia linked both to the labours of the months, although it is unusual to find only two months depicted.[2] Regardless, these men at work represent humankind's life of toil after the Fall and the ejection from the Garden of Eden. They are images that the laity in the public space outside the church building could relate to. Supporting the porch columns, cantilevered into the wall, so that they hover seemingly in mid-air, are a pair of lions, holding prey. The prey is badly eroded and difficult to identify, but they may be a boar and a goat, symbols of the devil.[3] Both prey animals seem to have the body of a serpent, a biblical symbol of temptation and the fall of humanity. Like the lions on the back of Elias's throne, these creatures are apotropaic; they guard the vulnerable entrance to the church, attacking any potential sources of evil. The north portal has a mixture of imagery that delights in variety and aims to hold the fascination of all kinds of laypeople: predominantly perhaps ordinary pilgrims and locals but also crusaders and the Norman elite.

In the archivolt above is a frieze that is generally accepted by scholars to be a depiction of an Arthurian legend (Figure 83). At the apex of the archivolt is a crenelated castle with a fortified door and two figures peeking over the battlements. On either side, mounted knights charge to fight the foot soldiers who are defending the castle. Both the knights and foot soldiers are dressed in standard Norman military costumes,

Figure 80 South portal, San Nicola, Bari. Photo: Author.

similar to those on the Charlemagne chess set (c. 1080s) and the Bayeux tapestry (1070s). The scene is almost identical to a corresponding frieze on a portal at the cathedral of Modena (Figure 84), where the castle is more ornate and the frieze more sparsely populated but clearly depicts the same narrative. At Modena, the figures are identified by inscriptions. Arthur of Bretagne and his knights are rescuing a woman, Winloge (presumably Guinevere), who has been kidnapped and imprisoned in a castle by a man called Mardoc. Therefore, we can deduce that the scene at Bari depicts the same story.

The story of King Arthur may have been brought to Bari by crusaders.[4] A contingent of the first crusade led by Robert Curthose, duke of Normandy, arrived in Bari late in 1096. With him were a number of Bretons, including the duke of Brittany and Archbishop Balderic of Dol. Unable to cross the Adriatic in the winter, they were forced to spend several months in Italy. Robert Curthose travelled to Calabria and spent the winter as a guest of Roger Borsa but was back in Apulia in March and set sail from Brindisi at Easter. At this point in their journey, the army was beginning to lose followers. The earliest desertions happened in Rome and continued in southern Italy, where many men sold their weapons and returned home as pilgrims, having already visited Rome and the shrines of St Benedict and St Nicholas.[5] Some members of the army probably stayed in Bari or nearby over the winter, some deserters may well have stayed longer or even set up home in Bari. The winter of 1096–7 (which coincides

Figure 81 North portal, San Nicola, Bari. Photo: Author.

Figure 82 Piacenza cathedral, west façade. Photo: Mongolo 1984 via Wikimedia.

Portal Sculpture   115

Figure 83 Arthurian archivolt, north portal, San Nicola, Bari. Photo: John McNeill.

Figure 84 Arthurian archivolt, Modena cathedral, porta della pescheria. Photo: Robert Aho via Wikimedia.

roughly with the probably decoration of the portals) would have provided the perfect opportunity to tell tales of King Arthur around the fire, but the story could just have easily come from the many ordinary pilgrims who passed through Bari (such as the Englishman Saewulf, who stopped in Bari on his way to Jerusalem in *c.* 1102). Stories about King Arthur must have captured the imagination of southern Italians and been disseminated widely because he appears again in the Otranto mosaic in the middle of the twelfth century (with an inscription).

The theory that Arthurian legends introduced to Italy in Bari is supported by the fact that the Bari archivolt is probably older than its counterpart at Modena. The portals at Bari must have been finished by 1106, when Paschal II declared the church to be 'perfect'. The animal supports are cantilevered into the walls, meaning that the portal sculpture was planned and executed along with the construction of the walls. The dating of Modena cathedral is more complex and contested. Begun in 1099, the relics were installed in 1106, but construction continued for several decades, possibly as late as 1140. The Arthurian scene seems to be part of the later phase of construction, but opinions differ as to how late.[6] The similarities in composition in the two friezes make it unlikely that they were produced entirely independently of each other. Most likely, the story was introduced to the Baresi by crusaders or pilgrims, sculpted onto the north portal and then somehow travelled to Modena. There are no stylistic similarities between the two, so we can exclude the possibility that the same sculptors worked on both. The most likely scenario is that a drawing of the Bari frieze made its way to Modena at some point in the early twelfth century, possibly along with the design for porch-portals.

The fact that the figures are labelled at Modena and unlabelled in Bari leads us to ponder whether and how viewers in Bari would have identified the figures. If the story was well known and retold often, locals would have been able to explain the portal sculpture to visitors. In Modena, the unfamiliar story may have required elucidation from inscriptions (or, perhaps the composition arrived on a drawing which was labelled and the labels were copied into the sculpted frieze). But another possible explanation for the lack of inscriptions at Bari is deliberate ambiguity, so that the scene could be interpreted in multiple ways. We will return to this idea below, but first I would like to put the Bari frieze in the broader context of how Arthurian images were used in sacred buildings.

The Bari and Modena friezes are part of an international group of roughly contemporary sculptures featuring Arthur. Each example seems to use King Arthur to set up a contrast between secular and ecclesiastical power. At St Jacques in Perros-Guirec in Brittany (*c.* 1100), Arthur is depicted with St Efflam, an Irish prince who settled in Brittany. In the sculpture, the saint calls Arthur to help him slay a dragon, but Arthur is defeated by the beast and Efflam has to step in, evoking Christ to successfully make the dragon disappear.[7] In this sculpture, Arthur is used as a tool to demonstrate that divine power is stronger than secular power.

At Modena, the Arthurian scene is on the *porta della pescheria* that leads into the church from fish market and the *via Emilia*, the major route through northern Italy, from the Alps to the Adriatic. Just like at Bari, the main audience for the Arthurian frieze were pilgrims and the local laity doing their business in the marketplace. On the opposite side of the cathedral is the bishop's entrance, the *porta dei principi*, which features St Geminiano, a fourth-century bishop of Modena, depicted removing a demon from the soul of a Byzantine princess and rewarded with gifts from the emperor.[8] The two friezes function as a pair: the secular King Arthur rescues Guinevere, while the saintly St Geminiano rescues the princess. Modena was at the heart of Matilda of Canossa's territory and therefore also at the heart of the investiture controversy, the power struggle between papal and imperial power. The contemporary power struggle between ecclesiastical and secular authority was a fraught political issue, referenced on the portals of the cathedral.[9] The two portal friezes at Modena parallel each other, but their placement on opposite sides of the cathedral sets them up in opposition to each other and the fact that the saint receives gifts from the emperor sends a message that an emperor's role is to support the church.

Gloria Allaire has argued that the archivolts at Modena and Bari and Caradoc of Llancarfan's text, *The Life of Gildas* (c. 1130), are based on a common oral legend, in which Guinevere is kidnapped by King Melwas (close enough to Mardoc) and imprisoned at Glastonbury Abbey, which is then besieged by Arthur.[10] In Caradoc's text, a peaceful resolution is brought about through the intervention of the abbot, who stands between the two armies and arranges for Guinevere to return to her husband. The two kings then pray together, give land to the abbey and promise to keep the peace and obey the abbot. The aim of Caradoc's text was probably to bolster the prestige of Glastonbury Abbey by giving it an Arthurian heritage, and it consequently created the legend that Arthur is buried at Glastonbury.[11] The text, which contrasts the wise and peacemaking abbot with the violent and hot-headed kings, is another example of Arthurian legend being used to demonstrate the superiority of ecclesiastical leaders over the laity.

Whereas at Modena, the two contrasting portals were used by different groups of people, at Bari the north and south portals were both used by the laity: one was an entrance and the other an exit. The south portal (Figure 80) – the exit – has no secular elements; it is decorated with the same imagery as the crypt capitals, evoking paradise through flora and fauna. It is also more classicizing than the north portal, with egg and dart moulding on the jambs and lintel and dentilation around the lunette, tying it visually to prestigious areas of the church with classicizing decoration (Elias's tomb and throne and the portal on the main façade, which I will address in this chapter). The two capitals, although badly damaged, are decorated with peacocks drinking from fountains (Figure 85).

The north and south portals contrast the secular with the sacred in a different way than the Arthurian scenes at Perros, Modena and in the *Life of Gildas*. Whereas those other examples pit sacred and secular power against each other, at Bari pilgrims 'travelled' from one to the other. They entered through the north portal, full of the cares of the earthly world, their minds on earthly issues. They emerged from the south portal, having visited the shrine, fortified by the prayers of St Nicholas, with their eyes more firmly fixed on the New Jerusalem represented by the church building. The contrasting imagery on the two portals was used as a visual manifestation of what we might call the 'spiritual cleansing' that the sacred space of the church could offer to pilgrims.

Figure 85 Capital, south portal, San Nicola, Bari. Photo: Author.

The Arthurian frieze is a profane story, added to help pilgrims to reflect on the spiritual experience of visiting the shrine. Thus it is used in the service of a religious message. The scene may be uninscribed because the story was familiar to the audience. But a viewer did not need to be able to identify the Arthurian origin in order for the image to serve its function. The fact that it is a scene of secular violence is sufficient for the north and south portals to work in tandem. There is also the possibility that the sculptors and patron wanted the scene to be imbued with multiple meanings.[12] On one level it is generic secular violence; on another level it is a specific Arthurian legend. On a third level, it could have been read as a depiction of recent events. The sculptors have depicted Arthur and his knights in Norman military dress, giving the story a contemporary setting and meaning that the frieze looked like a depiction of the Norman conquest. Only two decades had elapsed since the traumatic siege in which the Normans had ousted the Byzantines and it would have been fresh in the minds of many Baresi, including Elias. As we have seen throughout Part 2 of this book, the church of San Nicola was part of the community's response to and recovery from that siege. The end of Byzantine rule was the starting point for the construction of the church, just like the north portal is the beginning the pilgrim's visit to the shrine. Passing beneath a depiction of the Norman conquest before visiting the shrine may have been a healing trajectory for local visitors.

Yet another possibility is a parallel between the knights in the frieze and crusaders (both the foreigners who may have introduced the story and the southern Italians who fought in Bohemond's army). As we have seen, San Nicola began as an assertion of Lombard autonomy but became more and more responsive to other contemporary issues like crusade and reform, as construction progressed. Arthur rescuing Guinevere could also be read as the crusaders rescuing Jerusalem. A crusading meaning would put a more positive spin on the image, but the idea of spiritual transformation would hold true: the participation and approval of the church and the pope was what distinguished the crusade from any other war. Bohemond and his knights prayed at San Nicola before embarking for the Holy Land. In their minds, they may have entered the church as secular warriors and left it on a mission for God.

In Apulian sculpture, human figures are few and narrative scenes are incredibly rare. Its rarity would have made the frieze on the north portal very striking and thus probably a topic of conversation. The lack of inscriptions makes this a multivalent image, open to interpretation in a number of ways. Although the connection to Modena makes it likely that one of those interpretations was Arthurian, this is by no means certain. It remains possible that it is not King Arthur, and that the similarity between the composition of the Bari frieze and the Arthurian story was noticed only in Modena, where the two ideas were mixed together. The presence of King Arthur on the Otranto mosaic and the presence of Breton crusaders and pilgrims in Bari do strengthen the Arthurian connection, but it remains a possibility that the Bari frieze is not Arthurian. Regardless, the function of this image, in a liminal zone of the church, is to help the faithful understand the transformative potential of entering the sacred space.

West portal

If the four doors in the aisles were the practical, daily entrances for clergy and laity, designed to give access to different parts of the church, the west portal on the main façade is the processional, ceremonial entrance. The open space in front of the church must have been a gathering place for pilgrims and a stage for the civic and commercial life of the city. Standing in front of the open west door, the viewer looks down the nave, with its impressive rows of columns, through the arches of the templon screen to glimpse the altar. When the doors were closed (and even perhaps when they are open), the main portal and its sculpture become a focal point for engagement with the church from the outside. It is not surprising therefore that the imagery on the portal is focused on the Eucharist.

Like the side doors, the west door is a shallow porch-portal with a canopy supported by columns, this time resting on oxen rather than lions (Figure 86). There is a relief icon of St Nicholas in the lunette but it is not original; it was added in the seventeenth century. The portal makes use of spoliate sculpture: one of the capitals is from the fifth century, and the oxen stand on slices of a Roman cornice from the fourth century (Figure 87).[13] The cornice has a dentilated band, which is mirrored in the abacus of the

Figure 86 Oxen, west portal, San Nicola, Bari. Photo: Author.

Figure 87 Classical cornice reused in the west portal of San Nicola. Photo: Author.

capitals. The classicism continues in the band of egg and dart moulding that follows the arch of the doorway. The underside of the arch is decorated with a coffered motif (Figure 88), like the coffers found on Roman soffits and copied on the underside of the lunette on the *porta della pescheria* at Modena and on the main portal of Montecassino (and Montecassino the motif is diagonal).

At the base of the portal are a number of supporting creatures: the oxen are joined by telamons at the base of the jambs, kneeling on one knee just like their counterparts

Figure 88 Coffer motif on west portal, San Nicola, Bari. Photo: Author.

Figure 89 Telamons at the base of the west portal, San Nicola, Bari. Photo: Author.

on the throne, and elephants on the inside of the jambs (Figures 89 and 90) (echoing the throne in Canosa). On the backs of the elephants are chalices, out of which grow vines that unfurl up and around the arched portal. They are inhabited by an array of humans and animals, including a variety of birds. On the south side of the door, two nude figures stand on the back of the elephant. Pina Belli D'Elia identified them as Adam

Figure 90 Elephant at the base of the west portal, San Nicola, Bari. Photo: Author.

and Eve, and Marcello Angheban has argued that, along with other figures in portal sculpture, they can represent sinners.[14] Other figures include a knight in chainmail on horseback, a man riding a unicorn and a fantastical creature half-human half-animal eating grapes from the vine. Close to the apex of the arch, one on either side of it, are a pair of figures wrestling with lions, which could be Samson. On the gable is a winged quadraped with a human head; he is bearded with long hair and wears a Fatimid-style conical ridged hat, just like the mysterious central figure on the throne. The variety and intricacy of the inhabited vine scroll show influence from manuscripts.

The vines, already so plentiful in the side doors, take on a fuller sacramental significance here, evoking the Eucharistic wine and its salvific potential. At the apex of the doorway is a grape harvest, with a cart laden with grapes, pulled by oxen and driven by a man (Figure 91). Grape harvests are common in Romanesque art as part of the labours of the months, usually depicting people standing in a vat of grapes, crushing them with their feet, as in the depiction of October in the Otranto mosaic (1160s). Here, however, the iconography is quite different and has been taken from early Christian art rather than the labours of the months. A comparison can be made with the grape harvest in the ambulatory vault of Santa Costanza in Rome, built as a mausoleum for Constantine's daughters: Constantina and Helena. At Santa Costanza, a *putto* loads the grapes into a cart while another drives the oxen (Figure 92). Pagan Dionysiac imagery has been adapted into very early Christian iconography as an

Figure 91 Grape harvest, west portal, San Nicola, Bari. Photo: Author.

Figure 92 Grape harvest, Santa Costanza, Rome. Photo: Brad Hostetler.

allusion to Christ as the true vine, where the abundance and fertility of the harvest alludes not only to the Eucharist but also to the beauty and tranquillity of paradise.[15]

In the spandrels of the arched doorway are angels with veiled hands, holding discs representing consecrated hosts (Figure 93). Veiled hands are a ubiquitous sign of Eucharistic reverence in Byzantine art, seen in examples all over the empire, for instance the churches of St Sofia in Ohrid, St George in Sofia and La Martorana in Palermo.[16] Veiled hands are also found on the Bari Exultet 2, which was made early on in the Norman period. In the scroll, men with veiled hands crawl beneath the

Figure 93 Angels on the west portal of San Nicola, Bari. Photo: John McNeill.

Transfiguration, linked to Christ by rays of light which emanate down to touch their backs. Angels with veiled hands appear again in the baptism of Christ scene.

The angels on the portal are leaning in towards the doorway, as if inviting the viewer in. If the doors were open – and if the sunlight was not too bright – someone standing on the threshold would be able to see down the nave to the templon and beyond it to the ciborium and the altar. The ciborium was a late addition to San Nicola, probably added in the late 1120s or early 1130s. Its capitals are decorated, like the portal, with angels holding consecrated hosts. Thus there is a visual link between the portal sculpture and the celebration of the mass at the altar. Even when the doors were closed, the faithful would be able to look at the portal sculpture and feel the connection to Christ in the Eucharist.[17]

The inner arch and jambs are surrounded by a peculiar angled frame, not found on the other portals, nor at Salerno, Montecassino or Modena. This frame is adorned with palmettes interspersed with decorative motifs, some of which are interlace, others are spirals. This kind of decoration is found on numerous epistyles and closure panels of contemporary Byzantine templon screens. One such example comes from Byzantine Bari – several fragments of an epistyle are to be found scattered around San Nicola, one fragment has been re-used as an architrave in a doorway leading to the galleries above the nave, while another fragment was unearthed during the twentieth-century restorations and is now in the museum.[18] Similar examples are to be found further afield on the epistyle of a templon at Hosios Loukas and an epistyle at Blachernes at Arta that has been re-employed as a lintel.[19] This evocation of the idea of the templon is also pertinent for the Eucharistic meaning of the portal since part of the function of the templon is to articulate the sanctity of the altar and to frame the Eucharistic liturgy.

At the time of the construction of San Nicola, the church had recently been through a heated debate about the nature of the Eucharist. From shortly before 1050, Berengar of Tours began to formulate his explosive ideas about the nature of the sacrament. Berengar's thesis was that, although the consecrated bread and wine were in some sense the body and blood of Christ, they were still bread and wine, and furthermore, since Christ's body was present in a whole and pure form in heaven, it was not only impossible but also undignified that his blood and body should be physically present in such a fragmented form during the mass. His ideas were very unpopular, but he nonetheless caused widespread controversy and many theologians wrote tracts against his ideas, among them several southern Italians, including Alberic of Montecassino and Guitmund of Aversa.[20] The controversy came to a head at the Lenten council of 1079 in Rome, where Berengar recanted his controversial ideas at the Lenten council in 1079 and swore an oath that the bread and wine were transformed in substance at consecration.[21] The Lenten council settled the matter in Alberic and the pope's favour and was seen as a categorical defeat for Berengar, but it was by no means the end of the debate over the nature of the Eucharist.[22]

Guitmund of Aversa was a Benedictine monk from Normandy who wrote a Eucharistic treatise against Berengar in *c*. 1073, in which he countered Berengar's claim that is was impossible for Christ's body to be fragmented when the Eucharist took place in so many different churches. Guitmund argued that Christ could appear in many different forms.[23] He left Normandy on a pilgrimage to Rome and remained in Italy. He was present at the Council of Capua in 1087, where he debated with Desiderius of Montecassino and Odo, Bishop of Ostia, the future Urban II.[24] In 1089, at the Council of Melfi, Urban II appointed him bishop of Aversa, the early Norman stronghold between Capua and Naples.[25] Elias of Bari was also present at the Council of Melfi – where he had gone to invite Urban to come and consecrate the crypt – and so would have met Guitmund and had the opportunity to discuss theology with him at a crucial time in the planning of the basilica, when the crypt was finished and Elias was turning his attention to the design of the upper basilica.

In the eleventh century, while the Eucharist became more and more central to Christian devotion, there were also changes in the role of the clergy with regard to the sacraments.[26] Two things became very important: first, the Eucharist began to be perceived as the most important function of the clergy; and second it became increasingly important that it was administered by a priest who was not only properly ordained but also adhered to the reform movement's standards for priestly purity. At a time when there was a revolutionary shift in the role and identity of the clergy, it was not enough just to be ordained in order to perform the sacraments; a priest must also live and carry out his duties in an acceptable manner. These changes were echoed in the orthodox church where eleventh-century iconography became more focused on the power of the clergy and on the Eucharist.[27] Until the twelfth century the term *ordinatio* was understood to mean that a priest was appointed to a role within a particular community, and this role was not particularly associated with the Eucharist (it was even debated whether it was necessary for the Eucharist to be confected by an ordained priest). From the twelfth century onwards *ordinatio* came to mean that through ordination a man received the power to confect the Eucharistic sacrament.

This power was portable, it rested with the individual and could not be rescinded, thus the priest was able to perform his function (*ordo*) anywhere and it was not tied to a particular community.[28] In short, the Eucharist became the key to clerical identity during this period.

The heresy instigated by Berengar of Tours took place at a time when Eucharistic piety was increasing and the Gregorian reformers were placing an emphasis on the Eucharist as the primary sacrament and on sacerdotal ability to confect it. As early as the papacy of Gregory VII the laity was encouraged to boycott the Eucharist from simoniacal clerics.[29] Consequently the laity took communion less often and felt anxiety about its validity. Lay people took a keen interest in the Eucharistic debates and 'talked about it in the streets'.[30] Here on the portal are images facing into the secular space of the street, perfectly positioned to be discussed by the laity. The portal is both an image in the public space of the street where the laity can discuss and grapple with topical issues and a liminal zone which prepares them to enter the nave. The portal sculpture borrows features of templon screens to send the message that the doorway is the threshold of the Eucharistic space. With its emphasis on the Eucharist and particularly the reverence of the angels, perhaps the portal is intended to reassure the laity that the Eucharist is valid and pure. As we will see in Chapter 10, there are inscriptions on the steps leading to the sanctuary that admonish the clergy to behave well and, as we have already seen in Chapter 6, the imagery on the episcopal throne was also a way of regulating clerical behaviour. The portal sculpture may be another manifestation of the Gregorian Reform movement's concern with the purity of the clergy and, by extension, the sacraments they administered.

Sol invictus

At the apex of the gable is a male figure sitting in a chariot pulled by four horses (Figure 94). In his left hand he holds a palm branch and in his right a disc with a face on it surrounded by rays like the sun. This iconography can be traced back to the classical iconography of the rising sun, *sol invictus*. In early Christianity the iconography of *sol invictus* was adapted to fit a Christian message so that the cult of Christ could rival the cult of the sun god. In the third-century Tomb M in the Vatican catacombs is a depiction of Christ (with a cruciform nimbus) in a chariot pulled by horses surrounded by vines.[31] The iconography was also adapted for Constantine, who was depicted thus in his consecration coin.[32] The example from Bari, however, is not based on the early Christian iconography, since the man in the chariot does not have a cruciform nimbus (or indeed any nimbus) and is therefore unlikely to be Christ. Furthermore, the disc that he holds in his right hand (another Eucharistic host?) has rays emanating from it, linking him to solar imagery and divine light.

In the Middle Ages, the image of the personification of the sun appears on the Girona tapestry (Figure 95), where it represents the spring equinox as part of a calendar and the fourth day of creation when God separated night and day and created the celestial objects so that the passage of time could be marked.[33] The image shows a seated figure, crowned with rays of light, in a chariot drawn by four horses. Curiously, there was a

Figure 94 *Sol invictus*(?), west portal, San Nicola, Bari. Photo: Author.

Figure 95 Detail from the Girona Tapestry. Photo: Kippelboy via Wikimedia.

link between Puglia and Girona in the late eleventh century. Manuel Castiñeiras has concluded that the tapestry was probably made in the 1090s, for a church council held in 1097, by the nuns of San Daniel of Girona. Mafalda, daughter of Robert Guiscard and his second wife Sichelgaita, was married to the count of Barcelona, Ramon Berenger II, in 1078 and widowed in 1082. She made donations to San Daniel and retired there in 1105. Furthermore, between 1094 and 1099, the abbess of San Daniel was an Italian called Adelaide, who may have arrived in Catalonia as part of Mafalda's retinue.[34] The image of the personification of the sun at Bari was probably carved only a few years after the creation of the tapestry. The two depictions on the tapestry and the portal look nothing like each other, but the idea of the personification of the rising sun drawn from classical models may have been an idea that was shared through the links between Apulia and Catalonia. Recent research indicates that artistic links between southern Italy and Spain have been insufficiently studied, and further research in the future will hopefully illuminate connections with the western Mediterranean.[35]

It is also possible that the image of the sun at Bari had a double meaning, as a depiction of the prophet Elijah, who ascended to heaven in a chariot of fire and who is evoked on the tomb of Abbot Elias as his namesake.[36] In the next chapter we will read in Archbishop Elias's epitaph an explicit comparison between him and the prophet Elijah. The epitaph also announces that the church of San Nicola shines like a golden light. The idea of luminous churches was perhaps a Gregorian Reform idea because it is mirrored in Alfanus of Salerno's description of Montecassino as 'shining like the sun'.[37] The *sol invictus* on the portal is not Christ because he does not have a cruciform halo, but does carry a disc that could be a confluence of a Eucharistic host, Elijah, in his chariot of fire and the rising sun as embodiment of the light of Christ. The texts, Elias's epitaph and Alfanus's description of Montecassino, show that in this period the church itself was also considered to be luminous.

Conclusion

Above all, the portal sculpture at San Nicola was responsive to the contemporary world around it. The laity – pilgrims and locals – milling around the church would have seen images they could relate to, images that sparked debate and prompted them to reflect on entering the sacred space. The Eucharistic west portal may have caused arguments, anxiety or gossip about the sacramental purity of particular priests. The variety and liveliness of the images would have induced delight and curiosity. At the same time the Eucharistic elements would have induced feelings of devotion and reverence, bringing up memories and eager anticipation of communion. Much conversation and storytelling probably took place around the north door: romantic stories of a mythical king rescuing his wife, frightening stories of the Norman siege and exciting stories of crusader victories. For most pilgrims, drinking in the details on the north portal with its lions, knights and vines would have been a climactic moment, the culmination of their journey to Bari, the beginning of their encounter with St Nicholas, ripe with the possibility of healing, answered prayers and proximity to the divine. These sculptures do not have fixed or straightforward didactic meanings; rather, they are emotive and subjective experiences that engage the laity with the church.

9

Elias of Bari

Benedictine, bishop, builder

In previous chapters we met Elias: Benedictine Abbot, custodian of the relics, patron of the basilica, populist civic leader and archbishop of Bari and Canosa. He was probably from a prominent and established local family.[1] His relative Nicephorus was given some houses by Robert Guiscard. Nicephorus and Elias had another relative, Maraldus (possibly Elias' grandfather), who was an Armenian priest at San Giorgio degli Armeni.[2] Possibly he was a child oblate at the monastery at Cava dei Tirreni, just outside Salerno, where he would have been educated, particularly in law.[3] Another theory is that he received his training at Montecassino.[4] After ordination he returned to Bari as rector of the church of Santa Maria.[5] In 1071, in the midst of the Norman siege, Leucio, abbot of the Benedictine monastery in Bari, mindful of his advancing age, nominated Elias as his successor.[6] His appointment as abbot was confirmed by the Byzantine Catepan in one of his last administrative acts before capitulating to the Normans.[7] By the time he was installed as Abbot, the Normans had won the siege.[8] Gerardo Cioffari has argued that Elias was part of a faction within Bari who negotiated the Norman victory and ultimately opened the city gates to the Norman forces, but, if that is true, it is unlikely he did so out of any pro-Norman sentiment; more likely it would have been a pragmatic decision after a long siege.[9] The Catepan's endorsement might indicate that Elias's position in local politics was pro-Byzantine and anti-Norman, especially given his role in the civic conflict of 1087, as an opponent of the pro-Norman Ursus. Regardless, Elias's background and role as a civic leader seem to indicate that his real loyalty lay with the Lombard community. He probably saw both Byzantines and Normans as unwelcome outsiders but was willing to work with both when it was expedient. Seen in this light, he was the natural successor of Archbishop Bisantius, who, a generation earlier, had also advocated for the Lombard community through civic leadership and artistic patronage.

Elias steered the monastery through the first sixteen years of Norman rule before becoming the custodian of the relics of St Nicholas and project manager of San Nicola in 1087. Two years later, following the death of Ursus, Pope Urban II ordained him as archbishop of Bari and Canosa and lauded him as the 'special son of the Roman church'.[10] In 1095 the people of Bari swore a general oath of allegiance to him, in which they promised to listen to him and obey him for their communal salvation. Although he never played an official role in the secular government of the city, he became the unofficial leader of Bari and must have had a great deal of civic as well as ecclesiastical power.[11]

In 1091, Elias was once again involved in the development of the cult of saints in Bari. Before the arrival of St Nicholas, Bari and Canosa shared St Sabinus as their patron. In 1091, John Archdeacon of Bari (the same John who wrote the *translatio* text in favour of Ursus) wrote an *inventio* account in which he narrated how the relics of St Sabinus had been moved from Canosa to Bari in the ninth century, by Bishop Angelarius, then lost. The loss was a prelude to their rediscovery by Archbishop Elias in the crypt of Bari cathedral. Elias then had them re-interred, this time with an inscription marking their location.[12] John's suggestion that the relics were moved in the ninth century – when Bari was an Arab emirate – is completely implausible. Not only is it improbable that the relics would be moved from a Christian city to a Muslim city, there is also no trace of the relics in Bari.[13] John claimed that Bishop Angelarius moved the bones of three saints in 844: Sabinus, Rufinus and Memore (all three early bishops of Canosa). In 1994, when the altar in the crypt of Bari cathedral was opened, it contained bones belonging to only two men, both under sixty. Since Sabinus lived well into old age, the relics in the altar are almost certainly Rufinus and Memore.[14] It was probably this spurious attempt to claim St Sabinus's relics that prompted the rededication of the cathedral of Canosa to St Sabinus in 1101 (see Chapters 4 and 12).

The 'rediscovery' was therefore a conscious strategy by Elias and John to construct a new shrine to Sabinus in Bari cathedral. The aim may have been partly to boost the status of the cathedral within the city. The construction of San Nicola had created a new spiritual centre that must have, to a certain extent, eclipsed the cathedral. The new shrine to St Sabinus probably revived the cathedral as a devotional site for the Baresi. Although John's *translatio* text was supportive of Archbishop Ursus, John's true loyalty, as archdeacon, was probably to the cathedral and its community of clerics, rather than to a specific archbishop. John had been against the construction of a new church for St Nicholas because he wanted the cathedral to have the major new shrine. His *inventio* text attempted to shift the focus back to the cathedral. In 1091 Elias had become the archbishop, so his interests now aligned with John's. The new shrine to St Sabinus connected Elias more concretely to the historical episcopate. Elias and Sabinus became a pair: both bishops of Canosa, both builders of great churches. Elias's episcopate coincided with the increase in episcopal power in southern Italy that was a consequence of both the Norman conquest and the reform movement.[15] In Apulia in particular, bishops became stronger because the Norman conquest eliminated the tension between the Latin clergy's spiritual allegiance to the pope and their political allegiance to the empire. Alongside the change in episcopal status was the flourishing of local bishop saints. In Elias's fostering of the cult of St Sabinus, we see him participating in this trend to link contemporary bishops with their predecessors.

The developments in Bari could only have fuelled the rivalry with Canosa.[16] The people of Canosa and the cathedral clergy must have been irritated as best by Bari's new shrine to *their* saint. The rededication of Canosa cathedral to St Sabinus in 1101 was probably a response to the fake *inventio* in Bari, a reassertion that the relics were, and always had been, safe and sound in Canosa. The Museo dei Vescovi in Canosa

Figures 96 Liturgical gloves, Museo dei Vescovi, Canosa. Photo: Teresa Morrettoni via Wikimedia

has a pair of liturgical gloves, with embroidered medallions, probably worn by the bishop (Figure 96). They are ceremonial – the fingers are too short to be practical – but they have been worn extensively.[17] They probably date to the eleventh century.[18] The medallions are embroidered with silk thread and framed with a ring of pearls. One depicts Christ and the other an unidentified saint (St Sabinus?), both in the *orans* pose. They are self-referential because the gloves would have been most visible when the bishop lifted his own hands into the *orans* pose. They have traditionally been known as the 'gloves of San Sabinus', and it is possible that they were made at the time of the rededication in 1101, as a false memento of the saint.[19]

Elias' tomb

Given his status, it is no wonder that, when Elias died in 1105, he was given a lavish burial in the basilica he spent the later part of his life building. His tomb (Figure 97) is located at the threshold of the crypt, set into the wall at the bottom of the south staircase, close to the shrine of the saint and highly visible to those climbing the south staircase. If my supposition in Chapter 8 is correct and pilgrims entered through the north door and exited through the south door, they would pass Elias's tomb on their way out of the crypt. There are two questions we need to ask about the tomb: First, is it genuinely Elia's original tomb? And, if it is, what can it tell us about culture in Bari *c.* 1100? Ciofari has argued that Elias was venerated locally as a saint, even though he was not officially canonized.[20] Tombs were important in developing new cults, at a time when canonization was still by reputation and popular devotion, rather than a centralized process. Elias's lavish tomb may have been part of a grassroots movement to create a cult for him. In a quasi-hagiographic legend, Elias anointed the eyes of a blind boy with the manna of St Nicholas and the boy

Figures 97 Elias's tomb, San Nicola. Photo: Author

regained his sight.[21] In this story, the miracle happens because of a collaboration between St Nicholas and Elias, an indication that St Nicholas approved of Elias's veneration. The veneration lasted for many centuries and was described by local Barese Jesuit Antonio Beatillo, writing in the seventeenth century, who narrated how the women of Bari kissed and bowed to Elias's tomb. In 1570 the tomb was opened by the papal envoy Monsignor di Foligno who discovered that Elias's body emitted a sweet smell, just like St Nicholas's and St Sabinus's, leading to renewed calls for his canonization.[22]

The tomb is in two parts: above is a gabled tablet inscribed with a poetic tribute and below is piece of a classical sarcophagus, obtained perhaps from the ancient sites at Canosa, from the Byzantine palace or maybe given as a gift by Urban II along with the piece of marble that became Elias's throne. The sarcophagus is one of a group, known as the Sidmara type, in which figurative decoration is set within ornate microarchitectural niches. The group were made in Asia Minor in the Roman imperial period and exported all over the empire.[23] Elias's sarcophagus features toga-clad pagan philosophers, an iconography which was, from the fourth century, sometimes adapted for Christian occupants by placing Christ and the apostles in the niches, tying the figures to the micro-architecture by alluding to the apostles as columns or pillars of the church.[24] The philosophers on Elias's tomb are pagan philosophers, but they may have been interpreted as apostles when they were installed in San Nicola.

Perhaps not coincidentally, Elias's tomb may resemble the original tomb of St Nicolas in Myra, where there is a damaged Sidmara-type sarcophagus, often alleged to be the original tomb of the saint, although there is no concrete evidence that it was. A large chunk of the sarcophagus has been hacked away, possibly damaged by the merchants from Bari when they stole the relics. Even if it was not St Nicholas's original tomb, the Baresi may have initially believed it to be. In Chapter 5 we saw similarities in the veneration of the saint in Myra and Bari, and in Chapter 10 we will see encounter another set of similarities in the pavements. Individually, they would be no more than coincidences, but collectively, they seem to point to a conscious strategy to evoke the Myra church in Bari.

Classical sarcophagi were the most prized spoliate objects in the Middle Ages, and they were collected, traded and reused, particularly by the Benedictines.[25] It is generally asserted that elite burial in Roman sarcophagi was common practice by the end of the eleventh century, but this needs to be viewed with some caution since, in many cases, the burial cannot be securely dated and the identity of the corpse is only attributed through local legend. Collections of sarcophagi continued to grow throughout the Middle Ages, and bodies may have been moved into sarcophagi in later centuries. There is very little documentation of such burials early on.[26] The most famous and extensive collection is in the cathedral at Pisa, where the majority are thirteenth-century burials, although the earliest is thought to be from 1119.[27] In southern Italy it is often asserted that dukes of Apulia, Roger Borsa and his son William, are buried in classical sarcophagi located at the atrium of Salerno cathedral, but there is no evidence that they were buried in the specific sarcophagi traditionally assigned to them. Likewise there is no certainty about which members of the royal family are buried in which of the famous porphyry sarcophagi in Palermo.[28] Roger I, the first Count of Sicily and brother of Robert Guiscard, is said to have been buried in a spoliate sarcophagus, which was partially re-carved to Christianize the iconography, at the abbey of the SS. Trinità in Mileto in Calabria when he died in 1092. However, it is not certain that the sarcophagus was part of Roger's original burial because his tomb was altered in the thirteenth century.[29] The most secure example of contemporary burial in a classical sarcophagus is that of Pope Gregory VII, in Salerno cathedral, in 1085. His sarcophagus has a mismatched lid, which was partially re-carved with foliate decoration consistent with the style of contemporary sculpture in the cathedral.[30] The re-carving at the time of Gregory's death allows us to be fairly certain that it was part of an eleventh-century burial, although that the original occupant was Gregory VII is slightly less certain, since Orderic Vitalis claimed that he died in Benevento not Salerno.[31]

We therefore need to approach Elias's tomb with a degree of scepticism. At first glance, there are several reasons to doubt that this is the original form of Elias's tomb. The area at the bottom of the south staircase has been altered. Although the sculpted doorframe is original to the late eleventh century, the marble wall and floor cladding are modern. In my opinion the inscription has been moved. The way it intersects with the barrel vault above is very awkward. The corners of the square inscribed tablet have been cut diagonally to accommodate the vault and form a gable, which is stylistically decidedly not from the eleventh century. There is a cross on the gable, which looks early modern. If the inscription was moved, it was moved before the seventeenth century, when it is recorded in its current location.[32]

However, despite having been moved or altered, the inscription appears to have been an original part of Elias's burial, since the lettering is the same as that on the throne and the sanctuary steps.[33] The inscription reads,[34]

> Much of the world's honour lies buried here in peace. The kings have been bereft of a father, the laws of a judge. You lost your crowning glory, O Bari! Know that you were full of vigour as long as Bishop Elias was. A great father is enshrined in this beautiful tomb, he who guided you well and led you close to heaven. He was an equally good protector of all, of the known and the unknown, of those near and those far away. In the renown of his wisdom and of his building, equal to Solomon's and in the conduct of his pious life to be likened to saintly Elias [the prophet Elijah], he built this temple and it shone like a golden light. Here he went to sleep, while his spirit sought the stars.[35]

The text is classicizing and poetic; it was probably written by one of Elias's Benedictine brethren, possibly by his successor Eustasius. It was probably recited aloud at the annual commemoration of Elias's death, which is documented from the mid-thirteenth century, but almost certainly went back to 1105.[36] It contains some interesting intertextualities. The final phrase 'here he went to sleep, while his spirit sought the stars' also appears on the epitaph of Peter the Black, who was buried across the Adriatic, in the cathedral of Split.[37] In the 1080s Peter the Black founded the Benedictine monastery, St Peter's in Selo, Polijice, and his epitaph was composed by Dabrus the Deacon, who was probably a Benedictine.[38] Croatian Benedictine scribes at the time probably had a bank of stock phrases and ideas that they could draw on for epitaphs.[39] The second part of that phrase, 'his spirit sought the stars', also appears on the epitaph of the famous Benedictine, Hugh of Semur, abbot of Cluny, who died in 1109.[40] Hugh was a close friend of Gregory VII and an influential figure in the life of Urban II, his Cluniac contemporary.[41] These comparisons not only help to date Elias's inscription to around the time of his death but also place it within an international Benedictine literary culture.

Other, slightly more general, parallels can be found in the poetry of Alfanus of Salerno. Just as the author of Elias's epitaph addresses his poem to the city of Bari, Alfanus addressed praise of Desiderius to the Abbey of Montecassino.[42] The evocation of the city in such hyperbolic terms is a classicizing feature, found, for example, in the *laus urbis*, poems in praise of cities, a genre which continued into the Middle Ages, for example in the tenth-century poem 'O Roma Nobilis'.[43] In Elias's epitaph San Nicola is described as shining like a golden light. The symbolism of ecclesiastical institutions illuminating the world around them was a common one in Benedictine circles: Urban II described Cluny as a place that lit up the earth like a second sun and Alfanus described Montecassino as shining in the world like the sun shines in the sky.[44] The inscription therefore, is in keeping with contemporary Benedictine literature, in southern Italy and beyond, and should be regarded as an original part of Elias's tomb.

The comparisons to Solomon and Elijah are characteristic of the Gregorian reformers, who saw themselves as walking in the footsteps of the Old Testament prophets, full of holy zeal, rebuking kings for rejecting God, just as some reformers rebuked the Holy Roman Emperors and other secular leaders.[45] The comparisons between Elias, his namesake Elijah and Solomon are explicit. It is possible there were also more implicit comparisons made with St Nicholas. The prophet Elijah and Nicholas were both defenders of their faiths. On Mount Carmel Elijah defended the worship of the Hebrew God against the Canaanite worship of the deity Baal.[46] St Nicholas destroyed the pagan temple of Artemis and the demons who were said to dwell within it, and churches dedicated to Nicholas were sometimes built on the sites of Artemesian temples.[47] Elijah was taken up to heaven in a chariot of fire.[48] St Nicholas was also associated with fire. The meteorological phenomenon now known as St Elmo's Fire was named after St Nicholas in the Middle Ages. He was also associated with 'Greek fire', the Byzantine practice of setting fire to enemy ships during naval battles.[49] Elias, Nicholas and Solomon were all lauded for their sense of justice. Elias's inscription proclaims him as a judge, which is one of the ways he is linked to Solomon. St Nicholas was often seen as a defender of justice in the face of state injustice – he saved men who were condemned to state execution – part of his role as an exemplary secular bishop.[50] These similarities between Solomon and Elijah and St Nicholas are not explicitly mentioned in Elias's tomb, but it is hard to believe they were not noted, particularly the clergy, and perhaps incorporated into sermons. They are thematic threads that link the Old Testament figures, the early Christian bishop and the medieval bishop. The proximity of Elias's tomb with the shrine of St Nicholas must have fostered those connections, even though they are not explicit in the church today.

This discussion of Elias's tomb and career prompts the question, to what extent should he be seen as Gregorian reformer? Elias is not usually thought of as a reformer (he has rarely been considered at all outside the hyper local history of Bari). Louis Hamilton, on the other hand, sees him as a shrewd, pragmatic local leader who did not concern himself with the wider church outside Bari.[51] Paul Oldfield has also stressed Elias's role in forging civic identity and leadership, seeing his as a leader with a very local focus.[52] Graham Loud is the only historian to cautiously assert that Urban's appointment of Elias as archbishop was part of a reforming agenda.[53]

Elias may not have been well known beyond southern Italy and he did not have the singular focus of famous reformers like Bruno of Segni, Peter Damian, Anselm of Lucca, or the recognition given to his neighbours Alfanus of Salerno and Desiderius of Montecassino. In his government of the church in Bari and Canosa, Elias may not have made the kind of administrative changes that would class him as a reformer (as far as we know from the surviving evidence, which is not plentiful). But his artistic patronage of San Nicola tells a slightly different story. The construction and consecration of churches was a key characteristic of the ideal reforming cleric.[54] In that respect, Elias excelled himself as a proponent of reform. The many ways in which San Nicola has been modelled on early Christian churches demonstrate engagement with the broader desire for the church to 'return to her former beauty and stability', as Gregory VII put it, through *renovatio* and emulation of the early church.[55] The epitaph emphasizes Elias as a temple builder akin to Solomon, who was seen by reformers as the ideal patron of the arts.[56] Finally, Elias's strong relationship with Urban II and the implicit connections to other reforming Benedictines like Desiderius and Alfanus place him within the network of reformers.

There is no doubt that Elias had a different agenda to most reformers; his primary focus must have been steering his city through the gruelling Norman siege, departure of the Byzantines and the economic and political consequences. He had to contend with a powerful secular aristocracy, powerful merchants and the conflict between Bohemond and Roger Borsa. The arrival of St Nicholas and Bari's involvement in the first crusade gave the church in Bari (both the building and the institution) a distinctive character during Elias's episcopate. Administrative reform may not have been a priority, and issues that dominated art and ecclesiastical politics elsewhere were not present in Bari (e.g. the investiture crisis that defined northern Italy in this period was not a pressing concern in the south). Recent research on the Gregorian Reform movement is moving away from seeing it as a monolithic process imposed 'top down' by the papacy and instead moving towards emphasizing local variation and reform from below.[57] Bari should be incorporated into this new way of conceptualizing the reform movement. Archbishop Elias may not look like other reformers, but that does not mean that he was not participating in reform through the construction of his church.

10

Pavements

Adriatic connections underfoot?

This final chapter on San Nicola examines the pavements. For a modern audience, marble pavements are easy to overlook, but they are highly visible and valuable and were considered a prestigious part of the church building in the Middle Ages. They are also central to the experience of visiting the church. Every visitor has a physical and kinetic encounter with the church through the pavement. There are two impressive pavements in San Nicola: one in the crypt and another in the sanctuary of the upper basilica. The crypt pavement was almost certainly completed under Elias, but the sanctuary pavement was probably laid during the era of his successor, Eustasius (although it may have been planned or begun before Elias's death).[1] The pavements are mostly *opus sectile*, combined in the upper sanctuary with mosaic and marble inlay. In this chapter, I will explore what the pavements can tell us about artistic networks in southern Italy and the Mediterranean, arguing that the aim of the pavements was to evoke the authority of early Christian churches through the *opus sectile* technique. In doing so, the patrons of San Nicola were joining in a trend begun by Desiderius at Montecassino. However, the pavements in Bari are not derivative of Montecassino. Elias and Eustasius seem to have sought out their own artists and influences from local and international sources, drawing on Apulian models and looking east to the Adriatic and to St Nicholas's original shrine in Myra.

Civic and ecclesiastical leadership, 1105–23: Abbot Eustasius, Archbishop Riso and Prince Grimoald

It is worth beginning with a short synopsis of how Bari was governed after the death of Archbishop Elias. Elias died in 1105, and the leadership of San Nicola was assumed by Eustasius, who had founded and built the Benedictine monastery of Ognisanti di Cuti near Valenzano, 9km south of Bari, in the mid-eleventh century and was its abbot.[2] He was therefore another local, another Benedictine and someone who had experience of building projects. His role as 'decorator' of the new church is memorialized in an inscription on the sanctuary steps, which I will discuss in this chapter. With Elias's death the leadership San Nicola was once again split from the episcopacy. Eustasius persuaded Paschal II to place the church directly under papal authority, which separated it, to some extent, from local politics and ecclesiastical structures and gave Eustatius some independence.[3]

Elias's death had also left a vacancy in the episcopate but it was not filled until 1112, when an outsider arrived in Bari. The new archbishop, Riso, had previously been cardinal-priest of San Lorenzo in Damaso in Rome, where he had been involved in some dramatic events.[4] At this point in the papacy of Paschal II, the investiture crisis had reached a climactic point. In 1111, Emperor Henry V took Paschal II prisoner and forced him to sign the treaty of Ponte Mammolo, which granted the emperor the right to appoint bishops within his realm.[5] Paschal was strongly criticized by reformers who compelled the pope to revoke the treaty at the, highly unusual, Lateran Synod in March of 1112. Riso was at the synod and was one of the clerics who criticized the Pope. He was appointed archbishop of Bari only a few days later, at the beginning of April, possibly as a reward for his strong performance at the synod.[6]

Riso arrived in Bari at a fractious moment and brought his strong opinions and leadership with him from Rome.[7] Bohemond had died in 1111, leaving his widow Constance to act as regent for his infant sons. The city soon rebelled against Constance and had ousted her entirely by 1113.[8] Riso stepped into the power vacuum and, acting as a civic as well as religious leader (even more so than his predecessor), set up a civic commune.[9] There was a public fund which paid a civic militia, a democratic decision-making process, and money was raised to build fortifications (presumably to keep Constance and other Normans out). However, the commune was not a success and within a few years the city had descended into factionalism and violence.[10] Riso formed an alliance with Constance that put him in conflict with the anti-Norman faction.[11] The citizens considered that Riso was too close to Constance, and, in 1117 or 1118, while he was travelling (possibly fleeing) to Canosa, he was murdered by Argyros, a citizen of Bari, who led the anti-Norman faction.[12]

After Riso's death, Grimoald Alferanites, originally an ally of Riso's, seized control. A member of Bari's powerful, independent aristocracy, Grimoald came from a long-established elite family, who owned a lot of land in the city and had been in the household of the Byzantine governor Basil Boiannes, who had given them imperial titles.[13] Grimoald's family had almost certainly been pro-Byzantine during the Norman conquest and remained anti-Norman in the early twelfth century. He declared himself an autonomous prince of Bari in 1123, after he succeeded in forcing Bohemond II to give up his claim to the city.[14] Grimoald may have come to power in a time of chaos and violence but he became a successful and influential leader. He managed to ally himself with Pope Calixtus II and signed a diplomatic treaty with Venice in 1122.[15] He would later become a formidable opponent of Duke William and Roger II in the civil wars of the late 1120s and early 1130s, managing to keep Bari rebellious and independent of Norman control until 1132.[16] Like most Baresi, Grimoald had a special devotion to St Nicholas. He made donations to San Nicola, and styled himself 'Prince of Bari by the grace of God and St Nicholas'. When Nicholas's arm relic was stolen, it was said to be Grimoald himself who led the expedition to recover it.[17]

Inscription on the sanctuary steps

Despite the fact that the pope had made San Nicola and independent institution, all three of these men (Grimold, Riso and Eustasius) must have played some role in the life of San Nicola in the early twelfth century as the building was finished. At this stage, the church was more or less finished; Eustasius would perhaps have been overseeing the completion of the sculpture, particularly higher up in the building, and the finishing touches, such as lamps, screens, icons, liturgical objects, vestments and other textiles.

Eustasius's contribution is commemorated in an inscription on the steps leading up to the sanctuary, which describes him as the decorator of the church. The lettering matches that on Elias epitaph; both are written in large, clear capital letters, in emulation of classical public inscriptions.[18] The inscription (Figure 98) reads:

> These steps deny the arrogant access to heaven
> These steps permit the meek to seek heaven
> Therefore do not be afraid, you who wish to climb them
> Be humble, supplicating and virtuous and you will be high
> Like Father Elias who first built this temple
> And Father Eustasius who is now decorating and governing it.[19]

It is written in elegant verse and care has been taken to create rhyme and rhythm. Like the other inscriptions in this book, it demonstrates that the clergy of Bari were part of

Figure 98 Sanctuary steps, San Nicola, Bari. Photo: John McNeill.

a sophisticated intellectual culture. It seems likely that both this inscription and Elias's epitaph were written by Eustasius himself (or possibly by another Benedictine).

The sanctuary and its pavement were altered in the seventeenth century during a liturgical rearrangement. A drawing made before the alterations shows that the sanctuary steps originally extended straight across the space, from north to south, meaning that the altar platform was wider and the inscription on the steps was originally much more legible than it is now (Figure 99).[20] Although the inscription would have been visible from the nave and aisles, the only people able to actually climb the steps would have been clergy, who are admonished to emulate Elias and Eustasius in their humility and virtue and to avoid arrogance. As we shall see herein, the steps have been changed since the Middle Ages. The full inscription originally ran across the front of the sanctuary, whereas now the steps wrap around the altar on three sides, meaning that the inscription was originally much more legible. The size and clarity of the lettering mean it would have been clearly visible and legible to both the clergy, as they approached the steps at the beginning of the mass, and to the laity standing in the nave and aisles. In light of lay anxieties about clerical purity and the validity of the sacraments (see Chapter 8), the verses may have provided reassurance to the laity that their Eucharist was valid.

Were the clergy of Bari in particular need of this kind of character formation? In light of the fractious political situation, perhaps the inscription is a way of urging them to stay out of the turmoil. The language is typical of contemporary texts about clerical behaviour. Bruno of Segni, who uses Gregory VII and Leo IX as examples of ideal clergymen, describes them as humble, in his treatise against simony and contrasts them to the Normans, who are arrogant.[21] This seems to be a common comparison in reforming texts, contrasting the arrogance of secular rulers with the humility of

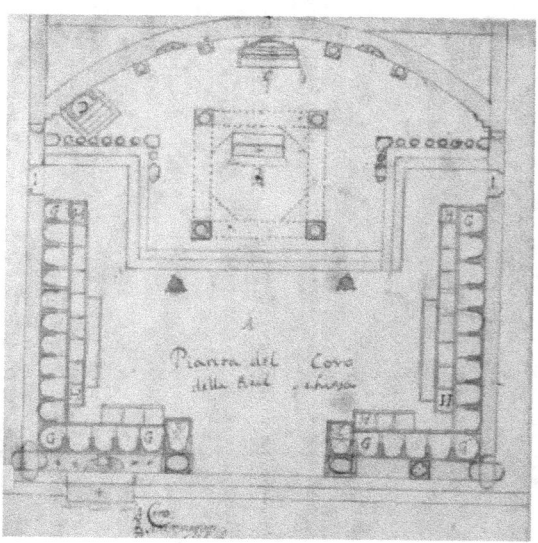

Figure 99 Drawing of the sanctuary in 1647 by Monsignor Antonio del Pezzo.

the clergy (a parallel to the way secular Arthurian legends were contrasted with the wisdom and peacemaking of ecclesiastical figures). To a contemporary audience, the inscription may have implied that the Barese clergy were humble and orthodox, in contrast to the bravado of Prince Grimoald and the squabbles of the political factions.

The second part of the inscription commemorates Elias and Eustasius as builders of the church but also exalts them as ideal priests. Eustasius was able to use Elias's status to bolster his own, by portraying them as a pair. What is interesting is the absence of any reference to St Nicholas, even though he too is an excellent role model for priests. The Baresi went to great effort to transport St Nicholas across the Mediterranean and build him an impressive church, and yet his presence is barely felt beyond the crypt. There is a very small depiction of him on one of the nave capitals, and he is depicted prominently on an enamel on the ciborium that was not part of the original decoration of the church (it was added in the 1130s). The absence of the saint may be part of the reason why a relief of him was added above the west portal in the seventeenth century. Of course much of the decoration of the original church has been lost and there could well have been depictions of Nicholas on icons, wall hangings and liturgical objects. It would be imprudent to make an argument based on an absence. Furthermore, the cult of saints is nurtured through more than just the visual: texts, sermons, liturgies, hymns, miracles and the constant devotion of the faithful no doubt focused on St Nicholas and kept the building focused on the cult. But it is worth noting that, in the decoration that survives, it is Elias, rather than Nicholas, who takes centre stage. With his prominent throne, tomb, epitaph and exaltation on the steps, he seems to have become the central focus for veneration, perhaps as the beginning of a canonization that was never realized.

I also wonder whether an international saint proved to be insufficient for the needs of the local community. Elsewhere in Apulia, and across southern Italy, most cities had local bishops as patron saints, which served a civic purpose. Local bishop saints were deeply connected to the place in which they had ministered and could be seen as continuing to provide pastoral care to their people long after their deaths, in a way that an outsider bishop like St Nicholas perhaps could not. St Nicholas had international fame and the prestige of having attended the Council of Nicea, and there is no doubt that St Nicholas's cult turned Bari into a major shrine in the following centuries and probably succeeded in drawing long-distance pilgrims away from other Apulian ports. But the fact he was an outsider and a newcomer may have limited the potency of his cult for locals. Elias's attempt to revive the cult of St Sabinus in Bari in the 1090s and the nascent cult surrounding Elias himself may be symptomatic of a local need for a local bishop saint.

The crypt pavement

The crypt was once entirely covered in an *opus sectile* pavement. Being a subterranean space mere metres from the sea, the crypt has faced the regular threat of flooding. As early as 1543, a raised floor was placed on top of the *opus sectile*, in the first of several attempts to prevent flooding, which had severely damaged the pavement.[22] The post-medieval floor was removed during the twentieth-century restorations, and the *opus sectile* was conserved as far as possible, but most of it has been lost.[23] The surviving parts are in the sanctuary (a pattern of interlaced squares and circles) (Figure 100) and the south apse (a quincunx looping around a diamond) (Figure 101). Although it is frustrating to have lost so much to water damage, the fact that it was covered by a post-medieval floor means that it escaped the nineteenth-century 'restorations' so common

Figure 100 *Opus sectile* around the shrine of St Nicholas, crypt, San Nicola, Bari. Photo: Sailko via Wikimedia.

Figure 101 Quincunx, *opus sectile*, south apse of the crypt, San Nicola, Bari. Photo: Author

in other pavements and therefore almost all of the surviving tesserae are original.[24] Since the crypt was built in merely two years, it is unlikely that the pavement was laid before the consecration in 1089. It was probably laid in the 1090s, or 1100s.

The pavement contains a number of distinctive features that help us to identify where the designs may have come from. The quincunx in a diamond design in the south apse is a very standard feature of *opus sectile* pavements, but the example at Bari is unusual in the way that the curves loop over and under the diamond frame. This playful design has loose parallels with Byzantine pavements at St John at Ephesus (fifth century), Hosios Loukas (eleventh century) (Figure 102) and under the dome at the Sagmata monastery (twelfth century).[25] The design in the sanctuary of the crypt is also unusual. The pattern stretches across the whole of the space without being contained in panels in a way that is antithetical to Byzantine pavements, where there was a strict relationship between the design of the pavement and the architectural structures above. In Byzantine churches, the floor is divided into panels according to the architectural divisions of space. Each bay of a church usually has its own self-contained panel;, thus, the pavement is an expression of both the architectural form of the building and a reflection of the ritual function of the space. In the crypt sanctuary in Bari, the correlation between architecture and pavement has been broken, as the pattern stretches across the sanctuary almost organically. But the pattern itself is more in keeping with Byzantine designs: the way the interlace combines squares and circles bears some similarity to monastic pavements in Constantinople: the Pantocrator (*c*. 1118) (Figure 103) and St John of Studion (*c*. 1130s–50s) (Figure 104). The examples in Constantinople were themselves inspired by late antique precedents, for example the

Figure 102 *Opus sectile* panel by the altar at Hosios Loukas, Boethia. Drawing from Schulz and Barnsley, *The Monastery of St Luke of Stiris*, p.30, figure 19.

144 From Byzantine to Norman Italy

Figure 103 Pavement of the south church of the Pantocrator monastery, Constantinople. Photo: Dumbarton Oaks.

Figure 104 Pavement, St John of Studion, Constantinople. Drawing: Wilhelm Salzenberg from the Fototeca Zeri, Università di Bologna.

sixth-century mosaic at San Vitale in Ravenna (Figure 105). However there are also similarities with a pavement in Myra, as we shall see herein.

Although *opus sectile* is an economical way of using scraps of spoliate marble that may be too small or too strangely shaped to be useable elsewhere, it is also a luxurious technique because it requires highly skilled artists, many different coloured marbles and a large quantity of stone to pave a whole church. It was so high status that was sometimes imitated in other media.[26] Elias's decision (or Eustasius's) to commission an *opus sectile* pavement for San Nicola was part of the desire to conjure up the prestige and authority of late antiquity. *Opus sectile* is a classical technique, which was used to pave the Constantinian basilicas in Rome that so inspired eleventh- and twelfth-century patrons.[27] The technique was infrequently used in Italy in the early Middle Ages but became very popular in Byzantium from the ninth century, because the aniconic designs were suitable for iconoclastic churches.

A new *opus sectile* workshop was set up at Montecassino, when Desiderius imported Byzantine artists from Constantinople to collaborate with an Italian workshop.[28] The overall design of the Montecassino pavement was derived from Italian floors, with an injection of patterns from the Byzantine workshop (Figure 106).[29] Thanks to this cross-cultural collaboration, the monks of Montecassino were trained in *opus sectile* and went on to set up their own prolific and accomplished workshop that laid pavements across southern Italy in the following decades.[30] The decision to pave San Nicola in *opus sectile* means that Elias or Eustasius was participating in the artistic trends begun at Montecassino and disseminated by that workshop. But was the Bari crypt pavement laid by the Montecassino workshop? As noted earlier, the extant contemporary parallels for the crypt pavement are exclusively within the Byzantine Empire, from Constantinople and Greece. The crypt pavement bears no similarity to the original Montecassino pavement, nor to the other pavements laid by that workshop. Although

Figure 105 San Vitale, Ravenna, mosaic pavement. Photo: Age of Stock.

Figure 106 Gattola's drawing of the Montecassino pavement.

the workshop's work was very varied and constantly innovating and they seem to have had regular injection of new designs from Byzantium, their work is often identifiable because of the reuse of patterns and the juxtaposition of Italian and Byzantine designs.[31] The Bari crypt pavement is more 'purely' Byzantine, perhaps meaning that Elias or Eustasius chose not to employ the Montecassino workshop, but instead hired a workshop from the Byzantine Empire, either from Constantinople or from across the Adriatic. The merchants of Bari certainly had the international connections to be able to do so. Montecassino is often seen as the source of inspiration for all southern Italian church building in the later eleventh century, but San Nicola seems to have been independent of it.

The sanctuary pavement in the upper basilica

The sanctuary of the upper basilica is paved with an equally impressive pavement which uses a mixture of *opus sectile*, mosaic and *opus interrasile*, marble inlay (Figure 107).[32] While the crypt pavement is related to Byzantine examples, the upper sanctuary pavement contains more mixed influences. The very different designs and

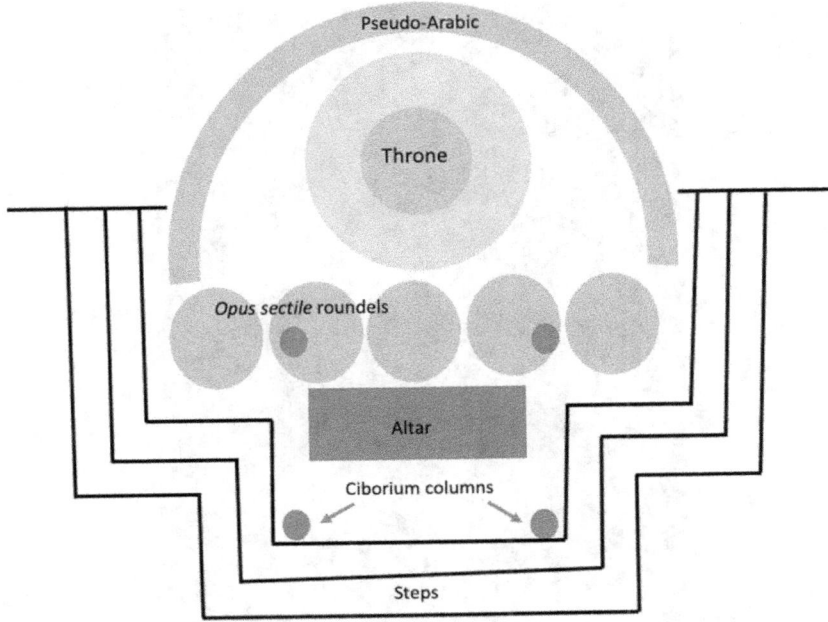

Figure 107 Sanctuary pavement, upper basilica, San Nicola, Bari. Drawn by the author.

influences, as well as the inscription by Eustasius, indicate that the upper pavement was laid later, by a different workshop. At the centre is Elias's throne, surrounded by a circular border and then the rest of the apse is filled in with a polychromatic zigzag and framed with the pseudo-Arabic mosaic (part of which was cut off when the steps were re-configured in the early modern period). Along the east side of the altar are five self-contained discs. The closest parallels for this row of discs are at San Giorgio a Velabro in Rome (ninth century), which has three roundels across the apse and San Menna in Sant'Agata dei Goti (c. 1100), which has a row of interlaced roundels on the west side of the altar. The San Menna pavement was laid by the Montecassino workshop.[33] Next to the throne is a small griffin (Figure 108). The griffin serves an apotropaic function, like the greyhounds that guarded the tomb of St Benedict at Montecassino and the animals found in analogous positions in Sant'Adriano at San Demetrio Corone in Calabria, the Cappella Palatina and at the Sagmata Monastery in Boethia.[34]

The *opus interrasile* on the risers of the steps is a Byzantine technique, not previously found in Italy.[35] The bottom riser is decorated with a series of trilobe palmettes, a decorative element derived from Sassanian art and commonly used in middle Byzantium, where it is found on enamels, sculpture, ceramics, manuscripts and silks.[36] On the middle riser is a repeated motif of birds inside stars. The technique was not used in Italy until the early twelfth century, when it appeared at San Nicola and in the Veneto at roughly the same time.[37]

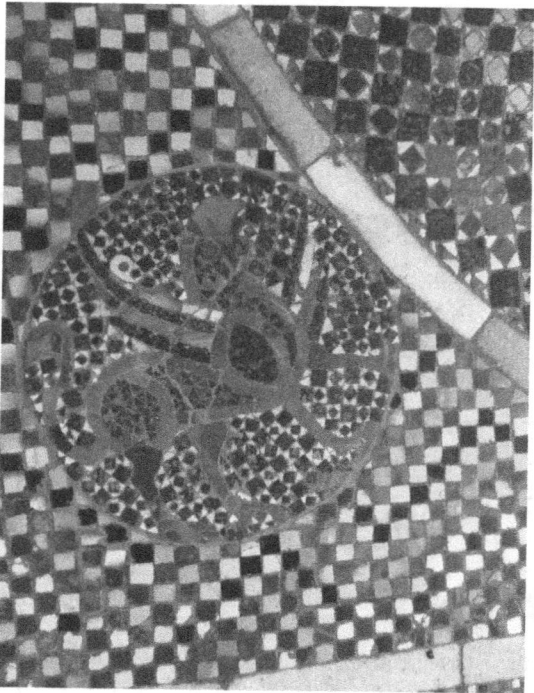

Figure 108 Griffin, sanctuary pavement, San Nicola, Bari. Photo: Author.

The juxtaposition of three different techniques is a distinctive feature of the upper sanctuary pavement and is another similarity with the art of the Veneto, where a number of early-twelfth-century pavements combine mosaic with *opus sectile*.[38] Some of the earliest are at San Marco (*c.* 1100–40), San Zaccharia in Venice (1120s?), followed by SS Maria and Donato in Murano (*c.* 1141), and there is another, further down the Adriatic, in Ravenna cathedral.[39] Scholarly opinion is divided on whether these pavements are inspired predominantly by late antique or middle Byzantine models, or a combination of the two.[40] However, the Venetian examples are pre-dated by other pavements in Apulia. The pavements at Bitonto (tenth century) and Santa Maria di Tremiti (early eleventh century) are mostly mosaic with very small pieces of *opus sectile*.[41] Certainly, the mixing of techniques and the introduction of *opus interrasile* link San Nicola to Venice. Venice is generally considered to be the artistic centre of the Adriatic, and it would be easy to assume that the idea for the San Nicola pavement came from San Marco, which was undoubtedly the largest construction project in the Adriatic at the time. However, Venetian artistic and economic dominance of the Adriatic was only just beginning in the early twelfth century; we should be careful not to make assumptions based on Venice's status in later centuries. The earlier examples of mixed-media pavements in Bitonto and the Tremiti could indicate that influence went the other way: that mixed-media pavements began in Apulia and that this particular aspect of the San Marco pavement was inspired by San Nicola.

Pavements

The crypt and upper sanctuary pavements were laid by different workshops, but both seem to point towards San Nicola as a site of independent artistic production, responsive to trends in southern Italy and the Adriatic but not derivative. The evidence is sketchy and any conclusions must necessarily be tentative; it is impossible to be certain about which workshop laid which pavement or how artistic influences circulated. However, the pavements at San Nicola raise the possibility that Elias eschewed the Benedictine Montecassino workshop in favour of seeking out Byzantine artists to pave the crypt. Later on, the upper pavement may have been laid by the Montecassino workshop, due to the similarities to San Menna and other Italian floors. But again, in the pavement we see independence and innovation in the mixing of techniques, the idea for which probably came from similar mixing on a smaller scale in other Apulian churches. That the same thing was happening in Venice at roughly the same time indicates intra-Adriatic artistic dialogue.

Links to Myra

There are some similarities with St Nicholas's church in Myra that are worth noting here. The church in Myra also has *opus sectile* pavements that were commissioned as part of restorations by Empress Zoe and Constantine IX Monomachos in the 1040s.[42]

One of the roundels on the east side of the main altar at San Nicola is similar to a roundel in Myra (Figures 109 and 110). The *opus sectile* panel on the west side of the altar in Myra has a diamond that loops around a square in a similar fashion to the panel in the south apse of the Bari crypt. This exact design occurs three times in Myra (Figure 111).

The biggest similarity between Myra and Bari lies in the liturgical configuration. From east to west, Myra has a tiered synthronon, an altar covered by a ciborium and then a templon supported by two columns (Figure 112). San Nicola had a similar

Figure 109 Roundel, sanctuary pavement, San Nicola, Bari. Photo: Author.

Figure 110 Roundel, St Nicholas, Myra. Photo: Dosseman via Wikimedia.

configuration. Originally there was probably a synthronon in the apse (as there is in the crypt below). San Nicola has a ciborium, although it is not original (it was made in the 1130s); it may have been added partly to enhance the similarity to Myra. Baldachin ciboria were not common in Italy at this time; in fact they were mostly limited to Apulia, and the San Nicola example is probably the oldest. Manuel Castiñieras has argued that they should be seen as echoing the ciboria of Papal Rome, but it seems to me that the idea for a ciborium at San Nicola may have come from Myra, as a way of evoking both St Nicholas's original shrine and the authority of early Christian Rome.[43] San Nicola also has a highly unusual templon screen consisting of three arches supported by two columns, originally with waist-height parapet screens to close off the lateral arches (Figure 113). The templon must be original, since stylistic analysis shows that the capitals were carved by the same sculptor who made Elias's throne. Of the Myra templon, only the columns survive, but it looks like it originally had three arches, just like the one in Bari. At Myra one of the columns is white marble but the other is dark grey granite, like both of the columns in Bari.

These similarities between Myra and San Nicola could be a coincidence. As we saw earlier, there are other parallels for the pavement and the liturgical arrangement could have been perceived as generically early Christian. But the unusual templon screen is a more concrete connection and we have seen other links to Myra in previous chapters, in Archbishop Elias's philosopher sarcophagus and in the miraculous manna produced by the relics, analogous in both sites. I noted in Chapter 9 the curious absence of references to St Nicholas in the upper basilica, but perhaps his cult was expressed through a connection to his original shrine. The people of Bari seem to have been planning the theft of his relics for some time before 1087. Merchants from Bari made

Figure 111 *Opus sectile* panel, St Nicholas, Myra. Photo: Dosseman via Wikimedia.

frequent trips to the eastern Mediterranean, probably stopping off in Myra often, able to visit the shrine and see that the relics were vulnerable since the Turkish conquest in the 1070s. There would have been plenty of information about the Myra shrine available to Elias as he planned the design of the new church, through oral stories and descriptions, perhaps even sketches drawn by travellers.

Emulating the Myra shrine would have lent a sense of authenticity and authority to the new shrine in Bari. St Nicholas is not an apostle and his shrine is later than the apostolic age, but as an early bishop saint who was present at the Council of Nicea, his shrine had the aura of being *ad limina apostolorum* (at the threshold of the apostles), a sense of the unbroken thread of apostolic succession that was particularly important during Gregorian Reform. In her discussion of the eleventh-century mosaics at Torcello, Liz James asserts that they were influenced by the late antique churches in Ravenna because Ravenna was seen as an authoritative artistic tradition that had power and authority across Christendom.[44] Myra could have played a similar role as an authoritative model for San Nicola. The pavements were a way of evoking the Christianity of late antiquity, which was seen as 'pure' and glorious by the reformers. Italian reformers saw Byzantine art as 'bridge' to early Christian art, a tool they could

Figure 112 Sanctuary, St Nicholas, Myra. Photo: Dosseman via Wikimedia.

Figure 113 Templon, San Nicola, Bari. Photo: Author.

use to achieve their goal of recapturing the church in Constantinian Rome. At Bari, Myra could have provided a specific model to achieve that.

Despite being Benedictines, grounded in the Latin church and preoccupied with issues facing Latin Christendom, in the pavements and liturgical arrangements of San Nicola, Elias and Eustasius were looking east. Although some in some aspects of San Nicola, Elias looked west to Salerno and north to Rome, when planning pavements, he looked out across the Adriatic and built artistic connections and dialogues with Myra, Venice and maybe with a workshop of Byzantine marble workers.

There may be further Adriatic connections in the materiality of the pavements. One of the biggest challenges in creating extensive marble pavements was the acquisition and transportation of materials. These kinds of pavements required large quantities of marble, and their polychromy depended on acquiring a large variety of marbles. Elias and Eustasius were probably responsible for acquiring the marble themselves, as Desiderius had done at Montecassino.[45] Desiderius made shopping trips to Rome, and Elias and Eustasius may also have visited ancient sites to collect materials. Elias's close relationship to Urban II, and Eustasius and Riso's links to Paschal II and Calixtus II, may have given them access to marble in Rome, although it may not have been necessary to look so far afield, since Canosa must have had plenty of Roman marble. Certainly they would have needed to draw on commercial relationships with merchants who dealt in stone and with the Norman lords whose permission may have been needed to move marble off their land. However, transporting marble by sea is more practical than transporting it by land and Bari's commercial shipping fleet and their knowledge of the Mediterranean ports may have been invaluable. It is quite likely therefore that at least some of the marble decoration in San Nicola came from the coastal areas of the Adriatic, such as Corfu or Butrint in Albania.

Conclusion to Part 2

In the roughly thirty years in which San Nicola was built and decorated, Bari went through a lot of changes and so did the church. Three phases can be identified: 1087–95, the immediate post-Byzantine phase; 1095–1105, in which the relationship between Elias and Urban II meant that the ideology of the first crusade was reflected in the building; and 1105–23, after Elias's death when the decoration was focused on the pavement in the upper sanctuary. In the first, post-Byzantine phase, the new church was a way for the citizens of Bari to assert their identity and power, ushering in a new era that was consciously post-Byzantine. At the same time, the citizens used the church as a way to assert their independence within the new Norman duchy, carving out a distinctive artistic and religious climate in Bari. As the building work progressed, that climate changed. The departure of southern Italians on crusade, the arrival of northern European crusaders passing through Bari, the influx of pilgrims, the visits of the Greek and Latin clergy for the Council of Bari in 1098, the continued relationship with Urban II and the news of crusader victories accompanied by the captured tent of Kerbogha of Mosul all shaped the church as it was being built. In this phase, the first crusade and the reform agenda came to dominate the church. In the third phase, under Abbot Eustasius, the church was mostly finished and Eustasius was only left to decorate it (although that process was possibly well underway when Elias died). The extent of Eustasius's contribution is uncertain, but at the very least he wrote a learned inscription on the sanctuary steps that reveals him to have been perhaps interested in reform issues.

This detailed examination of the construction of San Nicola has revealed that Bari was a major centre of artistic production that was distinctive and developed mostly independently of other centres of artistic innovation such as Montecassino and Salerno (although in the early phase of construction, Salerno was influential). San Nicola quickly became a model for other churches in Apulia. By the middle of the twelfth century, the southern Adriatic coast and its hinterland were scattered with buildings inspired by San Nicola. Bari deserves recognition alongside Montecassino, Salerno and Palermo as a nexus of innovation in southern Italian art. Elias of Bari deserves recognition as a major patron, alongside Desiderius, Alfanus, George of Antioch and Roger II.

Part 3

The Tomb of Bohemond I, Prince of Antioch

11

Crusader architecture

Constance of France and her Holy Sepulchre

For the third and final part of this book we return to Canosa, to investigate the tomb of Bohemond I, son of Robert Guiscard, lord of Bari and leader of the southern Italian contingent of the first crusade. During the crusade, Bohemond became prince of Antioch, in the Levant, but he died at home in Apulia and was buried in a small, but magnificent, chapel attached to Canosa cathedral. Analysis of the mausoleum is complicated by the loss of its interior decoration and its original dome. However, careful analysis of the extant parts of the building, together with other sources, can help us to reconstruct it to some extent. This chapter explores the architecture of the chapel and its patronage, arguing that it was commissioned by Bohemond's widow, Constance of France, as an imitation of Christ's empty tomb in the Holy Sepulchre. Chapter 12 looks at the highly innovative bronze doors, the first made in southern Italy since antiquity. In Chapter 13, I address the inscriptions written on the chapel itself and on the doors. When analysed together they reveal themselves to be part of the literary canon of the first crusade, not just a commemoration of Bohemond but also part of Constance's strategy to secure the inheritance of her son.

Who was Bohemond I?

Robert Guiscard and his first wife, Alberada of Buonalbergo, had a son, who they christened Mark. He was a big baby and Guiscard jokingly referred to the child as 'Bohemond' after hearing tales of an eponymous mythical giant.[1] In 1058, not long after Bohemond's birth, Guiscard divorced Alberada to marry the Lombard princess, Sichelgaita of Salerno, with whom he had another son Roger 'Borsa'.[2] Bohemond grew up to be a formidable knight and Guiscard's second in command during the Norman attacks on Byzantine territories in the Balkans.[3] It is, therefore, surprising that when Guiscard launched his Balkan attack, he named Roger Borsa as his heir to the Duchy of Apulia, Calabria and Sicily, thus disinheriting Bohemond. Perhaps his ultimate plan was to conquer the Balkans and divide his territory, leaving the Balkans to Bohemond and southern Italy to Roger Borsa.[4]

But Guiscard's Balkan campaign failed and when he died in 1085, Bohemond was left without any land, a vassal of his younger half-brother.[5] Bohemond challenged his brother, who was forced to give Bohemond extensive land in southern Apulia, including the whole of the Salento peninsula, as far north as Conversano. This made Bohemond one of the most powerful men in southern Italy and gave him access to the wealth of important port cities, such as Brindisi, Taranto, Monopoli and Conversano.[6] Not content, Bohemond launched a second attack on Roger Borsa's territories in Calabria and in August 1089 Roger Borsa was forced to give Bari to Bohemond, in return for relinquishing some of the cities he had taken in Calabria.[7] During these wars – and another in 1093 – although Roger Borsa made extensive concessions to Bohemond, he kept hold of the duchy because he had the support of his uncle, Count Roger of Sicily (later Roger II).[8] Once Bohemond had acquired the land in Apulia fraternal relations resumed, Bohemond even supported his brother against other rebels. As we saw in Chapter 5, although Bohemond's lordship of Bari was successful and fairly stable, he held power through collaboration with Bari's Lombard citizens and was not particularly involved in the day-to-day government of the city.

In 1096, Bohemond was helping Roger Borsa to besiege the rebellious city of Amalfi, when he announced his intention to join the first crusade. He mobilized an army from southern Italy, and they set sail from Brindisi. The status of Bohemond's southern Italian territories while he was away on the crusade is a little ambiguous. He may have left Roger Borsa as custodian of his lands, because when Canosa rebelled Roger Borsa quashed the revolt. Roger may have acted out of fraternal loyalty, but it could have been a way to expand his own power at his brother's expense.[9]

Bohemond's most notable achievement during the crusade was at the conquest of Antioch in the summer of 1098. Once Antioch was in crusader hands, Bohemond argued that, rather than returning the territory to the Byzantine emperor as promised, the crusaders should keep it for themselves, since Alexios had not fulfilled his promise to assist the crusade. He then proclaimed himself prince of Antioch. Bohemond did not continue to Jerusalem with the other crusaders, but he did make a pilgrimage later, when he spent Christmas in Bethlehem and visited Jericho, the River Jordan and the Roman temples at Baalbek.[10] He ruled Antioch until Byzantine forces invaded in 1104, although he spent most of that time as a prisoner of the Danishmend emir, Gümüshtigin Gazi.[11] In 1104, on the verge of defeat, Bohemond saw that the only way to retain the city was to get reinforcements from Latin Europe. He faked his own death to slip past the Byzantines and sailed for Italy, leaving his nephew Tancred as regent.[12]

To muster funds and military support, he planned a tour of France. Before he left, he went to Rome to ask Paschal II to grant a privilege to San Nicola in Bari. Paschal not only granted the privilege but also offered his support for the French tour, giving Bohemond the papal banner and offering Bruno of Segni, as papal legate, thus legitimizing the tour as a bona fide part of the crusade.[13] Bohemond and Bruno of Segni also travelled with a pretender to the Byzantine throne, who probably convinced nobody but served to 'authenticate' Bohemond's claim to Antioch. He toured France, 'preaching' to large audiences and donating gifts of silks and relics from the treasury at Antioch to religious foundations.[14] In the course of his tour, he married Constance, the daughter of the king of France.[15] He used his wedding day to make a charismatic speech to recruit knights and financial patrons, from the pulpit of Chartres cathedral.[16] His rhetoric was effective, and he returned to Puglia in August 1106 with enough resources to launch an attack against the Byzantine Empire in September 1107.[17] However, rather than returning to Antioch, Bohemond launched his attack in the east coast of the Adriatic, aiming to push further into the Balkans. The Balkan attack seems to have been a second attempt to conquer the land he had invaded with his father in the 1080s, perhaps pointing to a renewed ambition to conquer more land from the Byzantine Empire rather than just to hold onto Antioch (although some scholars have seen Antioch as his primary focus).[18] The Balkan campaign was a disaster; Bohemond was defeated by Alexios at Devol in September 1108 and forced to sign a treaty that relegated him to a vassal of the emperor. He was forced to pledge to provide the emperor with military assistance and to appoint a Greek-rite patriarch of Antioch.[19] However, there are many question marks over the Treaty of Devol. The only evidence for its contents is Anna Comnena's summary in the *Alexiad*. Crucially, the treaty stipulated that Bohemond's claim to Antioch was for his lifetime only; he could not pass it onto his sons.[20]

Bohemond and Constance had two sons: John (*c*. 1107–*c*. 1123) and Bohemond II (*c*. 1108–1130). Bohemond II outlived his older brother and eventually inherited Antioch. Although he died in childhood, John was Bohemond's intended heir and he was given a typically Greek name. Paula Hailstone has speculated that Bohemond wanted his heir to have a Byzantine name to make him a more suitable ruler for the ex-Byzantine city of Antioch. Since John was probably born after the Treaty of Devol, this might indicate that Bohemond was planning to break the terms of the treaty and launch a new conquest of Antioch.[21]

Sources disagree on the date of Bohemond's death. Local and Western sources, including the chroniclers of Montecassino and Romuald of Salerno, are in agreement that he died in 1111, fourteen days after his half-brother Roger Borsa. But William of Tyre and Anna Comnena (both writing at some distance from the events) inexplicably date his death to 1109. Anitra Gadolin has explained the discrepancy with the idea that Bohemond died in 1109 and was buried two years later.[22] However, the local sources are probably most reliable and 1111 is generally accepted as his date of death.[23]

To sum up, as Guiscard's oldest son, Bohemond expected to inherit the Duchy of Apulia and rule over the whole of southern Italy and Sicily. Instead he was usurped by his half-brother and defeated in the Balkans, leaving him with only part of Apulia, where his power was limited by the powerful Lombard population. Unlike most crusaders, who seem to have been motivated by genuine piety, Bohemond's motivations were more earthly (at least partially). He may have had felt a genuine religious impetus to join the crusade, but taking Byzantine land was an also an alluring prospect, one that seems to have dominated his life.

The burial chapel

San Nicola would have been the obvious place for Bohemond to be buried, but the instability in the wake of Elias's death may have ruled it out. The other logical option was the Hauteville family buried church, the SS Trinità in Venosa, but the second generation of Hautevilles had moved away from their early centres of power in Melfi and Venosa and away from the French-inspired architecture of the SS. Trinità (Roger Borsa was buried in Salerno instead). Bohemond seems to have had no particular connection to Canosa in life, although in the eighteenth century, Angelo Andrea Tortora claimed that he was a patron of the cathedral, that he had donated two thorns from the crown of thorns and left a will expressing his desire to be buried in Canosa (there is no trace of the thorns or the will today and Tortora's claim may be spurious).[24]

The decision to bury Bohemond at Canosa was probably because of its link to the burial church of the Byzantine emperors in Constantinople.[25] As we saw in Chapter 4, the cathedral was built by St Sabinus in the sixth century, modelled on the contemporary Holy Apostles in Constantinople. From Constantine the Great until the early part of the eleventh century, the Byzantine emperors were buried in two mausolea attached to the church, originally built for Constantine and Justinian.[26] The cathedral had been dedicated to Saints Paul and John the Evangelist until 1102 (when it was re-dedicated to Sabinus), and the memory of the original dedication and the architectural model must still have been fresh in people's minds.

Bohemond was buried in a small apsed, domed chapel attached to the south transept of the cathedral (Figure 114). It is clad with sheets of preconnesian marble. Comparisons with pieces in situ have shown that the marble came from the ruined temple of Giove Toro nearby.[27] The exterior is decorated with blind arcades and

Figure 114 Bohemond's burial chapel. Photo: John McNeill.

Figure 115 Semi-capital on Bohemond's burial chapel. Photo: Author.

sculpted semi-capitals, which are composite-Corinthian with foliage below and a rosette above, some with masks and volutes (Figure 115). Stylistically they bear some similarity to Acceptus's work inside the cathedral, but the long faces and prominent ears are much more similar to the masks on the ambulatory capitals in the unfinished dynastic burial church in Venosa (*c.* 1070–1100). The treatment of the foliage on the semi-capitals, and on the drum, is similar to capitals at San Benedetto in Brindisi (*c.* 1100).[28] These comparisons help to confirm that the building does indeed date to around the time of Bohemond's death. The current dome was constructed in 1904. Early photographs show that the original exterior of the dome was polygonal, rather than round, and there is evidence that it had once been gilded (like Constantine's mausoleum) (Figures 116 and 117).[29]

Today the interior has been whitewashed (Figures 118, 119 and 120), but it was originally lavishly decorated. A sixteenth-century description by Giovanni Battista Casati tells us that the interior was also clad in marble and some of it survives on the arches. Casati also reported that the chapel contained an altar, made of five pieces of marble and a marble tomb, which had been smashed to pieces.[30] Pratilli related that Bohemond's original tomb was a marble 'urn', raised about a metre off the ground.[31] The marble tomb was either an antique sarcophagus or an arcosolium, like most contemporary tombs, including that of Bohemond's mother Alberada at Venosa. Today, there is a tomb slab embedded in the floor of the chapel, inscribed simply *Boamundus*. Bohemond's bones were moved into the current grave in the floor in the nineteenth century, and it was described by the Inspector of Excavations and Antique Monuments, Vito Fontana in 1878, who reported that only two bones remained, which were sometimes shown to visitors, a practice which Fontana considered distasteful.[32]

An earlier description, from 1643, relates that the chapel had 'pictures in mosaic on the inside'.[33] 'Pictures' implies that the mosaics were figurative. The reference to mosaics

Figure 116 Early photograph of Bohemond's burial chapel. Late nineteenth century? Source unknown.

Figure 117 Engraving of Bohemond's burial chapel. Drawn by Louis-Jean Desprez, engraved by Berthault, published in Jean-Claude Richard de Saint-Non's, *Voyage Pittoresque ou Description des Royaumes de Naples et de Sicile*, volume 3.

Crusader Architecture 163

Figure 118 Interior, Bohemond's burial chapel. Photo: Author.

Figure 119 Interior of the dome, Bohemond's burial chapel. Photo: Author.

Figure 120 Interior of the apse, Bohemond's burial chapel. Photo: Author.

is repeated by Tortora, who implies that they were concentrated in the dome which, together with Casati's description, perhaps means that the walls were clad in marble, while the drum and dome (and probably the apse) were decorated with figurative mosaics.[34] The Byzantine convention would be to depict Christ as Pantocrator in the dome and the Theotokos in the apse. The presence of mosaics shows how lavish the building was originally. Figurative mosaics with a gold ground were expensive and specialist. The only other instance of mosaics in Apulia at this time was the small band of pseudo-Arabic in the San Nicola sanctuary pavement, and there were no other figurative mosaics in Apulia. Mosaicists must have been brought from further afield, possibly from the Montecassino-Salerno workshop; from Rome; from San Marco in Venice; or from Byzantium. As we shall see here there is reason to believe they may have come from Constantinople, although the other options are all possibilities.

Patronage

It is my contention that the patron of Bohemond's funerary chapel was his widow Constance.[35] One of the roles of an elite medieval widow was to memorialize her late husband, often for political reasons, and a good way to do that was through his tomb.[36] Bohemond's sons were still children (both under five when he died), so Constance acted as regent. One of the defining characteristics of Norman Italy was the preponderance of regencies. Constance of France, Adela of Flanders, Bertha of Loritello, Adelaide del Vasto and Margaret of Navarre all governed in place of their infant sons.[37] Sichelgaita of Salerno seems to have been almost a co-ruler with both her husband and her son, and she commanded troops independently.[38] In this section I want to argue for Constance as patron of the funerary chapel, but also to contextualize her patronage, demonstrating that she was far from exceptional.

Constance was the daughter of King Philip I of France (d. 1108). Her mother, Bertha of Holland, was repudiated by her father, just like Bohemond's mother Alberada of Buonalbergo. Constance married Count Hugh of Troyes and Champagne, from the house of Blois, in the early 1090s. Her sister-in-law was the formidable Adela of Blois, who gave her second son Thibaut to be brought up in Constance and Hugh's household as Hugh's heir. Adela was educated, wealthy in her own right and acted as regent when her husband was away for long periods. When Constance's marriage to Hugh was annulled in 1104, she resided at Adela's court.[39] When Constance married Bohemond in 1106, the wedding celebrations were hosted (and paid for) by Adela.[40] Adela seems to have had a great influence on Constance and could have been a role model, particularly during Constance's time as regent.

The inheritance of Constance's infant son was delicate in both Apulia and Antioch. The Apulian territories centred around Bari which, as we saw in Chapter 10, was unstable after the death of Archbishop Elias. At the point of Bohemond's death, Bari had been without an archbishop for six years and Bohemond's death destabilized it further: in the year following his death Archbishop Riso was appointed, Constance was exiled and the city adopted a communal government. The inheritance in the east was no easier. When he departed from Antioch in 1104, Bohemond had left his nephew Tancred as regent. The Treaty of Devol stipulated that Antioch would revert to the empire on Bohemond's death and that his son would receive another, unspecified, duchy from the emperor in recompense. But Tancred refused to return Antioch to the emperor and continued to rule independently after Bohemond's death.[41] Tancred died in 1112, and his nephew, Roger of Salerno, became the regent. Roger of Salerno would die in 1119, and the regency would pass to Baldwin II of Jerusalem until Bohemond II arrived to claim his inheritance in 1126, aged about eighteen (Constance died before this, in 1125).[42] But in 1111 when Bohemond died, it was not easy to see how his son would be able to rule Antioch successfully. Tancred was ambitious, and his relationship with his uncle Bohemond had been close but sometimes fractious. He sometimes defied Bohemond's orders, and, when Bohemond was captured by Gümüshtigin Gazi, Tancred waited three years to pay the ransom.[43] Therefore, at the point of Bohemond's death in 1111, his son John's inheritance was uncertain for two reasons. First, because the Treaty of Devol stated that he should receive a new duchy from the emperor as his vassal, but it was not clear which duchy or whether Alexios would even honour the agreement. Second, holding onto Antioch independently was preferable to receiving a hypothetical duchy as an imperial vassal, but Tancred was ruling Antioch and it is not clear whether he would step aside for John. Although Bohemond II did eventually claim Antioch successfully, that succession must have seemed very uncertain to Constance in the years immediately following Bohemond's death.

Léon-Robert Ménager, a usually meticulous and reliable historian, wrote about Constance's entry in the *Dizionario Biografico degli Italiani*, in which he claims that Constance went to Constantinople after Bohemond's death. He cites and quotes a document written or dictated by her in December 1112 in Constantinople and speculates that she may have gone there to ask for the emperor's help in securing the lands belonging to her son, although she must have been unsuccessful.[44] But Ménager does not give a source for this mysterious document, and I have not been able to find it. Without a source, naturally we should not draw conclusions about its veracity, but it is intriguing. Attempting to form an alliance with the Byzantine emperor would have been a surprising decision but potentially a very shrewd one. The Byzantines wanted to oust Tancred from Antioch and so did Constance. She may have attempted to persuade Alexios to send troops to oust Tancred or, if that failed, convince him to keep his promise and give her the promised alternative duchy. Either way, she was unsuccessful, if she was there at all. Ménager's suggestion also raises the possibility that Constance's trip to Constantinople may have provided artistic inspiration. She would have seen the Holy Apostles, the prototype for Canosa cathedral, and she would have been able to hire a workshop of mosaicists to decorate Bohemond's burial chapel.

Whether she went to Constantinople or not, in 1113 Constance was in Italy and the Baresi expelled her from their city, making Archbishop Riso their leader instead. Bari may have slipped from Constance's grasp, but she retained Canosa. A document from 1113 recounts that Constance had taken control of Canosa cathedral and was refusing to return it to Archbishop Riso. Eventually Pope Paschal II had to intervene and force Constance to allow the archbishop back into his own cathedral. The editor of the *Codice Diplomatico Barese*, Nitti di Vito, argued that the document might be false, but other scholars have accepted it as genuine.[45] Nitti di Vito thought that the document had been forged as part of a later claim that the cathedral should be under royal, rather than episcopal, authority. But Paschal II's intervention actually confirms episcopal oversight, so the forgery would have been counterproductive. The story is so extraordinary that it might just be true. In 1113, construction of Bohemond's tomb must have been underway, and the document is the best piece of evidence that Constance was the patron. The conflict with Riso might indicate that he was against the construction of the tomb, but Constance took control of the cathedral to build it anyway.

Not only was Constance in conflict with Archbishop Riso at this point, she was also challenged by the Counts of Conversano, distant cousins of Bohemond's, whose territory included Brindisi and was sandwiched between Constance's northern territories around Bari and Canosa and her southern territories in Taranto and the Salento. In 1116, Constance was kidnapped and imprisoned in Matera by Alexander of Conversano. When he eventually released her, she returned with 200 knights to ransack his lands.[46] She may have been back in Bari in 1117; at least she was on friendlier terms with Riso, because she made a donation to him.[47] This new alliance would be deadly for Riso, who was murdered soon after for being too close to Constance. In 1119 she was imprisoned again, this time by Grimoald Alferanites, self-declared prince of Bari, who released her only when Pope Calixtus II intervened, probably on the condition that she and her sons gave up all claim to Bari.[48]

Although ultimately she lost Bari, Constance succeeded in keeping hold of Bohemond's other territories, including Canosa. Like most widows, she preserved her authority partly by keeping her husband's memory alive by referring to him in the documents issued in her name. But she also asserted her own identity by referring frequently to her royal bloodline. While she was married to Hugh of Troyes, she had identified herself in charters as 'Constance, daughter of the King of France', as a way of boosting her husband's status.[49] After Bohemond's death, she began using the same phrase on documents in southern Italy. In two charters from San Lorenzo in Aversa in 1115, Constance identifies herself in the following way, 'I am Constance, daughter of King Philip of France and once the wife of Bohemond, the great and immortal prince of Antioch'.[50] It is interesting that her royal blood comes first and that she is 'once' the wife of Bohemond, even though he is 'immortal' because her authority to act independently comes from her widowed status. In her 1117 donation to Riso, she is the wife of 'Bohemond the invincible prince of Antioch.....acting with full authority and in place of my son who is still a boy'.[51] As we shall see in Chapter 13, this heroic memorialization of Bohemond as immortal and invincible is very similar to the inscriptions on the burial chapel, further evidence that it was Constance who was in charge of the construction of the chapel.

Did Constance have the money to build such an opulent tomb for her husband? There is conflicting evidence about Bohemond's resources at the end of his life. On the one hand he seems to have been impoverished after his defeat at Devol, his army were left unpaid and some of them may have been stranded in the Balkans.[52] He did not launch any more military campaigns after 1106, and Orderic Vitalis gives the impression that his resources were severely depleted.[53] On the other hand, William of Tyre (admittedly writing quite some time later) claimed that Bohemond was raising an army to return to the east when he died and Albert of Aachen reports that Alexios cemented the Treaty of Devol by giving Bohemond a huge quantity of gold, silver and purple silk, although it seems unlikely that Alexios would lavish gifts on a long-standing enemy and Albert may have been trying to lessen Bohemond's humiliation.[54] Even a cursory glance at Bohemond's biography tells us that, if Alexios did give him gold, silver and silks, Bohemond would have no hesitation in using that wealth to fund another attack on Alexios.

Even though they lost Bari, Constance and her sons inherited plenty of land in Apulia and perhaps that was enough to fund the construction of the chapel, but it is also possible that she had some financial help. One possible source of money is the French royal family. Nicholas Paul has written about how Bohemond's public image was constructed and manipulated by Constance's Capetian family, and that, after his death, the Capetians continued to concern themselves with Bohemond's image. They used written texts to create a lasting legacy for him. Their alliance with Bohemond was a crucial part of their involvement in the first crusade, and it was in their interests to keep promoting him as a hero. Constance might have asked her brother for money to build the chapel, but if Louis VI was not interested in preventing his sister from being imprisoned twice, it seems unlikely that he funded a chapel in a place so far from Paris.

A more likely source of money is Duke William, son and successor to Roger Borsa. Duke William was wealthy and is known to have been a weak leader. He had no children and Francesca Petrizzo has posited that he nominated his cousin Bohemond II – his closest male relative – as his heir.[55] Constance and Duke William had certainly formed some kind of alliance because in 1120 they besieged a castle together.[56] When Constance escaped from imprisonment by Alexander of Conversano and returned to take her revenge with 200 knights, I suspect that Duke William provided the knights. In 1118 Duke William gave some land to the Canosa cathedral so that the clergy would pray for his soul as well as the soul of his uncle Bohemond, who was already buried there. It seems likely that this donation was the final instalment in Duke William's financial support for the construction of the chapel.[57] Michele Cilla has argued the Duke William was the sole patron of the burial chapel, on the basis of the 1118 donation, but I hope I have shown that it was Constance who is much more likely to have instigated and managed the project, even if Duke William provided some or all of the funding.

Although neither Bohemond nor Roger Borsa was buried in their dynastic burial church of the SS. Trinità in Venosa, the Hautevilles continued to patronize the monastery at least up until the death of Roger Borsa.[58] It was probably funds from Robert Guiscard and Roger Borsa that helped to rebuild the abbey church in the French style, a project that was never finished.[59] As we saw earlier in this chapter, the sculpture on Bohemond's burial chapel is very similar to the capitals in the unfinished church at Venosa. As we shall see in the next chapter, the artist who made the bronze doors came from the region of Melfi and Venosa and was probably trained in metalworking at Venosa. These two links to Venosa demonstrate that Constance, in collaboration with Duke William, was looking towards Venosa, as the nexus of early Hauteville power, for inspiration and artists. The monastery's close connections and loyalty to the Hauteville family probably made it easy for Constance to form relationships with artists in Venosa and Melfi. There is one other link between Venosa and the chapel at Canosa. In the nave of the SS. Trinità is the tomb of Bohemond's mother, Alberada of Buonalbergo, who died *c*. 1122 (Figure 121). The tomb, which takes the form of an arcosolium, is inscribed 'Guiscard's wife Alberada is buried in this tomb. If you are looking for her son, he is in Canosa'.[60] The tomb has been linked to sculptors from Rome working in the 1120s; however, inscription is unusual and the tomb, which has gone through several restorations and alterations, may not even be medieval.[61] What is striking about it is the quantity of marble used to make it, including a large sheet of marble behind it, which is structurally unnecessary and therefore a great statement of lavishness. Alberada's marriage to Guiscard had ended long before her death, and it is puzzling that she would be given such a lavish burial. The large quantity of marble could be explained by dating the tomb to a much later period when marble was more plentiful. The monks of Venosa had reason, later on in the Middle Ages and early modern period, to try to emphasize or exaggerate their links to the Hauteville royal family, and Alberada's tomb could have been part of later manipulations of Hauteville memory.[62] However, leaving suspicions about date aside for a moment, the marble very similar to

Figure 121 Tomb of Alberada of Buonalbergo, SS Trinità di Venosa. Photo: Author.

the cladding of Bohemond's burial chapel, where we see large sheets of proconnesian marble of similar colour and pattern in the stone. If Alberada's tomb is medieval, and Alberada died in the 1120s soon after the burial chapel was complete, it may have been Constance who commissioned the tomb for her mother-in-law. Constance might have used the 'left over' marble from her husband's chapel to create a tomb in Venosa that not only pointed pilgrims to Canosa but also emphasized Bohemond's Hauteville lineage and therefore strengthened her son's claim to land in Apulia. If Duke William had nominated Bohemond II as his heir, it may have served both him and Constance to stress Bohemond II's lineage.

Since the women of Norman Italy have been so frequently neglected by scholars, I would like to contextualize Constance's patronage with a comparative discussion of her sister-in-law, Adela of Flanders. Adela outlived her husband Roger Borsa and acted as regent for her son Duke William until 1114, so she and Constance were regents at the same time.[63] There is no evidence that Constance's alliance with William started before his majority but, if – as seems very likely – Constance was already building the chapel in 1113 when she locked Riso out of the cathedral, she probably already had financial help and that financial help probably came from Adela. Adela may have been both a financial supporter and a role model for Constance, particularly in how she protected her son's inheritance. Adela had been queen of Denmark before she arrived in southern Italy. Her first husband was Cnut IV, who died in 1086. In 1092 she married Roger Borsa and boosted his status by bringing royalty into the Hauteville family (even if she was a former queen and only by marriage).[64] Cnut was canonized in 1100 by Paschal II, and Elisabeth van Houts has argued that it was Adela who persuaded him to approve the canonization, probably to increase the chances of her son Charles becoming king. She sent money and gifts to the shrine in Denmark.[65] She may have used a similar strategy in a less successful attempt to promote her second husband. Van Houts suggested that Adela commissioned William of Apulia to write the *Gesta Roberti Wiscardi* in praise of Guiscard, as propaganda to persuade Paschal II to give Roger Borsa a crown.[66] Commissioning texts was an important way that women exercised political influence in southern Italy. Matilda of Hauteville, sister of Roger II, commissioned Alexander of Telese's *Gesta Rogerii*, and Sichelgaita of Salerno commissioned, may even have been a co-author of, Amatus of Montecassino's chronicle.[67] Constance's decision to build a lavish tomb for Bohemond and commission inscriptions to decorate it, as a way to sure up her son's inheritance, may have been inspired by or even done in collaboration with Adela. It is reasonable to conclude that Constance and Adela formed an alliance while they were both regents (in the period 1111–1114) and that Constance continued the alliance with Duke William, once he began to rule independently.

Another, more distant, role model may have been Adelaide del Vasto, another regent and contemporary of Constance and Adela. Adelaide governed Sicily during the infancy of her son Roger II, until 1112, then became queen of Jerusalem by making an ambitious and strategic second marriage to Baldwin I (even though the marriage was annulled in 1117 and Adelaide returned to Sicily).[68] Adelaide's regency was successful despite the same kind of resistance and rebellions faced by Constance.

It is plausible and probable that Constance commissioned Bohemond's burial chapel and managed the project as part of a strategy to strengthen her position as regent and secure her son's inheritance. Immediately after Bohemond's death, she may have formed an alliance with Adela of Flanders to secure funding to build the chapel. She may have gone to Constantinople to attempt, unsuccessfully, to form another alliance with the Byzantine emperor. When she returned, she evicted the troublesome archbishop from the cathedral so that she could continue her project. In all this she may have been helped by her mother-in-law, Alberada di Buonalbergo, and when Alberada died, it may have been convenient for Constance to commission a tomb for Alberada in Venosa to solidify intergenerational connections to the early Hautevilles. I shall end this discussion of Constance's patronage with a tantalizing snippet of information from the eighteenth century. Tortora reported a description by an Abbot called Damadeno, who claimed there were two royal tombs on the south side of the cathedral: Bohemond's chapel and another adjacent to it.[69] This second tomb may have been at the other end of the loggia that was half demolished to make way for the eighteenth-century chapels. Marisa Petraglia and Pina Belli D'Elia have speculated that the second could have been Constance's own tomb.[70] The other possibility is that it may have been the tomb of Constance and Bohemond's son John, who died c. 1123, aged around sixteen. The construction of her son's tomb may have been Constance's final project before she died herself c. 1125.

Jerusalem in Apulia?

Having established that Bohemond's burial chapel was a richly decorated monument built by his widow, I want to turn my attention to the architecture and consider why it takes the form of a small domed building attached to a church, rather than a memorial inside the church. This kind of burial in a freestanding monument was highly unusual in this era, when the vast majority of elite burials in both Byzantium and the west took the form of arcosolia.[71] The building is usually described as a 'mausoleum', particularly in the Italian scholarship, which is misleading. Mausolea in the sense of independent centrally-planned commemorative structures, as employed by the Romans, had completely died out in the Christian world by the eleventh century, although they were very common in the Islamic world. The apse and altar in the building at Canosa mean that it is emphatically better described as a chapel.

Bohemond's chapel is attached to the south transept of the cathedral, which is unusual, but not unprecedented. In Slobodan Ćurčić's categorization of Byzantine subsidiary chapels, it would be described as a 'single satellite' chapel, comparable to the church of Bogorodica Eleousain in Veljusain in Macedonia (c. 1080), also a square, domed building with an apse to the east and an entrance to the south. Such subsidiary chapels were often used for funerary purposes, for example the two eastern chapels at Yilanca Bayir and the pair of chapels that flank the narthex of the Lavra monastery on Mount Athos (built after 961).[72] Comparable examples of subsidiary chapels are all Byzantine, which immediately places the chapel in the cultural orbit of the empire.

The models for Bohemond's chapel have been much debated and several possibilities have been proposed. It has been suggested that the building was designed by a Pisan architect, but beyond the generic blind arcading, the similarities seem arbitrary.[73] Under the label 'mausoleum', it has been associated with Islamic and classical prototypes. On the outskirts of Canosa are the ruins of a group of Roman mausolea which have been proposed as the inspiration.[74] No doubt the Roman monuments loomed large in the imaginations and civic pride of the people of Canosa but, other than being pavilions, they bear no resemblance to the chapel. Similarities with Islamic *quba* have also been explored, but they are vague and Bohemond's chapel is intrinsically a Christian building.[75] The suggestion that the chapel was originally open on three sides like an Islamic canopy tomb, and only enclosed later, is a bit far-fetched and not borne out by the architecture.[76] Timo Kirschberger's interpretation of the Canosa chapel is that it must be a reflection of Bohemond's links to Antioch, perhaps modelled on a building in Antioch.[77] Maria Callò Mariani and Antonio Cadei have gone further, suggesting that the monument was built by Arab artists who were brought from Antioch.[78] Although that would certainly have been a desirable way for Constance to strengthen ties to Antioch, it is not clear how much contact she had with Tancred and subsequently Roger of Salerno, and it seems unlikely that either of them would have cooperated with the project that drew attention to Bohemond II's claim to Antioch, thus weakening their own authority.

We have virtually no information about art and architecture in Antioch, which makes it difficult to assess the potential connections with Canosa. The city that Bohemond conquered no longer exists, and even excavations have revealed very little about its medieval fabric. The cathedral, famously founded and built by its first bishop St Peter, had a first class apostolic pedigree. In the Middle Ages it was believed that Peter had laid the foundations himself. By the time the crusaders arrived St Peter's original church, extensively rebuilt by Justinian, had become a crypt, with a new church built on top (coincidentally, like the cathedral of Bari).[79] The new church had been commissioned by the Byzantine emperor, John I, in the late tenth century and was modelled on Hagia Sophia in Constantinople.[80] Tancred was buried in the porch in 1112.[81] For the southern Italian Normans, the urban fabric of the city must have been impressive, especially the cathedral. The most impressive cities in mainland southern Italy – Bari, Benevento, Salerno – were affluent and historic, but they did not have the pedigree or scale of Antioch. So, while there may have been a chapel in Antioch that served as a prototype for the one in Canosa, the complete lack of evidence makes it impossible to discuss, even very speculatively.

Much more fruitful and specific are the comparisons with the Holy Sepulchre.[82] Some historians have seen Bohemond's recruiting rhetoric, both in 1096 and in 1106, as having a particular emphasis on the Holy Sepulchre as the focus of the crusade, even though he had very little involvement in its 'liberation'.[83] The first king of Jerusalem, fellow crusader, Godfrey of Boullion, was buried in the *triporticus* of the Holy Sepulchre in 1100, so there was a precedent for crusaders being associated with the sepulchre in death. The Canosa chapel is sometimes compared to the Anastasis rotunda, but the aedicule is a much more likely model. To assess the likelihood, we need to understand what the aedicule looked like in 1111 when Bohemond died. The church had been severely damaged by the Fatimids in 1009 but was restored by Byzantine emperor Constantine IX Monomachos, in the 1040s.[84] The aedicule, as described by Abbot Daniel of Kyiv in *c.* 1106, was covered in marble, surrounded by twelve columns and surmounted by a canopy that was gilded in silver (Figure 122).[85] This basic description tallies with the burial chapel, which is a similar pavilion, covered in marble, surmounted by a gilded dome, decorated with mosaics and with twelve

Figure 122 Hypothetical reconstruction of the aedicule as it may have been in *c.* 1100, Holy Sepulchre, Jerusalem. Drawing: Jelena Bogdanovic, after Martin Biddle.

pilasters on the exterior. The Latin rulers of Jerusalem later extensively rebuilt and restored the church of the Holy Sepulchre, but at the time of Bohemond's death, the aedicule looked a lot like the chapel in Canosa.[86]

A small liturgical object provides further evidence for the similarities between the burial chapel and the aedicule. It is an *artophorion* (a container for the Eucharist), made in Antioch in the tenth century, in the form of the aedicule: a cube, with an ornate door, an apse with arcading, a circular drum with alternating windows and blind arches and a dome (Figure 123). Inscriptions from the psalms associate the container with the heavenly Jerusalem.[87] The similarities to the chapel in Canosa are striking, especially in the basic structure.[88] Today it is in Aachen, but we do not know how it got there. It is possible that Bohemond took the artophorion with him from Antioch to Europe to give as a gift on his tour of France.

Of all the holy sites of Jerusalem, the burial chapel seems to be closest to the aedicule, but it is quite possible that it was a conflation of the aedicule and the Dome of the Rock.

Just as medieval architectural imitations are not exact copies of their prototypes, the prototypes themselves were perhaps not always clear or 'pure'.[89] The marble-clad, polygonal structure with blind arcading, interior mosaics and an octagonal drum surmounted by a metal-covered dome shares most of its features with the Dome of the Rock (Figure 124). Before the Dome of the Rock was adorned with ceramic tiles in the sixteenth century, the similarities would have been more immediately obvious. As

Figure 123 The Antioch artophorion, Aachen cathedral. Photo: Aachen cathedral treasury.

Figure 124 Dome of the Rock, Jerusalem. Photo: Andrew Shiva via Wikimedia.

we saw in Chapter 6, the Temple Mount and the Holy Sepulchre were almost equally important in the religious and political topography of Jerusalem.

Other imitations of the Holy Sepulchre help us to understand how the burial chapel might have been understood and used. Through the eleventh century, as pilgrimage to Jerusalem increased, so did imitations of the sepulchre in the west. It was often pilgrims returning from the Holy Land who instigated those copies. For example Fulk III of Anjou at Beaulieu-les-Loches; Bishop Leitbert at Cambrai; Odilo of Morhlon at Villeneuve D'Aveyron and Bishop Conrad at St Maurice's rotunda at Konstanz.[90] Fulk III of Anjou was buried at Beaulieu in a pavilion-like structure with a polygonal dome set in the cloister. The tomb was destroyed in the French Revolution, but an early modern drawing shows that it could have been modelled on the aedicule.[91] The early-eleventh-century tradition of building sepulchral churches, particularly in France, only grew once the crusade was underway. Some of Bohemond's fellow crusaders built sepulchral churches when they returned home: the octagonal baptistery of San Pietro in Consavia was originally an anastasis rotunda built by Bishop Landulf on his return from the Holy Land. The same is true of the St Sepulchre in Northampton, built by Simon of Senlis.[92]

The Byzantines also built imitations of the Holy Sepulchre. Most relevant of all examples is Constantine's mausoleum, which was attached to the Holy Apostles. Bohemond's life seems to have been dominated by his repeated audacious attempts to conquer land from the Byzantine Empire. Canosa cathedral was Bohemond's very own Holy Apostles, if his tomb was modelled on Constantine's, it would have created a triangular relationship between Canosa, Constantinople and Jerusalem, which was just as audacious as Bohemond himself and would have no doubt been pleasing to him.

Also in Constantinople, the Theotokos of Pharos, the personal church of the Byzantine emperors, housed the Passion relics and was thus connected to the death and burial of Christ. A visit to the Pharos was considered an adequate substitute for the Holy Sepulchre.[93] The Pharos is the church alluded to in Mesardonites' inscription commemorating the fortification of the Byzantine governor's palace in Bari and so its reputation was known in southern Italy, as it was throughout Europe because of the collection of Passion relics.[94] Among other relics, the Pharos held a piece of the rock from Christ's empty tomb slab, which was venerated at Easter.[95] A number of western pilgrims also took pieces of the tomb slab home with them. Among them Lancelin of Beauvais who built Saint-Sépulchre of Villers in 1060 and deposited his piece of the rock in it.[96] Fulk III of Anjou even bit off a piece of the sepulchre with his teeth, as if the rock itself were Eucharistic.[97] When Bohemond visited Jerusalem in 1099, he may have taken a piece of the Holy Sepulchre back to Antioch with him, and it is possible that the burial chapel included a similar contact relic. If Tortora's claim, that Bohemond donated thorns from the crown of thorns to Canosa cathedral, is correct. It may be that the burial chapel contained a small collection of Passion relics, just like the Pharos. The architectural models and cultural associations in Bohemond's burial chapel all seem to allude to a triangular relationship between Canosa, Constantinople and Jerusalem, which presents Bohemond as both an ideal crusader and, in some sense, a threat or heir to the Byzantine emperors. As we shall see in the next chapter, these associations continued in the inscriptions on the chapel.

Visiting the Pharos was considered to be a substitute for visiting Jerusalem, and Holy Sepulchre imitations in the west sometimes attracted pilgrims. Did Canosa begin to attract pilgrims to visit the sepulchre imitation? In Milan a church was constructed in 1030 dedicated to the Trinity, with a replica of Christ's tomb in the crypt. In 1100, following the crusader victory, it was re-dedicated to the Holy Sepulchre and the archbishop of Milan granted to any penitent who could not travel to Jerusalem one third of the indulgences bestowed on those who made the journey to the Holy Land. There was a similar arrangement at the Abbey of Neufmoustier in Flanders, founded by Peter the Hermit. At Palera in Catalonia, pilgrims were even granted the same indulgences as those who went all the way to Jerusalem.[98] Although there is no evidence for pilgrimage to Canosa, beyond local veneration of St Sabinus, it is entirely possible that Bohemond's lavish tomb did attract pilgrims and travellers. Like San Nicola, it would have been an intermediate stop on a longer journey, rather than a destination in its own right. Those travelling along the *via traiana* from Rome and Benevento to the new shrine of St Nicholas in Bari passed through Canosa on their way. Those travelling along the *via appia*, intending to embark for the east from the port at Brindisi or Taranto, could perhaps have been persuaded to take the *via traiana* instead, in order to see not only San Nicola di Bari but also the tomb of the heroic Bohemond. Perhaps some of the pilgrims to Monte Sant'Angelo were also re-rerouted to Canosa (possibly encouraged to do so when they visited Bohemond's foundation of San Leonardo at Siponto).

The possibility that the chapel attracted pilgrims is interesting in light of the nineteenth-century practice of showing Bohemond's remaining bones to visitors, as if they were relics. In 1738, Giacinto Giannuzzi recorded that it was common practice for visitors to chip off small pieces of marble from Bohemond's tomb to take away with them, just as Fulk and Lancelin of Beauvais had taken away pieces of the rock from the Holy Sepulchre. Indeed the exterior of the chapel is extensively chipped. Marisa Petraglia has speculated that the chapel was fenced off to make it inaccessible for most of the early modern period, to protect it, not only from thieves, but also from the veneration of the faithful, who wanted to take a piece of it as a souvenir.[99]

Holy Sepulchre imitations were used for liturgical and para-liturgical rituals. In some places the conquest of Jerusalem was celebrated liturgically on the 15th of July and feast days were inaugurated in certain places in response to the influx of Passion relics into the west.[100] The earliest copy of the *Gesta Francorum* had, as an appendix, a votive mass for the veneration of the Holy Sepulchre and a record of its dimensions. New hymns were composed evoking the events and emotions of the crusade; such hymns were probably used in the liturgy and in processions.[101] Sepulchres were also used in Easter liturgies and in the Easter re-enactment of the visitation of the women at the tomb (known as the *Visitatio sepulchri* or sometimes *Quem quearitis?* after the opening question when the angel asks the three Marys, 'whom do you seek?').[102] At Aquileia part of the Easter liturgy was to place a cross and a consecrated host inside the replica of the aedicule.[103] The complex of Santo Stefano in Bologna was modelled on the Holy Sepulchre and was part of a wider network of sites in Bologna that echoed Jerusalem. In Holy Week and Easter that sacred topography became the setting for several ritual re-enactments.[104] As a sepulchre imitation, the burial chapel in Canosa must also have been part of the Easter celebrations and possibly part of a commemoration of the conquest of Jerusalem. I cannot find any evidence that the conquest of Antioch was commemorated liturgically, and it would, of course, have far less religious significance, but it is a possibility.

The burial chapel is adjacent to a loggia, accessed through a door in the south transept of the cathedral. Inside the south transept, is a wall painting of the crucifixion, only recently discovered and in poor condition (Figures 125 and 126). The painting dates to the late twelfth century, although it is based on eleventh-century models from Campania.[105] The wall paintings, the two lancet windows in the south wall of the transept and the door that leads out to the burial chapel and the loggia were probably all made at the same time.[106] This project altered the relationship between the cathedral and the chapel. Originally, although the chapel was attached to the cathedral, it was effectively completely independent, only accessible from outside (we do not know what kind of space it stood in, whether it was on the street, in a piazza or more enclosed, in some kind of courtyard). But the alterations strengthened the relationship between the cathedral and the chapel. Although it was still accessible only by going outside, the door in the south transept created a (processional?) route from cathedral to tomb. The addition of the crucifixion scene probably reflected the way the chapel was already used during Holy Week and Easter. There were probably processions, re-enactments or stational devotions that took the faithful from the nave, through the transept where the crucifixion was marked, out to the 'aedicule' where the resurrection was celebrated.

Figure 125 Wall painting of the crucifixion in the south transept, Canosa cathedral. Photo: John McNeill.

Figure 126 Wall painting of the crucifixion, detail, south transept, Canosa cathedral. Photo: John McNeill.

The late-twelfth-century embellishments are roughly contemporary with some other relevant changes: the image of Bohemond with St Leonard that was carved on the portal of his foundation San Leonardo in Siponto; alterations to the tomb of Roger I in Mileto and the increased emphasis on the Hauteville tombs at Venosa.[107] Hauteville rule was waning and came to an end in 1189 with the death of King William II. The decline of Hauteville rule coincided with an increased memorialization of the early Hautevilles, including Bohemond, an attempt to draw on dynastic legacy at a time of uncertainty. The alterations are very roughly contemporary with the third crusade (1189–92), the attempt to recapture the Holy Land from the Ayyubids. The memory of Bohemond's success may have seemed all the more pertinent and heroic in the context to the third crusade.

Constance chose to bury Bohemond at Canosa cathedral, Apulia's imitation of the Holy Apostles in Constantinople, in a satellite chapel attached to the cathedral transept. The chapel itself is an imitation of the aedicule that stands over Christ's empty tomb. The chapel therefore has two interdependent prototypes: the tomb of Christ and the tomb of Constantine the Great, which was itself an imitation of the tomb of Christ. This amalgamation of two related models is an articulation of Bohemond's crusading tactics and rhetoric, which combined the desire to recapture the Holy Sepulchre with the desire to expand Norman power into the Byzantine Empire. As we shall see in Chapter 13, the inscriptions on the mausoleum reinforce those ideas.

12

Made in Italy

Innovations in bronze

At the entrance to the chapel stand a pair of bronze doors (Figures 127, 128, 129).[1] At first glance, they are unimpressive and poorly designed. They are cracked, strangely asymmetrical, the inscriptions are hard to decipher and some of the decoration has been lost. They are easy to overlook, but their importance cannot be overstated because they are crucial to the development of bronze work in southern Italy. In this chapter I will discuss their place in the history of medieval bronze doors, how they were made and what we can deduce about the artist, Roger the bell maker of Melfi. I will propose a re-construction of the original design of the doors and discuss how they relate to the chapel as an imitation of Christ's empty tomb.

Bronze and bronze doors in southern Italy

The Romans made monumental bronze doors using the technique of lost wax casting, for example those at the Pantheon or those that stood at the entrance to the Senate and were re-installed at the Lateran Basilica in the seventeenth century. These antique examples were emulated by Charlemagne, who commissioned doors cast in lost wax for his palace chapel at Aachen, as part of a general flourishing of bronze casting in the Carolingian Empire.[2]

The aedicule of the Holy Sepulchre probably had bronze doors in late antiquity, although we do not know if they were still there in the early twelfth century.[3] The Munich and Trivulzio ivories (both *c*. 400) show the doors of the aedicule as having figurative panels and lion door knockers. The early Christian lion door knockers would have been very similar to the late Roman examples now on display in the Museum of the Order of St John in London, which came from the Holy Sepulchre or its vicinity and were reused in the first hospital of the order in Jerusalem *c*. 1080.[4] The Antioch artophorion has ogee-shaped doors decorated with four crosses and may be more faithful to the appearance of the aedicule in the central Middle Ages. Some have speculated that the Aachen doors were intended to imitate those at that Holy Sepulchre.[5] The addition of bronze doors to Bohemond's chapel was therefore very much in keeping with its status as a 'copy' of Christ's empty tomb.

Figure 127 Doors to Bohemond's burial chapel. Photo: John McNeill.

In the eleventh century, there was a trend for importing bronze doors from Constantinople to Italy. In the early 1060s Pantaleone of Amalfi commissioned a pair of doors for Amalfi cathedral from a workshop in the Byzantine capital. A few years later, they caught the attention of Desiderius of Montecassino, who commissioned a pair for his own abbey church. There followed doors for San Paolo fuori le Mura in Rome (1070), the sanctuary of Monte Sant'Angelo in northern Apulia (1076), the cathedral of Salerno (c. 1085?), San Salvatore in Atrani (1087) and San Marco in Venice (which had two sets, c. 1080 and c. 1112).[6] These Italo-Byzantine doors were created through a fascinating collaboration between Italian patrons and the Byzantine artists. They are made from sheets of brass, wrapped around wooden panels and decorated using the Byzantine technique of *agemina*, whereby the designs were incised into the metal and then filled with thin strips of silver or other coloured materials. The iconography is mostly in keeping with contemporary Byzantine images, while the inscriptions are in Latin (presumably written by the Italian patrons and sent to the manufacturers Constantinople). Those at Amalfi, Montecassino, Rome and Monte Sant'Angelo were commissioned through the Comite Maurone family, merchants from Amalfi, who acted as middlemen between the Italian clergy and the Byzantine artists.[7] These doors began to be imported just after the Norman conquest, at a time when southern Italian merchants may have been anxious about economic disruption and

Figure 128 Doors to Bohemond's burial chapel. Drawing: Schulz, *Denkmäler*, plate 10.

keen to preserve trading connections with Constantinople.[8] As we saw in Chapter 5, the Norman conquest may have disrupted trade and bronze doors may have been one of the ways in which merchants from Amalfi sought to open up new commercial relationships. Bronze doors in this period are analogous to the technique of *opus sectile*. Both were perceived as prestigious forms of classical art that had been more or less lost in Italy and needed to be recuperated through Byzantium. Their importation from Byzantium was simultaneously responding to a classicizing trend in art and a need to foster diplomatic and commercial links with Constantinople.

The final set of Italo-Byzantine doors arrived in Venice *c.* 1112 and after that Italian metalworkers began to make doors in Italy. The Canosa doors are the first to be made using large-scale lost wax casting since antiquity.[9] However, the dating of the Canosa doors has not always been clear. Because they are designed very differently from one another, at one point, scholars considered the possibility that they were made separately, decades or even centuries apart. According to this theory, the right-hand door might be a spoliate, possibly even a Roman, while the left-hand door was made in the 1110s.[10] Recent analysis has excluded this as a possibility. The doors may not be symmetrical, but they are stylistically very similar and the metal alloys are a close enough match to conclude that they were made as a pair, by the same caster. The metallurgical analysis

Figure 129 Back of the doors to Bohemond's burial chapel. Photo: John McNeill.

concurs with stylistic analysis that the doors can be dated to the early twelfth century, shortly after Bohemond's death.[11]

Bohemond's doors ushered in a series of doors made in southern Italy, beginning with Oderisius of Benevento's doors at Troia cathedral (1119 and 1127), San Giovanni Battista delle Monache in Capua (1122) and San Bartolomeo in Benevento (1150).[12] Later in the century Roger II commissioned bronze doors for the Cappella Palatina, probably modelled on Charlemagne's, and later in the century Barisanus of Trani and Bonanno of Pisa created doors for the cathedrals of Pisa, Monreale, Trani and San Nicola in Bari (the latter no longer extant).[13] The doors at Canosa therefore mark a crucial turning point in the history of southern Italian metalworking. They are the point at which southern Italian patrons stopped importing doors from Constantinople and began to commission their own artists to create doors instead.

Making the Canosa doors

Large-scale casting of bronze objects like doors requires a considerable investment in resources. When Constance decided that the chapel should have bronze doors, she needed not only to employ a skilled caster, but also to gather the necessary materials, including a large quantity of wood to keep the furnace alight and the metals to create the alloy, in this case copper, tin and a small amount of silver.[14] Adding small amounts of silver to bronze alloys is a practice used by bell makers to obtain a distinctive sound when the bell is rung.[15] Due to metallurgical similarities to the Mari Cha Lion, we know that the copper used to create the bronze alloy in Canosa was mined in Cyprus, which demonstrates the commercial networks necessary to create the doors and the investment of time and money.[16]

An inscription tells us that the Canosa doors were made by a bell maker, called Roger of Melfi, who also made a candelabrum for the cathedral. This inscription is in keeping with the Italo-Byzantine doors, where the names of the makers are sometimes inscribed, although less often than the names of the patrons. The doors at San Paolo fuori le Mura in Rome have two signatures: of the caster and of the designer. The doors at Amalfi are signed by Simeon the Bronze caster.[17] The fact that Roger was a bell maker is worth dwelling on. Most western medieval bronze casters were Benedictine monks, and the two most famous metalworking centres were the abbeys at Hildesheim and Montecassino.[18] Although their origins are a little murky, monumental church bells seem to have emerged around the ninth century in Benedictine communities, to call monks to prayer from around the monastery and out in the fields.[19] It makes sense that the monks themselves developed the expertise for producing them. All of the early evidence for the identity of bell makers is that they were monks and that technical expertise was passed through monastic networks. Tancho, a monk at St Gall, made a bell for Charlemagne.[20] The tenth-century Anglo-Saxon saint Dunstan, abbot of Glastonbury, was a bell maker who taught his profession to fellow Benedictine St Ætholwold.[21]

By the turn of the twelfth century, most large Italian churches – monastic or not – possessed monumental cast bells.[22] There was a surge in the construction of bell towers and, no doubt, a corresponding need to train more bell makers. Perhaps at that point casting ceased to be mainly monastic because later on laymen were also making bells. The name of the caster and the date were often inscribed on the bell, and some in the thirteenth century were cast by fathers and sons, who must have been laymen, for example the bells at Santa Maria Maggiore in Rome and San Francesco in Assisi.[23] In short, although there is no hard evidence for it, bell casting was probably a monastic enterprise up to a certain point, when it expanded into lay workshops. Roger of Melfi was working at the time of the boom in bell making but before any evidence of lay production. It is impossible to say whether he was a monk, but I suspect he was and I would like to explore the possibility a little further.

Metalworking monks were often mobile; a good example is the Anglo-Saxon goldsmith who was struck by lightning at Montecassino in 1063.[24] Bell makers were necessarily itinerant because bells were cast on site, often inside a church.[25] It was easier for the bell casters to travel and set up a bell foundry on site than it was to transport a heavy bell and risk damaging it in transit. Casting our net of evidence very widely, as we are forced to do, there is evidence that lay and monastic metalworkers worked together collaboratively. Bell making is specialist and difficult; it requires a great deal of skill and resources. But a lot of the work – such as chopping wood, keeping the furnace alight and digging the casting pit – could be done by unskilled workers. At Nivelles in 1272, two lay metalworkers were engaged to make the shrine of St Gertrude, according to the sketches of Master Jacques, who was a goldsmith and a monk.[26] A similar arrangement could have been in place for Italian bell makers, whereby a skilled itinerant monk provided the necessary expertise and directed teams of local workers (we could hypothesize that, as bells became more popular, the local workers acquired more skills, took on more responsibility and were eventually able to set up their own workshops).

Bell casting was a delicate and lengthy process that could easily go wrong and sometimes took a few attempts. At Croxden Abbey in Staffordshire, a bell broke at Easter. Caster Henry Michael of Lichfield arrived soon after and worked all through the summer of 1303, finally casting the new bell at the feast of the nativity of the Virgin Mary in early autumn. That first cast failed, and he only managed to successfully cast a bell at the feast of All Saints in November.[27] The Croxden chronicle implies that Henry arrived alone and must have been assisted by the Croxden monks and perhaps local labourers. I imagine that this was the arrangement at Canosa in the 1110s: Roger of Melfi was probably a monk who was commissioned by Constance to design the doors, write the inscriptions and oversee a team of local workers and perhaps his own apprentices.

Since the name Roger was used exclusively by Normans in southern Italy, Roger of Melfi was either an immigrant or descended from one. Melfi, conquered in 1041, was an early Norman stronghold and effectively Robert Guiscard's first capital. Roger may have been a monk at one of the small Benedictine houses in Melfi, like San Giorgio and San Benedetto, or the larger San Michele in Monticchio close to Melfi. But it is likely that he learnt his profession at the nearby abbey of the SS Trinità in Venosa (only 20km from Melfi), one of the largest and richest monasteries in southern Italy and a site where metalworking is known to have taken place. In the nave of the first abbey church at Venosa are the remains of an eleventh-century bell foundry with two furnaces, and there is evidence for a continuing medieval metalworking practice on site.[28] The SS. Trinità was a monastery with a particularly Norman character. From 1073, the abbot was Berengar who had immigrated from Saint Évroul in Normandy to the monastery of Sant'Eufemia in Calabria founded by Robert Guiscard and the Norman abbot Robert of Grantmesnil, where many of the monks were Norman-born. Berengar was transferred to become Abbot of SS. Trinità.[29] Such an innovative and technically complicated project like the Canosa doors would have been entrusted only to a very experienced artist, so Roger of Melfi must have been a mature man in the 1110s. He is likely to have been part of the same generation as Bohemond, who was born c. 1058. If he were born in the 1050s, he would have been in his sixties at the time he made the doors. There are several possibilities for his biography. He could have been born in Normandy; perhaps he was a young monk who travelled to Italy with Berengar in the early 1070s. Alternatively, he could have been born in Melfi, perhaps a son of one of the knights who fought alongside Robert Guiscard.

Since the Canosa doors are the first medieval doors cast in southern Italy, presumably Roger had never made a door before. Although they are a pair, they are not identical or symmetrical. The left-hand door was made first and was cast as a single piece of bronze.[30]

The basic design is three medallions, with inscriptions in between them, surrounded by a vegetal border. The top two medallions were left blank in the casting process so that separately cast pieces could be attached them (more on that later in this chapter). The vegetal border – which is present on both doors – is almost identical to the decoration on a bell fragment from a nearby foundry as is the calligraphy in the inscriptions, which were carved into the bronze after casting, just like inscriptions on bells.[31] Large-scale bronze casting is difficult and sometimes hit and miss even for experienced casters, so it is hardly surprising that the first Canosa door was not a complete success. The left-hand door has structural weaknesses which caused two cracks to appear soon after casting: one very visible crack towards the bottom and another, less visible, in the centre. The central crack meant that the decoration in the central medallion had to be replaced, as did the small lion head on the border that functions as a handle. The two replacement lion heads are in keeping with the early-twelfth-century style.[32]

In response to the difficulties he encountered with the left-hand door, Roger was forced to use a different strategy for the right-hand door. It is possible that he originally cast two doors together and the original right-hand door had to be re-designed and re-cast because the structural problems were too great. Just like Henry of Lichfield at Croxden Abbey two centuries later, Roger may have been forced to abandon a first attempt. Whether there was a first attempt or not, the current right-hand door is designed in a different way to the earlier left-hand door. Roger abandoned the idea of casting a single piece and instead designed four panels, cast separately and then assembled them in a frame, to hide the joints.[33] On this second door, he also used a double casket cast, allowing him to cast foliate decoration on the back, as well as the front. The top and bottom panels are decorated with medallions, echoing the first door, while in the two central panels Roger has introduced figurative scenes in *agemina*, which were originally filled with silver.[34] Roger of Melfi's signature is in the bottom panel.

Both the *agemina* designs and the inscriptions have been carved into the metal after casting which, as we saw earlier, is a technique practiced by Byzantine metalworkers. However, the Byzantines made their doors from brass alloys that were easy to incise cold and developed special tools that allowed them to make smooth, precise grooves. Roger of Melfi obviously did not know about Byzantine techniques and tools because he used a bronze alloy, which is too hard to be cold-carved with ease. Fabrizio Vona has shown that the inscriptions and *agemina* grooves on the Canosa door are, when examined under a microscope, made up of fractured grooves, carved with a huge amount of effort using a hammer and chisel.[35] This is further evidence that the Canosa doors were experimental, the first to be made in Italy. By the time Oderisius of Benevento came to make the Troia doors, only a few years later in 1119, he used an alloy with a higher lead content, which is much easier to carve cold.[36]

Design

There are two original pieces of the doors which are now missing and I shall begin my discussion of design and iconography with these. On the left-hand door, the top medallion originally held a piece of cast decoration, which is now lost but the outline is still visible, along with an inscription telling us that it was a Madonna and child. The second panel down on the right-hand door has also lost some decoration. In this panel we see two figures kneeling beneath an empty space, with holes where something was attached. From the positions of the holes it was most likely a crucifixion, which would fit with the chapel's association with the Holy Sepulchre and probably use during Holy Week liturgies.[37]

The medallions on the doors feature two designs derived from Islamic objects: Arabic inscriptions and a star interlace design. The three medallions on the left-hand door have frames with Arabic lettering in them (Figures 130 and 131). These have usually been identified as pseudo-Arabic (including, erroneously, by me in a previous publication), but Ennio Napolitano has been able to read them as legible Arabic, a repetition of the word *yumm*, which means happiness.[38] Good wishes of this kind were often found on Islamic portable objects, such as silks, ceramics and metalwork. Circular inscriptions are common on medieval Islamic objects, and *al-yumm* commonly appears in circular inscriptions on Andalusian amulets made of lead from the tenth century to the fifteenth century.[39] The purpose of the amulets was apotropaic, and that is probably the purpose on the Canosa doors as well. The most pertinent comparison to the inscribed medallions on the doors is the bronze door knocker in the David Collection that was mentioned in earlier chapters. The knocker is thought to have been made in Sicily in the eleventh century, to adorn a mosque.[40] Identical or similar knockers were probably purchased for church doors in mainland southern Italy, where they would have been perceived as apotropaic, like the pseudo-Arabic mosaic in Bari.[41] Another object from Canosa provides a nice illustration of this perception: in the Museo dei Vescovi is a *flabellum*, a liturgical fan used to keep insects away from the Eucharist. The fan is made of parchment and is painted with a circular pseudo-Arabic inscription, surrounded by a foliate border.[42]

Figure 130 Detail of doors to Bohemond's burial chapel, showing the missing Marian relief. Photo: John McNeill.

Figure 131 Detail of the doors to Bohemond's burial chapel, showing one of the Arabic medallions. Photo: John McNeill.

The top and bottom medallions on the right-hand door are decorated with an interlace pattern with an eight-pointed star at the centre. Although it is difficult to see in photographs, the interlace is foliate; it sprouts tiny buds and shoots, like a vine. The foliage is inhabited by tiny horses and birds. Like the inscribed medallions, the star interlace probably comes from Islamic doors (Figure 132). The design is inspired by Fatimid wood carving, especially in the floriated interlace inhabited with animals.[43] The best parallel is the decoration on wooden panels now in Palazzo Abatellis in Palermo, which have a star interlace panels, inhabited by little animals.[44] The panels probably come from the royal palace built by King Roger II, from a door or ceiling, although there is a debate about whether it was carved in Sicily or Cairo.[45] In the foliate interlace decoration there is also a resemblance to the doors of La Martorana, carved in the 1140s.[46] Regardless of where they were made, they belong to the Fatimid cultural sphere, as do the star interlace medallions on the Canosa doors. Similar interlace appears in Fatimid metalwork, such as on a cylindrical box now in the Staatliche Museum in Berlin.[47]

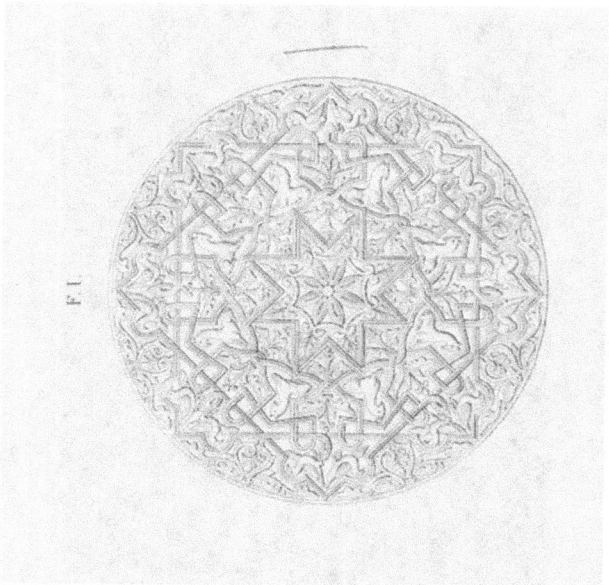

Figure 132 Star interlace medallion from the doors to Bohemond's burial chapel. Drawing: Schulz, *Denkmäler*, plate XLI.

Figurative panels

The most significant aspect of the figurative images (Figures 133 and 134) is that they were almost certainly not part of the original design for the doors. If we accept that the left-hand door was made first and that the design of the right-hand door had to be adapted to prevent it cracking, then it is unlikely that these figures were part of the original plan. The design of the left-hand door is aesthetically pleasing and harmonious: three medallions, inscriptions and a border. In the original design, the doors would have been symmetrical. On the right-hand door, the star medallions were probably part of the first design, with a third medallion between them (possibly another star or another lion head?) (Figure 135). Roger of Melfi's original design married Roman monumental bronze casting with designs from contemporary Islamic metalwork. The doors were classicizing, harking back to the early Christian art of Constantinian Rome but also incorporating designs from the Islamic areas of the Mediterranean that alluded either to southern Italy's role in international commerce or to the first crusade, or more likely to both. In this way, the Canosa doors are analogous to the Bari throne, which also marries classicism with Fatimid influences.

If my reconstruction of the original design for the doors is correct, both the *agemina* technique and the figures were an addition, an afterthought when the initial design proved impractical. This fact needs to be borne in mind when considering how the figures relate to the whole. Most scholars have made the assumption that the figures must be Bohemond and his family. This idea was first proposed in the

Figure 133 Kneeling figures, doors to Bohemond's burial chapel. Photo: John McNeill.

Figure 134 Trio of figures, doors to Bohemond's burial chapel. Photo: John McNeill.

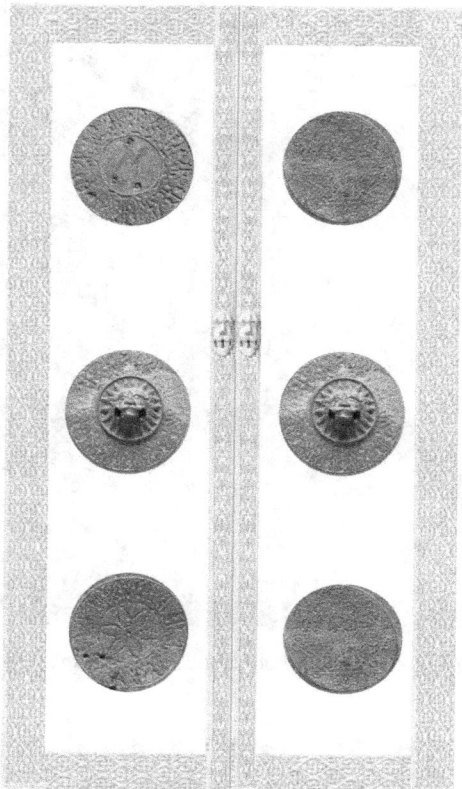

Figure 135 Original design of the Canosa doors, hypothetical reconstruction by the author.

nineteenth century and has been repeated many times. Luigi Russo sees the kneeling figures as Bohemond and Roger Borsa and the trio as their heirs: Bohemond II, Duke William and Tancred, Bohemond's nephew.[48] For Jean Flori the kneeling figures are Bohemond and his cousin, Richard of the Principate, while the trio are Bohemond, Tancred and Richard of the Principate again.[49] There are a number of problems with this mode of interpretation, and the first is illustrated by the fact that different scholars have been able to assign different identities to the various figures. It was rare for twelfth-century image makers to leave important figures unidentified in such a way. If these figures were Bohemond and other Hautevilles, they would be identifiable by inscriptions or incontrovertible visual clues. This is exemplified by the Italo-Byzantine doors, for example those at Monte Sant'Angelo, where all of the biblical and hagiographical scenes are carefully labelled with inscriptions. On the Canosa doors, the figures are not only unidentified by inscriptions, they are also unidentified visually. All five figures are identical to each other: they wear the same clothes, have the same hair style and the same body language. There is no hierarchy of scale or even any sense of pictorial space to give them some context. Furthermore there is no indication that the artist left the images unfinished or that they have suffered major damage, so what we see today must be as Roger of Melfi left it (minus the silver, which was used to fill the grooves, long since stolen). It is implausible that Roger of Melfi and Constance would have depicted Bohemond on the doors and then left the image so ambiguous.

If we exclude the idea that these figures are Hautevilles, we must ask who they are and what purpose they serve on the doors. They are dressed as laymen, with uncovered heads, long tunics and cloaks that fasten at the right shoulder. The key to understanding their function on the doors seems to be in their gestures. The two upper figures are kneeling, with their hands raised in prayer, supplication or exaltation. The trio below are more mysterious. None of the common trios in Christian iconography fit here; they are not the Magi, the three Hebrews in the fiery furnace or the visitation to Abraham. These are laymen, they have no halos, no wings, they bear no gifts. The three Marys at the tomb of Christ would fit well with the funerary nature of the chapel, but the figures here are clearly male. Each figure has one hand raised and the other lowered. The figure on the right is holding his cloak, pulling it away from his legs, with one foot in front of the other, indicating movement, as if he is about to stride out of the frame. This is even more pronounced in the other two figures, whose feet point more firmly to the right, meaning they are all moving in the same direction. The direction of feet indicates the direction of movement in other contemporary images, for example in the Easter procession in the Bari Benedictional scroll.[50]

Two of the people in the trio are holding hands, which is quite rare in medieval art. It can signify oath-taking or making a contract – like the modern handshake – but that doesn't seem to be the case here. It is not marriage, since the figures are male. The most common instances of hand-holding in medieval art are dancing scenes and the Anastasis, in which Christ pulls the souls of the faithful out of limbo. Both of these involve being led by the hand, and I think this is what is depicted in the Canosa doors. This is supported by numerous other examples of hand-holding in processions, entrances and exits. In the mosaics of Monreale (late twelfth century), God presents Eve to Adam by leading her towards him by the hand (Figure 136). On a capital of the Porte Miègeville at St Sernin in Toulouse (1100–1110) (Figure 137), the angel holds Adam's hand as he expels him and Eve from Eden. On the tympanum at Conques (early twelfth century), in the Last Judgement, numerous figures are led to their ultimate fate by the hand: not only is Charlemagne led by an abbot, there is also a procession of the elect holding hands, led through a door, into heaven by an angel. The reverse is the case in the tympanum at Saint Lazare at Autun, where the devil leads the damned by the hand. There are examples from later in the Middle Ages too, such as the procession of the elect in the Last Judgement in the stained glass windows of Bourges Cathedral. It is therefore a reasonable supposition to make that the trio on the Canosa doors are moving or processing. In the vein of the elect processing to heaven, this could be a depiction of Bohemond, perhaps with Hauteville relatives or other crusaders, taking his rightful place in paradise, but the anonymity of the figures still negates that possibility.

The meaning of the mysterious figures may lie in the inscriptions (which will be dealt with more thoroughly in the next chapter). The inscription on the left-hand door is divided into three parts, with the second and third part being opposite the two

Figure 136 God introduces Eve to Adam, Monreale. Photo: anonymous via Wikimedia.

Figure 137 Angel with Adam and Eve, Porte Miègeville, St Sernin, Toulouse. Photo: PierreSelim via Wikimedia.

figurative panels. I believe the inscriptions were intended to be read in conjunction with the figurative panels. Opposite the trio is inscribed, 'As you enter, look at the doors. May you see what is written. May you pray that Bohemond be given to heaven and offer his services there.'[51] Could it be that this verse, which gives instructions to the viewer, is being acted out in the panels opposite? Decoration on doors functions as both part of the exterior space and part of the liminality of the threshold, inviting the viewer to reflect on the space they are about to enter. Writing was used to connect the interior and exterior spaces.[52] The inscriptions at Canosa explicitly invite the viewer to enter the chapel. The trio of figures could be the faithful processing into the chapel, and the kneeling figures above could be praying for Bohemond's soul. This would tally with the figures' gestures, their anonymity and the fact that these panels were probably an emergency alteration to the original design of the doors.

Roger of Melfi's original design was one that combined the idea of monumental classical bronze doors with contemporary Islamic details. The original design, as evidenced by the left-hand door, resembles the classical doors at the Lateran and classicizing doors at Aachen. The idea was to create doors reminiscent of ancient Rome. The allusion to imperial Rome ties the chapel to the imperial mausolea in the Holy Apostles, asserting Bohemond as a conqueror of Byzantine territory. The addition of Islamic designs alludes to the contemporary Mediterranean world. Like the Bari throne, the doors combine the authority of antiquity with the cosmopolitanism of the twelfth-century Mediterranean. When this first design failed, Roger looked for solutions and inspiration in the Italo-Byzantine doors that were around him in southern Italy (perhaps he went to visit doors closest to Canosa in Monte Sant'Angelo, or those belonging to his fellow Benedictines at Montecassino). Out of his examination of the Italo-Byzantine doors, Roger developed the more successful panel construction with figurative *agemina* decoration.[53] He drew the figures in the same classicizing style as the Italo-Byzantine doors, with long, flowing garments, emphasizing the folds of drapery.[54]

The doors are imitations of the bronze doors of the aedicule (which may or may not have still been standing in the early twelfth century but would have been known through depictions and descriptions). Simultaneously, they are an imitation of the doors of the Constantinian age, in line with the chapel's other prototype, Constantine's mausoleum in the Holy Apostles. Like the architecture, and the rest of the decoration, they evoke the two contemporary and related tombs of Constantine and the Holy Sepulchre. But they are not only retrospective, they are also highly innovative, bringing the production of monumental bronze doors back to Italy, through the perseverance of Roger of Melfi.

13

Inscribing a crusader legacy

The burial chapel has inscriptions on the drum and on the bronze doors. For reasons that will become clear, these two inscriptions are best discussed together. The inscription on the drum takes the form of six rhyming hexameters. They are written, just underneath the dome, in clear capital letters, but the script is too small to be read from the ground, rendering the inscriptions redundant. Multiple descriptions of the chapel from before the twentieth-century report that the letters were carved into the marble and painted red.[1]

> The magnanimous prince of Syria lies under this vault, than whom no one better will after be born in the world.
> Greece conquered four times, Parthia, the greatest part of the world, felt long ago the spirit and strength of Bohemond.
> In ten battles he subdued by the reins of his valour hosts of thousands, which indeed the city of Antioch knows.[2]

On the doors, the inscriptions are written awkwardly, squashed into the upper part of the left-hand door. Jean Flori noted that they were written by two different calligraphic hands, which I have differentiated using bold font in the transcription that follows. Both hands are different from the signature of Roger of Melfi, which is in the bottom panel of the right-hand door.[3] The inscriptions on the doors begin with *unde....* (where), an odd way to begin something, and Fulvio delle Donne has interpreted this as a sign that the inscriptions on the doors follow on from those on the drum.[4]

> From this tomb the world proclaims how great was Bohemond; Greece bears witness, Syria counts the cost.
> He conquered Greece, protected Syria from the enemy.
> From this tomb, Greeks are laughing and Syria is grieving,
> Each of them rightly. Bohemond, may yours be a real salvation.
> **Bohemond conquered the powers of kings and the efforts of the powerful, and has earned by his own authority to be known by his name. He thundered over the world; since the globe succumbed to him. I cannot call him a man, yet I do not wish to call him a god.**
> In his life he strove to die for Christ, in dying he earned the grant of life. So let Christ's mercy grant to him that this man, his faithful warrior, should serve as a knight in heaven.

> As you enter, look at the doors. May you see what is written. May you pray that Bohemond be given to heaven and offer his services there.[5]

The history of the inscriptions is a complex puzzle to decipher. Although Francesco Magistrale has concluded that the inscriptions on both the doors and drum were inscribed by the same person in the 1110s, this conclusion is by no means certain, not least because they use different spellings of Bohemond and Syria.[6] On the drum, certain aspects of the lettering would be precocious for the early twelfth century and the word *magnanimus* is missing the first m, which delle Donne interprets as a transcription error. He concludes that the inscriptions were composed as a single text in the 1110s, but that the text was carved onto the drum at an unknown later date.[7] Delle Donne's theory is confirmed by Cesare Baronio, who transcribed the text now on the drum in 1607, but wrote that it was inscribed *in tabulis aereis*, on metal tablets, not on the building itself.[8] The inscription announces that Bohemond 'lies under this vault', so the tablets must have been displayed somewhere on the building. Since the inscription on the doors continues on from the other inscription, the tablets were probably on the exterior of the chapel, perhaps on either side of the doors, although there is no trace of how they were attached. This means that the inscriptions now on the drum were originally much or legible and accessible. Delle Donne also suggests that the text on the doors was carved in two phases: first the central part (in bold above), then the second hand slightly later as part of an attempt to emphasize Bohemond's crusading identity.[9] The idea of two phases of inscriptions on the doors is less substantiated by the evidence.

The following discussion of the models for the inscriptions supports the idea that they were composed together in the 1110s, even if the drum inscription was displayed on metal tablets at ground level until it was transcribed onto the drum at a much later date. Before looking at the models for the inscriptions, it is important to establish that the inscriptions paint Bohemond in a very different light to most contemporary southern Italian writers. Locals Lupo Protospatarius and Geoffrey Malaterra give him a very peripheral role in early Italo-Norman history. For them, the focus was on the dukes – Robert Guiscard, Roger Borsa, Duke William – as well as Roger I as conqueror of Sicily. Bohemond, who was disinherited and failed in his two big military campaigns in the Balkans, was relegated to a supporting role. He may have had success in the Levant, but that was not enough to make him a hero for southern Italian writers.[10] The Montecassino chroniclers Peter the Deacon and Leo of Ostia are more positive about Bohemond but only because they are essentially 'copying' the crusader text, the *Gesta Francorum*, or its derivatives.[11] In Italo-Norman culture in general Bohemond was marginalized, and there was a reluctance among most Italo-Normans to commemorate the first crusade.[12]

The inscriptions are not part of Italo-Norman literary culture; rather, they belong to the literary culture surrounding the first crusade. The inscriptions portray Bohemond as a great hero, which is not surprising given that epitaphs are always laudatory, but the way it is done reveals an elision with crusader ideology and other crusader texts, including the *Gesta Francorum*, written *c.* 1101 by someone in the southern Italian contingent of the crusade. There is a very general similarity to Godfrey of Bouillon's epitaph from 1100.

Here rests a Frankish pilgrim, who the place of holy Sion sought, a wondrous star, Duke Godfrey. He became the Egyptians's cause of fear, the Arab's rout, the Persian's trap. Elected king he would not choose the name nor yet the crown of King, but under Christ he chose to serve. His care was to restore once more the laws of Sion to herself. In Catholic faith to follow teaching true and see that it was followed. All dissent around him was destroyed and right prevailed. He thus was crowned with all the saints above. The soldier's pride, the people's strength, the clergy's hope.[13]

The listing of Godfrey's enemies and the reference to serving Christ are ideas echoed in Bohemond's inscriptions. Geoffrey is described as a wondrous star, something absent from Bohemond's inscriptions but present in the star interlace medallions on the doors. Bohemond's inscriptions do have a strong sense of the cosmos in 'he thundered over the world; since the globe succumbed to him', which together with the stars on the doors give a sense of Bohemond's dominion over the earth. The cosmos was important in crusader texts, particularly the sky. The victory of the crusade was said to have been foretold by signs in the sky, and the sun moon and stars were thought of as one of the ways God communicated with his people.[14] Both Bohemond and Geoffrey's epitaphs are part of the canon of early crusader texts that emphasized the agency of the secular leaders in bringing about the crusader victory. The success of the crusade was portrayed as being dependent on their leadership, piety and decision-making.[15] The strongest crusader aspects of Bohemond's inscriptions are lines, 'I cannot call him a man, yet I do not wish to call him a god. In his life he strove to die for Christ, in dying he earned the grant of life. So let Christ's mercy grant to him that this man, his faithful warrior, should serve as a knight in heaven'. Crusaders were considered to be the truest imitators of Christ and the words 'I cannot call him a man, yet I do not wish to call him a god' come very close to saying that Bohemond had reached a state of divine christomimesis.[16] The idea of Bohemond, almost as a martyr, part of an army of warriors in heaven is also part of the literary culture that developed over the course of the crusade.[17]

It has been suggested that, during Bohemond's lifetime, his image was carefully manipulated through the use of written texts.[18] Most recently Nicholas Paul has demonstrated that Bohemond began to use written texts for political purposes only after his marriage and that the textual manipulation of his image may have been instigated by Constance's family during his tour of France. The Capetians were keen to 'market' him as a hero for their own political purposes. This corpus of texts includes the *Gesta Francorum*, Orderic Vitalis's *Ecclesiastical History*, the hagiography of St Leonard and others such as a spurious letter from Alexios I claiming he would consider Latin rule in Constantinople.[19] Paul argues that the purpose of these texts was not just propaganda to fulfil short-term objectives but also the creation of a lasting legacy.[20]

One of these texts was a poem by Marbodus of Rennes, written in 1106, when Bohemond was in France, recounting his military triumphs and portraying him as a hero in the very same vein as the epitaph inscriptions. The end of Marbodus's poem is the exact same play on words that we find in the inscription on the doors: *Unde boat mundus, quanti fuerit Boamundus*.[21] Fulvio delle Donne has identified similarities with other texts such as the *Historia Hierosolimitana* by Robert of Reims (*c*. 1107) and the *Epistola VII* by Rudulphus Tortarius, both part of the French efforts to laud Bohemond from 1106 until his death.[22]

After his trip to France, there was also a change in the way that Bohemond styled himself. Before the first crusade, he sometimes used the title Prince of Taranto, but more commonly referred to himself simply 'Lord Bohemond'. On his two surviving charters from Antioch he is simply 'Bohemond' or 'Bohemond, son of Robert Guiscard duke of Apulia', and he continued to use the seal he had used in Italy, on which he is described as 'Bohemond, servant of Christ'.[23] However, after his trip to France, from 1106 onwards, he began to use the title Prince of Antioch and did so consistently until his death.[24] After 1111, Constance continued to refer to her late husband as Prince of Antioch. Between 1117 and 1119 charters were issued describing Bohemond II as 'son of the great Bohemond, Prince of Antioch' and 'son of the excellent Prince of Antioch lord Bohemond'.[25]

However, following the Treaty of Devol in 1108, Bohemond was not technically permitted to use the title of prince. The treaty stipulated that he would relinquish the title, instead styling himself as Duke of Antioch. The title prince was understood by the Byzantines as a ruler who acted independently, whereas, as a duke, Bohemond was integrated into the hierarchy of the empire, owing obedience to the emperor. Furthermore, the treaty stated that, after Bohemond's death, Antioch would revert to the emperor and Bohemond's heirs would receive another dukedom as compensation. After he signed the treaty, Bohemond never returned to Antioch and never instructed Tancred to honour it. This enabled Tancred to refuse to relinquish Antioch, on the grounds that Bohemond had never ordered him to do so.[26] Thus, use of the title prince on the burial chapel can be interpreted as a deliberate gesture of defiance of the Treaty of Devol and an assertion that Bohemond's son had the right, not just to rule Antioch, but to rule it independently.

The inscriptions were commissioned by Constance to perpetuate the image of Bohemond instigated in 1106 by her Capetian family. They are part of the literary culture of the first crusade. Ultimately the inscriptions, like the rest of the chapel, assert Bohemond's son's right to rule Antioch independently. But the chapel is not just about cementing inheritance, it is also about Constance asserting her own position as regent, and possibly also her own identity. Commissioning both the chapel and the texts was a way that Constance could make a contribution to the cultural life of the land she was ruling. It was also a way to make a contribution to the first crusade in her own right. Commissioning texts and memorials may have been considered an appropriate way for a woman to make a significant contribution to the crusade. Robert the Monk and Gilo of Paris put crusading ideas about martyrdom into the mouth of a grieving widow, who serves as a didactic literary device.[27] Other authors praise women who supported the crusade from their homes, such as Constance's sister-in-law, Adela of Blois, Ida of Boullion and Tancred's mother Emma (who Constance must have known personally).[28] Through both inscriptions and architecture, Constance joined that list.

Conclusion to Part 3

When her husband died, Constance of France found herself in a difficult situation. She was a foreign widow with two sons under five, and she was surrounded by hostility in Bari. Her sons' future depended on her ability to protect their inheritance until they were adults. In Apulia their inheritance was threatened by the anti-Norman, civic independence of the citizens of Bari and by her Norman neighbours, the Counts of Conversano. Antioch was even more uncertain. Tancred had control and would not relinquish it easily. Even without Tancred, there was the Byzantine Empire and the Treaty of Devol to contend with. After Bohemond's death, Constance may have gone to Constantinople in an attempt to form an alliance with the emperor. When that failed she returned to Italy and built a tomb for her husband in Canosa. In order to fund it, she formed an alliance with Duke William and his mother, Adela of Flanders. The burial chapel is, in essence, an assertion of her son's right to inherit Antioch and rule independently of the Byzantine emperor. It created an image of Bohemond almost as an *alter Christus* and set up Canosa as a substitute for Jerusalem. The chapel as an imitation of the Holy Sepulchre ensured Bohemond's continued fame and legacy because it probably became a focal point for Easter liturgies and a pilgrimage destination. The mosaics, bronze doors, copious spolia and inscriptions listing Bohemond's conquests evoke Constantinople, Jerusalem and ancient Rome.

Conclusion

Connections and retrospection

This book has explored the art and architecture of Bari and Canosa during the transition from Byzantine to Norman rule, but it is not a straightforward story of movement from one thing to another. The phrase in the title, 'from Byzantine to Norman', perhaps implies that Byzantine authority was replaced by Norman authority and Byzantine art by Norman art. In reality, 'Byzantine art' is a complex term, not easily defined, and distinctions between Byzantine and Lombard cultures were fuzzy throughout the period examined in this book. Despite Norman rule, Bari could never be described as culturally Norman. Art in Byzantine Apulia was hybrid and reflective of the mixed population. Byzantine officials commissioned art and buildings with strong associations with Constantinople, while the Lombards combined their Latin culture with Byzantinizing and Islamicizing elements that reflected Bari's status as a commercial port city and provincial capital in the Byzantine Empire.

The term 'Mediterranean art' is no more straightforward, but it is a useful term to describe an artistic culture that was shaped by Mediterranean connections, both contemporary commercial, diplomatic and artistic connections and the enduring legacy of the connectedness of the Roman Empire. Bari's identity as a commercial port city shaped the way the Lombard population saw themselves and how they wanted to present themselves to the world through their churches. The church of San Nicola contains a myriad of international connections, beginning with the relics of St Nicholas. The two most significant connections, apart from the relics, are the influence of luxury portable objects from the eastern Mediterranean, exemplified in the throne and crypt capitals, and the impact of the first crusade on the evolving construction project. San Nicola is, in many ways, a Latinizing project, a declaration of a new, post-Byzantine era but one that constantly refers back to Byzantine connections, not least through its very presence on the site of the former Byzantine palace.

One international connection is perhaps conspicuous by its absence. There seem to have been almost no artistic links between Bari and Venice. The one exception to this is in the pavements of San Nicola, where the marble inlay and mixed-media floors appear in Bari and the Veneto roughly contemporaneously. Given the Venice's increasing strength in the Adriatic and the size and significance of the construction project at San Marco, already underway when San Nicola was begun, one might expect to find more of a relationship between the two. It would be unwise to draw too many conclusions from the absence of a relationship, but it is nonetheless worth noting. It is perhaps indicative to the undoubted tension and competition between the two cities and another example of Bari's consistent commitment to asserting independence. A strong sense of autonomous civic identity is a defining feature of the Lombard community in Bari, and it was borne out in art and architecture in constant variety and innovation. Artists and patrons sought out new artistic models and combined various influences in new ways in Bari cathedral, San Nicola and in Bohemond's burial chapel.

Although international connectivity is the main focus of this book, it would be remiss to reduce these churches to 'just' manifestations of international connections. Other themes and distinctive features have also emerged. The hitherto unrecognized patronage of Constance of France in Canosa highlights the current lack art historical scholarship on women in southern Italy. Evidence of women's participation in the visual arts is very scant, but further research would no doubt illuminate other women patrons.

Another theme that has emerged is the extent to which Bari and Canosa were embedded in international Benedictine intellectual culture. This comes through particularly strongly in the many inscriptions, which are strikingly complex and scholarly for public texts of their time. It is particularly notable on the liturgical scrolls, the Canosa throne, the San Nicola sanctuary steps and on Archbishop Elias' tomb. These examples point to the importance and sophistication of the Benedictine monastery in Bari, which is rarely recognized. This book has been able to uncover some of its significance, even if it remains implicit.

On the other hand, Montecassino has proved to be less important than one might expect. The great Benedictine abbey of Montecassino is often considered to have had an all-encompassing dominance over the Latin church in southern Italy and a huge influence on the art and architecture of the mainland after Desiderius's reconstruction. Although the Benedictine monastery in Bari was a daughter house of Montecassino, the influence of Montecassino in Bari seems to have been slight. In particular, the *opus sectile* pavements (at least in the crypt) were probably a result of an independent collaboration with Byzantine marble workers, not mediated through the Montecassino workshop. There are stronger links with Salerno cathedral, which was linked to Montecassino, but Salerno is just one of many threads of influence in Bari.

There are two interconnected ideas that appear in every chapter of this book: contemporary international connections and a retrospective gaze back to late antiquity. The artists and patrons of Bari and Canosa wanted to harness the authority of antiquity and the purity of early Christianity and their contemporary international connections helped them to do so. Commercial and diplomatic relationships enabled them to acquire spolia, access late antique models and revitalize artistic techniques. Relationships with the Byzantine Empire were the key to importing artists and designs for *opus sectile* pavements, marble inlay and bronze doors. In this book I have argued that the retrospective trend in the art of Bari and Canosa should be seen as related to the Gregorian Reform movement. Bari was not (as far as we know) a hub for administrative or legislative reforms and the distinctive features of Barese culture mean that reform may have looked different in Bari than it did elsewhere. But the strong relationships with successive reforming popes, the consistent references to early Christian art and architecture, and to Jerusalem, and the participation in reforming Benedictine networks show that Bari – and Archbishop Elias in particular – was part of the artistic culture surrounding the reform movement. In Bari, participation in the reform movement was very closely tied to the re-Latinization of southern Italy following the Norman conquest and to the expansion of the Latin church through the first crusade, and those three ideas come together in San Nicola and Canosa cathedral.

Notes

Introduction

1. See, for example: Tronzo, *The Cultures of His Kingdom*; Bacile, 'The "Dynastic Mausolea" of the Norman Period in the South of Italy, c.1069–1189. A Study on the Form and Meaning of Burial Monuments in the Middle Ages'; Andaloro, *Nobiles Officinae*; Longo, 'The First Norman Cathedral in Palermo. Robert Guiscard's Church of the Most Holy Mother of God (With an Addendum by Jeremy Johns)'; Johns, *Arabic Administration in Norman Sicily*.
2. Bloch, *Monte Cassino in the Middle Ages*; Bloch, 'Origin and Fate of the Bronze Doors of Abbot Desiderius of Monte Cassino'; Braca, *Il Duomo di Salerno: Architettura e Culture Artistiche del Medioevo e dell'Età Moderna*; Cutler et al., *The Salerno Ivories*.
3. D'Onofrio, 'L'Abbatiale Normande Inachevée de Venosa'; Ungruh, *Das Bodenmosaik der Kathedrale von Otranto*; Caskey, 'Stuccoes from the Early Norman Period in Sicily'; Belli D'Elia, *Puglia Romanica*; Ronchi, *La Cattedrale di Trani*; Safran, *S. Pietro at Otranto. Byzantine Art in South Italy*; Belli D'Elia, *L'Angelo La Montagna Il Pellegrino. Monte Sant'Angelo e Il Santuario Di San Michele Del Gargano Dalle Origini Ai Nostri Giorni*.
4. Eastmond, 'The Limits of Byzantine Art'.
5. Kitzinger, *The Mosaics of St Mary's of the Admiral in Palermo*; Borsook, *Messages in Mosaic: The Royal Programmes of Norman Sicily, 1130–1187*; Tronzo, *The Cultures of His Kingdom*.
6. Belting, 'Byzantine Art among Greeks and Latins in Southern Italy'; Falla Castelfranchi, *Pittura Monumentale Bizantina in Puglia*; Wharton Epstein, *Art of Empire: Painting and Architecture of the Byzantine Periphery. A Comparative Study of Four Provinces*; Safran, *S. Pietro at Otranto. Byzantine Art in South Italy*; Safran, '"Byzantine" Art in Post-Byzantine South Italy? Notes on a Fuzzy Concept'; Safran, *The Medieval Salento*.
7. Porter, *Romanesque Sculpture of the Pilgrimage Roads*; Porter, 'Bari, Modena, and St.-Gilles'.
8. Conant, *Carolingian and Romanesque Architecture, 800 to 1200*; Fernie, *Romanesque Architecture*.
9. Belli D'Elia, *Puglia Romanica*; Bertelli, *Puglia Preromanica Dal V Secolo Agli Inizi Dell'XI*; Belli D'Elia, *Alle Sorgenti Del Romanico*; Garton, 'Early Romanesque Sculpture in Apulia'; Aceto, *Arte in Puglia Dal Medioevo al Settecento: Il Medioevo*.
10. Fernie, 'Definitions and Explanations of the Romanesque Style of Architecture from the 1960s to the Present Day'.
11. Barral i Altet, 'Arte Medievale e Riforma Gregoriana: Riflessioni Su Un Problema Storiografico'.
12. Quintavalle, 'Riforma Gregoriana e Origini Del "Romanico"'; Glass, *The Sculpture of Reform in North Italy, Ca. 1095–1130*; Kitzinger, 'The Gregorian Reform and the

Visual Arts'; Toubert, *Un Art Dirigé. Réforme Grégorienne et Iconographie*; Kessler, 'A Gregorian Reform Theory of Art?'
13. Folda, *The Art of the Crusaders in the Holy Land, 1098-1187*.
14. Horden and Purcell, *The Corrupting Sea: A Study of Mediterranean History*; Rosser-Owen, 'Mediterraneanism: How to Incorporate Islamic Art into an Emerging Field'.
15. One such exception is Castiñeiras, 'Compostela, Bari and Jerusalem: In Search of the Footsteps of a Figurative Culture on the Roads of Pilgrimage'.

Chapter 1

1. Todisco, *Bari Romana*; Martin, *La Pouille Du VIe Au XIIe Siècle*, 1993, 122; Nicols, 'Patronage and the Patrons of Canusium: A Case Study', 280-3.
2. Von Falkenhausen, *La Dominazione Bizantina nell'Italia Meridionale dal IX all'XI Secolo*, 112 and 130-2.
3. Von Falkenhausen, 20-2 and 32; Von Falkenhausen, 'Bari Bizantina: Profilo Di Un Capoluogo Di Provincia'; Von Falkenhausen, 'I Bizantini in Italia'.
4. Martin, 'Les Thèmes Italiens: Territoire, Administration, Population', 549.
5. Von Falkenhausen, *La Dominazione Bizantina nell'Italia Meridionale dal IX all'XI Secolo*, 111, 139-42 and 173-5.
6. Theotokis, *The Norman Campaigns in the Balkans, 1081-1108 AD*, 109-10; Shepard, 'Byzantium and the West c.900-c.1024', 622-3; Matheou, 'Hegemony, Elitedom and Ethnicity. "Armenians" in Imperial Bari, c.874 1071', 2.
7. Matheou, 'Hegemony, Elitedom and Ethnicity. "Armenians" in Imperial Bari, c.874 1071', 16.
8. Von Falkenhausen, *La Dominazione Bizantina nell'Italia Meridionale dal IX all'XI Secolo*, 158.
9. Von Falkenhausen, 173-5; Matheou, 'Hegemony, Elitedom and Ethnicity. "Armenians" in Imperial Bari, c.874 1071'.
10. Abulafia, 'The Italian Other: Greeks, Muslims and Jews', 230.
11. Martin, *La Pouille Du VIe Au XIIe Siècle*, 1993, 502; Bertelli, Fornaro, and Iorio, *S. Maria Que Est Episcopio*, 85-6; Cioffari, *Storia Della Chiesa Di Bari Dalle Origini Alla Fine Del Dominio Bizantino (1071)*, 11:122.
12. Copeta, 'Medieval Bari: A Multiethnic City', 155-6.
13. Copeta, 159.
14. Kreutz, *Before the Normans*, 38-9; Musca, *L'Emirato Di Bari 847-871*; Bondioli, 'Islamic Bari between the Aghlabids and the Two Empires'; Loud, *The Latin Church in Norman Italy*, 24.
15. Abulafia, 'Role of Trade in Muslim-Christian Contact during the Middle Ages', 18.
16. Depalo, 'S. Maria Del Carmine: La Chiesa Bizantina Riscoperta'; Lavermicocca, 'Fragmenta: La Chiesa Bizantina Di Palazzo Simi'.
17. John the Deacon, 'La Cronaca Veneziana Del Diacono Giovanni', 166-7.
18. Copeta, 'Medieval Bari: A Multiethnic City', 140.
19. Skinner, 'Room for Tension'.
20. Skinner, 161.
21. Martin, 'Settlement and the Agrarian Economy'; Guérin, 'Forgotten Routes?'
22. Abulafia, 'Trade and Crusade 1050-1250', 3; Abulafia, 'Moametto e Carlo Magno: Le Due Aree Monetarie Italiane Dell'Oro e Dell'Argento', 251.

Notes 205

23 Abulafia, 'Moametto e Carlo Magno: Le Due Aree Monetarie Italiane Dell'Oro e Dell'Argento', 229.
24 Tangheroni, 'Trade and Navigation', 129–30.
25 Nuzzo, 'Bari Prima Dei Normanni: La Città Nell'Alto Medioevo e La Documentazione Archeologica. Primi Dati Da Una Ricerca in Corso', 253–4 and 259; Neri et al., 'A Byzantine Connection: Eastern Mediterranean Glasses in Medieval Bari'.
26 Abulafia, 'Moametto e Carlo Magno: Le Due Aree Monetarie Italiane Dell'Oro e Dell'Argento', 229.
27 Von Falkenhausen, *La Dominazione Bizantina nell'Italia Meridionale dal IX all'XI Secolo*, 142–4.
28 Von Falkenhausen, 10–19.
29 Safran, *The Medieval Salento*, 141–3; Kreutz, *Before the Normans*, 128–9.
30 Von Falkenhausen, *La Dominazione Bizantina nell'Italia Meridionale dal IX all'XI Secolo*, 166–72.
31 Sinisi, 'The Marriage of the Year (1028)'.

Chapter 2

1 John the Deacon, 'La Cronaca Veneziana Del Diacono Giovanni', 165–7.
2 Guillou, 'Un Document Sur Le Gouvernement de La Province: L'Inscription Historique En Vers de Bari (1011)'.
3 My thanks to Kate Cook for her help with the translation into English. For the original, see Guillou.
4 Holmes, *Basil II and the Governance of Empire (976–1025)*, 438.
5 Shepard, 'Byzantium and the West c.900–c.1024', 622; Holmes, *Basil II and the Governance of Empire (976–1025)*, 435.
6 Giuliani, 'L'Edilizia Di XI Secolo Nella Puglia Centro-Settentrionale: Problemi e Prospettive Di Ricerca Alla Luce Di Alcuni Casi Di Studio', 193–5; Belli D'Elia, *Puglia Romanica*, 116–17.
7 Ciminale and Pellegrino, 'Interventi Di Restauro e Indagini Archeologiche Nell'Area Della Cattedrale e Della Basilica Di S. Nicola'; Ciminale, 'Nuove Acquisizioni Su Bari Tardoantica e Altomedievale Dalle Stratigrafie Dell'Area Di S. Nicola e Della Cattedrale'.
8 Nuzzo, Depalo, and Airò, 'Archeologia Urbana Nella "Cittadella Nicolaiana" Di Bari. Nuovi Dati Dal Riesame Delle Indagini Degli Anni Ottanta Nell'Area Del Pretorio Bizantino', 87–8.
9 Calia et al., 'Integrated Prospecting in the Crypt of the Basilica of Saint Nicholas in Bari, Italy', 275, figure 5.
10 Nuzzo, 'Bari: Il Pretorio Della Città Bizantina', 28–30.
11 Ševčenko, 'The Posthumous Miracles of St Eustratios on a Sinai Templon Beam'.
12 Garsoïan, 'The Problem of Armenian Integration into the Byzantine Empire', 56; Walter, *The Warrior Saints in Byzantine Art and Tradition*, 137.
13 Nitti di Vito, *Le Pergamene Di S. Nicola Di Bari. Periodo Greco (939–1071)*, 26–8, number 13.
14 Garton, 'Early Romanesque Sculpture in Apulia', 246.
15 For example, Matheou, 'Hegemony, Elitedom and Ethnicity. "Armenians" in Imperial Bari, c.874 1071', 5.

16 Belli D'Elia, *Puglia Romanica*, 283.
17 White, *Military Saints in Byzantium and Rus, 900–1200*, 66.
18 Ševčenko, 'The Posthumous Miracles of St Eustratios on a Sinai Templon Beam'.
19 Falla Castelfranchi, 'Iscrizione Greca Con L'Elogio Del Catapano Basilio Mesardonite'.
20 Lavermicocca, *Bari Bizantina*, 26.
21 Nuzzo, Depalo, and Airò, 'Archeologia Urbana Nella "Cittadella Nicolaiana" Di Bari. Nuovi Dati Dal Riesame Delle Indagini Degli Anni Ottanta Nell'Area Del Pretorio Bizantino', 81, note 10.
22 Goodchild, 'A Byzantine Palace at Apollonia (Cyrenaica)', 249.
23 Partrich, 'A Government Compound in Roman-Byzantine Caesarea'.
24 Niewöhner, 'The Late Antique Origins of Byzantine Palace Architecture'.
25 Goodchild, 'A Byzantine Palace at Apollonia (Cyrenaica)'.
26 My thanks to Emily Guerry for this idea.
27 Bertelli, 'Sul Reimpiego Di Elementi Architettonici Bizantini a Bari'.
28 Bertelli, 'Capitello-Imposta'; Harrison, *Excavations at Sarachane in Istanbul*.
29 Bertelli, 'Capitello-Imposta Su Colonna Spiralforme'.
30 Ousterhout, *Master Builders of Byzantium*, 142.
31 Bertelli, 'Sul Reimpiego Di Elementi Architettonici Bizantini a Bari'.
32 Bertelli, 'Epistilio Frammentario Di Iconostasi'; Bertelli, 'Capitellino Cubico'.
33 Belli D'Elia, 'Angelo Docente (La Divina Sapienza?)'.
34 Grabar, *Byzantine Painting*, 97; Solovyov, *Divine Sophia*, 49.
35 Meyendorff, 'L'Iconographie de La Sagesse Divine Dans La Tradition Byzantine'.
36 'Psalter', 7v; Kalavrezou, 'The Paris Psalter'.
37 Evans, 'The Arsenal Bible'.
38 Hanson, 'The Rise and Fall of the Macedonian Renaissance'; Westbrook, 'Architecture of Traces and Ascriptions: Interpreting the Vanished Great Palace of the Byzantine Emperors in Constantinople', 43–4; Magdalino, 'The Bath Leo the Wise and the "Macedonian Renaissance" Revisited: Topography, Iconography, Ceremonial, Ideology', 105–6.
39 Nitti di Vito, *Le Pergamene Di S. Nicola Di Bari. Periodo Greco (939–1071)*, 31, number 18; Von Falkenhausen, 'A Provincial Aristocracy: The Byzantine Provinces in Southern Italy (9th–11th Century)', 200, note 2.
40 Burnett, 'The Cult of St Nicholas in Medieval Italy', 137–9; Ötüken, 'La Basilica di San Nicola a Myra', 55–7.
41 Acta Sanctorum Bolondiana, 9 March II, 30B, par 11.
42 Safran, *S. Pietro at Otranto. Byzantine Art in South Italy*; Von Falkenhausen, 'A Provincial Aristocracy: The Byzantine Provinces in Southern Italy (9th–11th Century)', 213–15.
43 Tsitouridou, *The Church of the Panagia Chalkeon*, 10 and 15.

Chapter 3

1 Belting, 'Byzantine Art among Greeks and Latins in Southern Italy'.
2 Wharton Epstein, *Art of Empire: Painting and Architecture of the Byzantine Periphery. A Comparative Study of Four Provinces*.
3 See the discussion of Obolensky's 'Byzantine Commonwealth' in Boeck, *Imagining the Byzantine Past*, 11–13.

4   Jeffreys, Haldon, and Cormack, 'Byzantine Studies as an Academic Discipline', 11; Eastmond, 'The Limits of Byzantine Art'.
5   Boeck, *Imagining the Byzantine Past*, 11–13; Eastmond, *Art and Identity in Thirteenth-Century Byzantium: Hagia Sophia and the Empire of Trebizond*; Jones, *Between Islam and Byzantium: Aght'amar and the Visual Construction of Medieval Armenian Rulership*; Boeck, 'Simulating the Hippodrome: The Performance of Power in Kiev's St. Sophia'.
6   Safran, '"Byzantine" Art in Post-Byzantine South Italy? Notes on a Fuzzy Concept', 501 and 504.
7   Anderson, *Cosmos and Community in Early Medieval Art*, 52; Garrison, *Ottonian Imperial Art and Portraiture*, 123.
8   Muthesius, 'Silk, Power And Diplomacy In Byzantium', 102.
9   Göller, *1000 Jahre Bistum Bamberg 1007–2007: Unterm Sternenmantel*, 409; Baumgärtel-Fleischmann, 'Die Kaisermäntel Im Bamberger Domschatz', 383; Owen-Crocker and Coatsworth, 'The Star Mantle of Emperor Henry II'.
10 An exception is Volbach, 'Mantello Di Enrico II'.
11 Baumgärtel-Fleischmann, 'Die Kaisermäntel Im Bamberger Domschatz', 382–3; Von Pölnitz, *Die Bamberger Kaisermäntel*, 34.
12 Owen-Crocker and Coatsworth, 'The Star Mantle of Emperor Henry II'.
13 Dolezalek, *Arabic Script on Christian Kings*, 45.
14 Coatsworth and Owen-Crocker, 'The Coronation Mantle of King Stephen of Hungary'; Járó, 'Filati D'Oro: Techniche e Metologie'; Vernon, 'Dressing for Succession in Norman Italy: The Mantle of King Roger II'.
15 Owen-Crocker and Coatsworth, 'The Star Mantle of Emperor Henry II', 77; Vernon, 'Dressing for Succession in Norman Italy: The Mantle of King Roger II', 102.
16 Garrison, *Ottonian Imperial Art and Portraiture*, 123.
17 Garrison, 123.
18 Anderson, *Cosmos and Community in Early Medieval Art*, 52–4.
19 Ganz, 'Pictorial Textiles and Their Performance: The Star Mantle of Henry II'.
20 Martin, 'Jean, Archevêque de Trani et de Siponto, Syncelle Impérial', 26.
21 McClendon, *The Imperial Abbey of Farfa*, 99 and 172.
22 Boynton, *Shaping a Monastic Identity*, 168.
23 Boynton, 166–7.
24 McClendon, *The Imperial Abbey of Farfa*, 99 and 172.
25 Bertelli, *Puglia Preromanica Dal V Secolo Agli Inizi Dell'XI*, 91–3.
26 Anonimo Barese, 'Chronicle', 155; Bertelli, *Puglia Preromanica Dal V Secolo Agli Inizi Dell'XI*, 91–7.
27 Cioffari and Tateo, 'Annales Barensis', 32; Loud, *The Age of Robert Guiscard*, 70–1.
28 Nitti di Vito, *Le Pergamene Di S. Nicola Di Bari. Periodo Greco (939–1071)*, 31, number 18; Von Falkenhausen, 'A Provincial Aristocracy: The Byzantine Provinces in Southern Italy (9th–11th Century)', 200, note 2; Loud, *The Age of Robert Guiscard*, 71.
29 Loud, *The Age of Robert Guiscard*, 71.
30 Von Falkenhausen, *La Dominazione Bizantina nell'Italia Meridionale dal IX all'XI Secolo*, 166–72.
31 Von Falkenhausen, 171–2.
32 Matheou, 'Hegemony, Elitedom and Ethnicity. "Armenians" in Imperial Bari, c.874 1071', note 94.
33 Belli D'Elia, *Puglia Romanica*, 128.
34 Falcandus, *The History of the Tyrants of Sicily by Hugo Falcandus 1154–69*, 74.

35 Morizio, 'La Città in Età Romana: I Monumenti', 432.
36 Volbach, 'Bari Cattedrale', 108.
37 Vernon, 'Pseudo-Arabic and the Material Culture of the First Crusade in Norman Italy', 8–10.
38 Martin, 'Jean, Archevêque de Trani et de Siponto, Syncelle Impérial'.
39 Martin, *La Pouille Du VIe Au XIIe Siècle*, 1993, 592 and 625.
40 Shepard, 'Byzantium and the West c.900–c.1024', 622.
41 Nesbitt and Oikonomedes, *Catalogue of Byzantine Seals at Dumbarton Oaks and in the Fogg Museum of Art*, 2:96; Martin, 'Jean, Archevêque de Trani et de Siponto, Syncelle Impérial', 126.
42 Martin, *La Pouille Du VIe Au XIIe Siècle*, 1993, 594.
43 Martin, 'Jean, Archevêque de Trani et de Siponto, Syncelle Impérial', 123.
44 Oldfield, *Sanctity and Pilgrimage in Medieval Southern Italy, 1000–1200*, 32.
45 Belli D'Elia and Garton, 'Trani'.
46 Belli D'Elia and Garton, 71; Ronchi, *La Cattedrale di Trani*, 19–26. The inscription reads *eum possideat paradisium presul Iohannes*
47 Belli D'Elia, 'Abbazia Di San Benedetto'; Volbach, 'Bari', 109.
48 Belli D'Elia and Garton, 'Polignano'; Belli D'Elia and Garton, 'Santa Maria Di Colonna', 192; Belli D'Elia, 'Canosa', 72; Belli D'Elia, 'Coppia Di Sfingi Alate'.
49 Volbach, 'Bari', 109.
50 Walker, 'Textile with Roundels of Elephants, Senmurvs and Winged Horses'; Gonosovà, 'Textile Fragment with Double-Headed Eagles'; Alchermes, 'Two Stone Slabs'; Gonosovà, 'Textile Fragment with Senmurvs'; Gonosovà, 'Textile Fragment from the Reliquary of Saint Germanus'; Gonosovà, 'Textile Fragment from the Reliquary of Saint Siviard'.
51 Edwards, 'Reception and Reorientation: The Impact of Internationally Traded Objects in Italian Art & Architecture (950–1150)', 86–107.
52 Edwards, 'Patronage and Tradition in Textile Exchange and Use in the Early Norman South'; Edwards, 'Reception and Reorientation: The Impact of Internationally Traded Objects in Italian Art & Architecture (950–1150)', 82–5.
53 Lowe, *The Beneventan Script*, 150–2.
54 Volbach, 'Bari Cattedrale', 112; Sinisi, 'The Marriage of the Year (1028)'.
55 Ovid, 'Metamorphoses'; Vandi Kalogerakou, 'Ovid at the Crossroads. The Illustrations of the Metamorphoses in Apulia before 1071'.
56 Kelly, *The Exultet in Southern Italy*, 22 and 196.
57 Zchomelidse, *Art, Ritual, and Civic Identity in Medieval Southern Italy*, 45–58; 'Pontifical with Benediction of the Font'; 'Exultet'.
58 Kelly, *The Exultet in Southern Italy*, 135 and 155; Zchomelidse, *Art, Ritual, and Civic Identity in Medieval Southern Italy*, 40 and 56. The norm in the western rite is to chant the *lumen Christi* during the procession, but not in southern Italy.
59 Kelly, *The Exultet in Southern Italy*, 216.
60 'Exultet Roll'.
61 Kelly, *The Exultet in Southern Italy*, 227; 'Exultet Roll'.
62 Kelly, 169–70.
63 Pentcheva, 'Performative Images and Cosmic Sound in the Exultet Liturgy of Southern Italy', 466.
64 Kelly, *The Exultet in Southern Italy*, 197.
65 Kelly, 137–8.

66 Zchomelidse, 'Descending Word: Resurrecting Christ: Moving Images in Illuminated Liturgical Scrolls of Southern Italy', 20; Mayo, 'Vasa Sacra', 388; Kelly, *The Exultet in Southern Italy*, 214.
67 Kelly, *The Exultet in Southern Italy*, 202–4.
68 Pentcheva, 'Performative Images and Cosmic Sound in the Exultet Liturgy of Southern Italy', 427 and 466.
69 Kelly, *The Exultet in Southern Italy*, 192–3, 198 and 206.
70 Sinisi, 'Dressing the Earth: Eleventh-Century Garb in the Exultet Roll of Bari'.
71 Germanidou, 'The "Rose of the Winds" Illustration in the Exultet I Bari Roll (c.1025–1034) and Its Probable Neoplatonic Implications'.
72 Pentcheva, 'Performative Images and Cosmic Sound in the Exultet Liturgy of Southern Italy', 455.
73 Pentcheva, 400–1, 453 and 456.
74 Zchomelidse, 'Descending Word: Resurrecting Christ: Moving Images in Illuminated Liturgical Scrolls of Southern Italy', 20.
75 Cavallo, Orofino, and Percere, *Exultet: Rotoli Liturgici Del Medioevo Meridionale*, 54; Zchomelidse, *Art, Ritual, and Civic Identity in Medieval Southern Italy*, 54.
76 Volbach, 'Bari', 113; Belting, 'Byzantine Art among Greeks and Latins in Southern Italy', 5.
77 Speciale, 'Liturgia e Potere. Le Commemorazioni Finali Nei Rotoli Dell'Exultet', 196–7.
78 Parani, *Reconstructing the Reality of Images*, 23.
79 Belting, 'Byzantine Art among Greeks and Latins in Southern Italy'.
80 Zchomelidse, 'Descending Word: Resurrecting Christ: Moving Images in Illuminated Liturgical Scrolls of Southern Italy', 20–6; Speciale, 'Liturgia e Potere. Le Commemorazioni Finali Nei Rotoli Dell'Exultet', 198–9; Zchomelidse, *Art, Ritual, and Civic Identity in Medieval Southern Italy*, 60.
81 Mayo, 'Vasa Sacra', 385.
82 Mayo, 387–9.

Chapter 4

1 Jones, *The Geography of Strabo*, Book 6, chapter 3, section 9.
2 Campione, 'Sabino, Vescovo Di Canosa, Santo'.
3 Volpe, 'Architecture and Church Power in Late Antiquity: Canosa and San Giusto (Apulia)', 137; Volpe, 'Venerabilis Vir Restaurator Ecclesiarum', 29; Corrente, Giuliani, and Leone, 'Edilizia Paleocristiana Nell'Area Di Piano San Giovanni a Canosa Di Puglia', 1174–5.
4 Ughelli, *Italia Sacra, Sive de Episcopis Italiae*, 7:603.
5 Fernie, 'The Date, Iconography and Dedication of the Cathedral of Canosa'.
6 Belli D'Elia, *Puglia Romanica*, 93–106; Fernie, 'The Date, Iconography and Dedication of the Cathedral of Canosa'; Belli D'Elia, 'Canosa'.
7 Bertelli and Attolico, 'Analisi Delle Stutture Architettoniche Della Cattedrale Di San Sabino a Canosa: Primi Dati'; Falla Castelfranchi, 'La Cattedrale Di Canosa Non è Più Normanna'.
8 My thanks for Eric Fernie for pointing this out.

9. Ousterhout, *Eastern Medieval Architecture*, 203–5 and 251–2; Karydis, 'The Vaults of St. John the Theologian at Ephesos', 546–7.
10. Karydis, 'Justinian's Church of the Holy Apostles: A New Reconstruction Proposal', 125 and 127.
11. Matthews, *The Early Churches of Constantinople*, 28.
12. Karydis, 'Justinian's Church of the Holy Apostles: A New Reconstruction Proposal', 124.
13. Wharton Epstein, 'The Date and Significance of the Cathedral of Canosa in Apulia, South Italy'.
14. Wharton Epstein; Papacostas, 'The Medieval Progeny of the Holy Apostles', 396–8.
15. Krautheimer, 'Introduction to an "Iconography of Mediaeval Architecture"'.
16. Wharton Epstein, 'The Date and Significance of the Cathedral of Canosa in Apulia, South Italy'.
17. Cassano, 'Nuove Acquisizioni Sull'Architettura Canosina al Tempo Del Vescovo Sabino'.
18. Belli D'Elia, 'Canosa', 76–7.
19. Belli D'Elia and Garton, 'Pulpito'.
20. *Per iussionem domini mei guitberti venerabilis presbiteri ego acceptus peccator archidaconus feci hoc opus.*
21. Belli D'Elia, 'Acceptus'; Bertelli, 'Acceptus e Magister David a Siponto: Nuove Acquisizioni'; Wackernagel, 'La Bottega Dell'Archidiacono Acceptus, Sculptore Pugliese Dell'XI Secolo'.
22. *dmitte crimina Acceptus . . . rent mille triginta novem.*
23. Volbach, 'Monte Sant'Angelo', 40; Bertelli, 'Acceptus e Magister David a Siponto: Nuove Acquisizioni'.
24. Loud, *The Latin Church in Norman Italy*, 366.
25. Bréholles, *Recherches Sur Les Monument d'Histoire Des Normands et de La Maison Souabe Dans l'Italie Méridionale*, 42.
26. Cavell, 'Social and Symbolic Functions of the Romanesque Façade: The Example of Mâcon's Last Judgement Galilee', 84.
27. Belli D'Elia, *Puglia Romanica*, 253–6; Belli D'Elia, 'Acceptus'.
28. Doig, *Liturgy and Architecture*, 120–3.
29. D'Elia and Garton, 'Trono Vescovile'.
30. *Praesul ut eterna (eternam?) post hac potiare cathedram, quod vox exterius res ferat interius, quod geris in specie da(?) gestes lumen ut in re (?), lumen cum praestas, lumine ne careas.*
31. *Urso preceptor romaldus ad hec fuit actor.*
32. D'Elia and Garton, 'Trono Vescovile'.
33. Grabar, 'Trônes Épiscopaux Du XIème et XIIème Siècles En Italie Méridionale'.
34. Garton, 'Early Romanesque Sculpture in Apulia', 88; Nees, 'Forging Monumental Memories in the Early Twelfth Century', 775; Mola, 'Il Santuario e i Normanni', 76–80.
35. Transcription taken from Pierno, 'Artisti Nella Puglia Centro-Settentrionale Tra XI e XIII Secolo: Produzione Artistica Tra Stile, Identità Ed Autocoscienza', 18; Wackernagel, 'La Bottega Dell'Archidiacono Acceptus, Sculptore Pugliese Dell'XI Secolo', 6; Belli D'Elia and Garton, 'Siponto', 59.

    This little gift is given . . . greatly pious and . . . climb . . . soul . . . the sculptor commonly known as Acceptus . . . name attained . . . demands . . . none feels the sting(?).

    The archpriest of the cathedral of Santa Maria..... Master David made

Forgive Acceptus for his sins..... the year 1039
Ignatius(?) the priest and custodian of the church....
...... noble study......

36 The Monte Sant'Angelo inscription reads, *sedes hec numero differ a sede siponti ius et honor sedis que sunt sibi sunt quoque monti.*
37 Weinryb, 'The Inscribed Image: Negotiating Sculpture on the Coast of the Adriatic Sea', 325.
38 Genesis 1:3-4, John 8:12, John 12:35-6, 1 Thessalonians 5:5.
39 *Dum lucem habetis, credite in lucem, ut filii lucis sitis.*
40 Cary, *Outward Signs*, 144-6.
41 Old, *The Reading and Preaching of the Scriptures in the Worship of the Christian Church: The Medieval Chruch*, 305.
42 Gregory the Great, *Moral Reflections on the Book of Job*, Preface, page 59.
43 Dodwell, *The Pictorial Arts of the West, 800-1200*, 169.
44 Tracy, *Britain's Medieval Episcopal Thrones*, 8.

Chapter 5

1 For a history of the conquest see Loud, *The Age of Robert Guiscard*, chapters 2 and 3.
2 Ravegnani, *I Bizantini in Italia*, 202-12.
3 Loud, *The Age of Robert Guiscard*, 136; Oldfield, *City and Community in Norman Italy*, 18-21.
4 Oldfield, *City and Community in Norman Italy*, 25-7, 32 and 34; Nitti di Vito, *Le Pergamene Di S. Nicola Di Bari. Periodo Normanno*, 52 and 54.
5 Oldfield, *City and Community in Norman Italy*, 27.
6 Guérin, 'Forgotten Routes?', 91.
7 Oldfield, *City and Community in Norman Italy*, 27; Tenenti and Tucci, 'L'Impresa Marittima: Uomini e Mezzi', 636; Theotokis, *The Norman Campaigns in the Balkans, 1081-1108 AD*, 80-1; Stanton, 'The Norman Siege of Bari, 1068-71'.
8 Pozza and Ravegnani, *I Trattati con Bisanzio 992-1198*, 4:37-44, number 2; Frankopan, 'Byzantine Trade Privileges to Venice in the Eleventh Century', 3-13; Morossi, *Political and Economic Relations between Venice, Byzantium and Southern Italy (1081-1197)*, 16-24, 37 and 44.
9 Oldfield, *City and Community in Norman Italy*, 34.
10 Nitti di Vito, *Le Pergamene Di S. Nicola Di Bari. Periodo Normanno*, numbers 52 and 54.
11 Nitti di Vito, Numbers 22, 43, 51, 52, 54; Oldfield, *City and Community in Norman Italy*, 34.
12 Oldfield, *City and Community in Norman Italy*, 35.
13 Wilkinson, *Jerusalem Pilgrims before the Crusades*, 261-9; Birch, *Pilgrimage to Rome in the Middle Ages*, 157; Sensi, 'Santuario e Culto Di San Michele Nell'Italia Centrale', 270; Bettocchi and Aulisa, 'Il Santuario Dal IX al XI Secolo: Gli Affreschi e Conservazione', 51-2.
14 Wilkinson, *Jerusalem Pilgrims Before the Crusades*, 94.
15 Jones, *Saint Nicholas of Myra, Bari, and Manhattan: Biography of a Legend*, 79-82.
16 Otranto, *San Nicola di Bari e la Sua Basilica: Culto, Arte, Tradizione*, 65.
17 Burnett, 'The Cult of St Nicholas in Medieval Italy', 137-9; Ötüken, 'La Basilica di San Nicola a Myra', 55-7.

18. Burnett, 'The Cult of St Nicholas in Medieval Italy', 132–4; Falla Castelfranchi, *Pittura Monumentale Bizantina in Puglia*, 29 and 85; Sinclair, 'The Relationship between Art and Liturgy on the Periphery of the Byzantine Empire: the Cases of 10th century Cappadocia and Longobardia (Apulia)', 170.
19. Hayes, 'The Cult of St. Nicholas of Myra in Norman Bari, c. 1071–c. 1111', 494 and 499; Meisen, *Nikolauskult Und Nikolausbrauch Im Abendlande: Eine Kultgeographisch-Volkskundliche Untersuchung*, 66; Guerrieri, 'Dell'Antico Culto Di S. Nicola in Bari', 257; Jones, *Saint Nicholas of Myra, Bari, and Manhattan: Biography of a Legend*, 166.
20. Braca, *Il Duomo di Salerno: Architettura e Culture Artistiche del Medioevo e dell'Età Moderna*, 16; Caskey, 'Miracles and Matthew: Potential Contexts for the Salerno Ivories', 184.
21. Angold, *The Byzantine Empire, 1025–1204*, 21–6.
22. Pertusi, 'Ai Confini Tra Religione e Politica. La Contesa per Le Reliquie Di San Nicola Tra Bari, Venezia e Genova'; Grant, 'Byzantium's Ashes and the Bones of St Nicholas: Two Translations as Turning Points, 1087–1100'.
23. Nicephorus of Bari, *La Traslazione Di San Nicola*, 13–14; Nitti di Vito, 'Leggenda Di S. Nicola'.
24. Jones, *Saint Nicholas of Myra, Bari, and Manhattan: Biography of a Legend*, 189.
25. Cioffari and Tateo, 'Inventio of San Sabino of Canosa', 185.
26. Babudri, 'Le Note Autobiografiche Di Giovanni Arcidiacono Barese e La Cronologia Dell'Arcivescovato Di Ursone a Bari', 134–6.
27. Loud, *The Latin Church in Norman Italy*, 126.
28. Nitti di Vito, *Le Pergamene Di S. Nicola Di Bari. Periodo Normanno*, 73 and 280.
29. Geary, *Furta Sacra*, 101.
30. Cioffari, *L'Abate Elia. Il Benedettino che Costruì la Basilica di San Nicola.*, 55 and 90.
31. Nicephorus of Bari, Introduction.
32. Louis I Hamilton, *A Sacred City*, 139.
33. Geary, *Furta Sacra*, 98–9; Nitti di Vito, 'Leggenda Di S. Nicola'.
34. Nitti di Vito, 'Leggenda Di S. Nicola'.
35. Geary, *Furta Sacra*, 98–100.
36. Nicephorus of Bari, *La Traslazione Di San Nicola*, 40–1; Cioffari, *Storia della Basilica di S. Nicola di Bari*, 79.
37. Burnett, 'The Cult of St Nicholas in Medieval Italy', 157–8.
38. Nitto de Rossi and Nitti di Vito, *Le Pergamene Del Duomo Di Bari (952–1264)*, 59–61.
39. Skinner, '"Halt! Be Men!"', 631.
40. Corsi, 1987, 43, 82–3 and 121.
41. Jones, *Saint Nicholas of Myra, Bari, and Manhattan: Biography of a Legend*, 191.
42. Cioffari and Tateo, 'Inventio of San Sabino of Canosa', 81; Lupo Protospatharius, 'Annales', 60.
43. Loud, *The Latin Church in Norman Italy*, 212; Nitti di Vito, *Le Pergamene Di S. Nicola Di Bari. Periodo Normanno*, 61–3, number 33.
44. Burnett, 'The Cult of St Nicholas in Medieval Italy', 45–7; Osborne, 'The Hagiographic Programme of the Mosaics in the South Dome of San Marco at Venice', 21; Jones, *Saint Nicholas of Myra, Bari, and Manhattan: Biography of a Legend*, 37.
45. Ordeig i Mata, 'La Documentatació Del Monestri de Cuixà Referent a Olibai Als Anys Del Seu Abadiat', 46–50; Zimmermann, 'Sur La Terre Come Au Ciel: La Paix Chrétienne. Oliba (1008–1046), Pacificateur et Guide Des Âmes', 35–6; Castiñeiras, 'The Romanesque Portal as Performance'.

46 Ramseyer, *The Transformation of a Religious Landscape: Medieval Southern Italy, 850-1150*, 75; Cowdrey, *The Age of Abbot Desiderius: Montecassino, the Papacy and the Normans in the Eleventh and Easrly Twelfth Centuries*, 40-1; Louis I Hamilton, *A Sacred City*, 134.
47 Loud, *The Age of Robert Guiscard*, 141.
48 Braca, *Il Duomo di Salerno: Architettura e Culture Artistiche del Medioevo e dell'Età Moderna*, 16; Caskey, 'Miracles and Matthew: Potential Contexts for the Salerno Ivories', 184.
49 For the inscriptions at Salerno, Vescovi, 'Inscribing Presence', 139.
50 Ötüken, 'La Basilica di San Nicola a Myra', 47–8.
51 Campione, 'Sabino, Vescovo Di Canosa, Santo'.
52 Brazinski and Fryxell, 'The Smell of Relics'.
53 Schettini, *La Basilica di San Nicola di Bari*, 95–100.
54 Gerardo Cioffari and Marisa Milella, *Il Tesoro della Basilica di San Nicola. Catalogo della Mostra. Museo Storico di Stato*, Mosca, 22 Giugno – 28 Agosto 2005, 132, catalogue number 7 and Bacci, 2006, 257–8, catalogue number IV.3.
55 *Ora pro nobis beate Nicolae ut digni efficia mur promissione Christi.*
56 The crypt of Otranto cathedral is very similar to Salerno and San Nicola. It is likely that the Otranto and San Nicola were begun at roughly the same time, within a year or so of each other, both modelled on Salerno. Becker, *Die Architektur Der Normannen in Süditalien Im 11. Jahrhundert: Kontinuität Und Innovation Als Visuelle Strategien Der Legitimation von Herrschaft*, 146.
57 Kelly, 'La Musica, la Liturgia e la Tradizione nella Salerno del Dodicesimo Secolo', 190–6.
58 Krautheimer and Sandler, 'The Crypt of Sta. Maria in Cosmedin and the Mausoleum of Probus Anicius'.
59 Braca, *Il Duomo di Salerno: Architettura e Culture Artistiche del Medioevo e dell'Età Moderna*, 40 and 45; Caskey, 'Miracles and Matthew: Potential Contexts for the Salerno Ivories', 186–7; Krautheimer, 'San Nicola in Bari und die apulische Architektur des 12. Jahrhunderts', 161.
60 Caskey, 'Miracles and Matthew: Potential Contexts for the Salerno Ivories', 186–7; Rutishauser, 'Genèse et Développement de La Crypte à Salle En Europe Du Sud'; Dale, *Relics, Prayer, and Politics in Medieval Venetia*, 18–19.
61 Calò, 'Federico II e l'Elephante: Un Simbolo Cristologico per l'Anticristo Svevo', 98. There were other thrones with elephant supports in Trani, Calvi and Mazara del Vallo.
62 Sanders, *Ritual, Politics and the City in Fatimid Cairo*, 47, 49, 64 and 159.
63 Sanders, 106.
64 Walker, 'Textile with Roundels of Elephants, Senmurvs and Winged Horses'and For example the lusterware bowl in the Brooklyn Museum, museum number 69.122.1.
65 Edwards, 'Reception and Reorientation: The Impact of Internationally Traded Objects in Italian Art & Architecture (950–1150)', 147–73.
66 Blair and Bloom, *Cosmophilia: Islamic Art from the David Collection, Copenhagen*, 42–3, catalogue number 103; Northover and Meyer, 'A Newly Acquired Islamic Lion Door Knocker in the David Collection'.
67 Camber, 'The Mari Cha Lion in the Context of Apulian Romanesque Sculpture', 191.
68 Sanders, *Ritual, Politics and the City in Fatimid Cairo*, British Museum, 1923,1205.3.
69 For some of the most recent discussions, Shalem, *The Oliphant*; Rosser-Owen, 'The Oliphant: A Call for a Shift in Perspective'.

70 Hoffman, 'Pathways of Portability: Islamic and Christian Interchange from the Tenth to the Twelfth Century'; Eastmond, 'On Diversity in Southern Italy', 107–10.
71 Grabar, 'The Shared Culture of Objects'.
72 Boynton, *Shaping a Monastic Identity*, 168–74; Cutler et al., *The Salerno Ivories*.
73 Pace, 'Fra l'Islam e l'Occidente: Il Mistero Degli Olifanti'; Pace, 'Présence et Reflets de l'Art Islamique En Italie Méridionale Au Moyen Age'; Volbach, 'Bari', 126; Eastmond, 'Byzantine Oliphants?', 114.
74 Guérin, 'Forgotten Routes?'
75 Museum numbers: V&A 7935–1862, National Museum of Scotland A. 1956.562, Met 17.190.215.
76 British Museum, 1979,0701.1.
77 Volbach, 'Bari', 125–7; Fillitz, *Zwei Elfenbeinplatten Aus Süditalien*, 26; Eastmond, 'Byzantine Oliphants?', 114.
78 Eastmond, 'On Diversity in Southern Italy', 104; Guérin, 'Forgotten Routes?'
79 Eastmond, 'Byzantine Oliphants?', 95.
80 Copenhagen museum number 9140, Jászberény known as 'Lehel's Horn'.
81 Eastmond, 'Byzantine Oliphants?', 102.
82 Boeck, 'Simulating the Hippodrome: The Performance of Power in Kiev's St. Sophia', 287.
83 Eastmond, 'Byzantine Oliphants?', 113.
84 Muthesius, *Byzantine Silk Weaving*, 48–73.
85 Boeck, 'Simulating the Hippodrome: The Performance of Power in Kiev's St. Sophia'.
86 Boeck, 287.
87 Eastmond, 'Byzantine Oliphants?', 115.
88 Garton, 'Early Romanesque Sculpture in Apulia', 75 and 269; Cahn, *Romanesque Sculpture in American Collections: New York and New Jersey, Middle and South Atlantic States, the Midwest, Western and Pacific States*, 103.
89 Kinney, 'Spolia', 33.
90 Kinney, 25–33; Baer, *Sphinxes and Harpies in Medieval Islamic Art: An Iconographical Study*; Gelfer-Jørgensen, *Medieval Islamic Symbolism and the Paintings in the Cefalù Cathedral*, 116. For peacocks, St Augustine, *City of God*, book 21, chapter 4.
91 Kitzinger, 'The Arts as Aspects of a Renaissance: Rome and Italy', 642; Stroll, 'The Twelfth-Century Apse Mosaic in San Clemente in Rome and Its Enigmatic Inscription', 4; Guidobaldi, Barsanti, and Guiglia Guidobaldi, *San Clemente*.
92 Kitzinger, 'The Gregorian Reform and the Visual Arts', 92–3.
93 Stroll, 'The Twelfth-Century Apse Mosaic in San Clemente in Rome and Its Enigmatic Inscription', 4; Kitzinger, 'The Arts as Aspects of a Renaissance: Rome and Italy', 642. *Ecclesiam Christi viti similabimus isti + de ligno crucis jacobi dens ignatique: insuprascripti requiescunt corpore Christi + quam lex arentem set crus facit esse virentem*
94 Miramon, 'L'Invention de la Réforme Grégorienne. Grégoire VII au xixe Siècle, Entre Pouvoir Spirituel et Bureaucratisation de l'Église'.
95 Cushing, *Reform and the Papacy in the Eleventh Century*; Blumenthal, *The Investiture Controversy*.
96 Riley-Smith, *The First Crusade and the Idea of Crusading*, 1–11.
97 Loud, 'Abbot Desiderius of Montecassino and the Gregorian Papacy'.

Chapter 6

1. Lidov, 'Il Dio Russo', 87 and note 1.
2. Burnett, 'The Cult of St Nicholas in Medieval Italy', 42.
3. Loud, *The Latin Church in Norman Italy*, 215.
4. Pellegrini, 'Chronicon Ignoti Civis Barensis', 197.
5. *MLXXXXVIIII. Ind. VII. Tertia die intrante mense Octubris venit Papa Urbanus cum pluribus Archiepiscopi[s], et Episcopi[s], Abbatibus, et Commitibus; intraverunt in Bari, et suscepti sunt cum magna reverentia, et preparavit Domino Helia nostro Archiepiscopo mirificam sedem intus in Ecclesia Beatissimi Nicolay confessoris Christi.*
6. *Inclitus atque bonus sedet hac in sede patronus presul Barinus Helias et Canusinus.*
7. Greenhalgh, *Marble Past, Monumental Present: Building with Antiquities in the Mediaeval Mediterranean*, 192.
8. Kinney, 'Spolia from the Baths of Caracalla in Sta. Maria in Trastevere', 390.
9. Grabar, 'Trônes Épiscopaux Du XIème et XIIème Siècles En Italie Méridionale'; De Francovich, 'Wiligelmo Da Modena e Gli Inizii Della Scultura Romanica in Francia e in Spagna'; Porter, 'Bari, Modena, and St.-Gilles', 58.
10. Belli D'Elia, 'La Cattedra Dell'Abbate Elia'.
11. Those who have accepted Belli D'Elias's dating are Nees, 'Forging Monumental Memories in the Early Twelfth Century'; Kitzinger, 'The Arts as Aspects of a Renaissance: Rome and Italy', 667; Bornstein, 'Romanesque Sculpture in Southern Italy and Islam: A Revaluation'. Those who maintain that the throne was carved c.1100 are: Cioffari, 'Concilio Di Bari Del 1098: Uomini Ed Eventi', 114–15; Aceto, 'La Cattedra Dell'Abate Elia: Dalla Memoria Alla Storia'; Dorin, 'The Mystery of the Marble Man and His Hat: A Reconsideration of the Bari Episcopal Throne'.
12. Zarnecki, 'A Newly Discovered Head from Bury St Edmunds Abbey'.
13. Belli D'Elia, 'Maestro Della Cattedra Dell'Abate Elia. Coppie Di Schiavi e Maschere Sputaracemi'.
14. Calò Mariani, 'Considerazioni Sulla Scultura Artistica Nel Territorio a Sud-Est Di Bari Tra XI e XV Secolo', 391–5.
15. Appuhn, 'Beiträge Zur Geschichte Des Herrschersitzes Im Mittelalter II. Teil: Der Sogenannte Krodo-Altar Und Der Kaiserstuhl in Goslar'.
16. Hearn, *Romanesque Sculpture: The Revival of Monumental Stone Sculpture in the Eleventh and Twelfth Centuries*, 85.
17. 1 Kings, 10: 18–20 and 2 Chronicles, 9:17–19.
18. Iafrate, *The Wandering Throne of Solomon*, 9.
19. Tracy, *Britain's Medieval Episcopal Thrones*, 13.
20. Iafrate, *The Wandering Throne of Solomon*, 9 and 177.
21. Dagron, *Emperor and Priest*, 3.
22. Tracy, *Britain's Medieval Episcopal Thrones*, 9–10.
23. Grabar, 'Trônes Épiscopaux Du XIème et XIIème Siècles En Italie Méridionale'; Borsook, 'A Solomonic Throne for Salerno Cathedral?'. The Salerno ivories may have been originally made for a throne, which Borsook argues was Solomonic.
24. Iafrate, *The Wandering Throne of Solomon*, 39 and 49–50.
25. Hunter, 'Funerary Lions in Roman Provincial Art', 59 and 62; Hunter and Collard, 'The Cramond Lioness'.

26 Stroszeck, *Löwen-Sarkophage*, 1:26–34, Plates 28–71; Bacile, 'The "Dynastic Mausolea" of the Norman Period in the South of Italy, c.1069–1189. A Study on the Form and Meaning of Burial Monuments in the Middle Ages', 325; Koch and Wight, *Roman Funerary Sculpture. Catalogue of the Collections, John Paul Getty Museum, Malibu California*, 58–61.
27 Luidprandus, 'Antapodosis'.
28 Contadini and Camber, 'Acoustic Automata', 65.
29 Vernon, 'Pseudo-Arabic and the Material Culture of the First Crusade in Norman Italy', 25–6.
30 Belli D'Elia, *La Basilica Di S. Nicola a Bari: Un Monumento Nel Tempo*, 106–7, figure 163.
31 *sede patronus presul barinus.*
32 Iafrate, *The Wandering Throne of Solomon*, 60–73.
33 De Appolonia, 'Justice and Judgement in the Romanesque Column-Bearing Lions of Northern Italy', 170.
34 Oldfield, *City and Community in Norman Italy*, 36.
35 Robinson, *The Papacy, 1073–1198*, 179–80.
36 Cushing, *Reform and the Papacy in the Eleventh Century*, 85.
37 Robinson, *The Papacy, 1073–1198*, 124–7.
38 Cushing, *Reform and the Papacy in the Eleventh Century*, 35.
39 Kaplan, 'Black Africans in Hohenstaufen Iconography'.
40 Todisco and Chelotti, *La Scultura Romana Di Venosa e Il Suo Reimpiego*.
41 Bacile, 'The "Dynastic Mausolea" of the Norman Period in the South of Italy, c.1069–1189. A Study on the Form and Meaning of Burial Monuments in the Middle Ages', 313–26.
42 Moskowitz, *Nicola Pisano's Arca Di San Domenico and Its Legacy*, 9–13; Moskowitz, *Nicola and Giovanni Pisano: The Pulpits*, 35.
43 Meyer, 'La Figure de l'Atlante Dans La Sculpture Romane'.
44 De Souza, 'War, Slavery and Empire in Roman Imperial Iconography', 52.
45 De Souza, 39.
46 Zanker, *Roman Art*, 84 and 187; Spawforth, *Greece and the Augustan Cultural Revolution*, 104; Dowling, *Clemency and Cruelty in the Roman World*, 139; Schneider, *Bunte Barbaren Orientalenstatuen Aus Farbigem Marmor in Der Römischen Repräsentationskunst*.
47 De Souza, 'War, Slavery and Empire in Roman Imperial Iconography', 39–54.
48 Bindman and Gates, *The Image of the Black in Western Art I*, figure 328.
49 Vase with head of a man, terracotta, 4th century BC, Palazzo Jatta, Ruvo di Puglia, museum number 1113. http://www.imageoftheblack.com/gallery.html
50 British Museum, number 1926,0324.96. A project by King's College London to digitally re-construct the painted masks, makes it easier to see the facial features http://www.kvl.cch.kcl.ac.uk/masks/masks_archive/slave/19263-2496/19263-2496_01.html. My thanks to Jen Baird for pointing out the similarities between these masks and the Bari throne.
51 Gabrieli and Scerrato, *Gli Arabi in Italia*, 120, 159, figures 122 and 177; Baer, *Islamic Ornament*, 44–5, figures 51a and b.
52 Edwards, 'Reception and Reorientation: The Impact of Internationally Traded Objects in Italian Art & Architecture (950–1150)', 172–3.
53 Sanders, *Ritual, Politics and the City in Fatimid Cairo*, 49, 97, 159; Lev, 'David Ayalon and the History of Black Military Slavery in Medieval Islam'.
54 Dorin, 'The Mystery of the Marble Man and His Hat', 2008.
55 Dorin, 42–6.

56 Belli D'Elia, *Puglia Romanica*, 123.
57 Grabar, 'Trônes Épiscopaux Du XIème et XIIème Siècles En Italie Méridionale', 12–13.
58 Grabar, 12–3.
59 Dorin, 'The Mystery of the Marble Man and His Hat', 48.
60 Fynn-Paul, 'Empire, Monotheism and Slavery in the Greater Mediterranean Region from Antiquity to the Early Modern Era', 3–6.
61 Rotman, 'Migration and Enslavement', 393; Rotman, *Byzantine Slavery and the Mediterranean World*, 18–24.
62 Rio, 'Freedom and Unfreedom in Early Medieval Francia'.
63 Bramoullé, 'Recruiting Crews in the Fatimid Navy (909–1171)', 14; Jacoby, 'Venetian Commercial Expansion in the Eastern Mediterranean, 8th–11th Centuries', 380.
64 Smith, 'The Business of Human Trafficking', 538.
65 Smith, 531–3.
66 Smith, 536.
67 Guérin, 'Forgotten Routes?'
68 Smith, 'The Business of Human Trafficking', 539.
69 Nitti di Vito, *Le Pergamene Di S. Nicola Di Bari. Periodo Normanno*, 18.
70 Epstein, *Speaking of Slavery*, 85; Nitti di Vito, *Le Pergamene Di S. Nicola Di Bari. Periodo Normanno*, 128–30.
71 Epstein, 87; Nitti di Vito, 62.
72 Vernon, 'Pseudo-Arabic and the Material Culture of the First Crusade in Norman Italy'.
73 Krey, *The First Crusade*, 33–6. My italics.
74 Hagenmeyer, *Chronologie de la Première Croisade, 1094–1100*, 136; Krey, *The First Crusade*, 42–3.
75 Kostick, *The Social Structure of the First Crusade*, 287.
76 Hill, *Gesta Francorum et Aliorum Hierosolimitanorum. The Deeds of the Franks and the Other Pilgrims to Jerusalem*.
77 My thanks for John McNeill and Rose Walker for this idea.

Chapter 7

1 *Congrua iam aedificatione perfecta est.* Kappel, *S. Nicola in Bari Und Seine Architektonische Nachfolge. Ein Bautypus Des 11.-17. Jahrhunderts in Unteritalien Und Dalmatien*, 10; Belli D'Elia, *La Basilica Di S. Nicola a Bari: Un Monumento Nel Tempo*, 79–87.
2 Belli D'Elia, *Puglia Romanica*, 151.
3 Kappel, *S. Nicola in Bari Und Seine Architektonische Nachfolge. Ein Bautypus Des 11.-17. Jahrhunderts in Unteritalien Und Dalmatien*, 9.
4 Bressan, 'Le Iscrizioni Nella Bari Medievale: Un Itinerario Da Scoprire', 61.
5 Belli D'Elia, *Puglia Romanica*, 112.
6 Belli D'Elia, 112.
7 Fernie, *Romanesque Architecture*, 96.
8 Belli D'Elia, *La Basilica Di S. Nicola a Bari: Un Monumento Nel Tempo*, 42.
9 Willard and Conant, 'A Project for the Graphic Reconstruction of the Romanesque Abbey at Monte Cassino'.
10 Belli D'Elia, *La Basilica Di S. Nicola a Bari: Un Monumento Nel Tempo*, 228, figure 318.

11 Belli D'Elia, 19.
12 Kappel, *S. Nicola in Bari Und Seine Architektonische Nachfolge. Ein Bautypus Des 11.-17. Jahrhunderts in Unteritalien Und Dalmatien.*
13 Belli D'Elia, *La Basilica Di S. Nicola a Bari: Un Monumento Nel Tempo*, 40.
14 Conant, *Carolingian and Romanesque Architecture, 800 to 1200*, 347; von Winterfeld, *Die Kaiserdome: Speyer, Mainz, Worms*, 55–66.
15 Belli D'Elia, *La Basilica Di S. Nicola a Bari: Un Monumento Nel Tempo*, 45.
16 Milella, 'Il Rilievo Fotogrammetrico Digitale Multimmagine a Supporto Della Valorizzazione e Della Conoscenza Dei Beni Culturali', 94.
17 Belli D'Elia, *La Basilica Di S. Nicola a Bari: Un Monumento Nel Tempo*, 48.
18 Cassano, 'San Nicola', 420.
19 1 Kings VII, 13–21.
20 1 Kings VII, 25 and 29.
21 Barry, 'Disiecta Membra: Ranieri Zeno, the Imitation of Constantinople, the Spolia Style, and Justice at San Marco', 52.
22 Blunt, 'The Temple of Solomon with Special Reference to South Italian Baroque Art', 259.
23 Blunt, 259; Cahn, 'Solomonic Elements in Romanesque Art', 50–1.
24 Barry, 'Disiecta Membra: Ranieri Zeno, the Imitation of Constantinople, the Spolia Style, and Justice at San Marco'; Harrison, 'The Church of St. Polyeuktos in Istanbul and the Temple of Solomon', 276–9.
25 Kendall, *The Allegory of the Church*, 100.
26 *ut fuit introitus templi sancti salomonis + sic esst istius in medio bovis atque leonis.* Translation by Kendall (see previous note).
27 Iafrate, *The Wandering Throne of Solomon*, 39.
28 Wilkinson, *From Synagogue to Church.*
29 Schein, 'Between Mount Moriah and the Holy Sepulchre: The Changing Traditions of the Temple Mount in the Central Middle Ages', 175.
30 Ousterhout, 'New Temples and New Solomons: The Rhetoric of Byzantine Architecture', 226.
31 Schein, 'Between Mount Moriah and the Holy Sepulchre: The Changing Traditions of the Temple Mount in the Central Middle Ages', 187.
32 Balfour, *Solomon's Temple: Myth, Conflict and Faith*, 158.
33 Boas, *Jerusalem in the Time of the Crusades*, 109; Kedar, 'Intellectual Activities in a Holy City', 127–39.
34 Schein, 'Between Mount Moriah and the Holy Sepulchre: The Changing Traditions of the Temple Mount in the Central Middle Ages', 184.
35 Schein, 185.
36 Schein, 183–4.
37 Schein, 184–5.
38 Ousterhout, 'New Temples and New Solomons: The Rhetoric of Byzantine Architecture', 225.

Chapter 8

1 Bornstein, *Portals and Politics in the Early Italian City-State*, 32–4.
2 Belli D'Elia, *La Basilica Di S. Nicola a Bari: Un Monumento Nel Tempo*, 86.

3 Belli D'Elia, 87.
4 Loomis and Loomis, *Arthurian Legends in Medieval Art*.
5 Aird, *Robert 'Curthose', Duke of Normandy (C. 1050–1134)*, 168–70.
6 Silvestri, 'Una Rilettura Delle Fasi Costruttive Del Duomo Di Modena'; Glass, 'Prophesy and Priesthood at Modena'; Bornstein, *Portals and Politics in the Early Italian City-State*; Stiennon and Lejeune, 'La Légende Arthurienne Dans La Sculpture de La Cathédrale de Modène'; Allaire, 'Arthurian Art in Italy'; Muriel Whitaker, *The Legends of King Arthur in Art*; Loomis, 'The Story of the Modena Archivolt and Its Mythological Roots'; Putter, 'The Twelfth-Century Arthur'; Loomis, 'Modena, Bari, and Hades'. Silvestri offers a recent and thorough summary of the scholarship and a plausible new explanation for the various phases of construction. Bornstein and Glass date it to the very early twelfth century, while Lejeune and Stiennon think it is *c.* 1120. Whitaker and Allaire follow Lejeune and Steinnon.
7 Fox-Friedman, 'King Arthur in Art', 382.
8 Glass, 'Prophesy and Priesthood at Modena'.
9 Glass.
10 Allaire, 'Arthurian Art in Italy', 207.
11 Rouse and Rushton, 'Arthurian Geography', 229.
12 Monica Nari interpreted the Modena frieze as a denunciation of warfare, in keeping with the contemporary writings of Bernard of Clairvaux, so the Modena example may also have been interpreted on multiple levels. Chiellini Nari, 'Le Favole, i Simboli, Il "Ciclo Di Artù": Il Fronte Istoriato Nella "Porta Della Pescheria"'.
13 Cassano, 'San Nicola', 420 and 422.
14 Angheben, 'Les Animaux Stylophores Des Églises Romanes Apuliennes', 100; Belli D'Elia, *La Basilica Di S. Nicola a Bari: Un Monumento Nel Tempo*, 31.
15 Mackie, *Early Christian Chapels in the West*, 145–53, figure 73; Jensen, *Understanding Early Christian Art*, 60.
16 Parani, *Reconstructing the Reality of Images*, 306–7; Wharton Epstein, 'The Political Content of the Paintings of St Sophia at Ohrid', 315–29; Walter, *Art and Ritual in the Byzantine Church*, 175–6 and 190–8.
17 Similar associations may have been attached to porch-portals on northern Italian churches. Bornstein, *Portals and Politics in the Early Italian City-State*, 32.
18 Belli D'Elia, *La Basilica Di S. Nicola a Bari: Un Monumento Nel Tempo*, figures 3 and 4.
19 Vanderheyde, *La Sculpture Architecturale Byzantine Dans Le Thème de Nikopolis Du Xe Au Début Du XIIIe Siècle. Épire, Étolie-Acaranie et Sud de l'Albanie*, 104–7.
20 Saxon, *The Eucharist in Romanesque France*, 28–30; Macy, 'Theology of the Eucharist in the High Middle Ages', 371–2; Cowdrey, *Pope Gregory VII, 1073–1085*, 501.
21 Radding and Newton, *Theology, Rhetoric, and Politics in the Eucharistic Controversy, 1078–1079*, 52–6.
22 Radding and Newton, 64.
23 Saxon, 'Carolingian, Ottonian and Romanesque Art and the Eucharist', 312.
24 Dell'Omo, 'Per La Storia Dei Monaci-Vescovi Nell'Italia Normanna Del Secolo IX: Ricerche Biografiche Su Guitmondo Di La Croix-Saint-Leufroy, Vescovo Di Aversa', 8–9.
25 Somerville, *Pope Urban II, The Collectio Britannica, and the Council of Melfi (1089)*, 55–7.
26 Saxon, *The Eucharist in Romanesque France*, 45.

27. Hussey, *The Orthodox Church in the Byzantine Empire*, 358–9.
28. Macy, 'Theology of the Eucharist in the High Middle Ages', 366.
29. Saxon, 'Carolingian, Ottonian and Romanesque Art and the Eucharist', 280.
30. Saxon, 279–80.
31. Milburn, *Early Christian Art and Architecture*, 41 and 85, figures 22 and 51; Jensen, *Understanding Early Christian Art*, 42–3, figure 9.
32. Krautheimer, *Three Christian Capitals*, 65, figure 60.
33. Castiñeiras, *The Creation Tapestry*, 57 and 68.
34. Castiñeiras, 89–93.
35. Kapitaikin, '"The Daughter of al-Andalus": Interrelations between Norman Sicily and the Muslim West'; Rosser-Owen, 'Mediterraneanism: How to Incorporate Islamic Art into an Emerging Field'.
36. 2. Kings. 2.11.
37. Wollasch, *Neue Forschungen Über Cluny Und Die Cluniacenser*, 13; Alfano di Salerno, *Alfano Di Salerno. Il Carme Per Montecassino*, 28, lines 178–9.

Chapter 9

1. Pertusi, 'Ai Confini Tra Religione e Politica. La Contesa per Le Reliquie Di San Nicola Tra Bari, Venezia e Genova', 38; Houben, 'La Chiesa di Bari alla Fine dell'XI Secolo', 99, particularly note 43; Nitti di Vito, *Le Pergamene Di S. Nicola Di Bari. Periodo Normanno*, 3–5, number 1.
2. Nitti di Vito, *Le Pergamene Di S. Nicola Di Bari. Periodo Normanno*, 3–5, number 1; Houben, 'La Chiesa di Bari alla Fine dell'XI Secolo', 99, note 43; Matheou, 'Hegemony, Elitedom and Ethnicity. "Armenians" in Imperial Bari, c.874 1071'. Houben suggests that the document could be a forgery, but it has been accepted as genuine in the recent work by Matheou.
3. Cioffari, *L'Abate Elia. Il Benedettino che Costruì la Basilica di San Nicola*, 17–20.
4. Kamp, 'Vescovi e Diocesi dell'Italia Meridionale nel Passaggio dall Dominazione Bizantina allo Stato Normanno', 182.
5. Cioffari, *L'Abate Elia. Il Benedettino che Costruì la Basilica di San Nicola*, 17–20.
6. Bloch, *Montecassino in the Middle Ages*, 2:740; Kamp, 'Vescovi e Diocesi dell'Italia Meridionale nel Passaggio dall Dominazione Bizantina allo Stato Normanno', 182.
7. Bloch, *Monte Cassino in the Middle Ages*, 1:740.
8. Cioffari, *L'Abate Elia. Il Benedettino che Costruì la Basilica di San Nicola*, 25–9.
9. Cioffari, 25–9.
10. Kehr, *Italia Pontificia : sive repertorium privilegiorum et litterarum a Romanis Pontificibus ante annum MCLXXXXVIII: Italiae ecclesiis, monasteriis, civitatibus singulisque personis concessorum*, 9:319, number 7.
11. Oldfield, *City and Community in Norman Italy*, 36; Anonimo Barese, 'Chronicle', 154.
12. John the Deacon, 'Inventio S. Sabini'.
13. Musca, *L'Emirato Di Bari 847–871*.
14. Campione, 'Sabino, Vescovo Di Canosa, Santo'.
15. Ramseyer, *The Transformation of a Religious Landscape: Medieval Southern Italy, 850–1150*, 11.
16. Oldfield, *Sanctity and Pilgrimage in Medieval Southern Italy, 1000–1200*, 70.
17. Owen-Crocker, 'Episcopal Gloves (St Sabinus Gloves) from Canosa'.

18 Belli D'Elia, 'Canosa', 94.
19 Belli D'Elia, 94; Owen-Crocker, 'Episcopal Gloves (St Sabinus Gloves) from Canosa', 401.
20 Cioffari, *L'Abate Elia. Il Benedettino che Costruì la Basilica di San Nicola*, 32.
21 Cioffari, 127.
22 Beatillo, *Historia Della Vita, Miracoli, Traslatione, e Gloria Dell'Illustrissimo Confessore Di Christo San Nicolo Il Magno Archivescovo Di Mira, Patrone e Prottetore Della Città Di Bari*, 446.
23 Morey, *Roman and Christian Sculpture: The Sarcophagus of Claudia Antonia Sabina and the Asiatic Sarcophagi*, 5, part 1:46–50; Ghiandoni, 'Il Sarcofago Asiatico Di Melfi. Ricerche Mitologiche, Iconografiche e Stilistiche'.
24 Thomas, '"Houses of the Dead"? Columnar Sarcophagi as "Micro-Architecture"', 391; Hearn, *Romanesque Sculpture: The Revival of Monumental Stone Sculpture in the Eleventh and Twelfth Centuries*, 210.
25 Todisco, 'L'Eredità Dell'Antico Nella Cultura Materiale Di Bari Tra XI e XIII Secolo', 253–4.
26 My thanks to Rose Bacile for drawing my attention to this point in many discussions on the subject.
27 Greenhalgh, *The Survival of Roman Antiquities in the Middle Ages*, 193.
28 Bacile, 'The "Dynastic Mausolea" of the Norman Period in the South of Italy, c.1069–1189. A Study on the Form and Meaning of Burial Monuments in the Middle Ages', vii.
29 Bacile, 64–98.
30 Bacile, 92; Ingo Herklotz, *'Sepulcra' e 'Monumenta' Del Medioevo: Studi Sull'Arte Sepolcrale in Italia*, 147.
31 Braca, *Il Duomo di Salerno: Architettura e Culture Artistiche del Medioevo e dell'Età Moderna*, 103–14.
32 Beatillo, *Historia Della Vita, Miracoli, Traslatione, e Gloria Dell'Illustrissimo Confessore Di Christo San Nicolo Il Magno Archivescovo Di Mira, Patrone e Prottetore Della Città Di Bari*, 446.
33 Cavallo and Magistrale, 'Mezzogiorno Normanno e Scritture Esposte', 322; Todisco, 'L'Eredità Dell'Antico Nella Cultura Materiale Di Bari Tra XI e XIII Secolo', 254.
34 Bloch, *Montecassino in the Middle Ages*, 2:743.
35 *Orbis nour multus iacet his in pace sepultus / orbati reges patre sunt iudice leges / decidit o Barum rerum diadema tuarum / te viguisse scias viguit dum praesul Helias / clauditur hoc pulcro pater inclitus ille sepulcro / qui bene te super aethera vexxit / in commune bonus fuit omnibus ispe patronus / notis ignotis vicinis atque remotis / sensus laude boni fabricae quoque par salomoni / vitae more piae sancto simulandus heliae / hoc templum struxit quasi lampas et aurea luxit / hic abdormivit cum spiritus astra petivit.*
36 Cioffari, *L'Abate Elia. Il Benedettino che Costruì la Basilica di San Nicola*, 128.
37 Matijević Sokol, 'Epitafi Srednjega Vijeka: "knjige Života i Smrti"', 385–9. *hic abdormivit cum spiritus astra petivit.*
38 Fine, *When Ethnicity Did Not Matter in the Balkans*, 60; Pivčević, *The Cartulary of the Benedictine Abbey of St Peter of Gumay [Croatia] 1080–1187*.
39 Matijević Sokol, 'Epitafi Srednjega Vijeka: "knjige Života i Smrti"'.
40 Marrier, *Bibliotheca Cluniacensis*, 1643.
41 Kohnle, *Abt Hugo von Cluny (1049–1109)*.
42 Alfano di Salerno, *Alfano Di Salerno. Il Carme Per Montecassino*, 28, lines 180 and 186.
43 Brittain, 'O Roma Nobilis'.

44 Wollasch, *Neue Forschungen Über Cluny Und Die Cluniacenser*, 13; Alfano di Salerno, *Alfano Di Salerno. Il Carme Per Montecassino*, 28, lines 178–9.
45 Robinson, *The Papal Reform of the Eleventh Century*, 12–13; Paul of Bernried, 'Life of Pope Gregory VII', 263.
46 1 Kings 18.
47 Jones, *Saint Nicholas of Myra, Bari, and Manhattan: Biography of a Legend*, 20-1 and 24.
48 2 Kings 1: 11.
49 Jones, *Saint Nicholas of Myra, Bari, and Manhattan: Biography of a Legend*, 23.
50 Jones, 29–34 and 37.
51 Louis I Hamilton, *A Sacred City*, 142.
52 Oldfield, *City and Community in Norman Italy*, 36.
53 Loud, *The Age of Robert Guiscard*, 228. But 265–8 he is more cautious about whether or not Elias is a reformer.
54 Louis I Hamilton, *A Sacred City*, 69.
55 Cited and translated in Robinson, 'Reform and the Church, 1073 - 1122', 273. *Ad pristinum decorum et solidatatem redeat*.
56 Iafrate, *The Wandering Throne of Solomon*, 29.
57 Cushing, *Reform and the Papacy in the Eleventh Century*, 34.

Chapter 10

1 Most scholars agree on this dating. The lone voice of dissent is Rachele Carrino, who believes that Elias also commissioned the sanctuary pavement and that the inscription on the steps refers to Eustasius having paved the nave. Carrino, 'Il Pavimento Della Basilica Nicolaiana a Bari', 84–5.
2 Sada, *L'Abbazia Benedettina D'Ognisanti Di Cuti*, 41–4.
3 Cioffari, 'Dalle Origini a Bona Sforza', 143 and figure 122.
4 Hüls, *Kardinäle, Klerus Und Kirchen Roms: 1049–1130*, 179.
5 Robinson, 'Introduction', 91–2.
6 Robinson, *The Papacy, 1073–1198*, 129; McKeon, 'The Lateran Council of 1112, the Heresy of Lay Investiture and the Excommunication of Henry V'.
7 Romuald of Salerno, 'Romualdi Salernitani Chronicon', 206.
8 Anonimo Barese, 'Chronicle', 155–6 check page number.
9 Oldfield, 'Urban Government in Southern Italy, c.1085–c.1127', 600-1; Oldfield, *City and Community in Norman Italy*, 46; Martin, 'Les Communautes d'Habitants de la Pouille et leurs Rapports avec Roger II'.
10 Loud, *The Latin Church in Norman Italy*, 81; Oldfield, 'Urban Government in Southern Italy, c.1085–c.1127', 600-1.
11 Barile, 'La figlia del re di Francia e il principe normanno', 116–17.
12 Loud, *Roger II and the Creation of the Kingdom of Sicily*, 9.
13 Matheou, 'Hegemony, Elitedom and Ethnicity. "Armenians" in Imperial Bari, c.874 1071', 16; Skinner, 'Room for Tension', 170–5.
14 Oldfield, *City and Community in Norman Italy*, 47.
15 Nitti di Vito, *Le Pergamene Di S. Nicola Di Bari. Periodo Normanno*, numbers 69 and 69; Oldfield, *City and Community in Norman Italy*, 47–9.
16 Houben, *Roger II of Sicily*, 53–4.

17 Oldfield, *City and Community in Norman Italy*, 48; Poncelet, 'Miracula Sancti Nicolai a Monacho Beccensi', 426; Nitti di Vito, *Le Pergamene Di S. Nicola Di Bari. Periodo Normanno*, number 69.
18 Cavallo and Magistrale, 'Mezzogiorno Normanno e Scritture Esposte', 318; Magistrale, 'Forme e Funzioni Delle Scritte Esposte Nella Puglia Normanna'.
19 *His gradibus tumidis ascensus ad alta negatur, his gradibus blandis quaerere celsa datur, ergo ne timeas, qui sursum scandere quaeris, sis humilis supplex, plenus et altus eris, ut pater Helias hoc templum qui primus egit, quod pater Eustasius sic decorando regit.* With thanks to Andy Fox, Colin Whiting, Mark Thakkar, Andrew Buck, Neville Mogford and Francoise Charmaille for helping me decipher the inscription.
20 Milella, 'Il Rilievo Fotogrammetrico Digitale Multimmagine a Supporto Della Valorizzazione e Della Conoscenza Dei Beni Culturali', 94; Milella, 'Storia Dei Restauri'.
21 Sackur, 'Libelli de Lite'.
22 Fioretti et al., 'Study and Conservation of the St. Nicola's Basilica Mosaics (Bari, Italy) by Photogrammetric Survey', 162.
23 Schettini, *La Basilica di San Nicola di Bari*, 143.
24 Fioretti et al., 'Study and Conservation of the St. Nicola's Basilica Mosaics (Bari, Italy) by Photogrammetric Survey', 167.
25 Kier, *Der Mittelalterliche Schmuckfussboden Unter Besonderer Berücksichtigung Des Rheinlandes*, figures 298 and 319; Schulz and Barnsley, *The Monastery of Saint Luke of Stiris, in Phocis, and the Dependent Monastery of Saint Nicholas in the Fields, near Skripou in Boetia*, 30.
26 Greenhalgh, *Marble Past, Monumental Present: Building with Antiquities in the Mediaeval Mediterranean*, 247; Bowes, Francis, and Hodges, *Between Text and Territory: Survey and Excavations in the Terra of San Vincenzo al Volturno*.
27 Williams, *Italian Pavements: Patterns in Space*, 35, plate 1.
28 Amatus of Montecassino and Dunbar, *The History of the Normans by Amatus of Montecassino*, Book 3, page 107; Leo of Ostia, *Chronica Monasterii Casinensis*, 396, book 3.
29 Kier, *Der Mittelalterliche Schmuckfussboden Unter Besonderer Berücksichtigung Des Rheinlandes*, figures 1 and 2; Guiglia, 'Tradizione Locale Ed Influenze Bizantine Nei Pavimenti Cosmateschi'; Glass, *Studies on Cosmatesque Pavements*, 26; Bloch, *Monte Cassino in the Middle Ages*, 1:40–71; Cigola, 'Cosmatesque Pavement of Montecassino Abbey. History Through Geometric Analysis', 445–51; James, *Mosaics in the Medieval World*, 352; Mitchell, 'Giudizio Sul Mille: Rome, Monte Cassino, San Vincenzo al Volturno and the Beginnings of the Romanesque', 167–81.
30 Longo, 'Il Pavimento in Opus Sectile Della Chiesa Di San Menna. Maestranze Cassinesi a Sant'Agata de' Goti', 119–20; Longo, 'L'Opus Sectile Nei Cantieri Normanni - Una Squadra Di Marmorari Tra Salerno e Palermo'; Longo and Giarrusso, 'L'Impiego Del Palombino e Del Litotipo Artificiale Stracotto Nell'Opus Sectile Del Meridione Normanno'.
31 Longo, 'Il Pavimento in Opus Sectile Della Chiesa Di San Menna. Maestranze Cassinesi a Sant'Agata de' Goti', 114 and 121.
32 Fioretti et al., 'Study and Conservation of the St. Nicola's Basilica Mosaics (Bari, Italy) by Photogrammetric Survey', 167. The upper pavement, having been in continuous use since the twelfth century, has been much more heavily restored over the centuries than the crypt pavement. Consequently, although the marble is still mostly original, far more of the tesserae have been replaced.
33 Longo, 'Il Pavimento in Opus Sectile Della Chiesa Di San Menna. Maestranze Cassinesi a Sant'Agata de' Goti', 113 and 123.

34. Kier, *Der Mittelalterliche Schmuckfussboden Unter Besonderer Berücksichtigung Des Rheinlandes*, figure 319; Tronzo, *The Cultures of His Kingdom*, 34; Bloch, *Monte Cassino in the Middle Ages*, 1:47.
35. Barsanti, 'Una Note Sulla Diffusione Della Scultura a Incrostazione Nelle Regioni Adriatiche Del Meridione D'Italia Tra XI e XIII Secolo'; Macridy, 'The Monastery of Lips and the Burials of the Palaeologi', 187.
36. Vryonis, 'Jewelry from a Thessalonian Hoard'; Muthesius, *Byzantine Silk Weaving*, 38–9; Muthesius, *Studies in Byzantine, Islamic and Near Eastern Silk Weaving*, 98–206; Barsanti, 'Una Note Sulla Diffusione Della Scultura a Incrostazione Nelle Regioni Adriatiche Del Meridione D'Italia Tra XI e XIII Secolo', 525.
37. Zuliani, *Veneto Romanico*, 46 and 119; Barsanti, 'Una Note Sulla Diffusione Della Scultura a Incrostazione Nelle Regioni Adriatiche Del Meridione D'Italia Tra XI e XIII Secolo'.
38. Riccioni, 'I Mosaici Altomedievali Di Venezia e Il Monastero Di S. Ilario. Orditi "Venetico-Carolingi" Di Una Kionè Alto Adriatica', 279.
39. Minguzzi, 'I Pavimenti Antichi', 77 and 87; Barral i Altet, 'Genesi, Evoluzione e Diffusione Dei Pavimenti Romanici Delle Chiese Di Venezia', 46–55; Pinatsi, 'Regional Trends and International Exchange in the Art of Marble Pavements During the Middle-Byzantine Period', 110.
40. Barral i Altet, 'Genesi, Evoluzione e Diffusione Dei Pavimenti Romanici Delle Chiese Di Venezia'; Farioli-Campanati, 'Il Pavimento Di S. Marco a Venezia e i Suoi Rapporti Con L'Oriente', 11–19; Pinatsi, 'Regional Trends and International Exchange in the Art of Marble Pavements During the Middle-Byzantine Period', 110–11.
41. Carrino, 'Il Pavimento Della Basilica Nicolaiana a Bari', 89.
42. Ötüken, 'Myra-Demre Nikolaos Kilisesi Opus Sectile Yer Dösemesi ve Kazida Ortaya Çikan Opus Sectile Buluntular'; Ötüken, 'Konstantin IX - Solomon, Einzelkampfer, Siegesbringer Und Die Unbesiegbare Theotokos'.
43. Castiñeiras, 'The Baldachin-Ciborium: The Shifting Meanings of a Restricted Liturgical Furnishing in Romanesque Art'.
44. James, *Mosaics in the Medieval World*, 345.
45. Montecassino is the closest chronological and geographical parallel. In tenth-century Byzantium, it was also the patron who was responsible for acquiring materials. James, 103.

Chapter 11

1. Orderic Vitalis, *Ecclesiastical History of Orderic Vitalis*, 6, Books 11, 12 and 13:70–1.
2. Loud, *The Age of Robert Guiscard*, 141.
3. Savvidēs, *Byzantino-Normannica*, 48.
4. Yewdale, *Bohemond I, Prince of Antioch*, 23–4; Savvidēs, *Byzantino-Normannica*, 42; Upsher Smith, 'Nobilissimus and Warleader: The Opportunity and the Necessity behind Robert Guiscard's Balkan Expeditions'.
5. Savvidēs, *Byzantino-Normannica*; Theotokis, *The Norman Campaigns in the Balkans, 1081–1108 AD*.
6. Malaterra, *The Deeds of Count Roger of Calabria and Sicily and of His Brother Duke Robert Guiscard*, Book 4 (4? check this ref).
7. Theotokis, *The Norman Campaigns in the Balkans, 1081–1108 AD*, 185.

8   Theotokis, 185.
9   Romuald of Salerno, 'Chronicon'; Petraglia, 'La Cattedrale Di San Sabino a Canosa', 252.
10 Folda, *The Art of the Crusaders in the Holy Land, 1098–1187*, 36.
11 Friedman, *Encounter between Enemies: Captivity and Ransom in the Latin Kingdom of Jerusalem*, 134, 158 and 230.
12 Albu, 'Bohemond and the Rooster: Byzantines, Normans and the Artful Ruse'.
13 Yewdale, *Bohemond I, Prince of Antioch*, 109; Rowe, *The Jew, the Cathedral and the Medieval City*.
14 Riley-Smith, *The First Crusaders, 1095–1131*, 117–18; Orderic Vitalis, *Ecclesiastical History of Orderic Vitalis*, 6, Books 11, 12 and 13:69.
15 Abbot Suger, *The Deeds of Louis the Fat*, 43–5.
16 Orderic Vitalis, *Ecclesiastical History of Orderic Vitalis*, 6, Books 11, 12 and 13:71.
17 Abbot Suger, *The Deeds of Louis the Fat*, 45.
18 McQueen, 'Relations between the Normans and Byzantium 1071 - 1112'.
19 Hailstone, *Recalcitrant Crusaders?*, 103.
20 Asbridge, *The Creation of the Principality of Antioch, 1098–1130*, 94–8.
21 Hailstone, *Recalcitrant Crusaders?*, 107–8.
22 Gadolin, 'Prince Bohemund's Death and Apotheosis in the Church of San Sabino, Canosa Di Puglia'.
23 Flori, *Bohémond d'Antioche*, 287–8.
24 Tortora, *Relatio Status Sanctae Primatialis Ecclesiae Canusinae, Seu Historia Ex Romanorum Pontificum Constitutionibus*, 182.
25 Wharton Epstein, 'The Date and Significance of the Cathedral of Canosa in Apulia, South Italy'.
26 Dark and Özgümüş, 'New Evidence for the Byzantine Church of the Holy Apostles from Fatih Camii, Istanbul'; Downey, 'The Tombs of the Byzantine Emperors at the Church of the Holy Apostles in Constantinople'.
27 Cassano, *Principi, Imperatori, Vescovi: Duemila Anni Di Storia a Canosa*, 916.
28 Garton, 'Early Romanesque Sculpture in Apulia', 136.
29 Pratilli, *Della Aia Appia Riconosciuta e Descritta da Roma a Brindisi*, Book 4, Chapter 13, page 423; Richard de Saint-Non, *Voyage Pittoresque Ou Description Des Royaumes de Naples et de Sicile*.
30 Casati, 'Inventario Della Preposita Chiesa de S.to Savino e Delle Chiese Di Canosa'.
31 Pratilli, *Della Aia Appia Riconosciuta e Descritta da Roma a Brindisi*, 524–5.
32 Petraglia, 'La Cattedrale Di San Sabino a Canosa', 269–70; Fontana, '1 Versamento (1860–1890), Envelope 371, Relazione Del 9/05/1878, Sent by Vito Fontana, Ispettore Agli Scavi e Ai Monumenti Di Antichità to the Ministero Della Pubblica Istruzione'.
33 Cilla, *Caratteri e Restauri del Mausoleo di Marco Boemondo d'Altavilla*, 1–3; Vista, 'Curiosità Storiche: Canosa Nel 1643'.
34 Tortora, *Relatio Status Sanctae Primatialis Ecclesiae Canusinae, Seu Historia Ex Romanorum Pontificum Constitutionibus*, 352.
35 Flori, *Bohémond d'Antioche*, 289. Flori also argued that the chapel was built by Constance.
36 Van Houts, 'Changes of Aristocratic Identity: Remarriage and Remembrance in Europe 900–1200', 240.
37 Petrizzo, 'Band of Brothers: Kin Dynamics of the Hautevilles and Other Normans in Southern Italy and Syria, c.1030 - c.1140', 59; Hamilton, 'Women in the Crusader States: The Queens of Jerusalem (1100–1190)', 144–5; Houben, 'Adelaide Del Vasto Nella Storia Del Regno Di Sicilia'.

38 Skinner, '"Halt! Be Men!"'; Petrizzo, 'Band of Brothers: Kin Dynamics of the Hautevilles and Other Normans in Southern Italy and Syria, c.1030–c.1140', 54–5.
39 LoPrete, 'Adela of Blois: Familial Alliances and Female Lordship', 25.
40 LoPrete, 33.
41 Asbridge, *The Creation of the Principality of Antioch, 1098-1130*, 100.
42 Asbridge, 69 and 89–90.
43 Petrizzo, 'Band of Brothers: Kin Dynamics of the Hautevilles and Other Normans in Southern Italy and Syria, c.1030 - c.1140', 43–5; Robinson, *History and Cartulary of the Greek Monastery of St Elias and St Anastasius of Carbone*, 246–50 and 257–61. See the later for Constance's death.
44 Ménager, 'Costanza Di Francia'.
45 Nitti di Vito, *Le Pergamene Di S. Nicola Di Bari. Periodo Normanno*, number 38; Testi Cristiani, 'Sul Mausoleo Di Boemondo a Canosa', 111.
46 Petrizzo, 'Band of Brothers: Kin Dynamics of the Hautevilles and Other Normans in Southern Italy and Syria, c.1030–c.1140', 74–5; Romuald of Salerno, 'Romualdi Salernitani Chronicon', 208.
47 Nitti di Vito, *Le Pergamene Di S. Nicola Di Bari. Periodo Normanno*, number 64, 111.
48 Oldfield, *City and Community in Norman Italy*, 46–7; Musca, *Storia Di Bari*, 44; Romuald of Salerno, 'Romualdi Salernitani Chronicon', 206 and 210.
49 Doherty, 'Count Hugh of Troyes and the Prestige of Jerusalem', 884–5.
50 Paul, 'A Warlord's Wisdom', 564, note 170. *Ego Constancia Francorum Regis filippi filia et quondam domini Boamundi antiocheni principis magne et inmortalis memorie uxor*
51 Nitti di Vito, *Le Pergamene Di S. Nicola Di Bari. Periodo Normanno*, number 64, 111. *Boamundi invictissimi Antiocheni principis......auctoritate agens plenariam potestatem et vicem filii mei aduc pueri.*
52 Yewdale, *Bohemond I, Prince of Antioch*, 131.
53 Orderic Vitalis, *Ecclesiastical History of Orderic Vitalis*, 6, Books 11, 12 and 13:101–5.
54 William of Tyre, *A History of Deeds Done Beyond the Sea*, 472; Flori, *Bohémond d'Antioche*, 287; Asbridge, *The Creation of the Principality of Antioch, 1098-1130*, 95; Albert of Aachen, *Historia Ierosolimitana: History of the Journey to Jerusalem*, 758–9.
55 Petrizzo, 'Band of Brothers: Kin Dynamics of the Hautevilles and Other Normans in Southern Italy and Syria, c.1030–c.1140', 58.
56 Petrizzo, 75.
57 Petraglia, 'La Cattedrale Di San Sabino a Canosa', 251.
58 Houben, *Il Libro Del Capitolo Del Monastero Della SS. Trinità Di Venosa (Cod. Casin. 334)*, 34–5.
59 Bacile, McNeill, and Vernon, 'Venosa, Acerenza and "Norman" Architecture in Southern Italy'.
60 *Guiscardi coniux Aberada hac conditur arca. Si genitum quaeres, hunc Canusinus habet.*
61 Bloch, 'A New Fascination with Ancient Rome', 620–1; Bacile, 'The "Dynastic Mausolea" of the Norman Period in the South of Italy, c.1069–1189. A Study on the Form and Meaning of Burial Monuments in the Middle Ages', 54–5.
62 Houben, 'Da Venosa a Monreale: I Luoghi Di Memoria Dei Normanni Nel Sud', 53; Bacile, 'The "Dynastic Mausolea" of the Norman Period in the South of Italy, c.1069–1189. A Study on the Form and Meaning of Burial Monuments in the Middle Ages', 56–9.
63 Hailstone, *Recalcitrant Crusaders?*, 81.

64 Van Houts, 'Changes of Aristocratic Identity: Remarriage and Remembrance in Europe 900–1200', 239.
65 Van Houts, 238–9.
66 Van Houts, 240–1.
67 Petrizzo, 'Band of Brothers: Kin Dynamics of the Hautevilles and Other Normans in Southern Italy and Syria, c.1030–c.1140', 105–6; Skinner, '"Halt! Be Men!"'
68 Houben, 'Adelaide Del Vasto Nella Storia Del Regno Di Sicilia'; Pontieri, 'La Madre Di Re Ruggiero, Contessa Di Sicilia, Regina Di Gerusalemme'.
69 Tortora, *Relatio Status Sanctae Primatialis Ecclesiae Canusinae, Seu Historia Ex Romanorum Pontificum Constitutionibus*, 8–9.
70 Petraglia, 'La Cattedrale Di San Sabino a Canosa', 338.
71 Ousterhout, *Master Builders of Byzantium*, 120–1.
72 Ćurčić, 'Architectural Significance of Subsidiary Chapels in Middle Byzantine Churches'; Babić, *Les Chapelles Annexes Des Églises Byzantines: Fonction Liturgique et Programmes Iconographiques*.
73 Cadei, 'La Prima Committenza Normanna', 366, note 21.
74 Chelotti, 'Tipologia dei Monumenti', 274–6; Greenhalgh, *Marble Past, Monumental Present: Building with Antiquities in the Mediaeval Mediterranean*, 218.
75 Cilla, *Caratteri e Restauri del Mausoleo di Marco Boemondo d'Altavilla*; Bertaux and Prandi, *L'Art Dans l'Italie Méridionale. Aggiornamento Dell'Opera Di Émile Bertaux*; Herklotz, 'Lo Spazio Della Morte e Lo Spazio Della Sovranità', 325.
76 Cilla, *Caratteri e Restauri del Mausoleo di Marco Boemondo d'Altavilla*; Testi Cristiani, 'Sul Mausoleo Di Boemondo a Canosa'.
77 Kirschberger, *Erster Kreuzzug Und Ethnogenese*.
78 Cadei, 'La Prima Committenza Normanna', 366; Calò Mariani, 'Sulle Relazioni Artistiche Tra La Puglia e l'Oriente Latino', 47.
79 Eger, '(Re)Mapping Medieval Antioch', 104.
80 Eger, 104.
81 Folda, *The Art of the Crusaders in the Holy Land, 1098–1187*, 52.
82 Testi Cristiani, 'Sul Mausoleo Di Boemondo a Canosa', 107–16.
83 Morris, *The Sepulchre of Christ and the Medieval West*, 183; Housley, 'Jerusalem and the Development of the Crusade Idea 1099–1128', 30–1.
84 Ousterhout, 'Rebuilding the Temple'; Boas, *Jerusalem in the Time of the Crusades*, 103.
85 Wilson, *The Pilgrimage of the Russian Abbot Daniel in the Holy Land, 1106–1107 A.D.*, 4:12.
86 Morris, *The Sepulchre of Christ and the Medieval West*, 190–3.
87 Grabar, 'Le Reliquaire Byzantin de La Cathédrale d'Aix-La-Chapelle'; Saunders, 'The Aachen Reliquary of Eustathius Maleinus, 969–70'; Ousterhout, 'Reliquary of St Anastasios the Persian'.
88 Salvarani, *La Fortuna Del Santo Sepolcro Nel Medioevo*, 154; Herklotz, 'Lo Spazio Della Morte e Lo Spazio Della Sovranità', 325.
89 Krautheimer, 'Introduction to an "Iconography of Mediaeval Architecture"'.
90 Moore, *The Architecture of the Christian Holy Land: Reception from Late Antiquity through the Renaissance*, 67 and 69; Morris, *The Sepulchre of Christ and the Medieval West*, 164.
91 Moore, *The Architecture of the Christian Holy Land: Reception from Late Antiquity through the Renaissance*, 67.
92 Moore, 75.
93 Lidov, 'A Byzantine Jerusalem: The Imperial Pharos Chapel as the Holy Sepulchre', 77.

94 Lidov, 66 and 71.
95 Lidov, 85–9.
96 Bartal, 'Relics of Place'.
97 Halphen and Poupardine, *Chronica de Gestis Consulum Andegavorum, Chronique Des Comtes d'Anjou et Des Seigneurs d'Amboise*, 51.
98 Moore, *The Architecture of the Christian Holy Land: Reception from Late Antiquity through the Renaissance*, 69 and 75.
99 Petraglia, 'La Cattedrale Di San Sabino a Canosa', 262.
100 John, 'The "Feast of the Liberation of Jerusalem"'.
101 Gaposchkin, 'The Echoes of Victory'.
102 Moore, *The Architecture of the Christian Holy Land: Reception from Late Antiquity through the Renaissance*, 69.
103 Ousterhout, 'The Church of Santo Stefano', 316.
104 Ousterhout, 'The Church of Santo Stefano'; Ousterhout, 'Sacred Geographies and Holy Cities: Constantinople as Jerusalem', 3–4.
105 Menduni, 'Ricerche Sui Restauri Della Basilica Cattedrale Di S. Sabino a Canosa a Partire Dal XIX Secolo Sino All'Inizio Del XX Secolo. L'Affresco Della Crocifissione Del Redentore Sul Calvario'; Petraglia, 'La Cattedrale Di San Sabino a Canosa', 334.
106 Petraglia, 'La Cattedrale Di San Sabino a Canosa', 335 and 340.
107 Richardson, 'Between the Limousin and the Holy Land'; Bacile, 'The "Dynastic Mausolea" of the Norman Period in the South of Italy, c.1069–1189. A Study on the Form and Meaning of Burial Monuments in the Middle Ages', 56–9 and 73–102; Bacile, McNeill, and Vernon, 'Venosa, Acerenza and "Norman" Architecture in Southern Italy'; Houben, 'Roberto Il Guiscardo e Il Monachesimo'; Houben, 'Da Venosa a Monreale: I Luoghi Di Memoria Dei Normanni Nel Sud', 53.

Chapter 12

1 Schulz, *Denkmäler Der Kunst Des Mittelalters in Unteritalien*, Plate 10.
2 Weinryb, *The Bronze Object in the Middle Ages*, 16.
3 Conant, 'The Original Buildings at the Holy Sepulchre in Jerusalem', Plate 15.
4 Weetch, 'The Mystery of the Bronze Lion Heads at the Museum of the Order of St John'; 'Lion Head Door Knocker or Handle (LDOSJ 5617)'.
5 Doig, 'Charlemagne's Palace Chapel at Aachen: Apocalyptic and Apotheosis', 189.
6 Matthiae, *Le Porte Bronzee Bizantine in Italia*.
7 Matthiae, 13.
8 Guérin, 'Forgotten Routes?', 91.
9 It should be noted that the doors of San Zeno in Verona were made earlier, in the 1080s, but the technique is very different. Weinryb, *The Bronze Object in the Middle Ages*, 112.
10 Cadei, 'La Prima Committenza Normanna'.
11 Vona, 'Le Porte Di Monte Sant'Angelo e Di Canosa: Tecnologie a Confronto', 378–80; Vona, 'La Porta Del Mausoleo Di Boemondo'.
12 Bloch, *Monte Cassino in the Middle Ages*, 1:495 and 553; Vona, 'Le Porte Di Monte Sant'Angelo e Di Canosa: Tecnologie a Confronto'.
13 Weinryb, *The Bronze Object in the Middle Ages*, 82; Iacobini, '"Barisanus......Me Fecit" Nuovi Documenti Sull'Officina Di Barisanus Da Trani'.

14 Vona, 'Le Porte Di Monte Sant'Angelo e Di Canosa: Tecnologie a Confronto', 378; Vona, 'Persistenza Della Tradizione Tecnologica Di Bisanzio Nei Bronzi Medievali Pugliesi', 28.
15 Vona, 'Le Porte Di Monte Sant'Angelo e Di Canosa: Tecnologie a Confronto', 378.
16 Camber, 'The Mari Cha Lion in the Context of Apulian Romanesque Sculpture', 186; Fasnacht, 'Copper on Cyprus'.
17 Iacobini, 'Le Porte Bronzee Bizantine in Italia: Arte e Tecnologia Nel Mediterraneo Medievale', 18.
18 Weinryb, *The Bronze Object in the Middle Ages*, 49–50, 56–7 and 87.
19 Arnold and Goodson, 'Resounding Community', 103–11.
20 Grant, *Early Lives of Charlemagne by Eginhard and the Monk of St Gall*, 94, chapter 29.
21 Hudson, *Historia Ecclesie Abbendonensis*, 1:339.
22 Christie, 'On Bells and Belltowers. Origins and Evolutions in Italy and Britain, AD 700-1200', 16–23.
23 De Blaauw, 'Campanae Supra Urbem: Sull'Uso delle Campane nella Roma Medievale', 410–14.
24 Dodwell, *Anglo-Saxon Art*, 61.
25 Arnold and Goodson, 'Resounding Community', 119.
26 Dodwell, *Anglo-Saxon Art*, 66–7.
27 Hills, 'Croxden Abbey and Its Chronicle', 301.
28 Cirsone, 'La Basilica Della SS. Trinità Di Venosa Dalla Tarda Antichità All'Età Moderna (II Parte)', 102–3.
29 Occhiato, 'Rapporti Culturali e Rispondenze Architettoniche Tra Calabria e Francia in Età Romanica'; Houben, 'Melfi e Venosa: Due Città Sotto Il Dominio Normanno-Svevo'.
30 Vona, 'Persistenza Della Tradizione Tecnologica Di Bisanzio Nei Bronzi Medievali Pugliesi', 29.
31 Vona, 'Le Porte Di Monte Sant'Angelo e Di Canosa: Tecnologie a Confronto', 376 and 378; Giannichedda et al., 'Attività Fusoria Medievale a Canosa'.
32 Vona, 'Le Porte Di Monte Sant'Angelo e Di Canosa: Tecnologie a Confronto'; Vona, 'Persistenza Della Tradizione Tecnologica Di Bisanzio Nei Bronzi Medievali Pugliesi'.
33 Vona, 'Le Porte Di Monte Sant'Angelo e Di Canosa: Tecnologie a Confronto', 376.
34 Vona, 'Persistenza Della Tradizione Tecnologica Di Bisanzio Nei Bronzi Medievali Pugliesi', 29.
35 Vona, 25, 28, 31–3.
36 Vona, 31–3. But Oderisius's superior alloy may have been serendipity rather than intention, as Vona believes that he used a melted down Roman bronze, rather than a newly made alloy. Even if Oderisius stumbled upon an alloy better suited to cold carving, his doors are still structurally stronger, larger and more confident than those of Roger of Melfi's.
37 Henry Swinburne's eighteenth-century description reports that the figures are kneeling below a Madonna but I think Swinburne was probably conflating this image with the Madonna on the other door. Henry Swinburne, *Travels in the Two Sicilies, by Henry Swinburne, Esq. in the Years 1777, 1778, 1779, and 1780*, 410; Petraglia, 'La Cattedrale Di San Sabino a Canosa', 266.
38 Napolitano, 'Le Iscrizioni Arabe della Porta del Mausoleo di Boemondo a Canosa'; Vernon, 'Pseudo-Arabic and the Material Culture of the First Crusade in Norman Italy'.

39. Gaspariño Garcìa, 'Amuletos Andalusíes. Nuevas Adiciones', 79; D'Ottone Rambuch, 'Aubin-Louis Millin e La Civiltà Islamica Attraverso Disegni e Appunti Inediti', 156.
40. Blair and Bloom, *Cosmophilia: Islamic Art from the David Collection, Copenhagen*, 42–3; Northover and Meyer, 'A Newly Acquired Islamic Lion Door Knocker in the David Collection'; Raby, 'The Inscriptions on the Pisa Griffin and the Mari-Cha Lion: From Banal Blessings to Indices of Origin'.
41. Vernon, 'Pseudo-Arabic and the Material Culture of the First Crusade in Norman Italy', 3–4 and 25–6; Erdmann, *Arabische Schriftzeichen Als Ornamente in Der Abendländischen Kunst Des Mittelalters*.
42. Garton, 'Early Romanesque Sculpture in Apulia', 302.
43. Barrucand, *Trésors fatimides du Caire*, 91 and 94–5; 'Panel with Horse Heads (11.205.2), Metropolitan Museum of Art, New York'.
44. Delogu, *La Galleria Nazionale Di Sicilia*, figure 96; Ventrone Vassallo, 'Pannello Ligneo'.
45. Marsiglia, 'Elementi Erratici Lignei Di Epoca Medievale in Sicilia', 85–6.
46. Gabrieli and Scerrato, *Gli Arabi in Italia*, 117, figures 114–6.
47. Barrucand, *Trésors fatimides du Caire*, 124–5; *Bronze Cylindrical Box, I.3679, Staatliche Museum, Berlin*. Apparently there is a similar box in the cathedral museum in Bari, but I have not been able to see it.
48. Russo, *Boemondo*, 200.
49. Flori, *Bohémond d'Antioche*, 293.
50. Mayo, 'Vasa Sacra'.
51. I have used Paula Hailstone's translation. See the following chapter for the full inscription. Hailstone, *Recalcitrant Crusaders?*, 112.
52. Debiais, 'Writing on Medieval Doors: The Surveyor Angel on the Moissac Capital (ca.1100)', 285.
53. Bloch, 'Origin and Fate of the Bronze Doors of Abbot Desiderius of Monte Cassino'; Iacobini, 'Le Porte Bronzee Bizantine in Italia: Arte e Tecnologia Nel Mediterraneo Medievale'.
54. Bertelli, 'La Porta Del Santuario Di S. Michele a Monte Sant'Angelo: Aspetti e Problemi', 300.

Chapter 13

1. Petraglia, 'La Cattedrale Di San Sabino a Canosa', 274.
2. Translation by Paula Hailstone.

   Magnanimus siriae iacet hoc sub tegimine princeps,
   Quo nullus melior nascetur in orbe deinceps,
   Grecia victa quater, pars mazima partia mundi
   Ingenium et vires sensere diu Boemundi
   Hic acie in dena vicit virtutis abena
   Agimina millena, quod et urbs sapit anthiocena

3. Flori, *Bohémond d'Antioche*, 295.
4. Delle Donne, 'Le Fonti Letterarie Latine Su Boemondo', 181.
5. *Unde boat mundus, quanti fuerit Boamundus*

   Graecia testatur, Syria denumerat
   Hanc expugnavit, illam protexit ab hoste;

Hinc rident Graecia, Syria damna tua.
Quod Graecus ridet, quod Syrus luget, uterque
Iuste, vera tibi sit, Boamunde, salus.
Vicit opes regum Boamundus opusque potentum
Et meruit dici nomine iure suo:
Intonuit terris. Cui cum succumberet orbis,
Non hominem possum dicere, nolo deum.
Qui vivens studit, ut pro Christo moreretur
Promeruit, quod ei morienti vita daretur.
Hoc ergo Christi clementia conferat isti
Militet ut coelis suus hic athleta fidelis.
Intrans cerne fores; videas, quid scribatur; ores
Ut celo detur Boamundus ibique locetur.

6 Magistrale, 'Forme e Funzioni Delle Scritte Esposte Nella Puglia Normanna', 38; Delle Donne, 'Le Fonti Letterarie Latine Su Boemondo', 181.
7 Delle Donne, 'Le Iscrizioni Del Mausoleo Di Boemondo D'Altavilla a Canosa', 9 and 17.
8 Baronio, *Annales Ecclesiastici*, 12:89.
9 Delle Donne, 'Le Iscrizioni Del Mausoleo Di Boemondo D'Altavilla a Canosa', 17; Delle Donne, 'Le Fonti Letterarie Latine Su Boemondo', 182.
10 Russo, 'Oblio e Memoria Di Boemondo d'Altavilla Nella Storiografia Normanna'; Delle Donne, 'Le Fonti Letterarie Latine Su Boemondo', 185.
11 Delle Donne, 'Le Iscrizioni Del Mausoleo Di Boemondo D'Altavilla a Canosa', 188.
12 Russo, 'Bad Crusaders? The Normans of Southern Italy and the Crusading Movement in the Twelfth Century'.
13 Folda, *The Art of the Crusaders in the Holy Land, 1098-1187*, 38.
14 Packard, 'Remembering the First Crusade: Latin Narrative Histories 1099 - c.1300', 50.
15 Packard, 47-8.
16 Packard, 40.
17 Cowdrey, 'Martyrdom and the First Crusade', 48; Packard, 'Remembering the First Crusade: Latin Narrative Histories 1099 - c.1300', 44.
18 Flori, *Bohémond d'Antioche*, 717-46; Carrier, 'Pour En Finir Avec Les Gesta Francorum'; Paul, 'A Warlord's Wisdom'.
19 Friedman, *Encounter between Enemies: Captivity and Ransom in the Latin Kingdom of Jerusalem*, 231.
20 Paul, 'A Warlord's Wisdom', 565.
21 Delle Donne, 'Le Fonti Letterarie Latine Su Boemondo', 177 and 180-1; Marbodus of Rennes, 'Carmina Varia, 38, Commendatio Jerosolymitanae'.
22 Delle Donne, 'Le Fonti Letterarie Latine Su Boemondo', 175-6.
23 Jamison, 'The Norman Administration of Apulia and Capua: More Especially under Roger II. and William I. 1127-1166', 225-6.
24 Asbridge, *The Creation of the Principality of Antioch, 1098-1130*, 130-2.
25 Nitto de Rossi and Nitti di Vito, *Le Pergamene Del Duomo Di Bari (952 - 1264)*, 72, number 38; Nitti di Vito, *Le Pergamene Di S. Nicola Di Bari. Periodo Normanno*, number 64.
26 Asbridge, *The Creation of the Principality of Antioch, 1098-1130*, 95-6 and 132-3.
27 Packard, 'Remembering the First Crusade: Latin Narrative Histories 1099 - c.1300', 72-3.
28 Packard, 71.

Bibliography

Abbot, Suger. *The Deeds of Louis the Fat*. Translated by Richard Cusimano and John Moorhead. Washington, DC: Catholic University of America Press, 1992.

Abulafia, David. 'Moametto e Carlo Magno: Le Due Aree Monetarie Italiane Dell'Oro e Dell'Argento'. In *Economia Naturale, Economia Monetaria*, edited by Ruggerio Romano and Ugo Tucci, 221–70. Storia D'Italia: Annali 6. Turin: Einaudi, 1983.

Abulafia, David. 'Role of Trade in Muslim-Christian Contact during the Middle Ages'. In *The Arab Influence in Medieval Europe*, edited by Richard Hitchcock and Dionisius A. Agius, 1–24. Reading, MA: Ithaca Press, 1994.

Abulafia, David. 'The Italian Other: Greeks, Muslims and Jews'. In *Italy in the Central Middle Ages 1000–1300*, edited by David Abulafia, 215–36. Oxford: Oxford University Press, 2004.

Abulafia, David. 'Trade and Crusade 1050–1250'. In *Cross Cultural Convergences in the Crusader Period*, edited by Michael Goodich, Sylvia Schein, and Sophia Menache, 1–20. New York: Peter Lang, 1995.

Aceto, Francesco, ed. *Arte in Puglia Dal Medioevo al Settecento: Il Medioevo*. Rome: De Luca, 2010.

Aceto, Francesco. 'La Cattedra Dell'Abate Elia: Dalla Memoria Alla Storia'. In *Medioevo: Imagine e Memoria. Atti Del Convegno Internazionale Di Studi, Parma, 23–28 Settembre 2008*, edited by Arturo Carlo Quintavalle, 132–43. Milano: Electa, 2009.

Aird, William M. *Robert 'Curthose', Duke of Normandy (C. 1050–1134)*. Woodbridge: Boydell Press, 2011.

Albert of Aachen. *Historia Ierosolimitana: History of the Journey to Jerusalem*. Edited by Susan B. Edgington. Oxford: Oxford University Press, 2007.

Albu, Emily. 'Bohemond and the Rooster: Byzantines, Normans and the Artful Ruse'. In *Anna Komnene and Her Times*, edited by Thalia Gouma-Peterson, 157–68. New York; London: Garland Publishing, 2000.

Alchermes, Joseph D. 'Two Stone Slabs'. In *Glory of Byzantium: Art and Culture of the Middle Byzantine Era, A.D. 843–1261*, edited by Helen C. Evans and William D. Wixom, 326–27. New York: Metropolitan Museum of Art, 1997.

Alfano di Salerno. *Alfano Di Salerno. Il Carme Per Montecassino*. Edited by Nicola Acocella. Salerno, 1963.

Allaire, Gloria. 'Arthurian Art in Italy'. In *The Arthur of the Italians: Arthurian Legend in Medieval Italian Literature and Culture*, edited by F. Regina Psaki and Gloria Allaire, 205–32. Cardiff: University of Wales Press, 2014.

Amatus of Montecassino, and Prescott N. Dunbar. *The History of the Normans by Amatus of Montecassino*. Woodbridge: Boydell Press, 2004.

Andaloro, Maria, ed. *Nobiles Officinae: Perle, Filigrane e Trame Di Seta Dal Palazzo Reale Di Palermo*. Catania: G. Maimone, 2006.

Anderson, Benjamin. *Cosmos and Community in Early Medieval Art*. New Haven: Yale University Press, 2017.

Angheben, Marcel. 'Les Animaux Stylophores Des Églises Romanes Apuliennes: Étude Iconographique'. *Arte Medievale* 1, no. 2 (2002): 97–117.

Angold, Michael. *The Byzantine Empire, 1025–1204: A Political History*. London: Longman, 1997.

Anonimo, Barese. 'Chronicle'. In *Antiche Cronache Di Terra Di Bari*, edited by Gerardo Cioffari and Rosa Lupoli Tateo. Bari: Centro studi Nicolaiani, 1991.

Appuhn, Horst. 'Beiträge Zur Geschichte Des Herrschersitzes Im Mittelalter II. Teil: Der Sogenannte Krodo-Altar Und Der Kaiserstuhl in Goslar'. *Aachener Kunstblätter* 54/55 (1986): 69–98.

Arnold, John H., and Caroline Goodson. 'Resounding Community: The History and Meaning of Medieval Church Bells'. *Viator* 43, no. 1 (2012): 99–130. https://doi.org/10.1484/J.VIATOR.1.102544.

Asbridge, Thomas S. *The Creation of the Principality of Antioch, 1098–1130*. Woodbridge: Boydell & Brewer, 2000.

Babić, Gordana. *Les Chapelles Annexes Des Églises Byzantines: Fonction Liturgique et Programmes Iconographiques*. Paris: Klincksieck, 1969.

Babudri, Francesco. 'Le Note Autobiografiche Di Giovanni Arcidiacono Barese e La Cronologia Dell'Arcivescovato Di Ursone a Bari'. *Archivio Storico Pugliese* 2 (1949): 134–46.

Bacile, Rosa. 'The "Dynastic Mausolea" of the Norman Period in the South of Italy, c.1069–1189: A Study on the Form and Meaning of Burial Monuments in the Middle Ages'. D.Phil thesis, University of Oxford, 2010.

Bacile, Rosa, John McNeill, and Clare Vernon. 'Venosa, Acerenza and "Norman" Architecture in Southern Italy'. *Arte Medievale* 4, no. 11 (2021): 27–59.

Baer, Eva. *Islamic Ornament*. New York: New York University Press, 1998.

Baer, Eva. *Sphinxes and Harpies in Medieval Islamic Art: An Iconographical Study*. Jerusalem: Israel Oriental Society, 1965.

Balfour, Alan. *Solomon's Temple: Myth, Conflict and Faith*. Chichester: Wiley-Blackwell, 2012.

Barile, Nicola Lorenzo. 'La Figlia del Re di Francia e il Principe Normanno: Il Matrimonio di Costanza e Boemondo d'Altavilla (1106)'. In *Con Animo Virile: Donne e Potere nel Mezzogiorno Medievale, Secoli XI-XV*, edited by Patrizia Mainoni, 85–137. Rome: Viella, 2011.

Baronio, Cesare. *Annales Ecclesiastici*. Vol. 12. Rome, 1607.

Barral i Altet, Xavier. 'Arte Medievale e Riforma Gregoriana: Riflessioni Su Un Problema Storiografico'. *Hortus Artium Medievalium* 16 (2010): 73–82.

Barral i Altet, Xavier. 'Genesi, Evoluzione e Diffusione Dei Pavimenti Romanici Delle Chiese Di Venezia'. In *Storia Dell'Arte Marciana: Sculture, Tesoro, Arrazzi*, edited by Renato Polacco, vol. 2, 46–55. Venice: Marsilio, 1997.

Barrucand, Marianne, ed. *Trésors Fatimides du Caire*. Ghent and Paris: Snoeck-Ducaju & Zoon, Institut du Monde Arabe, 1998.

Barry, Fabio. 'Disiecta Membra: Ranieri Zeno, the Imitation of Constantinople, the Spolia Style, and Justice at San Marco'. In *San Marco, Byzantium, and the Myths of Venice*, edited by Henry Maguire and Robert Nelson, 7–62. Washington, DC: Dumbarton Oaks, 2010.

Barsanti, Claudia. 'Una Note Sulla Diffusione Della Scultura a Incrostazione Nelle Regioni Adriatiche Del Meridione D'Italia Tra XI e XIII Secolo'. In *La Sculpture Byzantine VIIe - XIIe Siècles*, edited by Charalambos Pennas and Catherine Vanderheyde. Bulletin de Correspondence Hellénique 49, 515–557. Athens: École Française d'Athènes, 2008.

Bartal, Renana. 'Relics of Place: Stone Fragments of the Holy Sepulchre in Eleventh-Century France'. *Journal of Medieval History* 44, no. 4 (2018): 406–21. https://doi.org/10.1080/03044181.2018.1487872.

Baumgärtel-Fleischmann, Renate. 'Die Kaisermäntel Im Bamberger Domschatz'. In *Kaiser Heinrich II. 1002–1024*, edited by Josef Kirmeier, 379–87. Bamberg: Bayerische Landesausstellung, 2002.

Beatillo, Antonio. *Historia Della Vita, Miracoli, Traslatione, e Gloria Dell'Illustrissimo Confessore Di Christo San Nicolo Il Magno Archivescovo Di Mira, Patrone e Prottetore Della Città Di Bari*. Venice: Nicolò Pezzana, 1705.

Becker, Oliver. *Die Architektur Der Normannen in Süditalien Im 11. Jahrhundert: Kontinuität Und Innovation Als Visuelle Strategien Der Legitimation von Herrschaft*. Affalterbach: Didymos-Verlag, 2018.

Belli D'Elia, Pina. 'Abbazia Di San Benedetto'. In *Alle Sorgenti Del Romanico. Puglia XI Secolo*, edited by Pina Belli D'Elia, 193–4. Bari: Dedalo, 1987.

Belli D'Elia, Pina. 'Acceptus'. In *Enciclopedia Dell'Arte Medievale*, 85–7. Rome: Istituto della Enciclopedia Italiana, 1991.

Belli D'Elia, Pina, ed. *Alle Sorgenti Del Romanico: Puglia XI Secolo*. Bari: Edizioni Dedalo, 1987.

Belli D'Elia, Pina. 'Angelo Docente (La Divina Sapienza?)'. In *Arte in Puglia Dal Medioevo al Settecento: Il Medioevo*, edited by Francesco Abbate, 121–2. Rome: De Luca Editori d'Arte, 2010.

Belli D'Elia, Pina. 'Canosa'. In *Alle Sorgenti Del Romanico. Puglia XI Secolo*, edited by Pina Belli D'Elia, 72–9. Bari: Dedalo, 1987.

Belli D'Elia, Pina. 'Coppia Di Sfingi Alate'. In *Arte in Puglia Dal Medioevo al Settecento: Il Medioevo*, edited by Francesco Abbate, 123–7. Rome: De Luca Editori d'Arte, 2010.

Belli D'Elia, Pina. *La Basilica Di S. Nicola a Bari: Un Monumento Nel Tempo*. Galatina: Congedo, 1985.

Belli D'Elia, Pina. 'La Cattedra Dell'Abbate Elia'. *Bolletino D'Arte* 59 (1974): 1–17.

Belli D'Elia, Pina, ed. *L'Angelo La Montagna Il Pellegrino. Monte Sant'Angelo e Il Santuario Di San Michele Del Gargano Dalle Origini Ai Nostri Giorni*. Foggia: Claudio Grenzi, 1999.

Belli D'Elia, Pina. 'Maestro Della Cattedra Dell'Abate Elia. Coppie Di Schiavi e Maschere Sputaracemi'. In *Arte in Puglia Dal Medioevo al Settecento: Il Medioevo*, edited by Francesco Abbate, 127–8. Roma: De Luca Editori d'Arte, 2010.

Belli D'Elia, Pina. *Puglia Romanica*. Milan: Jaca, 2003.

Belli D'Elia, Pina, and Tessa Garton. 'Polignano'. In *Alle Sorgenti Del Romanico. Puglia XI Secolo*, edited by Pina Belli D'Elia, 207. Bari: Dedalo, 1987.

Belli D'Elia, Pina, and Tessa Garton. 'Pulpito'. In *Alle Sorgenti Del Romanico: Puglia XI Secolo*, edited by Pina Belli D'Elia, 80–2. Bari: Dedalo, 1987.

Belli D'Elia, Pina, and Tessa Garton. 'Santa Maria Di Colonna'. In *Alle Sorgenti Del Romanico. Puglia XI Secolo*, edited by Pina Belli D'Elia, 190–2. Bari: Dedalo, 1987.

Belli D'Elia, Pina, and Tessa Garton. 'Siponto'. In *Alle Sorgenti Del Romanico. Puglia XI Secolo*, edited by Pina Belli D'Elia, 47–67. Bari: Dedalo, 1987.

Belli D'Elia, Pina, and Tessa Garton. 'Trani'. In *Alle Sorgenti Del Romanico. Puglia XI Secolo*, edited by Pina Belli D'Elia, 68–71. Bari: Dedalo, 1987.

Belli D'Elia, Pina and Francesco Tateo. *Storia di Bari Dalla Conquista Normanna al Ducato Sforzesco*. Rome: Laterza, 1987

Belting, Hans. 'Byzantine Art among Greeks and Latins in Southern Italy'. *Dumbarton Oaks Papers* 28 (1974): 1–29. https://doi.org/10.2307/1291353.

Bertaux, Émile, and Adriano Prandi. *L'Art Dans l'Italie Méridionale. Aggiornamento Dell'Opera Di Émile Bertaux*. Rome: École Française de Rome, 1978.

Bertelli, Gioia. 'Acceptus e Magister David a Siponto: Nuove Acquisizioni'. In *'A Mari Usque Ad Mare' Cultura Visuale e Materiale Dall'Adriatico All'India. Scritti in Memoria

Di Gianclaudio Macchiarella, edited by Mattia Guidetti and Sara Mondini, 63–72. Venice: Edizioni Ca'Foscari - Digital Publishing, 2016.

Bertelli, Gioia. 'Capitellino Cubico'. In *Arte in Puglia dal Medioevo al Settecento: il Medioevo*, edited by Francesco Abbate 53. Rome: De Luca Editori d'Arte, 2010.

Bertelli, Gioia. 'Capitello-Imposta'. In *Arte in Puglia Dal Medioevo al Settecento: Il Medioevo*, edited by Francesco Abbate, 47–8. Rome: De Luca Editori d'Arte, 2010.

Bertelli, Gioia. 'Capitello-Imposta Su Colonnia Spiralforme'. In *Arte in Puglia Dal Medioevo al Settecento: Il Medioevo*, edited by Francesco Abbate, 48. Rome: De Luca Editori d'Arte, 2010.

Bertelli, Gioia. 'Epistilio Frammentario Di Iconostasi'. In *Arte in Puglia Dal Medioevo al Settecento: Il Medioevo*, edited by Francesco Abbate, 57–8. Rome: De Luca Editori d'Arte , 2010.

Bertelli, Gioia. 'La Porta Del Santuario Di S. Michele a Monte Sant'Angelo: Aspetti e Problemi'. In *Le Porte Di Bronzo Dall'Antichità al Secolo XIII*, edited by Salvatorino Salomi, 293–306. Rome: Istituto della Enciclopedia Italiana, 1990.

Bertelli, Gioia. *Puglia Preromanica Dal V Secolo Agli Inizi Dell'XI*. Milan: Jaca, 2004.

Bertelli, Gioia. 'Sul Reimpiego Di Elementi Architettonici Bizantini a Bari'. Edited by Giuliano Volpe. *Puglia Paleocristiana e Altomedievale* 6 (1991): 137–70.

Bertelli, Gioia, and Angelofabio Attolico. 'Analisi Delle Stutture Architettoniche Della Cattedrale Di San Sabino a Canosa: Primi Dati'. In *Canosa. Ricerche Storiche Decennio 1999–2009*, edited by Liana Bertoldi Lenoci, 723–58. Martina Franca: Edizioni Pugliesi, 2011.

Bertelli, Gioia, Arcangelo Fornaro, and Raffaele Iorio. *S. Maria Que Est Episcopio: La Cattedrale Di Bari Dalle Origini al 1034*. Bari: Edipuglia, 1994.

Bettocchi, Silvia, and Immacolata Aulisa. 'Il Santuario Dal IX al XI Secolo: Gli Affreschi e Conservazione'. In *Angelo La Montagna Il Pellegrino*, edited by Pina Belli D'Elia, 50–6. Foggia: Claudio Grenzi, 1999. http://www.claudiogrenzieditore.it/scheda_libro.asp?id_libro=288.

Bindman, David, and Henry Louis Gates, eds. *The Image of the Black in Western Art I: From the Pharaohs to the Fall of the Roman Empire*. Publications of Menil Foundation. Cambridge MA: Harvard University Press, 1976.

Birch, Debra. *Pilgrimage to Rome in the Middle Ages: Continuity and Change*. Woodbridge: Boydell & Brewer Ltd, 2000.

Blair, Sheila S., and Jonathan M. Bloom. *Cosmophilia: Islamic Art from the David Collection, Copenhagen*. Chesnut Hill, MA: McMullen Museum of Art, Boston College, 2006.

Bloch, Herbert. 'A New Fascination with Ancient Rome'. In *Renaissance and Renewal in the Twelfth Century*, edited by Robert Louis Benson and Giles Constable, 615–36. Oxford: Clarendon Press, 1982.

Bloch, Herbert. *Monte Cassino in the Middle Ages*. Vol. 1. Roma: Edizioni di Storia e Letteratura, 1986.

Bloch, Herbert. *Montecassino in the Middle Ages*. Vol. 2. 2 vols. Rome: Edizioni di Storia e Letteratura, 1986.

Bloch, Herbert. 'Origin and Fate of the Bronze Doors of Abbot Desiderius of Monte Cassino'. *Dumbarton Oaks Papers* 41 (1987): 89–102. https://doi.org/10.2307/1291548.

Blumenthal, Uta-Renate. *The Investiture Controversy: Church and Monarchy from the Ninth to the Twelfth Century*. University Park, PA: University of Pennsylvania Press, 2010.

Blunt, Anthony. 'The Temple of Solomon with Special Reference to South Italian Baroque Art'. In *Kunsthistorische Forschungen Otto Pâcht Zu Seinem 70. Geburtstag*, edited by Artur Rosenauer and Gerold Weber, 258–65. Salzburg: Verlag, 1972.

Boas, Adrian J. *Jerusalem in the Time of the Crusades: Society, Landscape, and Art in the Holy City Under Frankish Rule*. London and New York: Routledge, 2001.

Boeck, Elena N. *Imagining the Byzantine Past: The Perception of History in the Illustrated Manuscripts of Skylitzes and Manasses*. Cambridge: Cambridge University Press, 2015.

Boeck, Elena N. 'Simulating the Hippodrome: The Performance of Power in Kiev's St. Sophia'. *Art Bulletin* 91, no. 3 (2009): 283–301.

Bondioli, Lorenzo M. 'Islamic Bari between the Aghlabids and the Two Empires'. In *The Aghlabids and Their Neighbors: Art and Material Culture in Ninth-Century North Africa*, edited by Glaire D. Anderson, Corisande Fenwick, and Mariam Rosser-Owen, 470–90. Leiden: Brill, 2017.

Bornstein, Christine Verzár. *Portals and Politics in the Early Italian City-State: The Sculpture of Nicholaus in Context*. Parma: Università degli Studi di Parma, Istituto di storia dell'arte Centro di studi Medievali, 1988.

Bornstein, Christine Vezár. 'Romanesque Sculpture in Southern Italy and Islam: A Revaluation'. In *The Meeting of Two Worlds Cultural Exchange Between East and West During the Crusades*, edited by Vladimir Goss, 285–93. Kalamazoo: Medieval Institute Publications, 1986.

Borsook, Eve. 'A Solomonic Throne for Salerno Cathedral?' Edited by Elisabetta Scirocco and Gerhard Wolf. *Convivium. Exchanges and Interactions in the Arts of Medieval Europe, Byzantium, and the Mediterreanean. The Italian South: Transcultural Perspectives 500 – 1500* 5, no. 1 (2018): 36–49.

Borsook, Eve. *Messages in Mosaic: The Royal Programmes of Norman Sicily, 1130–1187*. Woodbridge: Boydell Press, 1998.

Bowes, Kimberly Diane, Karen Francis, and Richard Hodges, eds. *Between Text and Territory: Survey and Excavations in the Terra of San Vincenzo al Volturno*. London: British School at Rome, 2006.

Boynton, Susan. *Shaping a Monastic Identity: Liturgy & History at the Imperial Abbey of Farfa, 1000–125*. Ithaca: Cornell University Press, 2006.

Braca, Antonio. *Il Duomo di Salerno: Architettura e Culture Artistiche del Medioevo e dell'Età Moderna*. Salerno: Laveglia, 2003.

Bramoullé, David. 'Recruiting Crews in the Fatimid Navy (909–1171)'. *Medieval Encounters* 13, no. 1 (2007): 4–31.

Brazinski, Paul, and Allegra Fryxell. 'The Smell of Relics: Authenticating Saintly Bones and the Role of Scent in the Sensory Experience of Medieval Christian Veneration'. *Papers from the Institute of Archaeology* 23, no. 1 (2013): 1–15. https://doi.org/10.5334/pia.430.

Bressan, Luigi. 'Le Iscrizioni Nella Bari Medievale: Un Itinerario Da Scoprire'. In *Studi in Onore Di Giosuè Musca*, edited by Cosimo Damiano Fonseca and Sivo Vito, 53–72. Bari: Dedalo, 2000.

Brittain, Frederick, ed. 'O Roma Nobilis'. In *Medieval Latin and Romance Lyric to A.D. 1300*, vol. 88. Cambridge: Cambridge University Press, 1951.

Bronze Cylindrical Box, I.3679, Staatliche Museum, Berlin. Accessed 20 January 2022. http://www.smb-digital.de/eMuseumPlus?service=direct/1/ResultDetailView/result.tab.link&sp=10&sp=Scollection&sp=SfieldValue&sp=0&sp=1&sp=3&sp=SdetailView&sp=1&sp=Sdetail&sp=0&sp=F&sp=SdetailBlockKey&sp=2.

Burnett, Sarah. 'The Cult of St Nicholas in Medieval Italy'. Ph.D thesis, University of Warwick, 2009.

Cadei, Antonio. 'La Prima Committenza Normanna'. In *Le Porte Di Bronzo Dall'Antichità al Secolo XIII*, edited by Salvatorino Salomi, 357–72. Rome: Istituto della Enciclopedia Italiana, 1990.
Cahn, Walter. *Romanesque Sculpture in American Collections: New York and New Jersey, Middle and South Atlantic States, the Midwest, Western and Pacific States*. Turnhout: B. Franklin, 1999.
Cahn, Walter. 'Solomonic Elements in Romanesque Art'. In *The Temple of Solomon: Archaeological Fact and Medieval Tradition in Christian, Islamic and Jewish Art*, edited by Joseph Gutmann, 45–72. Missaula: Scholars Press for the American Academy of Regligion and the Society of Biblial Literature, 1976.
Calia, Angela, Giovanni Leucci, Nicola Masini, Loredana Matera, Raffaele Persico, and Maria Sileo. 'Integrated Prospecting in the Crypt of the Basilica of Saint Nicholas in Bari, Italy'. *Journal of Geophysics and Engineering* 9, no. 3 (2012): 271. https://doi.org/10.1088/1742-2132/9/3/271.
Calò, Francesco. 'Federico II e l'Elephante: Un Simbolo Cristologico per l'Anticristo Svevo'. In *II Ciclo Di Studi Medievali, Atti Del Convegno (Firenze, 27–28 Maggio 2017)*, edited by Gruppo della Ricerca NUME, 86–111. Florence: Arcore, 2017.
Calò Mariani, Maria Stella. 'Considerazioni Sulla Scultura Artistica Nel Territorio a Sud-Est Di Bari Tra XI e XV Secolo'. In *Arte in Puglia Dal Medioevo al Settecento: Il Medioevo*, edited by Francesco Abbate, 385–428. Roma: De Luca, 2010.
Calò Mariani, Maria Stella. 'Sulle Relazioni Artistiche Tra La Puglia e l'Oriente Latino'. In *Roberto Il Guiscardo e Il Suo Tempo. Relazioni e Comunicazioni Nelle Prime Giornate Normanno-Sveve (Bari, Maggio 1973)*, edited by Centro di Studi Normanno-Svevo, 33–66. Roma: Il Centro di Ricerca, 1975.
Camber, Richard. 'The Mari Cha Lion in the Context of Apulian Romanesque Sculpture'. In *The Pisa Griffin and the Mari-Cha Lion: Metalwork, Art and Technology in the Medieval Islamicate Mediterranean*, edited by Anna Contadini, 179–96. Pisa: Pacini, 2018.
Campione, Ada. 'Sabino, Vescovo Di Canosa, Santo'. In *Dizionario Biografico Degli Italiani*. Istituto Enciclopedia Treccani. Accessed 29 November 2021. https://www.treccani.it/enciclopedia/sabino-vescovo-di-canosa-santo_%28Dizionario-Biografico%29/.
Carrier, Marc. 'Pour En Finir Avec Les Gesta Francorum: Une Réflexion Historiographique Sur l'État Des Rapports Entre Grecs et Latins Au Début Du XIIe Siècle et Sur l'Apport Nouveau d'Albert d'Aix'. *Crusades* 7 (2008): 13–34. https://doi.org/10.4324/9781315271606-4.
Carrino, Rachele. 'Il Pavimento Della Basilica Nicolaiana a Bari'. *La Mosaïque Gréco-Romaine, Collection de l'École française de Rome* 352, no. 9 (2005): 79–97.
Cary, Phillip. *Outward Signs: The Powerlessness of External Things in Augustine's Thought*. Oxford: Oxford University Press, 2008.
Casati, Giovanni Battista. 'Inventario Della Preposita Chiesa de S.to Savino e Delle Chiese Di Canosa', 1599. Archivio Storico Prevostale di Canosa.
Caskey, Jill. 'Miracles and Matthew: Potential Contexts for the Salerno Ivories'. In *The Salerno Ivories: Objects, Histories, Contexts*, edited by Francesca Dell'Acqua, Anthony Cutler, Avinoam Shalem, Herbert L. Kessler, and Gerhardt Wolf, 179–90. Berlin: Gebr. Mann Verlag, 2016.
Caskey, Jill. 'Stuccoes from the Early Norman Period in Sicily: Figuration, Fabrication and Integration'. *Medieval Encounters* 17, no. 1–2 (1 January 2011): 80–119. https://doi.org/10.1163/157006711X561730.
Cassano, Raffaella. 'Nuove Acquisizioni Sull'Architettura Canosina al Tempo Del Vescovo Sabino'. In *Storia Dell'Archeologia Della Daunia in Ricordo Di Marina Mazzei*, edited

by Giuliano Volpe, Maria José Strazulla, and Danilo Leone, 305-26. Bari: Edipuglia, 2008.

Cassano, Raffaella. *Principi, Imperatori, Vescovi: Duemila Anni Di Storia a Canosa*. Bari: Marsilio, 1992.

Cassano, Raffaella. 'San Nicola'. In *Archeologia Di Una Città. Bari Dalle Origini al X Secolo*, edited by Giuseppe Andreassi and Francesca Radina, 405-24. Bari: Edipuglia, 1988.

Castiñeiras, Manuel. 'The Romanesque Portal as Performance'. *Journal of the British Archaeological Association* 168, no. 1 (2015): 1-33.

Castiñeiras, Manuel A. 'Compostela, Bari and Jerusalem: In Search of the Footsteps of a Figurative Culture on the Roads of Pilgrimage'. *Ad Limina. Revista de Investigación Del Camino de Santiago y Las Peregrinaciones* 1 (2010): 15-51.

Castiñeiras, Manuel A. 'The Baldachin-Ciborium: The Shifting Meanings of a Restricted Liturgical Furnishing in Romanesque Art'. In *The Regional and Transregional in Romanesque Europe*, edited by Richard Plant and John McNeill, 1-47. Abingdon: Routledge, 2021.

Castiñeiras, Manuel A. *The Creation Tapestry*. Girona: Catedral de Girona, 2011.

Cavallo, Guglielmo, and Francesco Magistrale. 'Mezzogiorno Normanno e Scritture Esposte'. In *Epigrafia Medievale Greca e Latina. Ideologia e Funzione*, edited by Cyril Mango and Guglielmo Cavallo, 293-329. Spoleto: Centro Italiano di Studi sull'Alto Medioevo, 1995.

Cavallo, Guglielmo, Giulia Orofino, and Oronzo Percere. *Exultet: Rotoli Liturgici Del Medioevo Meridionale*. Rome: Istituto Poligrafico e Zecca dello Stato, 1994.

Cavell, Leslie Joan. 'Social and Symbolic Functions of the Romanesque Façade: The Example of Mâcon's Last Judgement Galilee'. Ph.D thesis, University of Michigan, 1997.

Chelotti, Marcella. 'Tipologia dei Monumenti'. In *Le Epigrafi Romane di Canosa*, edited by Marcella Chelotti, Marina Silvestrini, Rosanna Gaeta, and Vincenza Morzio, vol. 2, 267-92. Bari: Edipuglia, 1990.

Chiellini Nari, Monica. 'Le Favole, i Simboli, Il 'Ciclo Di Artù': Il Fronte Istoriato Nella "Porta Della Pescheria"'. In *La Porta Della Pescheria Nel Duomo Di Modena*, edited by Chiara Frugoni, Monica Chiellini Nari, and Cristina Acidini Luchinat, 35-53. Modena: Pannini, 1991.

Christie, Neil. 'On Bells and Belltowers. Origins and Evolutions in Italy and Britain, AD 700-1200'. *Church Archaeology* 5-6 (2004): 13-30.

Cigola, Michela. 'Cosmatesque Pavement of Montecassino Abbey. History Through Geometric Analysis'. In *Computational Modelling of Objects Represented in Images: Fundamentals, Methods and Applications III: Proceedings of the International Symposium CompIMAGE 2012, Rome, Italy, 5-7 September 2012*, edited by Paolo Di Giamberardino, 445-51. Boca Raton: CRC Press, 2012.

Cilla, Michele. *Caratteri e Restauri del Mausoleo di Marco Boemondo d'Altavilla*. Lavello: Alfagrafica Volonnino, 1993.

Ciminale, Dario. 'Nuove Acquisizioni Su Bari Tardoantica e Altomedievale Dalle Stratigrafie Dell'Area Di S. Nicola e Della Cattedrale'. In *Paesaggi e Insediamenti Urbani in Italia Meridionale Fra Tardoantico e Altomedioevo*, edited by Giuliano Volpe and Roberta Giuliani, 107-28. Bari: Edipuglia, 2010.

Ciminale, Dario, and Emilia Pellegrino. 'Interventi Di Restauro e Indagini Archeologiche Nell'Area Della Cattedrale e Della Basilica Di S. Nicola'. In *Bari Sotto La Città: Luoghi Di Memoria*, edited by Maria Rosaria Depalo and Francesca Radina, 99-108. Bari: Mario Adda Editore, 2008.

Cioffari, Gerardo. 'Concilio Di Bari Del 1098: Uomini Ed Eventi'. In *Il Concilio Di Bari Del 1098*, edited by Salvatore Palese and Giancarlo Locatelli, 108–21. Bari: Edipuglia, 1999.
Cioffari, Gerardo. 'Dalle Origini a Bona Sforza'. In *San Nicola Di Bari e La Sua Basilica. Culto, Arte, Tradizione*, edited by Giorgio Otranto, 150–95. Milan: Electa, 1987.
Cioffari, Gerardo. *L'Abate Elia. Il Benedettino che Costruì la Basilica di San Nicola*. Matera: Barile, 2007.
Cioffari, Gerardo. *Storia della Basilica di S. Nicola di Bari*. Bari: Centro studi nicolaiani della Basilica di S. Nicola, 1984.
Cioffari, Gerardo. *Storia Della Chiesa Di Bari Dalle Origini Alla Fine Del Dominio Bizantino (1071)*. Vol. 11. Memorie e Documenti. Bari: Centro Studi Nicolaiani, 1992.
Cioffari, Gerardo, and Rosa Lupoli Tateo, eds. 'Annales Barensis'. In *Antiche Cronache Di Terra Di Bari*. Bari: Centro studi Nicolaiani, 1991.
Cioffari, Gerardo, and Rosa Lupoli Tateo, eds. 'Inventio of San Sabino of Canosa'. In *Antiche Cronache Di Terra Di Bari*. Bari: Centro Studi Nicolaiani, 1991.
Cirsone, Giacomo. 'La Basilica Della SS. Trinità Di Venosa Dalla Tarda Antichità All'Età Moderna (II Parte)'. *La Capitanata. Rivista Semestrale Della Biblioteca Provinciale Di Foggia Anno L* 27, no. 27 (June 2012): 99–141.
Coatsworth, Elizabeth, and Gale Owen-Crocker. 'The Coronation Mantle of King Stephen of Hungary'. In *Clothing the Past: Surviving Garments from Early Medieval to Early Modern Western Europe*, 81–3. Brill, 2018.
Conant, Kenneth John. *Carolingian and Romanesque Architecture, 800 to 1200*. New Haven: Yale University Press, 1993.
Conant, Kenneth John. 'The Original Buildings at the Holy Sepulchre in Jerusalem'. *Speculum* 31, no. 1 (1956): 1–48.
Contadini, Anna, and Richard Camber. 'Acoustic Automata'. In *The Pisa Griffin and the Mari-Cha Lion: Metalwork, Art, and Technology in the Medieval Islamicate Mediterranean*, edited by Anna Contadini, 63–76. Pisa: Pacini Editore, 2018.
Copeta, Clara. 'Medieval Bari: A Multiethnic City'. *Plurimondi* 4, no. 9 (2011): 139–64.
Corrente, Marisa, Roberta Giuliani, and Danilo Leone. 'Edilizia Paleocristiana Nell'Area Di Piano San Giovanni a Canosa Di Puglia'. In *La Cristianizzazione in Italia Tra Tardoantico Ed Altomedioevo*, edited by Emma Vitale and Rosa Maria Buonacasa Carra, vol. 2, 1167–200. Palermo: Saladino, 2007.
Cowdrey, Herbert E. J. 'Martyrdom and the First Crusade'. In *Crusade and Settlement*, edited by Peter Edbury, 46–56. Cardiff: University College Cardiff Press, 1985.
Cowdrey, Herbert E. J. *Pope Gregory VII, 1073–1085*. Oxford: Clarendon Press, 1998.
Cowdrey, Herbert E. J. *The Age of Abbot Desiderius: Montecassino, the Papacy and the Normans in the Eleventh and Easrly Twelfth Centuries*. Oxford: Oxford University Press, 1983.
Ćurčić, Slobodan. 'Architectural Significance of Subsidiary Chapels in Middle Byzantine Churches'. *Journal of the Society of Architectural Historians* 36, no. 2 (1977): 94–110. https://doi.org/10.2307/989106.
Cushing, Kathleen G. *Reform and the Papacy in the Eleventh Century: Spirituality and Social Change*. Manchester: Manchester University Press, 2005.
Cutler, Anthony, Francesca Dell'acqua, Herbert L. Kessler, Avinoam Shalem, and Gerhard Wolf, eds. The Salerno Ivories: Objects, Histories, Contexts. Berlin: Dietrich Reimer, 2016.
Dagron, Gilbert. *Emperor and Priest: The Imperial Office in Byzantium*. Cambridge: Cambridge University Press, 2003.

Dale, Thomas E. A. *Relics, Prayer, and Politics in Medieval Venetia: Romanesque Painting in the Crypt of Aquileia Cathedral*. Princeton: Princeton University Press, 1997.

Dark, Ken, and Ferudun Özgümüş. 'New Evidence for the Byzantine Church of the Holy Apostles from Fatih Camii, Istanbul'. *Oxford Journal of Archaeology* 21, no. 4 (2002): 393–413. https://doi.org/10.1111/1468-0092.00170.

De Appolonia, Giovanna. 'Justice and Judgement in the Romanesque Column-Bearing Lions of Northern Italy'. *IKON* 2 (2009): 167–76.

De Blaauw, Sible. 'Campanae Supra Urbem: Sull'Uso delle Campane nella Roma Medievale'. *Rivista di storia della Chiesa in Italia* 47, no. 1 (1993): 367–415.

De Francovich, Géza. 'Wiligelmo Da Modena e Gli Inizii Della Scultura Romanica in Francia e in Spagna'. *Rivista Del R. Istituto d'Archeologia e Storia Dell'Arte* 7 (1940): 225–94.

De Souza, Philip. 'War, Slavery and Empire in Roman Imperial Iconography'. *Bulletin of the Institute of Classical Studies* 54, no. 1 (2011): 31–62.

Debiais, Vincent. 'Writing on Medieval Doors: The Surveyor Angel on the Moissac Capital (ca.1100)'. In *Writing Matters: Presenting and Perceiving Monumental Inscriptions in Antiquity and the Middle Ages*, edited by Irene Berti, Katharina Bolle, Fanny Opdenhoff, and Fabian Stroth, 285–308. Materiale Textkulturen 14. Berlin: De Gruyter, 2013.

D'Elia, Pina Belli, and Tessa Garton. 'Trono Vescovile'. In *Alle sorgenti del romanico Puglia XI secolo*, edited by Pina Belli D'Elia, 86–91. Bari: Dedalo, 1987.

Delle Donne, Fulvio. 'Le Fonti Letterarie Latine Su Boemondo'. In *'Unde Boat Mundus Quanti Fuerit Boamundus' Boemondo I Di Altavilla Un Normanno Tra Occidente e Oriente*, edited by Cosimo Damiano Fonseca and Pasquale Ieva, 175–91. Bari: Società di Storia Patria per la Puglia, 2015.

Delle Donne, Fulvio. 'Le Iscrizioni Del Mausoleo Di Boemondo D'Altavilla a Canosa'. *ArNos Archivio Normanno-Svevo* 3 (December 2011): 7–18.

Dell'Omo, Mariano. 'Per La Storia Dei Monaci-Vescovi Nell'Italia Normanna Del Secolo IX: Ricerche Biografiche Su Guitmondo Di La Croix-Saint-Leufroy, Vescovo Di Aversa'. *Benedictina* 40 (1993): 9–34.

Delogu, Raffaello. *La Galleria Nazionale Di Sicilia*. Rome: Istituto Poligrafico dello Stato, 1962.

Depalo, Maria Rosaria. 'S. Maria Del Carmine: La Chiesa Bizantina Riscoperta'. In *Bari Sotto Città: Luoghi Di Memoria*, 117–20. Bari: Mario Adda Editore, 2008.

Dodwell, Charles Reginald. *Anglo-Saxon Art: A New Perspective*. Manchester: Manchester University Press, 1982.

Dodwell, Charles Reginald. *The Pictorial Arts of the West, 800–1200*. New Haven: Yale University Press, 1993.

Doherty, James. 'Count Hugh of Troyes and the Prestige of Jerusalem'. *History* 102, no. 353 (2017): 874–88. https://doi.org/10.1111/1468-229X.12521.

Doig, Allan. 'Charlemagne's Palace Chapel at Aachen: Apocalyptic and Apotheosis'. In *Bishop Robert Grosseteste and Lincoln Cathedral: Tracing Relationships between Medieval Concepts of Order and Built Form*, edited by Nicholas Temple, John Shannon Hendrix, and Christian Frost, 179–200. London and New York: Routledge, 2016.

Doig, Allan. *Liturgy and Architecture: From the Early Church to the Middle Ages*. Farnham: Routledge, 2017.

Dolezalek, Isabelle. *Arabic Script on Christian Kings: Textile Inscriptions on Royal Garments from Norman Sicily*. Berlin and Boston: Walter de Gruyter GmbH & Co KG, 2017.

D'Onofrio, Mario. 'L'Abbatiale Normande Inachevée de Venosa'. In *L'architecture Normande Au Moyen Age 1 Regards Sur l'art de Bâtir, Actes Du Colloque Du Cerisy-La-Salle (28 Septembre -2 Octobre 1994)*, edited by Maylis Baylé, 111–24. Caen: Presses Universitaires de Caen, 1997.

Dorin, Rowan. 'The Mystery of the Marble Man and His Hat: A Reconsideration of the Bari Episcopal Throne'. *Florilegium* 25 (2008): 29–52.

D'Ottone Rambuch, Arianna. 'Aubin-Louis Millin e La Civiltà Islamica Attraverso Disegni e Appunti Inediti'. *Arte Medievale* 4 (2018): 151–66.

Dowling, Melissa Barden. *Clemency and Cruelty in the Roman World*. Ann Arbor: University of Michigan Press, 2006.

Downey, Glanville. 'The Tombs of the Byzantine Emperors at the Church of the Holy Apostles in Constantinople'. *The Journal of Hellenic Studies* 79 (1959): 27–51. https://doi.org/10.2307/627920.

Eastmond, Antony. *Art and Identity in Thirteenth-Century Byzantium: Hagia Sophia and the Empire of Trebizond*. Burlington, VT: Ashgate, 2004.

Eastmond, Antony. 'Byzantine Oliphants?' In *ΦΙΛΟΠΑΤΙΟΝ Spaziergang Im Kaiserlichen Garten: Schriften Uber Byzanz Und Seine Nachbarn*, edited by Neslihan Asutay-Effenberger and Falko Dalm, 95–118. Mainz: Verlag des Römisch-Germanischen Zentralmuseums, 2012.

Eastmond, Antony. 'On Diversity in Southern Italy'. In *The Salerno Ivories. Objects, Histories, Contexts*, edited by Anthony Cutler, Francesca Dell'Acqua, Herbert L. Kessler, Avinoam Shalem, and Gerhard Wolf, 97–109. Berlin: Reimer Verlag-Gebr. Mann, 2015.

Eastmond, Antony. 'The Limits of Byzantine Art'. In *A Companion to Byzantium*, edited by Liz James, 313–22. Oxford: Wiley-Blackwell, 2010.

Edwards, Emma. 'Patronage and Tradition in Textile Exchange and Use in the Early Norman South'. edited by Emily A. Winkler, Liam Fitzgerald, and Andrew Small, 89–113. Woodbridge: Boydell Press, 2020.

Edwards, Emma. 'Reception and Reorientation: The Impact of Internationally Traded Objects in Italian Art & Architecture (950–1150)'. PhD Thesis, Courtauld Institute of Art, 2016.

Eger, A Asa. '(Re)Mapping Medieval Antioch: Urban Transformations from the Early Islamic to the Middle Byzantine Periods'. *Dumbarton Oaks Papers* 67 (2013): 95–134.

Epstein, Steven. *Speaking of Slavery: Color, Ethnicity, and Human Bondage in Italy*. Ithaca: Cornell University Press, 2001.

Erdmann, Kurt. *Arabische Schriftzeichen Als Ornamente in Der Abendländischen Kunst Des Mittelalters*. Wiesbaden: Verlag der Akademie der Wissenschaften und der Literatur, 1954.

Evans, Helen C. 'The Arsenal Bible'. In *Byzantium: Faith and Power (1261 - 1557)*, edited by Helen C. Evans, 42–43. New York: Yale University Press, 2004.

'Exultet'. Scroll. Benevento, c 969. Vatican Library.

'Exultet Roll'. Liturgical scroll. Bari, c 1000. John Rylands Library, Manchester. https://www.digitalcollections.manchester.ac.uk/view/MS-LATIN-00002/1.

Falcandus, Hugo. *The History of the Tyrants of Sicily by Hugo Falcandus 1154–69*. Translated by Graham A. Loud and Thomas Wiedermann. Manchester: Manchester University Press, 1998.

Falla Castelfranchi, Marina. 'Iscrizione Greca Con L'Elogio Del Catapano Basilio Mesardonite'. In *Arte in Puglia Dal Medioevo al Settecento: Il Medioevo*, edited by Francesco Abbate, 103–4. Rome: De Luca Editori d'Arte, 2010.

Falla Castelfranchi, Marina. 'La Cattedrale Di Canosa Non è Più Normanna'. In *Canosa. Ricerche Storiche Decennio 1999–2009*, edited by Liana Bertoldi Lenoci, 677–88. Martina Franca: Edizioni Pugliesi, 2011.

Falla Castelfranchi, Marina. *Pittura Monumentale Bizantina in Puglia*. Milano: Electa, 1991.

Farioli-Campanati, Raffaella. 'Il Pavimento Di S. Marco a Venezia e i Suoi Rapporti Con L'Oriente'. In *Storia Dell'Arte Marciana: I Mosaici*, edited by Renato Polacco, 11–19. Venice: Marsilio, 1997.

Fasnacht, Walter. 'Copper on Cyprus'. In *The Pisa Griffin and the Mari-Cha Lion: Metalwork, Art, and Technology in the Medieval Islamicate Mediterranean*, edited by Anna Contadini, 129–38. Arte. Ospedaletto (Pisa): Pacini editore, 2018.

Fernie, Eric. 'Definitions and Explanations of the Romanesque Style of Architecture from the 1960s to the Present Day'. In *A Companion to Medieval Art: Romanesque and Gothic in Northern Europe*, edited by Conrad Rudolph, 407–16. Chichester: Wiley, 2019.

Fernie, Eric. *Romanesque Architecture: The First Style of the European Age*. New Haven: Yale University Press, 2014.

Fernie, Eric. 'The Date, Iconography and Dedication of the Cathedral of Canosa'. In *Romanesque and the Mediterranean Patterns of Exchange Across the Latin, Greek and Islamic Worlds c.1000–c.1250*, 167–72. London: Routledge, 2017.

Fillitz, Herman. *Zwei Elfenbeinplatten Aus Süditalien*. Bern: Abegg-Stiftung, 1967.

Fine, John V. A. (Jr). *When Ethnicity Did Not Matter in the Balkans: A Study of Identity in Pre-Nationalist Croatia, Dalmatia, and Slavonia in the Medieval and Early-Modern Periods*. Ann Arbor: University of Michigan Press, 2006.

Fioretti, Giovanna, Pasquale Acquafredda, Silvia Calò, Mariagrazia Cinelli, Germano Germanò, Alessandro Laera, and Angelo Moccia. 'Study and Conservation of the St. Nicola's Basilica Mosaics (Bari, Italy) by Photogrammetric Survey: Mapping of Polychrome Marbles, Decorative Patterns and Past Restorations'. *Studies in Conservation* 65, no. 3 (2020): 160–71.

Flori, Jean. *Bohémond d'Antioche: Chevalier d'Aventure*. Paris: Payot, 2007.

Folda, Jaroslav. *The Art of the Crusaders in the Holy Land, 1098–1187*. Cambridge: Cambridge University Press, 1995.

Fontana, Vito. *1 Versamento (1860–1890), Envelope 371, Relazione Del 9/05/1878, Sent by Vito Fontana, Ispettore Agli Scavi e Ai Monumenti Di Antichità to the Ministero Della Pubblica Istruzione*. Roma: Archivio Centrale dello Stato, 1878.

Fox-Friedman, Jeanne. 'King Arthur in Art'. In *A Companion to Arthurian Literature*, edited by Helen Fulton, 381–99. Chichester: Wiley-Blackwell, 2009.

Frankopan, Peter. 'Byzantine Trade Privileges to Venice in the Eleventh Century: The Chrysobull of 1092'. *Journal of Medieval History* 30, no. 2 (2004): 135–60. https://doi.org/10.1016/j.jmedhist.2004.03.005.

Friedman, Yvonne. *Encounter between Enemies: Captivity and Ransom in the Latin Kingdom of Jerusalem*. Leiden: Brill, 2002.

Fynn-Paul, Jeffrey. 'Empire, Monotheism and Slavery in the Greater Mediterranean Region from Antiquity to the Early Modern Era'. *Past & Present* 205, no. 1 (2009): 3–40. https://doi.org/10.1093/pastj/gtp036.

Gabrieli, Francesco, and Umberto Scerrato. *Gli Arabi in Italia: Cultura, Contatti e Tradizioni*. Milano: Garzanti and Scheiwiller, 1989.

Gadolin, Anitra R. 'Prince Bohemund's Death and Apotheosis in the Church of San Sabino, Canosa Di Puglia'. *Byzantion* 52 (1982): 124–53.

Ganz, David. 'Pictorial Textiles and Their Performance: The Star Mantle of Henry II'. In *Dressing the Part: Textiles as Propaganda in the Middle Ages*, edited by Kate Dimitrova and Margaret Goehring, 13–29. Turnhout: Brepols, 2014.

Gaposchkin, M. Cecilia. 'The Echoes of Victory: Liturgical and Para-Liturgical Commemorations of the Capture of Jerusalem in the West'. *Journal of Medieval History* 40, no. 3 (2014): 237–59. https://doi.org/10.1080/03044181.2014.912830.

Garrison, Eliza. *Ottonian Imperial Art and Portraiture*. London and New York: Routledge, 2012.

Garsoïan, Nina G. 'The Problem of Armenian Integration into the Byzantine Empire'. In *Studies on the Internal Diaspora of the Byzantine Empire*, edited by Hélène Ahrweiler and Angeliki E. Laiou, 53–124. Washington, DC: Dumbarton Oaks, 1998.

Garton, Tessa. 'Early Romanesque Sculpture in Apulia'. PhD thesis, Courtauld Institute of Art, 1975.

Gaspariño Garcìa, Sebastián. 'Amuletos Andalusíes. Nuevas Adiciones'. *Manquso. Gacetilla de Estudios Epigráficos y Numismáticos Andalusíes* 8 (2017): 79–82.

Geary, Patrick J. *Furta Sacra: Thefts of Relics in the Central Middle Ages*. Princeton and Oxford: Princeton University Press, 1990.

Gelfer-Jørgensen, Mirjam. *Medieval Islamic Symbolism and the Paintings in the Cefalù Cathedral*. Leiden: Brill, 1986.

Germanidou, Sophia. 'The "Rose of the Winds" Illustration in the Exultet I Bari Roll (c.1025 - 1034) and Its Probable Neoplatonic Implications'. In *Εν Σοφία Μαθητεύσαντες Essays in Byzantine Material Culture and Society in Honour of Sophia Kalopissi-Verti*, edited by Charikleia Diamanti and Anastasia Vassiliou, 100–11. Oxford: Archaeopress, 2019.

Ghiandoni, Olivia. 'Il Sarcofago Asiatico Di Melfi. Ricerche Mitologiche, Iconografiche e Stilistiche'. *Bolletino D'Arte* 89–90 (1995): 1–6.

Giannichedda, Enrico, Fabrizio Vona, Roberta Giuliani, and Erminia Lapadula. 'Attività Fusoria Medievale a Canosa'. *Archeologia Medievale* 22 (2005): 157–71.

Giuliani, Roberta. 'L'Edilizia Di XI Secolo Nella Puglia Centro-Settentrionale: Problemi e Prospettive Di Ricerca Alla Luce Di Alcuni Casi Di Studio'. In *La Capitanata e l'Italia Meridionale Nel Secolo XI Da Bisanzio Ai Normanni*, edited by Pasquale Favia and Giovanni De Venuto, 189–232. Bari: Edipuglia, 2011.

Glass, Dorothy. 'Prophecy and Priesthood at Modena'. *Zeitschrift für Kunstgeschichte* 63 (2000): 326–38.

Glass, Dorothy F. *Studies on Cosmatesque Pavements*. B.A.R International Series 82. Oxford: British Archaeological Reports, 1980.

Glass, Dorothy F. *The Sculpture of Reform in North Italy, Ca. 1095-1130: History and Patronage of Romanesque Façades*. Farnham: Ashgate, 2010.

Göller, Luitgar. *1000 Jahre Bistum Bamberg 1007-2007: Unterm Sternenmantel*. St Petersburg: Imhof Verlag, 2007.

Gonosovà, Anna. 'Textile Fragment from the Reliquary of Saint Germanus'. In *Glory of Byzantium: Art and Culture of the Middle Byzantine Era, A.D. 843-1261*, edited by William D. Wixom and Helen C. Evans, 224–6. New York: Metropolitan Museum of Art, 1997.

Gonosovà, Anna. 'Textile Fragment from the Reliquary of Saint Siviard'. In *Glory of Byzantium: Art and Culture of the Middle Byzantine Era, A.D. 843-1261*, edited by Helen C. Evans and William D. Wixom, 226. New York: Metropolitan Museum of Art, 1997.

Gonosovà, Anna. 'Textile Fragment with Double-Headed Eagles'. In *Glory of Byzantium: Art and Culture of the Middle Byzantine Era, A.D. 843-1261*, edited by Helen C.

Evans and William D. Wixom, 413–14. New York: Metropolitan Museum of Art, 1997.
Gonosovà, Anna. 'Textile Fragment with Senmurvs'. In *Glory of Byzantium: Art and Culture of the Middle Byzantine Era, A.D. 843–1261*, edited by Helen C. Evans and William D. Wixom, 224. New York: Metropolitan Museum of Art, 1997.
Goodchild, Richard. 'A Byzantine Palace at Apollonia (Cyrenaica)'. *Antiquity* 34, no. 136 (1960): 246–58. https://doi.org/10.1017/S0003598X00035535.
Grabar, André. *Byzantine Painting: Historical and Critical Study*. London: MacMillan, 1979.
Grabar, André. 'Le Reliquaire Byzantin de La Cathédrale d'Aix-La-Chapelle'. In *Karolingische Und Ottonische Kunst. Werden, Wesen, Wirkung. 6. Internationaler Kongreß Für Frühmittelalterforschung. Deutschland, 31 Aug. - 9. Sept. 1954*, edited by Hermann Schnitzler, 282–97. Wiesbaden: Steiner, 1957.
Grabar, André. 'Trônes Épiscopaux Du XIème et XIIème Siècles En Italie Méridionale'. *Wallraf-Richartz Jarbuch* 16 (1954): 7–52.
Grabar, Oleg. 'The Shared Culture of Objects'. In *Islamic Visual Culture, 1100 –1800: Constructing the Study of Islamic Art*, vol. 2, 115–29. Hampshire: Ashgate, 2006.
Grant, Alasdair C. 'Byzantium's Ashes and the Bones of St Nicholas: Two Translations as Turning Points, 1087–1100'. In *Trends and Turning Points. Constructing the Late Antique and Byzantine World*, edited by Matthew Kinloch and Alex MacFarlane, 247–65. Leiden: Brill, 2019. https://doi.org/10.1163/9789004395749_016.
Grant, Arthur James, ed. *Early Lives of Charlemagne by Eginhard and the Monk of St Gall*. London: De La More Press, 1905. https://www.gutenberg.org/ebooks/48870.
Greenhalgh, Michael. *Marble Past, Monumental Present: Building with Antiquities in the Mediaeval Mediterranean*. Leiden: Brill, 2009.
Greenhalgh, Michael. *The Survival of Roman Antiquities in the Middle Ages*. London: Duckworth, 1989.
Gregory the Great. *Moral Reflections on the Book of Job*. Translated by Brian Kerns. Cistercian Studies Series 249. Minnesota: Liturgical Press, 2014.
Guérin, Sarah M. 'Forgotten Routes? Italy, Ifrīqiya and the Trans-Saharan Ivory Trade'. *Al-Masāq* 25, no. 1 (2013): 70–91.
Guerrieri, Ferruccio. 'Dell'Antico Culto Di S. Nicola in Bari'. *Rassegna Pugliese* 19 (1902): 257–62.
Guidobaldi, Federico, Claudia Barsanti, and Alessandra Guiglia Guidobaldi. *San Clemente*. Rome: Romae, 1992.
Guiglia, Alessandra. 'Tradizione Locale Ed Influenze Bizantine Nei Pavimenti Cosmateschi'. *Bolletino D'Arte* 26 (1984): 57–72.
Guillou, André. 'Un Document Sur Le Gouvernement de La Province: L'Inscription Historique En Vers de Bari (1011)'. In *Studies on Byzantine Italy*, 1–13. London: Variorum Reprints, 1970.
Hagenmeyer, Heinrich. *Chronologie de la Première Croisade, 1094–1100*. Hildesheim: Georg Olms Verlag, 1973.
Hailstone, Paula Z. *Recalcitrant Crusaders?: The Relationship Between Southern Italy and Sicily, Crusading and the Crusader States, c. 1060–1198*. 1st edn. Abingdon and New York: Routledge, 2019.
Halphen, Louis, and René Poupardine, eds. *Chronica de Gestis Consulum Andegavorum, Chronique Des Comtes d'Anjou et Des Seigneurs d'Amboise*. Paris: Auguste Picard, 1913.
Hamilton, Bernard. 'Women in the Crusader States: The Queens of Jerusalem (1100–1190)'. *Studies in Church History Subsidia* 1 (1978): 143–74.

Hanson, John. 'The Rise and Fall of the Macedonian Renaissance'. In *A Companion to Byzantium*, edited by Liz James, 338–50. Chichester: Wiley-Blackwell, 2010. https://doi.org/10.1002/9781444320015.ch26.

Harrison, Martin, ed. *Excavations at Saraçhane in Istanbul*. Vol. 1. Princeton and Washington: Princeton University Press and Dumbarton Oaks, 1986.

Harrison, Richard Martin. 'The Church of St. Polyeuktos in Istanbul and the Temple of Solomon'. *Harvard Ukrainian Studies* 7 (1983): 276–79.

Hayes, Dawn Marie. 'The Cult of St. Nicholas of Myra in Norman Bari, c. 1071 –c. 1111'. *The Journal of Ecclesiastical History* 67 (2016): 492–512. https://doi.org/10.1017/S0022046915003371.

Hearn, Millard F. *Romanesque Sculpture: The Revival of Monumental Stone Sculpture in the Eleventh and Twelfth Centuries*. Ithaca: Cornell University Press, 1981.

Henry, Swinburne. *Travels in the Two Sicilies, by Henry Swinburne, Esq. in the Years 1777, 1778, 1779, and 1780*. Dublin: printed for Messrs Price, Sleater, Whitestone, Cross, Colles and 6 others in Dublin-86, 1783.

Herklotz, Ingo. 'Lo Spazio Della Morte e Lo Spazio Della Sovranità'. In *I Normanni: Popolo d'Europa, 1030-1200*, edited by Mario D'Onofrio, 321–6. Venice: Marsilio, 1994.

Hill, Rosalind, ed. *Gesta Francorum et Aliorum Hierosolimitanorum. The Deeds of the Franks and the Other Pilgrims to Jerusalem*. Oxford: Oxford University Press, 1967.

Hills, Gordon. 'Croxden Abbey and Its Chronicle'. *Journal of the British Archaeological Association* 21 (1865): 294–315.

Hoffman, Eva Rose F. 'Pathways of Portability: Islamic and Christian Interchange from the Tenth to the Twelfth Century'. *Art History* 24, no. 1 (February 2001).

Holmes, Catherine. *Basil II and the Governance of Empire (976–1025)*. Oxford: Oxford University Press, 2005.

Horden, Peregrine, and Nicholas Purcell. *The Corrupting Sea: A Study of Mediterranean History*. Oxford: Wiley-Blackwell, 2000.

Houben, Hubert. 'Adelaide Del Vasto Nella Storia Del Regno Di Sicilia'. In *Bianca Lancia Di Agliano Tra Il Piemonte e Il Regno Di Sicilia (Atti Del Convegno Internazionale Di Agliano, 28–29 Aprile 1990)*, edited by Renato Bordone, 121–45. Alessandria: Edizioni dell'Orso, 1992.

Houben, Hubert. 'Da Venosa a Monreale: I Luoghi Di Memoria Dei Normanni Nel Sud'. In *Memoria: Ricordare e Dimenticare Neela Cultura Del Medioevo*, edited by Michael Borgolte, Cosimo Damiano Fonseca, and Hubert Houben. Bologna: Mulino, 2005.

Houben, Hubert. *Il Libro Del Capitolo Del Monastero Della SS. Trinità Di Venosa (Cod. Casin. 334)*. Lecce: Congedo, 1984.

Houben, Hubert. 'La Chiesa di Bari alla Fine dell'XI Secolo'. In *Il Concilio di Bari del 1098: Atti del Convegno Storico Internazionale e Celebrazioni del IX Centenario del Concilio*, edited by Salvatore Palese and Giancarlo Locatelli, 91–107. Bari: Edipuglia, 1999.

Houben, Hubert. 'Melfi e Venosa: Due Città Sotto Il Dominio Normanno-Svevo'. In *Mezzogiorno Normanno-Svevo: Monasteri e Castelli, Ebrei e Musulmanni*, edited by Hubert Houben, 319–36. Naples: Liguori, 1996.

Houben, Hubert. 'Roberto Il Guiscardo e Il Monachesimo'. *Benedictina* 32, no. 2 (1985): 495–520.

Houben, Hubert. *Roger II of Sicily: A Ruler Between East and West*. Cambridge: Cambridge University Press, 2002.

Housley, Norman. 'Jerusalem and the Development of the Crusade Idea 1099–1128'. In *Crusading and Warfare in Medieval and Renaissance Europe*, edited by Norman

Housley, Variorum collected studies series, 27–40. Aldershot: Ashgate, 2001. https://contentstore.cla.co.uk/secure/link?id=235F1308-20DB-E511-80BD-0CC47A6BDDEB.

Hudson, John, ed. *Historia Ecclesie Abbendonensis: The History of the Church of Abingdon.* Vol. 1. Oxford: Clarendon Press, 2007.

Huillard-Bréholles, Jean-Louis-Alphonse. *Recherches Sur Les Monument d'Histoire Des Normands et de La Maison Souabe Dans l'Italie Méridionale.* Paris: Panckoucke, 1844.

Hüls, Rudolf. *Kardinäle, Klerus Und Kirchen Roms: 1049–1130.* Tübingen: Bibliothek des Deutschen Historischen Instituts in Rom, 1977.

Hunter, Fraser. 'Funerary Lions in Roman Provincial Art'. In *Romanisation Und Resistenz in Plastik, Architektur Und Inshriften Der Provinzen Des Imperium Romanum*, edited by Peter Noelke, 59–65. Mainz am Rhein: Verlag Philip von Zabern, 2003.

Hunter, Fraser, and Mark Collard. 'The Cramond Lioness'. *Current Archaeology* 155 (1997): 404–7.

Hussey, Joan M. *The Orthodox Church in the Byzantine Empire.* Oxford: Oxford University Press, 2010.

Iacobini, Antonio. '"Barisanus......Me Fecit" Nuovi Documenti Sull'Officina Di Barisanus Da Trani'. In *Medioevo: Le Officine*, edited by Arturo Carlo. Quintavalle, 190–206. Milan: Electa, 2010.

Iacobini, Antonio. 'Le Porte Bronzee Bizantine in Italia: Arte e Tecnologia Nel Mediterraneo Medievale'. In *Le Porte Del Paradiso: Arte e Tecnologia Bizantina Tra Italia e Mediterraneo*, edited by Antonio Iacobini, 15–54. Roma: Campisano, 2009.

Iafrate, Allegra. *The Wandering Throne of Solomon: Objects and Tales of Kingship in the Medieval Mediterranean.* Leiden: Brill, 2015.

Ingo, Herklotz. *'Sepulcra' e 'Monumenta' Del Medioevo: Studi Sull'Arte Sepolcrale in Italia.* Naples: Liguori, 2001.

Jacoby, David. 'Venetian Commercial Expansion in the Eastern Mediterranean, 8th–11th Centuries'. In *Medieval Trade in the Eastern Mediterranean and Beyond*, 371–91. Farnham: Ashgate, 2009.

James, Liz. *Mosaics in the Medieval World: From Late Antiquity to the Fifteenth Century.* Cambridge: Cambridge University Press, 2017.

Jamison, Evelyn. 'The Norman Administration of Apulia and Capua: More Especially under Roger II. and William I. 1127–1166'. *Papers of the British School at Rome* 6, no. 6 (1913): 211–481.

Járó, Márta. 'Filati D'Oro: Techniche e Metologie'. In *Nobiles Officinae: Perle, Filigrane e Trame Di Seta Dal Palazzo Reale Di Palermo*, vol 2, edited by Maria Andaloro, 163–70. Catania: G. Maimone, 2006.

Jeffreys, Elizabeth, John F. Haldon, and Robin Cormack. 'Byzantine Studies as an Academic Discipline'. In *Oxford Handbook of Byzantine Studies*, edited by Elizabeth Jeffreys, John F. Haldon, and Robin Cormack, 1–19. Oxford: Oxford University Press, 2008.

Jensen, Robin Margaret. *Understanding Early Christian Art.* Abingdon: Routledge, 2000.

John, Simon. 'The "Feast of the Liberation of Jerusalem": Remembering and Reconstructing the First Crusade in the Holy City, 1099–1187'. *Journal of Medieval History* 41, no. 4 (2015): 409–31. https://doi.org/10.1080/03044181.2015.1084353.

John the Deacon. 'Inventio S. Sabini'. In *Antiche Cronache Di Terra Di Bari*, edited by Gerardo Cioffari and Rosa Tateo, 279–81. Bari: Centro Studi Nicolaiani, 1991.

John the Deacon. 'La Cronaca Veneziana Del Diacono Giovanni'. In *Cronache Veneziane Antichissime*, edited by Giovanni Monticolo, 57–174. Rome: Forzani, 1890.

Johns, Jeremy. *Arabic Administration in Norman Sicily: The Royal Diwan*. Cambridge: Cambridge University Press, 2002.

Jones, Charles Williams. *Saint Nicholas of Myra, Bari, and Manhattan: Biography of a Legend*. Chicago: University of Chicago Press, 1978.

Jones, H. L., ed. *The Geography of Strabo*. Cambridge MA: Harvard University Press, 1924.

Jones, Lynn. *Between Islam and Byzantium: Aght'amar and the Visual Construction of Medieval Armenian Rulership*. Aldershot: Ashgate, 2007.

Kalavrezou, Ioli. 'The Paris Psalter'. In *The Glory of Byzantium: Art and Culture of the Middle Byzantine Era*, edited by William D. Wixom and Helen C. Evans, 240–2. New York: Metropolitan Museum of Art, 1997.

Kamp, Norbert. 'Vescovi e Diocesi dell'Italia Meridionale nel Passaggio dalla Dominazione Bizantina allo Stato Normanno'. In *La Chiesa di Taranto: Studi Storici in Onore di Mons. Guglielmo Motolese, Arcivescovo di Taranto, nel XXV Anniversario del Suo Episcopato*, edited by Cosimo Damiano Fonseca, vol. 2, 165–87. Galatina: Congedo, 1977.

Kapitaikin, Lev. "'The Daughter of al-Andalus': Interrelations between Norman Sicily and the Muslim West'. *Al-Masāq: Journal of the Medieval Mediterranean* 25, no. 1 (2013): 113–34.

Kaplan, Paul H. D. 'Black Africans in Hohenstaufen Iconography'. *Gesta* 26, no. 1 (1987): 29–36.

Kappel, Kai. *S. Nicola in Bari Und Seine Architektonische Nachfolge. Ein Bautypus Des 11.-17. Jahrhunderts in Unteritalien Und Dalmatien*. Römische Studien Der Bibliotheca Hertziana 13. Worms: Wernersche Verlagsgesellschaft, 1996.

Karydis, Nikolaos. 'Justinian's Church of the Holy Apostles: A New Reconstruction Proposal'. In *The Holy Apostles: A Lost Monument, a Forgotten Project, and the Presentness of the Past*, edited by Robert G. Ousterhout and Margaret Mullett, 99–131. Washington, DC and Cambridge, MA: Dumbarton Oaks and Harvard University Press, 2020.

Karydis, Nikolaos. 'The Vaults of St. John the Theologian at Ephesos: Visualizing Justinian's Church'. *Journal of the Society of Architectural Historians* 71, no. 4 (2012): 524–51. https://doi.org/10.1525/jsah.2012.71.4.524.

Kedar, Benjamin Z. 'Intellectual Activities in a Holy City: Jerusalem in the Twelfth Century'. In *Sacred Space: Shrine, City, Land*, edited by Benjamin Z. Kedar and R. J. Zwi Werblowsky, 127–39. London: Palgrave Macmillan, 1998. https://doi.org/10.1007/978-1-349-14084-8_9.

Kehr, Paul Fridolin. *Italia Pontificia : sive repertorium privilegiorum et litterarum a Romanis Pontificibus ante annum MCLXXXXVIII: Italiae ecclesiis, monasteriis, civitatibus singulisque personis concessorum*. Vol. 9. Berolini: Weidmann, 1906.

Kelly, Thomas Forrest. 'La Musica, la Liturgia e la Tradizione nella Salerno del Dodicesimo Secolo'. In *Salerno nel XII Secolo: Istituzioni, Società, Cultura: Atti del Convegno Internazionale: Raito di Vietri sul Mare, Auditorium di Villa Guariglia, 16/20 giugno 1999*, edited by Paolo Delogu and Paolo Peduto, 188–212. Salerno: Centro Studi Salernitani, 2004.

Kelly, Thomas Forrest. *The Exultet in Southern Italy*. Oxford: Oxford University Press, 1996.

Kendall, Calvin B. *The Allegory of the Church: Romanesque Portals and Their Verse Inscriptions*. Toronto: University of Toronto Press, 1998.

Kessler, Herbert L. 'A Gregorian Reform Theory of Art?' In *Roma e La Riforma Gregoriana: Tradizioni e Innovazioni Artistiche (XI - XII Secolo)*, edited by Serena Romano and Julie Enckell Julliard, 25–48. Rome: Viella, 2007.

Kier, Hiltrud. *Der Mittelalterliche Schmuckfussboden Unter Besonderer Berücksichtigung Des Rheinlandes*. Düsseldorf: Rheinland-Verl, 1970.

Kinney, Dale. 'Spolia'. In *St. Peter's in the Vatican*, edited by William Tronzo, 16–47. Cambridge; New York: Cambridge University Press, 2008.

Kinney, Dale. 'Spolia from the Baths of Caracalla in Sta. Maria in Trastevere'. *The Art Bulletin* 68, no. 3 (1986): 379–97. https://doi.org/10.2307/3050973.

Kirschberger, Timo. *Erster Kreuzzug Und Ethnogenese: In Novam Formam Commutatus - Ethnogenetische Prozesse Im Fürstentum Antiochia Und Im Königreich Jerusalem*. Nova Mediaevalia, Band 13. Göttingen: V & R unipress, 2015.

Kitzinger, Ernst. 'The Arts as Aspects of a Renaissance: Rome and Italy'. In *Renaissance and Renewal in the Twelfth Century*, edited by Robert L Benson and Giles Constable, 637–71. Toronto: University of Toronto Press, 1999.

Kitzinger, Ernst. 'The Gregorian Reform and the Visual Arts: A Problem of Method: The Prothero Lecture'. *Transactions of the Royal Historical Society* 22 (1972): 87–102. https://doi.org/10.2307/3678830.

Kitzinger, Ernst. *The Mosaics of St Mary's of the Admiral in Palermo*. Boston: Harvard University Press, 1991.

Koch, Guntrum, and Karol Wight, eds. *Roman Funerary Sculpture. Catalogue of the Collections, John Paul Getty Museum, Malibu California*. Malibu: J. Paul Getty Museum, 1988.

Kohnle, Armin. *Abt Hugo von Cluny (1049–1109)*. Sigmaringen: Thorbecke, 1993.

Kostick, Conor. *The Social Structure of the First Crusade*. Leiden: Brill, 2008.

Krautheimer, Richard. 'Introduction to an "Iconography of Mediaeval Architecture"'. *Journal of the Warburg and Courtauld Institutes* 5 (1942): 1–33. https://doi.org/10.2307/750446.

Krautheimer, Richard. 'San Nicola in Bari und die apulische Architektur des 12. Jahrhunderts'. *Wiener Jahrbuch fur Kunstgeschichte* 9 (1934): 16–19.

Krautheimer, Richard. *Three Christian Capitals: Topography and Politics*. Berkeley: University of California Press, 1983.

Krautheimer, Richard, and Lucy Freeman Sandler. 'The Crypt of Sta. Maria in Cosmedin and the Mausoleum of Probus Anicius'. In *Essays in Memory of Karl Lehmann*, edited by Lucy Freeman Sandler. New York: Institute of Fine Arts, 1964.

Kreutz, Barbara. *Before the Normans: Southern Italy in the Ninth and Tenth Centuries*. Philadelphia: University of Pennsylvania Press, 1996.

Krey, August C. *The First Crusade: The Accounts of Eyewitnesses and Participants*. Princeton, NJ: Princeton University Press, 1921.

Lavermicocca, Nino. *Bari Bizantina: Origine, Declino, Eredità Di Una Capitale Mediterranea*. Bari: Edizioni di Pagina, 2017.

Lavermicocca, Nino. 'Fragmenta: La Chiesa Bizantina Di Palazzo Simi'. In *Bari Sotto La Città: Luoghi Della Memoria*, edited by Maria Rosaria Depalo and Francesca Radina, 61–4. Bari: M. Adda, 2008.

Leo of Ostia. *Chronica Monasterii Casinensis*. Edited by Hartmut Hoffmann. Monumenta Germaniae Historica, Scriptores 34. Hannover: Hahnsche Buchhandlung, 1980.

Lev, Yaacov. 'David Ayalon and the History of Black Military Slavery in Medieval Islam'. *Der Islam* 90, no. 1 (2013): 21–43.

Lidov, Aleksei. 'A Byzantine Jerusalem: The Imperial Pharos Chapel as the Holy Sepulchre'. In *Jerusalem as Narrative Space: Erzählraum Jerusalem*, edited by Gerhard Wolf and Annette Hoffmann, 63–103. Leiden: Brill, 2012.

Lidov, Aleksej Michajlovic. 'Il Dio Russo'. In *San Nicola. Splendori d'Arte d'Oriente e d'Occidente*, edited by Michele Bacci, 77–88. Milan: Skiro, 2006.
Longo, Ruggero. 'Il Pavimento in Opus Sectile Della Chiesa Di San Menna. Maestranze Cassinesi a Sant'Agata de' Goti'. In *La Chiesa Di San Menna a Sant'Agata de' Goti. Atti Del Convegno Di Studi, 9 Giugno 2010*, edited by Franco Iannotta, 113–46. Salerno: ARCI Postiglione, 2014.
Longo, Ruggero. 'L'Opus Sectile Nei Cantieri Normanni - Una Squadra Di Marmorari Tra Salerno e Palermo'. In *Medioevo. Le Officine*, edited by Arturo Carlo Quintavalle, 179–89. I Convegni Di Parma 12. Milan: Electa, 2010.
Longo, Ruggero. 'The First Norman Cathedral in Palermo. Robert Guiscard's Church of the Most Holy Mother of God (With an Addendum by Jeremy Johns)'. *Convivium* 5, no. 1 (2018): 16–35. https://doi.org/10.1484/J.CONVI.4.2018022.
Longo, Ruggero, and Renato Giarrusso. 'L'Impiego Del Palombino e Del Litotipo Artificiale Stracotto Nell'Opus Sectile Del Meridione Normanno'. In *Aiscom, Atti Del XVI Colloquio Dell'Associazione Italiana per Lo Studio e La Conservazione Del Mosaico, Palermo, 17-19 Marzo 2010*, edited by Claudia Angelelli, 229–42. Tivoli: Scripta Manent, 2011.
Loomis, Roger Sherman. 'Modena, Bari, and Hades'. *The Art Bulletin* 6, no. 3 (1924): 71–4.
Loomis, Roger Sherman. 'The Story of the Modena Archivolt and Its Mythological Roots'. *Romanic Review* 15 (1924): 266–84.
Loomis, Roger Sherman, and Laura Hibbard Loomis. *Arthurian Legends in Medieval Art*. New York: Modern Language Association of America, 1938.
LoPrete, Kimberly A. 'Adela of Blois: Familial Alliances and Female Lordship'. In *Aristocratic Women in Medieval France*, edited by Theodore Evergates, 7–43. Philadelphia: University of Pennsylvania Press, 1999.
Loud, G. A. *The Latin Church in Norman Italy*. Cambridge: Cambridge University Press, 2007.
Loud, Graham. *The Age of Robert Guiscard: Southern Italy and the Northern Conquest*. Abingdon: Routledge, 2000.
Loud, Graham A. 'Abbot Desiderius of Montecassino and the Gregorian Papacy'. *The Journal of Ecclesiastical History* 30, no. 3 (1979): 305–26.
Loud, Graham A. *Roger II and the Creation of the Kingdom of Sicily*. UK edn. Manchester: Manchester University Press, 2012.
Louis I, Hamilton. *A Sacred City: Consecrating Churches and Reforming Society in Eleventh-Century Italy*. Manchester Medieval Studies. Manchester: Manchester University Press, 2010.
Lowe, Elias Avery. *The Beneventan Script: A History of the South Italian Minuscule*. Rome: Edizioni di Storia e Letteratura, 1980.
Luidprandus. 'Antapodosis'. In *MGH Scriptores Rerum Germanicarum*, vol. 41 edited by George Waltz, 54. Hannover: MGH, 1877.
Lupo Protospatharius. 'Annales'. In *Monumenta Germaniae Historica, Scriptores*, edited by Georg Heinrich Pertz 5, Annales et Chronica aevi Salici, 52–63. Hannover, 1844.
Mackie, Gillian Vallance. *Early Christian Chapels in the West: Decoration, Function and Patronage*. Toronto: University of Toronto Press, 2003.
Macridy, Theodore. 'The Monastery of Lips and the Burials of the Palaeologi'. *Dumbarton Oaks Papers* 18 (1964): 253–77.
Macy, Gary. 'Theology of the Eucharist in the High Middle Ages'. In *A Companion to the Eucharist in the Middle Ages*, edited by Ian Christopher Levy, Kristen Van Ausdall, and Gary Macy, 365–99. Leiden: Brill, 2012.

Magdalino, Paul. 'The Bath Leo the Wise and the 'Macedonian Renaissance' Revisited: Topography, Iconography, Ceremonial, Ideology'. *Dumbarton Oaks Papers* 42 (1988): 97–118.

Magistrale, Francesco. 'Forme e Funzioni Delle Scritte Esposte Nella Puglia Normanna'. *Scrittura e Civiltà* 16, no. 1992 (1992): 5–75.

Malaterra, Geoffrey. *The Deeds of Count Roger of Calabria and Sicily and of His Brother Duke Robert Guiscard*. Translated by Kenneth Baxter Wolf. Ann Arbor: University of Michigan Press, 2005.

Marbodus of Rennes. 'Carmina Varia, 38, Commendatio Jerosolymitanae'. In *Patrologia Latina*, edited by Jaques Paul Migne, vol. 171, 1672. Paris, 1854.

Marrier, Martinus. *Bibliotheca Cluniacensis: In Qua SS. Patrum Abb. Clun. Vitae, Miracula, Scripta, Statuta, Priuilegia, Chronologiaque Duplex*. Lutetiae Parisiorum: Sumptibus Sebastiani Cramoisy, 1614.

Marsiglia, Nunzio. 'Elementi Erratici Lignei Di Epoca Medievale in Sicilia'. In *La Ricostruzione Congetturale Dell'Architettura. Storia, Metodi, Esperienze Applicative*, 82–92. Architettura e Storia 8. Palermo: Grafill, 2013.

Martin, Jean-Marie. 'Jean, Archevêque de Trani et de Siponto, Syncelle Impérial'. In *Byzance et Ses Périphéries (Mondes Grec, Balkanique et Musulman). Hommage à Alain Ducellier*, edited by Christophe Picard and Bernard Doumerc, 123–30. Toulouse: Presses Universitaires du Midi, 2004.

Martin, Jean-Marie. *La Pouille Du VIe Au XIIe Siècle*. Rome: École française de Rome, 1993.

Martin, Jean-Marie. 'Les Communautes d'Habitants de la Pouille et leurs Rapports avec Roger II'. In *Società, Potere e Popolo nell'Età di Ruggero II*, edited by Centro Studi Normanno Svevi, 73–98. Giornate Normanno-Seveve 3. Bari: Dedalo, 1979.

Martin, Jean-Marie. 'Les Thèmes Italiens: Territoire, Administration, Population'. In *Histoire et Culture Dans L'Italie Byzantine: Acquis et Nouvelles Recherches*, edited by Jean-Marie Martin, André Jacob, and Ghislaine Noyé, 1–43. Collection de l'École Française de Rome 363. Rome: Ecole Francaise de Rome, 2006.

Martin, Jean-Marie. 'Settlement and the Agrarian Economy'. In *The Society of Norman Italy*, 17–46. Leiden: Brill, 2002. https://www.bookdepository.com/The-Society-of-Norman-Italy-Graham-Loud-Professor-Alex-Metcalfe/9789004125414?ref=bd_ser_1_1.

Matheou, Nicholas S.M. 'Hegemony, Elitedom and Ethnicity. "Armenians" in Imperial Bari, c.874 1071'. In *Italy and the East Roman World in the Medieval Mediterranean*, edited by Nicholas S.M. Matheou and Thomas J. MacMaster, 245–72. London: Routledge, 2021.

Matijević Sokol, Mirjana. 'Epitafi Srednjega Vijeka: 'knjige Života i Smrti''. In *Smrt u Opusu Vladana Desnice i Europskoj Kulturi: Poetički, Povijesni i Filozofski Aspekti. Zbornik Radova s Međunarodnoga Znanstvenog Skupa Desničini Susreti 2017*, edited by Drago Roksandic and Ivana Cvijovic Javorina, 381–99. Zagreb: Filozofski fakultet Sveučilišta u Zagrebu, Centar za komparativnohistorijske i interkulturne studije; Beograd: Institut za književnost i umetnost, 2018.

Matthews, Thomas F. *The Early Churches of Constantinople: Architecture and Liturgy*. University Park, PA: Pennsylvania State University Press, 971. https://catalog.library.vanderbilt.edu/discovery/fulldisplay/alma991018515069703276/01VAN_INST:vanui.

Matthiae, Guglielmo. *Le Porte Bronzee Bizantine in Italia*. Rome: Officina Edizioni, 1971.

Mayo, Penelope C. 'Vasa Sacra: Apostolic Authority and Episcopal Prestige in the Eleventh-Century Bari Benedictional'. *Dumbarton Oaks Papers* 41 (1987): 375–89.

McClendon, Charles B. *The Imperial Abbey of Farfa: Architectural Currents of the Early Middle Ages*. New Haven: Yale University Press, 1987.

McKeon, Peter R. 'The Lateran Council of 1112, the Heresy of Lay Investiture and the Excommunication of Henry V'. *Medievalia et Humanistica* 17 (1966): 3–12.

McQueen, William B. 'Relations between the Normans and Byzantium 1071–1112'. *Byzantion* 56 (1986): 427–76.

Meisen, Karl. *Nikolauskult Und Nikolausbrauch Im Abendlande: Eine Kultgeographisch-Volkskundliche Untersuchung*. Düsseldorf: Schwann, 1981.

Ménager, Léon-Robert. 'Costanza Di Francia'. In *Dizionario Biografico Degli Italiani*. Vol. 30, 1984. https://www.treccani.it/enciclopedia/costanza-di-francia_(Dizionario-Biografico)/.

Menduni, Michele. 'Ricerche Sui Restauri Della Basilica Cattedrale Di S. Sabino a Canosa a Partire Dal XIX Secolo Sino All'Inizio Del XX Secolo. L'Affresco Della Crocifissione Del Redentore Sul Calvario'. In *Canosa Ricerche Storiche. Decennio 1999 - 2009*, edited by Liana Bertoldi Lenoci, 827–76. Martina Franca: Edizioni Pugliesi, 2011.

Meyendorff, Jean. 'L'Icongraphie de La Sagesse Divine Dans La Tradition Byzantine'. *Cahiers Archéologiques* 10 (1959): 259–77.

Meyer, Bella. *La Figure de l'Atlante Dans La Sculpture Romane*. Paris: Université Paris IV, 1986.

Milburn, Robert. *Early Christian Art and Architecture*. Berkeley and Los Angeles: University of California Press, 1988.

Milella, Nicola. 'Il Rilievo Fotogrammetrico Digitale Multimmagine a Supporto Della Valorizzazione e Della Conoscenza Dei Beni Culturali'. In *Marmora Apuliae. Atti Giornata Studi Marmora. Politecnico Di Bari, 11 Ottobre 2018*, edited by Giovanna Fioretti, 91–7. Bari: Digilabs srls, 2019.

Milella, Nicola. 'Storia Dei Restauri'. In *San Nicola Di Bari e La Sua Basilica. Culto, Arte, Tradizione*, edited by Giorgio Otranto, 212–58. Milan: Electa, 1987.

Minguzzi, Simonetta. 'I Pavimenti Antichi'. In *'In Centro et Oculis Urbis Nostre'. La Chiesa e Il Monastero Di San Zaccaria*, edited by Chiese Di Venezia, Nuove Prospettive Di Ricerca, 75–94. Venice: Marcianum, 2015.

Miramon, Charles de. 'L'Invention de la Réforme Grégorienne. Grégoire VII au xixe Siècle, Entre Pouvoir Spirituel et Bureaucratisation de l'Église'. *Revue de l'Histoire des Religions* 236, no. 2 (2019): 283–315.

Mitchell, John. 'Giudizio Sul Mille: Rome, Monte Cassino, San Vincenzo al Volturno and the Beginnings of the Romanesque'. In *Rome across Time and Space: Cultural Transmission and the Exchange of Ideas, c. 500–1400*, edited by Claudia Bolgia, 167–81. Cambridge: Cambridge University Press, 2011.

Mola, Stefania. 'Il Santuario e i Normanni'. In *L'Angelo, La Montagna, Il Pellegrino*, edited by Pina Belli D'Elia, 66–83. Foggia: Claudio Grenzi, 1999.

Moore, Kathryn Blair. *The Architecture of the Christian Holy Land: Reception from Late Antiquity through the Renaissance*. Cambridge: Cambridge University Press, 2017.

Morey, Charles Rufus. *Roman and Christian Sculpture: The Sarcophagus of Claudia Antonia Sabina and the Asiatic Sarcophagi*. Vol. 5, part 1. Sardis: Publications of the American Society for the Excavation of Sardis; Princeton, NJ: The American Society for the Excavation of Sardis, 1924.

Morizio, Vincenza. 'La Città in Età Romana: I Monumenti'. In *Archaeologia Di Una Città: Bari Dalle Origini al X Secolo*, edited by Giuseppe Andreassi and Francesca Radina, 395–438. Bari: Edipuglia, 1988.

Morossi, Daniele. 'Political and Economic Relations between Venice, Byzantium and Southern Italy (1081–1197)'. Ph.D Thesis, University of Leeds, 2018.
Morris, Colin. *The Sepulchre of Christ and the Medieval West: From the Beginning to 1600*. Oxford and New York: Oxford University Press, 2005.
Moskowitz, Anita Fiderer. *Nicola and Giovanni Pisano: The Pulpits*. London and Turnhout: Harvey Miller, n.d.
Moskowitz, Anita Fiderer. *Nicola Pisano's Arca Di San Domenico and Its Legacy*. University Park, PA: Pennsylvania State University Press, 1994.
Muriel, Whitaker. *The Legends of King Arthur in Art*. Woodbridge: Brewer, 1990.
Musca, Giosuè. *L'Emirato Di Bari 847–871*. Bari: Dedalo, 1967.
Museum of the Order of St John, London. 'Lion Head Door Knocker or Handle (LDOSJ 5617)'. Accessed 28 January 2022. https://museumstjohn.org.uk/collections/lion-head-door-knocker-or-handle/.
Muthesius, Anna. *Byzantine Silk Weaving: AD 400 to AD 1200*. Vienna: Verlag Fassbaender, 1997.
Muthesius, Anna. 'Silk, Power And Diplomacy In Byzantium'. In *Textiles in Daily Life*, edited by Beverley Gordon and Suzanne Baizerman, 99–110. Textile Society of America, Symposium Proceedings. St Paul Minnesota: Dos Tejedoras, 1992. https://digitalcommons.unl.edu/cgi/viewcontent.cgi?article=1579&context=tsaconf.
Muthesius, Anna. *Studies in Byzantine, Islamic and Near Eastern Silk Weaving*. London: Pindar Press, 2008.
Napolitano, Ennio G. 'Le Iscrizioni Arabe della Porta del Mausoleo di Boemondo a Canosa'. *Spolia. Journal of Medieval Studies* 3 (2017): 1–14.
Nees, Lawrence. 'Forging Monumental Memories in the Early Twelfth Century'. In *Memory and Oblivion. Acts of the XXIX International Congress of the History of Art, Amsterdam 1996*, edited by Adriaan Wessel Reinink and Jeronen Stumpel, 773–82. Dordrecht: Kluwer, 1999.
Neri, Elisabetta, Nadine Schibille, Michele Pellegrino, and Donatella Nuzzo. 'A Byzantine Connection: Eastern Mediterranean Glasses in Medieval Bari'. *Journal of Cultural Heritage* 38 (2019): 253–60.
Nesbitt, John, and Nicholas Oikonomedes. *Catalogue of Byzantine Seals at Dumbarton Oaks and in the Fogg Museum of Art: South of the Balkans, the Islands, South of Asia Minor*. Vol. 2. Washington, DC: Dumbarton Oaks, 1991.
Nicephorus of Bari. *La Traslazione Di San Nicola: Le Fonti*. Edited by Pasquale Corsi. Bari: Centro studi Nicolaiani, 1987.
Nicols, John. 'Patronage and the Patrons of Canusium: A Case Study'. In *Civic Patronage in the Roman Empire*, 279–311. Leiden: Brill, 2014. https://doi.org/10.1163/9789004261716_09.
Niewöhner, Philipp. 'The Late Antique Origins of Byzantine Palace Architecture'. In *The Emperor's House: Palaces from Augustus to the Age of Absolutism*, edited by Michael Featherstone, Jean-Michel Spieser, Gülru Tanman and Ulrike Wulf-Rheidt, 31–52. Berlin: De Gruyter, 2015.
Nitti di Vito, Francesco, ed. *Le Pergamene Di S. Nicola Di Bari. Periodo Greco (939–1071)*. Codice Diplomatico Barese 4. Trani: Società di Storia Patria per la Puglia, 1900.
Nitti di Vito, Francesco, ed. *Le Pergamene Di S. Nicola Di Bari. Periodo Normanno*. Codice Diplomatico Barese 5. Trani: Società di Storia Patria per la Puglia, 1902.
Nitti di Vito, Francesco. 'Leggenda Di S. Nicola'. *Iapigia* 8 (1937): 317–35.

Nitto de Rossi, Giambattista, and Francesco Nitti di Vito, eds. *Le Pergamene Del Duomo Di Bari (952 -1264)*. Codice Diplomatico Barese 1. Bari: Commissione Provinciale di Archeologia e Storia Patria, 1897.

Northover, Peter, and Joachim Meyer. 'A Newly Acquired Islamic Lion Door Knocker in the David Collection'. *The Journal of the David Collection* 1 (2003): 48–71.

Nuzzo, Donatella. 'Bari: Il Pretorio Della Città Bizantina'. In *Citadella Nicolaiana 1: Archeologia Urbana a Bari Nell'Area Della Basilica Di San Nicola*, edited by Donatella Nuzzo, Maria Rosaria Depalo, and Giacomo Disantarosa, 25–35. Bari: Edipuglia, 2015.

Nuzzo, Donatella. 'Bari Prima Dei Normanni: La Città Nell'Alto Medioevo e La Documentazione Archeologica. Primi Dati Da Una Ricerca in Corso'. In *Storia e Archeologia Globale Dei Paesaggi Rurali in Italia Fra Tardoantico e Medioevo*, edited by Giuliano Volpe, 253–68. Insulae Diomedeae Collana Di Ricerche Storiche e Archeologiche 34. Bari: Edipuglia, 2018.

Nuzzo, Donatella, Maria Rosaria Depalo, and Sara Airò. 'Archeologia Urbana Nella "Cittadella Nicolaiana" Di Bari. Nuovi Dati Dal Riesame Delle Indagini Degli Anni Ottanta Nell'Area Del Pretorio Bizantino'. *Temporis Signa: Archeologia Della Tarda Antichità e Del Medioevo* 7 (2012): 79–106.

Occhiato, Giuseppe. 'Rapporti Culturali e Rispondenze Architettoniche Tra Calabria e Francia in Età Romanica'. *Mélanges de l'École Française de Rome* 93, no. 2 (1981): 565–603.

Old, Hughes Oliphant. *The Reading and Preaching of the Scriptures in the Worship of the Christian Church: The Medieval Chruch*. Grand Rapids, Michigan: Eerdmans, 1999.

Oldfield, Paul. *City and Community in Norman Italy*. Cambridge: Cambridge University Press, 2009.

Oldfield, Paul. *Sanctity and Pilgrimage in Medieval Southern Italy, 1000–1200*. Cambridge: Cambridge University Press, 2014.

Oldfield, Paul. 'Urban Government in Southern Italy, c.1085–c.1127'. *The English Historical Review* 122, no. 497 (2007): 579–608.

Ordeig i Mata, Ramón. 'La Documentatació Del Monestri de Cuixà Referent a Olibai Als Anys Del Seu Abadiat'. *Cahiers de St-Michel de Cuxa* 40 (2009): 39–51.

Orderic, Vitalis. *Ecclesiastical History of Orderic Vitalis*. Translated by Marjorie Chibnall. Vol. 6, Books 11, 12 and 13. Oxford: Clarendon Press, 1978.

Osborne, John. 'The Hagiographic Programme of the Mosaics in the South Dome of San Marco at Venice'. *Revue d'Art Canadienne, Canadian Art Review (RACAR)* 22, no. 1–2 (1995): 19–28.

Otranto, Giorgio. *San Nicola di Bari e la Sua Basilica: Culto, Arte, Tradizione*. Milano: Electa, 1987.

Ötüken, Semiha Yildiz. 'Konstantin IX - Solomon, Einzelkampfer, Siegesbringer Und Die Unbesiegbare Theotokos'. In *Byzantine Constantinople: Monuments, Topography and Everyday Life*, edited by Nevra Necipoğlu, 175–85. Leiden: Brill, 2001.

Ötüken, Semiha Yildiz. 'La Basilica di San Nicola a Myra'. In *San Nicola: Splendori d'Arte d'Oriente e d'Occidente*, edited by Michele Bacci, 47–61. Milano: Skira, 2006.

Ötüken, Semiha Yildiz. 'Myra-Demre Nikolaos Kilisesi Opus Sectile Yer Dösemesi ve Kazida Ortaya Çikan Opus Sectile Buluntular'. In *Anatolia at Daylight, Essays in Honour of Prof. Dr. Cevdet Bayburtluoğlu*, edited by Coşkun Özgünel, 182–9. Istanbul: Homer Kitabevi ve Yayincilik, 2001.

Ousterhout, Robert. *Eastern Medieval Architecture: The Building Traditions of Byzantium and Neighboring Lands*. Oxford: Oxford University Press, 2019.

Ousterhout, Robert. 'New Temples and New Solomons: The Rhetoric of Byzantine Architecture'. In *The Old Testament in Byzantium*, edited by Paul Magdalino and Robert Nelson, 223–53. Washington, DC: Dumbarton Oaks Research Library and Collection, 2010.

Ousterhout, Robert. 'Rebuilding the Temple: Constantine Monomachus and the Holy Sepulchre'. *Journal of the Society of Architectural Historians* 48, no. 1 (1989): 66–78. https://doi.org/10.2307/990407.

Ousterhout, Robert. 'Reliquary of St Anastasios the Persian'. In *Glory of Byzantium: Art and Culture in the Middle Byzantine Era*, edited by Helen C. Evans and William D. Wixom, 460–1. New York: Metropolitan Museum of Art, 1997.

Ousterhout, Robert G. *Master Builders of Byzantium*. Princeton, NJ: Princeton University Press, 1999.

Ousterhout, Robert G. 'Sacred Geographies and Holy Cities: Constantinople as Jerusalem'. In *Hierotopy: The Creation of Sacred Space in Byzantium and Medieval Russia*, edited by Aleksej Michajlovic Lidov, 98–116. Moscow: Indrik, 2006.

Ousterhout, Robert G. 'The Church of Santo Stefano: A "Jerusalem" in Bologna'. *Gesta* 20, no. 2 (1981): 311–21. https://doi.org/10.2307/766940.

Ovid. 'Metamorphoses'. Bari, c 1050. Biblioteca Malatestiana, Cesena.

Owen-Crocker, Gale. 'Episcopal Gloves (St Sabinus Gloves) from Canosa'. In *Clothing the Past: Surviving Garments from Early Medieval to Early Modern Western Europe*, edited by Elizabeth Coatsworth and Gale Owen-Crocker, 400–4. Leiden: Brill, 2018.

Owen-Crocker, Gale R., and Elizabeth Coatsworth. 'The Star Mantle of Emperor Henry II'. In *Clothing the Past: Suviving Garments from Early Medieval to Early Modern Western Europe*, 75–7. Leiden: Brill, 2018.

Pace, Valentino. 'Fra l'Islam e l'Occidente: Il Mistero Degli Olifanti'. In *Studi in Onore Di Umberto Scerrato per Il Suo Settantacinquesimo Compleanno*, edited by Maria Vittoria Fontana and Bruno Genito, 609–27. Naples: Istituto Italiano per L'Africa e L'Oriente, 2003.

Pace, Valentino. 'Présence et Reflets de l'Art Islamique En Italie Méridionale Au Moyen Age'. *Cahiers de St-Michel de Cuxa* 35 (2004): 57–70.

Packard, Barbara. 'Remembering the First Crusade: Latin Narrative Histories 1099 - c.1300'. PhD Thesis, Royal Holloway, University of London, 2011. https://core.ac.uk/download/pdf/28897102.pdf.

'Panel with Horse Heads (11.205.2), Metropolitan Museum of Art, New York'. Accessed 20 January 2022. https://www.metmuseum.org/art/collection/search/446191.

Papacostas, Tassos. 'The Medieval Progeny of The Holy Apostles'. In *The Byzantine World*, edited by Paul Stephenson, 386–405. Oxford: Routledge, 2010. https://doi.org/10.4324/9780203817254.ch28.

Parani, Maria G. *Reconstructing the Reality of Images: Byzantine Material Culture and Religious Iconography 11th–15th Centuries*. Leiden: Brill, 2003.

Partrich, Joseph. 'A Government Compound in Roman-Byzantine Caesarea'. *Proceedings of the World Congress of Jewish Studies*, edited by Ron Margolin, 35–44, 1997.

Paul, Nicholas L. 'A Warlord's Wisdom: Literacy and Propaganda at the Time of the First Crusade'. *Speculum* 85, no. 3 (2010): 534–66. https://doi.org/10.1017/S0038713410001284.

Paul of Bernried. 'Life of Pope Gregory VII'. In *The Papal Reform of the Eleventh Century. The Lives of Pope Leo IX and Pope Gregory VII.*, translated by Ian Stuart Robinson, 262–364. Manchester; New York: Manchester University Press, 2004.

Pellegrini, Camillo. 'Chronicon Ignoti Civis Barensis'. In *Historia Principum Langobardorum*, vol. 2, 185–200. Naples, 1643.
Pentcheva, Bissera V. 'Performative Images and Cosmic Sound in the Exultet Liturgy of Southern Italy'. *Speculum* 95, no. 2 (2020): 396–466.
Pertusi, Agostino. 'Ai Confini Tra Religione e Politica. La Contesa per Le Reliquie Di San Nicola Tra Bari, Venezia e Genova'. *Quaderni Medievali* 5 (1978): 6–56.
Petraglia, Marisa. 'La Cattedrale Di San Sabino a Canosa'. Ph.D thesis, Sapienza, Università di Roma, 2012.
Petrizzo, Francesca. 'Band of Brothers: Kin Dynamics of the Hautevilles and Other Normans in Southern Italy and Syria, c.1030 - c.1140'. Ph.D thesis, University of Leeds, 2018.
Pierno, Marida. 'Artisti Nella Puglia Centro-Settentrionale Tra XI e XIII Secolo: Produzione Artistica Tra Stile, Identità Ed Autocoscienza'. *Venezia Arti* 26 (2017): 17–35.
Pinatsi, Christina. 'Regional Trends and International Exchange in the Art of Marble Pavements During the Middle-Byzantine Period'. In *Architecture of Byzantium and Kievian Rus from the 9th to the 12th Centuries*, edited by Oleg Ioannissian and Denis Jolshin, 101–17. St Petersburg: State Hermitage Publishers, 2012.
Pivčević, Edo. *The Cartulary of the Benedictine Abbey of St Peter of Gumay [Croatia] 1080-1187*. Bristol: Arthur, 1984.
Poncelet, A, ed. 'Miracula Sancti Nicolai a Monacho Beccensi'. In *Catalogus Codicum Hagiographicorum Latinorum Bibliotheca Nationali Parisiensi*, vol. 2edited by Société des Bollandistes, 405–32. Brussels: Hagiographi Bollandiani, 1890.
Pontieri, Ernesto. 'La Madre Di Re Ruggiero, Contessa Di Sicilia, Regina Di Gerusalemme'. In *Atti Del Convegno Internazionale Di Studi Ruggeriani*, vol. 1, 327–432. Palermo: Società Siciliana per la Storia della Patria, 1955.
'Pontifical with Benediction of the Font'. Scroll, c 969. Biblioteca Casanatense.
Porter, Arthur Kingsley. 'Bari, Modena, and St.-Gilles'. *Burlington Magazine* 43, no. 245 (1923): 58–67.
Porter, Arthur Kingsley. *Romanesque Sculpture of the Pilgrimage Roads*. Vol. 1. Boston: Marshall Jones, 1923.
Pozza, Marco, and Giorgio Ravegnani, eds. *I Trattati con Bisanzio 992-1198*. Vol. 4. Venezia: Il cardo, 1993.
Pratilli, Francesco Maria. *Della Aia Appia Riconosciuta e Descritta da Roma a Brindisi*. Naples: G. di Simone, 1745.
'Psalter'. Constantinople, 10th century. Gr.139. Bibliothèque Nationale de France. https://gallica.bnf.fr/ark:/12148/btv1b10515446x/f18.item.
Putter, Ad. 'The Twelfth-Century Arthur'. In *The Cambridge Companion to the Arthurian Legend*, edited by Ad Putter and Elizabeth Archibald, 36–52. Cambridge: Cambridge University Press, 2009.
Quintavalle, Arturo Carlo. 'Riforma Gregoriana e Origini Del 'Romanico''. In *Compostela e L'Europa. La Storia Di Diego Gelmirez*, edited by Manuel A. Castiñeiras, 204–31. Milan, 2010.
Raby, Julian. 'The Inscriptions on the Pisa Griffin and the Mari-Cha Lion: From Banal Blessings to Indices of Origin'. In *The Pisa Griffin and the Mari-Cha Lion: Metalwork, Art, and Technology in the Medieval Islamicate Mediterranean*, edited by Anna Contadini, 305–62. Pisa: Pacini Editore, 2018.
Radding, Charles, and Francis Newton. *Theology, Rhetoric, and Politics in the Eucharistic Controversy, 1078-1079: Alberic of Monte Cassino Against Berengar of Tours*. New York: Columbia University Press, 2003.

Ramseyer, Valerie. *The Transformation of a Religious Landscape: Medieval Southern Italy, 850–1150*. Ithaca: Cornell University Press, 2006.

Ravegnani, Giorgio. *I Bizantini in Italia*. Bologna: Il Mulino, 2004.

Riccioni, Stefano. 'I Mosaici Altomedievali Di Venezia e Il Monastero Di S. Ilario. Orditi 'Venetico-Carolingi' Di Una Kionè Alto Adriatica'. In *The Age of Affirmation. Venice, the Adriatic and the Hinterland between the 9th and 10th Centuries*, edited by Stefano Gasparri and Sauro Gelichi, 277–322. Turnhout: Brepols, 2017.

Richard de Saint-Non, Jean-Claude. *Voyage Pittoresque Ou Description Des Royaumes de Naples et de Sicile*. Vol. 3. 4 vols. Paris: Clousier, 1781.

Richardson, Jessica N. 'Between the Limousin and the Holy Land: Prisoners, Performance, and the Portal of San Leonardo at Siponto'. *Gesta* 54, no. 2 (2015): 165–94. https://doi.org/10.1086/681953.

Riley-Smith, Jonathan. *The First Crusade and the Idea of Crusading*. London: Continuum, 1993.

Riley-Smith, Jonathan. *The First Crusaders, 1095–1131*. Cambridge: Cambridge University Press, 1997.

Rio, Alice. 'Freedom and Unfreedom in Early Medieval Francia: The Evidence of the Legal Formulae'. *Past & Present* 193, no. 1 (2006): 7–40.

Robinson, Gertrude. *History and Cartulary of the Greek Monastery of St Elias and St Anastasius of Carbone*. Rome: Pont. Institutum Orientalium Studiorum, 1928.

Robinson, Ian Stuart. 'Introduction'. In *The Papal Reform of the Eleventh Century: Lives of Pope Leo IX and Pope Gregory VII. Selected Sources Translated and Annotated*, edited by Ian Stuart Robinson, 1–96. Manchester: Manchester University Press, 2004.

Robinson, Ian Stuart. 'Reform and the Church, 1073–1122'. In *The New Cambridge Medieval History, c.1024 - c.1198*, edited by David Luscombe and Jonathan Riley-Smith 4, part 1:268–334. Cambridge: Cambridge University Press, 2004.

Robinson, Ian Stuart. *The Papacy, 1073–1198: Continuity and Innovation*. Cambridge: Cambridge University Press, 1990.

Robinson, Ian Stuart. *The Papal Reform of the Eleventh Century: Lives of Pope Leo IX and Pope Gregory VII*. Manchester; New York: Manchester University Press, 2004.

Romuald of Salerno. 'Chronicon'. In *Roger II and the Creation of the Kingdom of Sicily*, edited by Graham Loud. Manchester; New York: Manchester University Press, 2012.

Romuald of Salerno. 'Romualdi Salernitani Chronicon'. In *Rerum Italicarum Scriptores, Nuova Edizione*, edited by Carlo Garufi, 1–246. Città di Castello: Muratori, 1935.

Ronchi, Benedetto. *La Cattedrale di Trani*. Fasano: Schena, 1985.

Rosser-Owen, Mariam. 'Mediterraneanism: How to Incorporate Islamic Art into an Emerging Field'. *Journal of Art Historiography* 6 (2012): 2–33.

Rosser-Owen, Mariam. 'The Oliphant: A Call for a Shift in Perspective'. In *Romanesque and the Mediterranean*, edited by John McNeill and Rosa Bacile, 15–58. Abingdon: Routledge, 2015.

Rotman, Youval. *Byzantine Slavery and the Mediterranean World*. Cambridge MA: Harvard University Press, 2009.

Rotman, Youval. 'Migration and Enslavement: A Medieval Model'. In *Migration Histories of the Medieval Afroeurasian Transition Zone*, edited by Johannes Preisler-Kapeller, Lucien Reinfandt, and Yannis Stouritis, 387–412. Leiden: Brill, 2020.

Rouse, Robert Allen, and Cory James Rushton. 'Arthurian Geography'. In *The Cambridge Companion to the Arthurian Legend*, edited by Elizabeth Archibald and Ad Putter, 218–34. Cambridge: Cambridge University Press, 2009.

Rowe, Nina. *The Jew, the Cathedral and the Medieval City: Synagoga and Ecclesia in the Thirteenth Century*. Cambridge: Cambridge University Press, 2011.

Russo, Luigi. 'Bad Crusaders? The Normans of Southern Italy and the Crusading Movement in the Twelfth Century'. *Anglo-Norman Studies* 38 (2015): 169–80.

Russo, Luigi. *Boemondo: figlio del Guiscardo e principe di Antiochia*. Avellino: E. Sellino, 2009.

Russo, Luigi. 'Oblio e Memoria Di Boemondo d'Altavilla Nella Storiografia Normanna'. *Bulletino Dell'Istituto Storico Italiano per Il Medioevo* 106, no. 1 (2004): 137–65.

Rutishauser, Samuel. 'Genèse et Développement de La Crypte à Salle En Europe Du Sud'. *Cahiers de St-Michel de Cuxa* 24 (1993): 37–52.

Sackur, E., ed. 'Libelli de Lite'. In *Monumenta Germaniae Historica*, edited by George Waitz, 542–eeeee6. Hannover, 1892.

Sada, Luigi. *L'Abbazia Benedettina D'Ognisanti Di Cuti*. Bari: Società di Storia Patria per la Puglia, 1974.

Safran, Linda. "'Byzantine' Art in Post-Byzantine South Italy? Notes on a Fuzzy Concept'. *Common Knowledge, Special Issue: Fuzzy Studies: A Symposium on the Consequence of Blur, Part 3* 18, no. 3 (2012): 487–504.

Safran, Linda. *S. Pietro at Otranto. Byzantine Art in South Italy*. Rome: Edizioni Rari Nantes, 1992.

Safran, Linda. *The Medieval Salento: Art and Identity in Southern Italy*. Philadelphia: University of Pennsylvania Press, 2014.

Salvarani, Renata. *La Fortuna Del Santo Sepolcro Nel Medioevo*. Milan: Jaca, 2008. https://books.google.com/books/about/La_fortuna_del_Santo_Sepolcro_nel_Medioe.html?id=1palh81YLOIC.

Sanders, Paula. *Ritual, Politics and the City in Fatimid Cairo*. Albany, NY: State University of New York Press, 1994.

Saunders, W. B. R. 'The Aachen Reliquary of Eustathius Maleinus, 969–970'. *Dumbarton Oaks Papers* 36 (1982): 211–19. https://doi.org/10.2307/1291468.

Savvidēs, Alexēs G. K. *Byzantino-Normannica: The Norman Capture of Italy (to A.D. 1081) and the First Two Invasions in Byzantium (A.D. 1081–1085 and 1107–1108)*. Leuven: Uitgeverij Peeters en Departement Oosterse Studies, 2007.

Saxon, Elizabeth. 'Carolingian, Ottonian and Romanesque Art and the Eucharist'. In *A Companion to the Eucharist in the Middle Ages*, edited by Ian Levy, Gary Macy, and Kristen Van Ausdall, 251–324. Leiden: Brill, 2012.

Saxon, Elizabeth. *The Eucharist in Romanesque France: Iconography and Theology*. Woodbridge: Boydell, 2006.

Schein, Sylvia. 'Between Mount Moriah and the Holy Sepulchre: The Changing Traditions of the Temple Mount in the Central Middle Ages'. *Traditio* 40 (1984): 175–95.

Schettini, Franco. *La Basilica di San Nicola di Bari*. Bari: Laterza, 1967.

Schneider, Rolf Michael. *Bunte Barbaren Orientalenstatuen Aus Farbigem Marmor in Der Römischen Repräsentationskunst*. Worms: Wernersche Verlagsgesellschaft, 1986.

Schulz, Heinrich Wilhelm. *Denkmäler Der Kunst Des Mittelalters in Unteritalien*. Dresden: Wilhelm K.H. Schulz, 1860.

Schulz, Robert Weir, and Sidney Barnsley. *The Monastery of Saint Luke of Stiris, in Phocis, and the Dependent Monastery of Saint Nicholas in the Fields, near Skripou in Boetia*. Athens: British School at Athens, 1901.

Sensi, Mario. 'Santuario e Culto Di San Michele Nell'Italia Centrale'. In *Culto e Santuari Di San Michele Nell'Europa Medievale*, edited by Pierre Bouet, Giorgio Otranto, and André Vauchez, 241–81. Bari: Edipuglia, 2007.

Ševčenko, Nancy Patterson. 'The Posthumous Miracles of St Eustratios on a Sinai Templon Beam'. In *Byzantine Religious Culture: Studies in Honor of Alice-Mary Talbot*, edited by Denis Sullivan, Elizabeth Fisher, and Stratis Papaioannou, 267–87. Leiden: Brill, 2012.

Shalem, Avinoam. *The Oliphant: Islamic Objects in Historical Context*. Leiden: Brill, 2004.

Shepard, Jonathan. 'Byzantium and the West c.900 - c.1024'. In *The New Cambridge Medieval History*, edited by Timothy Reuter, vol. 3, 605–23. Cambridge: Cambridge University Press, 2000. https://doi.org/10.1017/CHOL9780521364478.

Silvestri, Elena. 'Una Rilettura Delle Fasi Costruttive Del Duomo Di Modena'. *Atti e Memorie* 11, no. 35 (2013): 117–49.

Sinclair, Susan. 'The Relationship between Art and Liturgy on the Periphery of the Byzantine Empire: the Cases of 10th century Cappadocia and Longobardia (Apulia)'. Ph.D thesis, Courtauld Institute of Art, 2003.

Sinisi, Lucia. 'Dressing the Earth: Eleventh-Century Garb in the Exultet Roll of Bari'. In *Refashioning Medieval and Early Modern Dress: A Tribute to Robin Netherton*, edited by Gale Owen-Crocker and Maren Clegg-Hyer, 29–44. Cambridge: Cambridge University Press, 2019.

Sinisi, Lucia. 'The Marriage of the Year (1028)'. Edited by Gale R. Owen-Crocker and Robin Netherton. *Medieval Clothing and Textiles* 9 (2013): 45–54.

Skinner, Patricia. "Halt! Be Men!': Sikelgaita of Salerno, Gender and the Norman Conquest of Southern Italy'. *Gender & History* 12, no. 3 (2000): 622–41. https://doi.org/10.1111/1468-0424.00203.

Skinner, Patricia. 'Room for Tension: Urban Life in Apulia in the Eleventh and Twelfth Centuries'. *Papers of the British School at Rome* 66 (1998): 159–76. https://doi.org/10.1017/S0068246200004268.

Smith, Romney David. 'The Business of Human Trafficking: Slaves and Money Between Western Italy and the House of Islam Before the Crusades (c.900–c.1100)'. *Journal of Medieval History* 45, no. 5 (2019): 523–52.

Solovyov, Vladimir Sergeyevich. *Divine Sophia: The Wisdom Writings of Vladimir Solovyov*. Ithaca: Cornell University Press, 2009.

Somerville, Robert. *Pope Urban II, The Collectio Britannica, and the Council of Melfi (1089)*. Oxford: Oxford University Press, 1996.

Spawforth, Antony. *Greece and the Augustan Cultural Revolution*. Cambridge: Cambridge University Press, 2015.

Speciale, Lucinia. 'Liturgia e Potere. Le Commemorazioni Finali Nei Rotoli Dell'Exultet'. *Mélanges de l'Ecole Française de Rome* 112, no. 1 (2000): 191–224.

Stanton, Charles D. 'The Norman Siege of Bari, 1068–71'. In *Rethinking Norman Italy: Studies in Honour of Graham A. Loud*, edited by Paul Oldfield and Joanna Drell, 265–83. Manchester: Manchester University Press, 2021.

Stiennon, Jacques, and Rita Lejeune. 'La Légende Arthurienne Dans La Sculpture de La Cathédrale de Modène'. *Cahiers de Civilisation Médiévale* 6 (1963): 281–96.

Stroll, Mary. 'The Twelfth-Century Apse Mosaic in San Clemente in Rome and Its Enigmatic Inscription'. *Storia e Civiltà* 4 (n.d.): 3–17.

Stroszeck, Jutta. *Löwen-Sarkophage: Sarkophage mit Löwenköpfen, schreitenden Löwen und Löwen-Kampfgruppen*. Vol. 1. Die antiken Sarkophagreliefs 6. Berlin: Gebr Mann, 1998.

Tangheroni, Marco. 'Trade and Navigation'. In *Italy in the Central Middle Ages: 1000–1300*, edited by David Abulafia, 127–46. Oxford and New York: Oxford University Press, 2004.

Tenenti, Alberto, and Ugo Tucci. 'L'Impresa Marittima: Uomini e Mezzi'. In *Storia Di Venezia: Dalle Origini Alla Caduta Della Serenissima*, vol. 2, edited by Giorgio Cracco and Gherardo Ortalli, 627–56. Rome: Istituto della Enciclopedia Italiana, 1996.

Testi, Cristiani, Maria Laura. 'Sul Mausoleo Di Boemondo a Canosa'. In *Boemondo. Storia Di Un Principe Normanno*, edited by Franco Cardini, Bendetto Vetere, and Nunzio Lozito, 107–16. Martina Franca: Congedo, 2003.

Theotokis, Georgios. *The Norman Campaigns in the Balkans, 1081-1108 AD*. Woodbridge: Boydell Press, 2014.

Thomas, Edmund. 'Houses of the Dead'? Columnar Sarcophagi as "Micro-Architecture"'. In *Life, Death and Representation: Some New Work on Roman Sarcophagi*, edited by Jas Elsner and Janet Hutchinson, 387–435. Berlin: De Gruyter, 2011.

Todisco, Luigi. *Bari Romana*. Rome: L'Erma di Bretschneider, 2017.

Todisco, Luigi. 'L'Eredità Dell'Antico Nella Cultura Materiale Di Bari Tra XI e XIII Secolo'. In *Scultura Antica e Reimpiego in Italia Meridionale, I: Puglia, Basilicata, Campania*, edited by Luigi Todisco, 239–70. Bari: Edipuglia srl, 1994.

Todisco, Luigi, and Marcella Chelotti. *La Scultura Romana Di Venosa e Il Suo Reimpiego*. Rome: Bretschneider, 1996.

Tortora, Angelo Andrea. *Relatio Status Sanctae Primatialis Ecclesiae Canusinae, Seu Historia Ex Romanorum Pontificum Constitutionibus*. Rome: Ex typographia Komarek, 1758.

Toubert, Hélène. *Un Art Dirigé. Réforme Grégorienne et Iconographie*. Paris: Cerf, 1990.

Tracy, Charles. *Britain's Medieval Episcopal Thrones*. Oxford; Philadelphia: Oxbow Books, 2014.

Tronzo, William. *The Cultures of His Kingdom: Roger II and the Cappella Palatina in Palermo*. Princeton: Princeton University Press, 1997.

Tsitouridou, Anna. *The Church of the Panagia Chalkeon*. Thessaloniki: Institute for Balkan Studies, 1985.

Ughelli, Ferdinando. *Italia Sacra, Sive de Episcopis Italiae*. Vol. 7. 10 vols. Venice: apud Sebastianum Coleti, 1721.

Ungruh, Christine. *Das Bodenmosaik der Kathedrale von Otranto*. 1st edn. Affalterbach: Didymos-Verlag, 2013.

Upsher Smith, Richard. 'Nobilissimus and Warleader: The Opportunity and the Necessity behind Robert Guiscard's Balkan Expeditions'. *Byzantion* 70 (2001): 507–26.

Van Houts, Elisabeth. 'Changes of Aristocratic Identity: Remarriage and Remembrance in Europe 900–1200'. In *Memory and Commemoration in Medieval Culture*, edited by Meredith Cohen, Elma Brenner, and Mary Franklin-Brown, 221–41. London: Routledge, 2013.

Vanderheyde, Catherine. *La Sculpture Architecturale Byzantine Dans Le Thème de Nikopolis Du Xe Au Début Du XIIIe Siècle. Épire, Étolie-Acaranie et Sud de l'Albanie*. Athens: École Française d'Athènes, 2005.

Vandi Kalogerakou, Loretta. 'Ovid at the Crossroads. The Illustrations of the Metamorphoses in Apulia before 1071'. In *After the Carolingians: Re-Defining Manuscript Illumination in the Tenth and Eleventh Centuries*, edited by Beatrice Kitzinger and Joshua O'Driscoll, 302–35. Berlin: De Gruyter, 2019.

Ventrone Vassallo, Giovanna. 'Pannello Ligneo'. In *Eredità Dell'Islam: Arte Islamica in Italia*, edited by Giovanni Curatola, 197–8. Cinisello Balsamo, Milan: Silvana Editoriale, 1993.

Vernon, Clare. 'Dressing for Succession in Norman Italy: The Mantle of King Roger II'. *Al-Masāq: Journal of the Medieval Mediterranean* 31, no. 1 (2019): 95–110.

Vernon, Clare. 'Pseudo-Arabic and the Material Culture of the First Crusade in Norman Italy: The Sanctuary Mosaic at San Nicola in Bari'. *Open Library of Humanities* 4, no. 1 (2018): 1–43.

Vescovi, Michele Luigi. 'Inscribing Presence: Script, Relics, Space in Salerno Cathedral'. In *Sacred Scripture / Sacred Space. The Interlacing of Real Places and Conceptual Spaces in Medieval Art and Architecture*, edited by Tobias Frese, Wilfried E. Keil, and Kristina Krüger, 137–64. Berlin and Boston: De Gruyter, 2019. https://doi.org/10.1515/9783110629156-007.

Vista, Francesco Saverio. 'Curiosità Storiche: Canosa Nel 1643'. *Rassegna Pugliese* 22, no. 7–8 (1905): 239.

Volbach, Fritz. 'Bari'. In *Alle Sorgenti Del Romanico. Puglia XI Secolo*, edited by Pina Belli D'Elia, 107–17. Bari: Dedalo, 1987.

Volbach, Fritz. 'Bari Cattedrale'. In *Alle Sorgenti Del Romanico: Puglia XI Secolo*, edited by Pina Belli D'Elia, 99–105. Bari: Dedalo, 1987.

Volbach, Fritz. 'Mantello Di Enrico II'. In *Alle Sorgenti Del Romanico: Puglia XI Secolo*, edited by Pina Belli D'Elia, 128–30. Bari: Dedalo, 1975.

Volbach, Fritz. 'Monte Sant'Angelo'. In *Alle Sorgenti Del Romanico. Puglia XI Secolo*, edited by Pina Belli D'Elia, 36–46. Bari: Dedalo, 1987.

Volpe, Giuliano. 'Architecture and Church Power in Late Antiquity: Canosa and San Giusto (Apulia)'. *Late Antique Archaeology* 3, no. 1 (2006): 131–68. https://doi.org/10.1163/22134522-90000063.

Volpe, Giuliano. 'Venerabilis Vir Restaurator Ecclesiarum'. In *Canosa Ricerche Storiche 2007, Atti Del Convengo (16 - 18.2.2007)*, edited by L. Bertoldi Lenoci, 23–52. Martina Franca: Edizioni Pugliesi, 2008.

Von Falkenhausen, Vera. 'A Provincial Aristocracy: The Byzantine Provinces in Southern Italy (9th–11th Century)'. In *The Byzantine Aristocracy, IX to XIII Centuries*, edited by Michael Angold, 211–35. B.A.R International Series 221. Oxford: B.A.R., 1984.

Von Falkenhausen, Vera. 'Bari Bizantina: Profilo Di Un Capoluogo Di Provincia'. In *Spazio, Società, Potere Nell'Italia Dei Comuni*, edited by Gabriella Rossetti, 199–203. Florence: Liguori, 1986.

Von Falkenhausen, Vera. 'I Bizantini in Italia'. In *I Bizantini in Italia*, edited by Guglielmo Cavallo, Vera Von Falkenhausen, and Raffaella Farioli-Campanati, 3–136. Milan: Garzanti, 1982.

Von Falkenhausen, Vera. *La Dominazione Bizantina nell'Italia Meridionale dal IX all'XI Secolo*. Bari: Ecumenica editrice, 1978.

Von Pölnitz, Sigmund. *Die Bamberger Kaisermäntel*. Bamberg: Bamberger Dom, 1973.

Vona, Fabrizio. 'La Porta Del Mausoleo Di Boemondo'. In *Canosa Ricerche Storiche 2003*, edited by L. Bertoldi Lenoci, 105–12. Fasano: Schena, 2003.

Vona, Fabrizio. 'Le Porte Di Monte Sant'Angelo e Di Canosa: Tecnologie a Confronto'. In *Le Porte Del Paradiso: Arte e Tecnologia Bizantina Tra Italia e Mediterraneo*, edited by Antonio Iacobini, 375–410. Roma: Campisano, 2009.

Vona, Fabrizio. 'Persistenza Della Tradizione Tecnologica Di Bisanzio Nei Bronzi Medievali Pugliesi'. In *L'Héritage Byzantin En Italie (VIIIe-XIIe Siècle). III Décor Monumental, Objets, Tradition Textuelle*, edited by Jean-Marie Martin, Sulamith Brodbeck, Annick Peters-Custot, and Vivien Prigent, 23–37. Rome: École Française de Rome, 2015.

Vryonis, Speros P. 'Jewelry from a Thessalonian Hoard'. In *The Glory of Byzantium: Art and Culture of the Middle Byzantine Era, A.D. 843–1261*, edited by Helen C. Evans and William D. Wixom, 243–44. New York: Metropolitan Museum of Art, 1997.

Wackernagel, Martin. 'La Bottega Dell'Archidiacono Acceptus, Sculptore Pugliese Dell'XI Secolo'. *Bolletino D'Arte* 2, no. 4 (1908): 143–50.
Walker, Daniel. 'Textile with Roundels of Elephants, Senmurvs and Winged Horses'. In *Glory of Byzantium: Art and Culture of the Middle Byzantine Era, A.D. 843–1261*, edited by Helen C. Evans and William D. Wixom, 414–16. New York: Metropolitan Museum of Art, 1997.
Walter, Christopher. *Art and Ritual in the Byzantine Church*. London: Variorum, 1982.
Walter, Christopher. *The Warrior Saints in Byzantine Art and Tradition*. Aldershot: Routledge, 2016.
Weetch, Rosie. 'The Mystery of the Bronze Lion Heads at the Museum of the Order of St John'. *Bearers of the Cross: Material Religion in the Crusading World, 1095 - c.1300* (blog), 7 September 2016. https://www.bearersofthecross.org.uk/mystery-bronze-lion-heads-museum-order-st-john/.
Weinryb, Ittai. *The Bronze Object in the Middle Ages*. Cambridge: Cambridge University Press, 2016.
Weinryb, Ittai. 'The Inscribed Image: Negotiating Sculpture on the Coast of the Adriatic Sea'. *Word & Image* 27, no. 3 (2011): 322–33. https://doi.org/10.1080/02666286.2011.541133.
Westbrook, Nigel. 'Architecture of Traces and Ascriptions: Interpreting the Vanished Great Palace of the Byzantine Emperors in Constantinople'. *Fabrications: The Journal of the Society of Architectural Historians, Australia and New Zealand* 6, no. 1 (2006): 43–61.
Wharton Epstein, Annabelle J. *Art of Empire: Painting and Architecture of the Byzantine Periphery. A Comparative Study of Four Provinces*. University Park, PA: Pennsylvania State University Press, 1988.
Wharton Epstein, Annabelle J. 'The Date and Significance of the Cathedral of Canosa in Apulia, South Italy'. *Dumbarton Oaks Papers* 37 (1983): 79–90. https://doi.org/10.2307/1291478.
Wharton Epstein, Annabelle J. 'The Political Content of the Paintings of St Sophia at Ohrid'. *Jahrbuch Der Österreichischen Byzantinistik* 29 (1980): 315–29.
White, Monica. *Military Saints in Byzantium and Rus, 900–1200*. Cambridge: Cambridge University Press, 2013.
Wilkinson, John. *From Synagogue to Church: The Traditional Design: Its Beginning, Its Definition, Its End*. London: Routledge, 2002.
Wilkinson, John. *Jerusalem Pilgrims Before the Crusades*. Warminster: Aris & Phillips, 2002.
Willard, Henry M., and Kenneth John Conant. 'A Project for the Graphic Reconstruction of the Romanesque Abbey at Monte Cassino'. *Speculum* 10, no. 2 (1935): 144–6.
William of Tyre. *A History of Deeds Done Beyond the Sea*. Translated by Emily Atwater Babcock and August C. Krey. New York: Columbia University Press, 1943.
Williams, Kim. *Italian Pavements: Patterns in Space*. Houston, Texas: Anchorage Press, 1997.
Wilson, Charles William, ed. *The Pilgrimage of the Russian Abbot Daniel in the Holy Land, 1106–1107 A.D.* London: Palestine Pilgrims Text Society, 1897.
Winterfeld, Dethard von. *Die Kaiserdome: Speyer, Mainz, Worms*. Regensburg: Verlag Schnell & Steiner, 2000.
Wollasch, Joachim. *Neue Forschungen Über Cluny Und Die Cluniacenser*. Freiburg: Herder, 1959.
Yewdale, Ralph Bailey. *Bohemond I, Prince of Antioch*. New York: AMS Press, 1980.
Zanker, Paul. *Roman Art*. Los Angeles: The J. Paul Getty Museum, 2010.

Zarnecki, George. 'A Newly Discovered Head from Bury St Edmunds Abbey'. In *Arte d'Occidente: Temi e Metodi. Studi in Onore Di Angiola Maria Romanini*, edited by Antonio Cadei, Marina Righetti Tosti-Croce, and Anna Segagni Malacart, 319–26. Roma: Edizioni Sintesi Informzione, 1999.

Zchomelidse, Nino. 'Descending Word: Resurrecting Christ: Moving Images in Illuminated Liturgical Scrolls of Southern Italy'. In *Meaning in Motion: The Semantics of Movement in Medieval Art*, edited by Nino Zchomelidse and Giovanni Freni, 3–34. Princeton: Princeton University Press, 2011.

Zchomelidse, Nino M. *Art, Ritual, and Civic Identity in Medieval Southern Italy*. University Park, PA: Pennsylvania State University Press, 2014.

Zimmermann, Michel. 'Sur La Terre Come Au Ciel: La Paix Chrétienne. Oliba (1008–1046), Pacificateur et Guide Des Âmes'. *Cahiers de St-Michel de Cuxa* 40 (2009): 7–38.

Zuliani, Fulvio, ed. *Veneto Romanico*. Italia Romanica. Milan: Jaca, 2008.

Index

Aachen 173, 179, 193
Acceptus 31, 47–52, 67, 72, 161
Acerenza 30
Acre 20
Adelaide del Vasto 165, 170
Adela of Blois 165, 197
Adela of Flanders 165, 169–70, 198
Albania 153
Alberada of Buonalbergo 57, 157, 161, 165, 168–70
Alexandria 12, 99
Alferada, Lombard, woman of Bari 13, 33
Amalfi 3, 12, 57, 69, 71, 158, 180–1, 183
    Comite Maurone family 180
Andalusia 186
Andrew, Archbishop of Bari and Canosa, see Bari, Archbishops of Bari and Canosa
Andria, Sant'Agostino 108
angels 124
Angelus, mason 102–3
Anna Comnena 159
Antioch 100, 157–9, 165–6, 171–3, 175, 194, 197–8
    artophorion, now in Aachen (see under metalwork)
Apollonia, Libya 16
apotropaic 88–90, 112, 147, 186
Aquiliea 88
Arabic 69, 186, see also pseudo-Arabic
Argyros, son of Melus 9–10, 21, 24
Armenians 10, 13, 15, 129
Arta, Blanchernes church 124
Arthur, king 113, 116–19
Assisi 183
Athos, Lavra monastery 15, 171
Atrani 180
Autun, Saint Lazare 191
Aversa 125, 167

Baalbek, Roman temples 158
Bamberg 22–4
Bari
    Archbishops of Bari and Canosa
        Andrew 10
        Angelarius 130
        Bisantius 25–31, 35, 38–44
        Elias
            Archbishop 81, 118
            Benedictine 41, 59, 111
            biography 129–30
            death and legacy 55, 85, 139–41, 159, 165
            ecclesiastical judge 81, 91
            involvement in the Gregorian reform movement 75, 78, 91, 151
            patron of San Nicola 61–2, 75, 78–80, 101–3, 108, 117, 137, 145–6, 149, 151–2
            throne 81–5
            tomb and epitaph 128, 131–6, 150, 200
        Nicholas 26–31, 35, 42–3, 46, 51, 67, 81
        Riso 55, 138–9, 153, 165–9
        Romuald 25
        Ursus 49–50, 59–62, 67, 79–81, 129, 130
    churches in Bari
        Benedictine monastery 11, 32–4, 41, 51, 59, 67, 129
        Holy Wisdom 15, 19
        St Basil 15
        St Demetrios 15
        St Eustratios 15, 26, 59–61
        St Gregory 15
        St Mark of the Venetians 10
        San Giorgio 11
        San Pietro 'Raveddise', La Vallisa 10
        Santa Maria del Buonconsiglio 11

Santa Maria del Carmine 11
Santa Pelagia of the Cypriots 10
Santa Teresa dei Maschi 11
Theotokos, St John the Evangelist and St John the Baptist, monastery 25
Council of Bari 81, 84–5, 100, 110, 153
rectors of San Nicola
Elias (*see* Archbishops of Bari and Canosa)
Eustasius 55, 134, 137–41, 145–6, 152–3
Basil Mesardonites, *see* Byzantine governors of Bari
Benevento 9, 14, 15, 33, 38–52, 175, 182
Landulf, archbishop and his manuscript patronage 33, 35–9
Bertha of Loritello 165
Bethlehem 158
Bisantius of Bari, *see* Bari, Archbishops of Bari and Canosa
Bitetto 75
Bitonto 102, 106, 148
boars 112
Bohemond I, Prince of Antioch
biography 157–9
as a crusader 110, 119, 173, 175, 194–8
death and burial 5–6, 47, 138, 159–61, 164–9, 178, 188, 191, 200
political role in southern Italy 57, 61–2, 106, 110
soul 193
Bohemond II, Prince of Antioch 138, 159, 165, 169, 171, 190, 197
Bologna, Santo Stefano 176
Bourges, Cathedral 191
Brindisi 9, 31, 75, 106, 113, 158, 161, 166, 175
San Benedetto 106, 161
Sant'Andrea dell'Isola 75
Brittany, St Jacques in Perros-Guirec 116–17, *see also* Arthur, king
Bulgaria 101
St George's church, Sofia 123

Bury St Edmunds 85–6
Byzantine emperors
Alexios I Comnenas 158, 165, 167, 196
Basil II 15, 38
Constantine VII Porphyrygenitos 19
Constantine VIII 38
Constantine IX Monomachos 20, 58, 149, 172
John I 172
Byzantine governors of Bari 199
Basil Boiannes 138
Basil Mesardonites 14–20
Christopher 20
Pothos Argyros 26–7
Byzantine imperial iconography 38

Cairo 6, 12, 69, 95, 99, 187
Calabria 12, 56, 102, 113, 133, 147, 157–8, 184
San Demetrio Corone 147
Sant'Eufemia 184
Canosa
Archbishops (*see under* Bari)
churches
San Giovanni, baptistery 42
San Pietro 42
Santa Maria, early cathedral 42
SS Cosma e Damiano 42
temples
Giove Toro 160
Capetians 196–7, *see also* Constance of France
Louis VI 167
Philip I 165, 167
Capua 125, 182
Catalonia
Girona tapestry 126
Monastery of San Daniel 127, 128
Adelaide, Abbess 128
Ramon Berenger, count of Barcelona 127
ceramics 69, 94, 147, 173, 186
Chartres, cathedral 159
Cnut IV, King of Denmark 169
Concordia Sagittaria, 'Basilica E' 106
Conques 191
Constance of France 6, 138, 157–9, 164–70, 184, 191, 196–8, 200

Constantinople
  artistic production   18–19, 23, 29, 41, 108, 146, 180
  automaton throne   87–8, 90
  Chalke Gate   16
  Chalkoprateia   45
  Hagia Sophia   16, 19, 38, 45, 172
  Hippodrome   72, 74–5
  Holy Apostles   42–6, 160–1, 166, 174–5, 178, 193
  mosaicists   164
  palace   9, 15–16, 20, 87
  Pantocrator monastery   143
  Pharos church   15–16, 175
  relationship to Apulia   12, 21, 24, 26, 199
  St John of Studion   143
  St Polyeuktos   16, 109
  status   6
  trade   12–13, 99, 181–2
  travel to   9–10, 24, 42, 45, 56, 166, 170, 198
  Yilanca Bayir   171
Conversano   158, 198
  Alexander, count of   166, 168
  San Benedetto   75
Cordoba   6
Corfu   153
Cremona   111
Croxden Abbey   184–5
crusading
  events of first crusade   81, 88, 157–9
  Jerusalem   110
  relationship to art
    Bari   3–6, 81, 98–101, 110, 113, 119, 153
    Canosa   3–6, 178
    elsewhere   174
    textual culture   176, 195–7
    third crusade   178
Cyprus   11, 183

Dalmatia   10, 33, 99, 101, 102
Damascus, Great Mosque   95
Dattus, brother-in-law of Melus   21–3
Devol, treaty   159, 165, 167, 197–8
Durrës   12

eagles   48
early Christian art and architecture
  architecture   106
  Bari   25, 37
  episcopal thrones   51, 88
  iconography   126–8
  Jerusalem   179
  Myra   79
  pavements   137, 150
  relationship to the Gregorian reform movement   4, 75, 135, 151, 200–1
  Rome   67, 78, 107, 111, 122, 145, 188
Easter   33–5, 38, 40, 110, 113, 176, 184, 191, 198
Egypt   10, 19, 71, 99
El Djem, Tunisia   90
elephants   48–9, 67–9, 95–7, 121–2
Elias of Bari, *see* Bari, Archbishops of Bari and Canosa
Emma of Hauteville   197
enamel   141, 147
Ephesus, church of St John   143
ethnicity   86, 91, 94, 97
Eucharist   30, 48, 119–28, 140, 173, 175, 186
Exultet scrolls   34–42, 123, 191

Farfa abbey   24
Fatimid art and architecture   95–101, 122, 187–8
Fatimid empire   4, 172
Frederick II   93

Genoa   59
George of Antioch   154
Glastonbury Abbey   117, 183
goats   16, 112
gold, *see* metalworking
Goslar   85–6
Grado, Santa Maria delle Grazie   106
Gregorian reform movement
  ideology   91, 125, 151
  intersection with the first crusade   62, 153
  relationship to art   4, 200–1
  relationship to art in Bari   6, 52, 75–8, 80, 126, 135–6, 153

textual culture 128
Urban II 62, 80
griffins 67, 75-6, 147-8
Grimoald Alferanties, Prince of Bari 138-9, 141, 167
Gümüshtigin Gazi, Danishmend ruler 158, 165

Hauteville family 56, 159, 168, 170, 178, 190-1
Hildesheim 183
Holy Week 36, 176, 186
Hosios Loukas 38, 124, 143
Hospitallers, Order of St John 179
Hugh, Count of Troyes and Champagne 165, 167
Hungarian coronation mantle 23

Ida of Bouillon 197
India 12
ivory and bone 87, 99
 'Charlemagne' chess set 69, 95, 97, 113
 early Christian 179
 Farfa Casket 71
 Fatimid 69, 95-8
 oliphants and horns 71-5
 Southern Italy 69, 71

Jericho 158
Jerusalem
 al-Aqsa mosque 109-10
 crusader conquest 100-1, 109, 119, 198
 Dome of the Rock 109-10, 173
 heavenly Jerusalem 173
 Holy Sepulchre 6, 109-10, 157, 171-9, 186, 193, 198
  imitations 174-5
 kings 173
  Baldwin I 170
  Baldwin II 165
  Godfrey of Bouillon 109, 172, 195-6
 Nea Ekklesia 108
 New Jerusalem 117
 pilgrimage 116, 175
 Temple Mount 87, 100-2, 108-10, 173
 trade 12

Jews 11, 57, 61, 99, 101, 109
John, Archbishop of Trani 30-1
John of Hauteville, son of Bohemond I 159, 165, 170
Jordan, river 158

Kerbogha of Mosul 100, 153
Krodo altar 86
Kyiv 74, 81

labours of the months 112, 122
lions
 doors 69-71, 179, 185, 188
 Elias's throne 86-93
 judgement 88-93
 Mari Cha Lion 183
 protection 69-71, 88-93, 112, 179, 185
 Samson wrestling a lion 122
 San Nicola, crypt 69-71, 75
 St Mark 40
 temple of Solomon 108-9
 throne of Solomon 49, 86-7
Lucera, portrait of Johannes Maurus 91

Macedonia
 Bogorodica Eleousain, church in Veljusain 171
 Leo, archbishop of Ohrid 30
 St Sofia's church, Ohrid 123
Mafalda of Hauteville 127-8
marble
 Alberada's tomb 168-9
 Bohemond's burial chapel 160-1, 164, 168-9, 176, 194
 columns 150
 Elias's throne 82-5, 87, 100
 Elias's tomb 132-3
 Eucharistic 175
 Holy Sepulchre 172-3, 175-6
 liturgical furniture, Canosa 48-9
 modern replacement 133
 pavements 137, 145-6, 199-200
 significance as spolia 87, 100, 132, 160, 168
 trade and transportation 153
 visual similarity to ivory 87
Margaret of Navarre 165
Matilda of Canossa 117
Matilda of Hauteville 170

Melfi   62, 159, 168, 184
   Council of Melfi   56, 62, 82, 125
   Roger of Melfi (*see* metalwork)
Melus, husband of Alferada of Bari   33
Melus, Lombard nobleman of Bari   9–10, 14–15, 21–6, 30, 41, 102
metalwork
   agemina   180, 185, 188, 193
   artophorion   173, 179
   bells   183–5
   Bonanno of Pisa   182
   bronze, lucidity   109
   bronze doorknocker, David Collection   69, 186
   bronze doors   6, 157, 179–93, 198, 200
   candelabrum   183
   gold   12, 22–4, 36, 69, 86–7, 99, 128, 134, 164, 167, 172, 183–4
   Mari Cha Lion   183
   Oderisius of Benevento   182, 185
   Roger of Melfi, bellmaker   168, 179, 183–94
   silver   167, 172
   Simeon the bronze caster   183
Mileto   3, 133, 178
Modena   85, 113, 116–20, 124
   Wiligelmus of Modena, sculptor   111
Monopoli   85, 158
Monreale   182, 191
Montecassino
   architecture   107
   Desiderius, abbot   103, 125, 134–5, 137, 153–4, 180, 200
   historiography   3
   influence   103–4, 146–7, 149, 154, 200
   intellectual culture   125, 128
   metalwork   183, 193
   mosaics   164
   reconstruction   47, 145
   relationship to San Benedetto in Bari   11, 129
   scriptorium   33
   sculpture   120, 124
Monte Sant'Angelo
   ambo   47
   artistic centre   3, 51–2
   bronze doors   180, 190, 193
   pilgrimage   58, 175
   throne   49, 82, 87

mosaics   4, 19, 25, 75, 78, 89–90, 101, 116, 119, 122, 137, 145–51, 161, 164–6, 172–3, 186, 191, 198
Myra   1, 58, 60, 63, 132–3, 137, 149–53

Naples, church of Sant'Aspreno al Porto   32
Nicholas of Bari, *see* Bari, Archbishops of Bari and Canosa
Normandy   67
   Bayeux tapestry   113
   Robert Curthouse, Duke of Normandy   113
   St Évroul, monastery   184
Normans
   conquest   2, 56, 118, 136, 180–1, 199
   expansion   178
   government of Bari   80, 112, 153
   immigration   184
   opposition to Norman rule   138, 140, 198

Oderisius of Benevento, *see under* metalwork
Ofanto, river   42
opus interrasile   146
opus sectile   4, 88, 137, 141–53, 181
Otranto   3, 20, 58, 70, 99, 116, 119, 122
Ovid   33
oxen   109, 119–20, 122

Palermo   3, 6, 12, 41, 93, 95, 123, 147, 154, 182, 187
Paris, St Denis   23
peacocks   75–6, 111
pearls   99, 131
pendentive domes   43–5
Piacenza   109, 111
Pietrabbondante   92
pilgrimage
   Bari   107, 111, 116, 119, 129, 131, 141, 153
   Constantinople   175
   crusaders as pilgrims   113, 116, 119
   intersection with art and architecture   6
   Jerusalem   116, 175
   Rome   113, 124, 125

Pisa
   Bonanno of Pisa (*see under* metalwork)
   cathedral 133
   Nicola Pisano 94
   possible artistic link to Canosa 171
Poitiers, Notre-Dame des Moreaux 109
Polignano, Benedictine monastery 32
Pompei 92
Popes
   Alexander II 30
   Calixtus II 138, 153, 167
   Gregory VII 57, 59, 78, 87, 91, 126, 133–4, 140
   Leo IX 58, 140
   Nicholas II 56
   Paschal II 102, 116, 138, 153, 158, 166, 170
   Urban II 62, 78, 80, 82–4, 87, 91, 100, 110, 125, 129, 134, 153
pseudo-Arabic 29, 89, 100–1, 147, 164, 186

Ravello 10
Ravenna 17, 87, 145, 148
Red Sea 12
relics 81, 129, 130, 133, 158, 175–6, 199
Richard of the Principate 190
Robert Guiscard, Duke of Apulia 56, 58–9, 62, 127, 129, 133, 157–8, 168, 184, 195, 197
rock crystal 99
Roger Borsa, Duke of Apulia 57, 61–2, 113, 133, 157–60, 168–70, 190, 195
Roger I, Count of Sicily 133, 178, 186, 195
Roger II, King of Sicily 3, 23, 41, 93, 138, 154, 158, 170, 182, 187
Roger of Melfi, *see under* metalwork
Roger of Salerno, regent of Antioch 165, 171
Rome
   ancient Rome 198
   ciboria 150
   early Christian art 188
   Lateran 78, 109, 193
   Lateran Synod 138
   Lenten council of 1079 125
   Mosaicists 164
   Old St Peter's 76, 102
   O Roma Nobilis, poem 134
   pilgrimage 113, 124
   St Alessio 23
   San Clemente 78
   San Giorgio a Velabro 147
   San Lorenzo fuori le Mura 108
   San Lorenzo in Damaso 138
   San Paolo fuori le Mura 180, 183
   Santa Costanza 122
   Santa Maria in Cosmedin 67
   Santa Maria Maggiore 183
   sculpture 86
   spolia 83, 88, 101, 153
Romuald, sculptor 49, 69, 75, 78–9
Ruvo di Puglia 108

Sagmata monastery, pavement 143, 147
Sainte Marie d'Oloron 101
St Gall 183
Saints
   St Ætholwold 183
   St Benedict 113, 147
   St Cataldus 57
   St Dunstan 183
   St Efflam 116
   St Germiniano 117
   St Gertrude 184
   St Leonard 178
   St Leucius 31
   St Matthew 57
   St Memore 130
   St Nicholas
      Byzantine saint 81, 88
      cult and shrine in Myra 63, 79, 137, 150
      devotion to 62, 110, 119, 135, 138, 141
      ecumenism 1, 81
      Gregorian Reform 79
      miracles 131–2
      pilgrimage 113, 117, 175
      relics 1, 58, 79, 129, 130, 132, 138, 199
   St Rufinus 130
   St Sabinus 43–6, 58, 130–2, 141, 160, 175
   St Secundinus 57
Salento 12, 158, 166

Salerno
  Alfanus, archbishop   57, 62, 103, 128, 134–5, 154
  cathedral   57
    atrium   107–8, 133
    bronze doors   180
    consecration   62
    crypt   63, 65–7, 106
    influence on Bari   104, 110, 154, 200
    mosaics   78
    papal throne   87
    sculpture   90, 124
    tomb of Gregory VII   133
    tomb of Roger Borsa   160
  Cava dei Tirreni   129
  cult of St Matthew   57–8, 65
  ivories   3, 69, 71
Sant'Agata dei Goti, church of San Menna   147, 149
Sant'Angelo in Formis   103, 108
San Vincenzo al Volturno   33
sarcophagi   94, 132–3, 150, 161
serpents   112
Sichelgaita, princess of Salerno and duchess of Apulia   61, 157, 170
Sicily   2–4, 6, 10, 29, 56, 69, 86, 95, 157, 159, 170
Siena, cathedral   109
silk, *see* textiles
Siponto   47, 51, 87
  San Leonardo   175
slavery   81, 98–101
Slavs   60, 99–101
sol invictus   126–8
Solomon, king   81, 87, 90, 101, 102, 134–5
  temple   88, 108–10
  throne   86–7, 109
Sorrento, cathedral   32
Speyer, cathedral   106
Split, Dalmatia   16
  Peter the Black, epitaph   134
spolia   81–4, 181, 198
star mantle of Henry II   23

Tancred of Hauteville   100, 158, 165–6, 171, 190, 198
Taranto   57, 60, 158, 166, 197
telamons   85, 91–2, 94, 97–101

textiles   5, 24, 69, 95, 113, 126
  clothing   12, 13, 20, 38, 67, 69, 72, 91, 97, 101, 112, 118, 131, 190–1
  silk   23–5, 32, 39, 41, 71, 97, 99, 131, 147, 158, 167, 186
  tents   100, 153
Thessaloniki, church of Panagia Chalkeon   20
Toulouse, St Sernin   191
Trani   3, 30–2, 51, 58, 60, 87, 182
  Santa Maria di Colonna, monastery   32, 67
Tremiti islands   24, 148
Troia   30, 57, 91, 182, 185

Valenzano, Ognisanti di Cuti, monastery   137
Venice
  alliance with Bari   138
  artistic links to Bari   147–9, 153, 164, 199–200
  competition with Bari   14, 56–7, 63
  involvement in the slave trade   99
  San Marco   109, 148, 199
  San Niccolò al Lido   63
  San Zaccaria   148
  SS Maria e Donato, Murano   148
  Torcello   88, 151
  Venetians in Bari   10
Venosa
  artistic centre   3
  Hauteville dynastic burial church   159–61, 168–70, 178
  metalworking   184
  source of spolia   92–3
via Egnazia   9
via Emilia   116
via Traiana   42, 175
vines   111, 122, 128

wall paintings   176
William, Duke of Apulia   133, 138, 168–70, 190, 195, 198
William I, King of Sicily   26, 28
William II, king of Sicily   178
wood   97, 183, 186
Wurtzburg, cathedral   109

Yemen   12

www.ingramcontent.com/pod-product-compliance
Lightning Source LLC
Chambersburg PA
CBHW052219300426
44115CB00011B/1751